Literature in America

The Founding of a Nation

Literature

General Editor, ROBERT C. ALBRECHT

THE FOUNDING OF A NATION • KENNETH SILVERMAN
A CENTURY OF EXPANSION • DON HAUSDORFF
THE MODERN AGE • CHARLES KAPLAN

 THE FREE PRESS • New York
COLLIER-MACMILLAN LIMITED • London

in America

The Founding of a Nation

Edited by Kenneth Silverman

The Free Press
A Division of The Macmillan Company
866 Third Avenue, New York, New York 10022

Collier-Macmillan Canada Ltd., Toronto, Ontario

Library of Congress Catalog Card Number: 73–139984

printing number
1   2   3   4   5   6   7   8   9   10

CONTENTS

I

The Puritans

v

II

The Colonial South and the Middle Colonies

III

The Revolution and After

Two Slave Poets

Other Eighteenth-Century Poets

Selective Table of Contents. Arranged by Topics

Foreword

Our main goal in editing this anthology was to produce three volumes of manageable size that would (especially when supplemented by paperback editions of novels and plays) enable students to gain a sense of the variety and shape of American literature. We also wanted to avoid burdening readers with a heft of scholarly apparatus that would tend to make critics of them—or bore them—before they could enjoy what they were reading. To achieve these aims we have been highly selective in choosing works for these books and in confining ourselves to footnotes and bibliographies that are useful and helpful.

Although I assisted at various points in all the volumes, each of the three editors is responsible for his contribution alone: Kenneth Silverman, Volume I; Don Hausdorff, Volume II; Charles Kaplan, Volume III. The books are not rigidly uniform and have, in fact, been planned so that they can be used independently in appropriate courses as well as together in a complete survey of American literature. From the beginning we agreed that each editor should have as much freedom as possible in preparing his own volume, aware that the literature of the various centuries might require different presentations.

The organization of each book reflects a bias of the editors. Dissatisfied with a strictly chronological presentation of American literature, we have chosen to organize the selections on more significant bases. For instance, the geographic divisions of the country had important consequences which are visible in the literature of early America; hence the use of such divisions in organizing the first volume. (Incidentally, many selections in Volume I present a significant problem: Students not accustomed to reading the prose and poetry of the seventeenth and eighteenth centuries find them difficult to study. I have therefore supplied headnotes which, along with the editor's excellent introductions, may help many readers in their first encounters with these selections.) The more cosmopolitan character of the later nineteenth-century literature is reflected in the structuring of the second volume. The makeup of the third volume posed a problem because the history of the literature of this century has not been charted to the satisfaction of many scholars. Organizing the selections in the final book in the series by significant topics indicates some of the recurrent concerns but does not impose a wholly artificial pattern and does avoid the deceptive implications of mere chronological ordering.

This anthology is not a social history despite an organization of topics that could be considered extra-literary. For example, slavery and theology were important to authors of the early period, and they wrote about them in works of indisputable worth. On such issues, we have carefully chosen selections that reflect both the concern of the authors and the quality of their work. We accept a broad definition of literature yet insist upon the substantial differences between a social-problems reader and a literature anthology.

We have used texts that are both readable and reliable. If a text seemed particularly unreadable in its original state, a reliable modern version was substituted. We have also sought to compile an open anthology, one in which the interpretation of works is left to the readers instead of imposed by the editors. We recognize that a complete survey of American literature must include major and minor authors and fiction, drama, and poetry. In limiting this anthology to a reasonable length we have, as we have said, necessarily been selective. When in doubt, we chose the author who seemed most representative of a period or of a group of writers. We have included no novels, and fewer dramas than we believe should be read in most courses. Readers will understand the necessity for such omissions.

We wish to thank Thomas O. Gay of *The Free Press* for his most helpful assistance at every stage in the preparation of this text.

Robert C. Albrecht
General Editor

Eugene, Oregon

PREFACE

The teacher of a course in early American literature is likely to face the same problem that has vexed every anthologist of the period, namely the problem of organization. None of the traditional literary approaches—Major Writers, Thematic, Genres, Literary History—helps one to discover the shapes and the imaginative vocabulary of American writing between 1630 and 1800. The Major Writers approach fails because major writers in the period are few. The Thematic approach is likely to be quite ephemeral. Changes in current ideology demand new versions of the past, and "themes" are here today and gone tomorrow. The other two approaches fail for a more serious reason that accounts for the design of the present anthology. They ignore what seems to be, empirically, the main concern of American literature, at least until this moment—the search for a national identity in a pluralistic nation. They fail to reveal both real differences and ideals of union. This anthology takes shape from a sense of the pluralism of early American life—the puritanism of the Puritans, the southernness of the South, less distinctly the middleness of the Middle colonies, the federalism of the Federalists—a pluralism never more pronounced than in its constant imaginings of what a single America might be like. Thus while this is an anthology of early American literature, it is also about early America.

Of the other organizations, the thematic probably provides the most intellectually stimulating view of the period. Thus the materials have been arranged with a dual table of contents, so that they may be considered by themes as well—the frontier, science, slavery, witchcraft, and so on. Any organization, of course, both admits and omits. I regret the omission of such important writers as John Smith, John Winthrop, Benjamin Tompson, Mary Rowlandson, the Puritan elegists, and particularly of Tom Paine and Thomas Jefferson among the later writers. Here limitations of space as well as of design took their toll. On the other hand, I have included some infrequently anthologized but significant writers and works: the very lively early American drama, Royall Tyler, the southern gazetteers, Edwards'

Miscellanies and "On the Medium of moral Government," Crèvecoeur's Indian tales, Fisher Ames' *American Literature*, the more Villon-like poems of Freneau, Dwight's *Epistle . . . to Col. Humphreys*, and quite a few others. As a supplement to this anthology, the semester or trimester survey of early American literature ought to include a number of the following classic works, to be read whole. They are all available in inexpensive editions: Hugh Henry Brackenridge, *Modern Chivalry*; William Bradford, *Of Plymouth Plantation*; Charles Brockden Brown, *Wieland* or *Edgar Huntley*; J. Hector St. John De Crèvecoeur, *Letters from an American Farmer*; Jonathan Edwards, *The Nature of True Virtue* or *The Freedom of the Will*; Benjamin Franklin, *The Autobiography*.

Special bibliographies appear at the end of each preface. Some useful general works on the period are: Daniel Boorstin, *The Americans: The Colonial Experience* (New York, 1958); Howard Mumford Jones, *O Strange New World. American Culture: The Formative Years* (New York, 1964); Winthrop D. Jordan, *White over Black: American Attitudes Toward the Negro 1550–1812* (Chapel Hill, N.C., 1968); Harrison T. Meserole, *Seventeenth-Century American Poetry* (New York, 1968); Roy Harvey Pearce, *The Continuity of American Poetry* (Princeton, N.J., 1961); Max Savelle, *Seeds of Liberty: The Genesis of the American Mind* (New York, 1948); Kenneth Silverman, *Colonial American Poetry* (New York, 1968); Moses Coit Tyler, *A History of American Literature during the Colonial Time* (New York, 1878); Louis B. Wright, *The Cultural Life of the American Colonies* (New York, 1957).

Kenneth Silverman
New York University
New York City, January 1970

Note: The brief textual headnotes were written by Robert Albrecht of The Free Press. The footnotes, like the introductory essays, are the editor's.—K.S.

ACKNOWLEDGMENTS

BROWN, CHARLES BROCKDEN: "Walstein's School of History" from Harry R Warfel, ed., *The Rhapsodist and other Uncollected Writings* (New York, 1943), reprinted by permission of Harry R. Warfel.

BYRD, WILLIAM: "Diary" from Louis B. Wright and Marion Tinling, eds., *The Great American Gentleman* (New York, 1963), reprinted with permission of Louis B. Wright and Mrs. Marion Tinling. "London Diary" from Louis B. Wright and Marion Tinling, eds., *The London Diary (1717–1721) and other writings of William Byrd* (New York, 1958), reprinted by permission of Louis B. Wright and Mrs. Marion Tinling. "Inamorato L'Oiseaux" from Marion Tinling and Maude Woodfin, eds., *Another Secret Diary of William Byrd* (Richmond, 1942), reprinted by permission of Mrs. Marion Tinling and Camilla Patton. "The History of the Dividing Line" reprinted by permission of the publishers from pp. 158–62, 204–5, 217–9, 221–2, 230, 277–8, 279–80 of Louis B. Wright, ed., *The Prose Works of William Byrd of Westover*, The Belknap Press of Harvard University Press, copyright © 1966 by the President and Fellows of Harvard College.

DE CRÈVECOEUR, HECTOR ST. JOHN: "Hoppajewot" from Percy G. Adams, trans. and ed., *Crèvecoeur's Eighteenth-Century Travels in Pennsylvania and New York* (Lexington, 1961), reprinted with permission of the University Press of Kentucky.

EDWARDS, JONATHAN: "The Future Punishment of the Wicked" from Clarence Faust and Thomas H. Johnson, eds., *Jonathan Edwards Representative Selections* (New York, 1935), reprinted by permission of Clarence Faust and Thomas H. Johnson. "Miscellanies" from Harvey G. Townsend, ed., *The Philosophy of Jonathan Edwards from his Private Notebooks* (Eugene, Ore., 1955) reprinted with permission of University of Oregon Books.

FRANKLIN, BENJAMIN: "Silence Dogood, No. 7" from Leonard W. Labaree, ed., *The Papers of Benjamin Franklin*, I (New Haven, 1959); "Verses on the Virginia Capitol Fire" from Labaree, *Papers*, III (New Haven, 1961). Both reprinted with permission of the Yale University Press. "Parody of a Meditation" identified as Franklin's and published in Alfred Owen Aldridge, "A Religious Hoax by Benjamin Franklin," *American Literature*, XXXVI (1964), reprinted with permission of Alfred Owen Aldridge and the Duke University Press. "Letter to Mary Stevenson" from I. Bernard Cohen, ed., *Benjamin Franklin's Experiments* (Cambridge, 1941), reprinted with permission of Harvard University Press.

FRENEAU, PHILIP: "To a New-England Poet" and "Verses Written on Leaving a Great House" from Lewis Leary, ed., *The Last Poems of Philip Freneau* (New Brunswick, 1945), reprinted by permission of the Rutgers University Press.

HAMILTON, ALEXANDER: Text from J. A. Leo Lemay, "Hamilton's Literary History of the *Maryland Gazette*," *William and Mary Quarterly*, 3d ser., XXIII (1966), reprinted with permission of J. A. Leo Lemay and the *William and Mary Quarterly*.

MATHER, COTTON: "The Pigeons," from *Curiosa Americana*, reprinted by courtesy of the Massachusetts Historical Society. "Bonifacius" reprinted by permission of the publishers from David Levin, ed., *Cotton Mather's "Bonifacius: An Essay upon the Good*," The Belknap Press of Harvard University Press, copyright © 1966 by the President and Fellows of Harvard College.

REID, JAMES: "The Religion of the Bible" from Richard Beale Davis, ed., *The Colonial Virginia Satirist*, Volume 57 (1967), *Transactions of the American Philosophical Society*, reprinted with permission of Richard Beale Davis and the American Philosophical Society.

TAYLOR, EDWARD: "Meditation 47" from Thomas H. Johnson, "Some Edward Taylor Gleanings," *New England Quarterly*, XVI (1943), reprinted with their permission. "Meditation 5" and "Meditation 150" from Donald Stanford, ed., *The Poems of Edward Taylor* (New Haven, 1960). Copyright © 1960 by Yale University Press and reprinted with their permission. "Gods Determinations" from *The Poetical Works of Edward Taylor*, ed. Thomas H. Johnson (Princeton Paperback, 1966). Copyright © Rockland, 1939; Princeton University Press, 1943. Reprinted by permission of Princeton University Press. The text followed here is that of the Yale University Press, with their permission. "Treatise Concerning the Lord's Supper" from Norman S. Grabo, ed., *Edward Taylor's Treatise Concerning the Lord's Supper* (East Lansing, 1966), reprinted by permission of the Michigan State University Press. Special thanks to the Yale University Press for permitting the use here of their edition of Edward Taylor's poems, for the sake of presenting a unified text.

TRUMBULL, JOHN: "An Essay on the Use and Advantages of the Fine Arts" from Clarence Arthur Brown, ed., *Achievement of American Criticism* (New York, 1954). Copyright © The Ronald Press Company, New York, and reprinted with their permission.

TYLER, ROYALL: "The Prologue" and "Ode Composed for the Fourth of July" from Marius B. Peladeau, ed., *The Verse of Royall Tyler* (Charlottesville, 1968), originally published in the *Publications of the Colonial Society of Massachusetts*, reprinted by permission of Marius B. Peladeau and the Colonial Society of Massachusetts.

I

The Puritans

MIDWAY through *Gods Determinations*, the Puritan poet Edward Taylor offers some advice that is astonishing in its arrogance. The dramatic situation is this: a Saint—a man assured of his salvation —addresses a Soul that despairs of salvation because it is convinced of its sinfulness. To guide and comfort the distressed Soul, the Saint advises:

> Do all Good Works, work all good things you know
> As if you should be sav'd for doing so.
> Then undo all you've done, and it deny
> And on a naked Christ alone rely.

The arrogance of this, again, is astonishing. The Saint recommends a course of action presumably simple enough to reduce to a motto. But the motto offers no comfort or advice because it is incomprehensible. Why should the Soul do good works "as if" they will save it? How can the Soul "undo" and "deny" its good works? And why and how do them if only to undo them? Despite his consolatory tone, the Saint answers the Soul's questions with a question. He presents a riddle as a rule and recommends a paradox as a way of life.

Yet to savor that paradox is to savor the marrow of Puritan experience. Paradox, doubt, and uncertainty constituted the essence of Puritan life. The Saint *is* offering comfort and advice, for to a Puritan anxiety was a style of life. To come to see the paradox as deliberate advice, however, one must revise the popular but mistaken equation between religious orthodoxy and conformity. All Puritans, we say, believed that a man was damned or saved from the beginning of time; then why does the Saint urge the Soul to do good works (or does he?)? All Puritans believed that a man ought to lead a harshly pious life; then why does the Saint tell the Soul to undo and deny its pious acts (or does he?)?

The fact is that different Puritan thinkers had different answers to such questions as whether good works could lead one to salvation. Puritans, like us, felt different ways about different things. Puritan society allowed for and encouraged a variety of responses to admittedly perplexing issues. Indeed, diversity was inherent in the Protestant Reformation of the sixteenth century; and it was from the Reformation's attacks upon Catholicism that puritanism emerged. By questioning the need for an intricate church hierarchy to mediate between the

2

believer and God, the Reformation gave some sanction to the believer who would find his own way. Even the earliest days of the Reformation saw a constant splintering of Protestant opinion that resulted in a proliferation of sects—Baptists, Methodists, Lutherans, Calvinists, Presbyterians, Brownists, Baxterites. In Puritanism, diversity became an institutional principle. The Puritan form of church organization— Congregationalism—granted to each separate church the power, within limits, to organize and worship as it pleased, free of the directives of some overseeing federation of churches. These churches or congregations, and the individuals who composed them, moreover, changed with time and altered their views as circumstances changed. And some communities, some churches, some individuals in New England changed their views more or less than others. Isolated inland communities, for example, changed more slowly than coastal communities with their swelling cities and open harbors. There was no single, unchanging Puritan view.

The Puritans did, just the same, exist. But what, in the final analysis, made them Puritans were less the answers they gave than the problems they attempted to solve. Puritans gave different answers, but they were all staring at the same problems. Essentially the same issues occupied Thomas Hooker in 1640, Edward Taylor in 1695, and Jonathan Edwards in 1740, providing the clearest possible continuity from one to the other, and making them all Puritans. This century-long devotion of its intellectual energy to solving the same problems, and an air of mind-wracking strain which tells how deeply felt but tormentingly complex the problems were, give American Puritan writing its distinctively dialectical, dynamic look and feel. The straining, anxious, problematic atmosphere of Puritan life was the product of turning problems into codes, of trying to reconcile, and to live by, some equally valued but conflicting ideals of behavior.

Most of these conflicting ideals are embraced by the terms "freedom" and "restraint." Perhaps the deepest problem for Puritanism was how a man could be true to his deepest self while remaining a responsible and responsive social being. The wilderness of the New World aggravated the problem. Its openness spurred the hope that in America a man could be truly himself, while its perils made communal rule and solidarity even more strictly necessary than in Europe. Under "freedom" and "restraint" can be classed other conflicting ideals that the Puritans found difficult but imperative to resolve: free will and determinism, pure faith and pure works, inspiration and technique, emotion and logic. In this essay "Puritan" refers to no one resolution of these conflicts, but to the many differing resolutions and to the people in whose minds such conflicts vitally counted. Some of the more influential and artful solutions appear in the selections that follow.

i The Earlier American Puritans

Although dissension broke out even among the first generation of Puritans who arrived in Massachusetts in 1630—when 108 settlers asked to be made freemen—this group as a whole shared a clearer sense of social purpose and a stronger common identity than would exist in later Puritan generations. Its relative unity grew from a need to band together before persecution in England and before the unexpected trials of wilderness America. A large number of the 25,000 settlers who arrived in the 1630's seem to have been literate and intelligent, and many were graduates of the chief English universities. A decade after arriving, they had founded a college (Harvard) and erected a printing press; another decade and their companions in England had beheaded a king and taken over a government by revolution. Thus the first generation was an extraordinary group, a community of intellectuals who yet were social activists, and mystics in addition. Because the avowed purposes of the first generation served as a touchstone by which later Puritans often tried the success and health of their own society, some features of its life deserve comment here: its providential view of itself, the Hebraic flavor of Puritan life, and the Puritans' passionate communal sense.

All three characteristics appear in the writings of JOHN COTTON (1584–1652), the grandfather of Cotton Mather and one of the most influential of all Puritan ministers. With an M.A. from Cambridge University and fame in England for his writing and preaching, Cotton fled to Massachusetts in 1633 to become a teacher at the Boston Church and the leading spokesman for the early form of church government in New England. In his sermon *Gods Promise to His Plantation* he reminded the first, heavy-hearted group of Puritan emigrants to depart for Massachusetts that behind their daring exodus lay the controlling hand of Providence. Cotton, like every other Puritan, never questioned the absolute sovereignty of God. Not a hair turns gray, not a sparrow falls to earth anywhere, but God causes it. (Since most Puritans also felt that man must answer for his actions, the unquestionable sovereignty of God created momentous social and theological problems.) Accordingly, although Cotton's account of the motives behind the emigration is complex enough to include the congestion, widespread poverty, and religious persecutions of England, he sees the Puritans' flight from the Old World as divinely appointed, providential. New England was to be, in Governor John Winthrop's famous phrase, a "city on the hill," an example on high to the rest of the world and, to some Puritans at least, the beginning of God's kingdom on earth.

Cotton justifies the Puritans' departure by repeatedly citing scriptural illustrations and arguments. For Puritans like Cotton the Bible was the final authority, the source of all law, although Puritans recognized that human interpretation of God's word could err. In the Bible, God had made known part of His intention toward mankind. Many Puritans saw themselves repeating in modern times the history of the ancient Jews, and they regarded the events of the Old Testament as a prophecy of their lives in the New World. Not all Puritans believed this. Some regarded the events of the Old Testament as prophecies ("types") only of events fulfilled in the New Testament ("anti-types"), and no more than similar to their lives in America. The Puritan attempt to harmonize the Old Testament with the New—begun in medieval Christianity—gave birth to a further range of intellectual problems, such as how the wrathful Old Testament Yahweh can be one with the more merciful God of the New Testament. The narrower dispute over "typology" went into creating the controversy between John Cotton and Roger Williams; this, in turn, led to Williams's leaving Massachusetts and founding Rhode Island. The more noticeable and lasting effect of thus viewing the Bible as the source of all law was the Hebraic cast of Puritan life. Many Puritans were fluent Hebraists, studied Hebrew at Harvard, alluded to their leaders as Joshua or Moses, considered the Indians one of the ten lost tribes of Israel, and called their settlements The Wilderness Zion or Christian Israel—the ancestors of many nineteenth-century American towns named Canaan and Bethel. Conservative Puritans also proposed equating civil law with the scriptural law handed down to Moses—including the harsh criminal law described in Exodus—and merging church and state into a sort of Bible state, or theocracy.

One social idea of the Old Testament proved troublesome to Puritanism in theory, and in practice contributed to its decline: the idea of the Covenant. The books of the Pentateuch describe God's entering into a quasi-legal contract with such Jewish leaders as Abraham and with whole Jewish tribes. In these contracts God promises to reward the Jews for their obedience to Him. Reading human history and building society in terms of this contract left the Puritans with two exasperating contradictions. The Covenant binds a party—God—who cannot be bound; how can God retain His absolute sovereignty yet remain legally obliged to man? The Covenant also collided with the Calvinist-Augustinian strain in Puritanism. Calvin and Augustine argued that man can do nothing to affect his salvation, since because of his corrupt nature he lacks the power to love God. But the Covenant implies that man *can* work toward his salvation by living up to the terms of the contract. The Puritans took from the Old Testament not only this individual covenant—the Covenant of Grace—but also the social covenant, in which the community as a group agrees to abide by the terms of the contract. Puritans acknowledged the covenant publicly in church, on days set aside specifically to allow the congregation to reaffirm its contract. The tribal "they" of John Cotton's text—"they shall have peaceable and quiet resting there"—derives from the social covenant, and its corollary the Covenant of Peace: in return for following His ordinances as set forth in the Old Testament, God would reward the community by immunizing it from the plague of war consuming Europe. Throughout Puritan social thought resounds the hope that America, unlike Europe, will live in peace.

The social covenant legislated into being the fervently communal spirit of the early Puritans. By the terms of the contract, the entire community would be punished for the sins of any one member; God would punish all for the failings of any. Thus each Puritan took upon himself the fate of the entire community. He became responsible in his own life for the destiny of his neighbors; anyone's business became everyone's business. Communal disasters pointed back to private sins. Earthquakes, the passing of great men, Indian attacks—all became signs of God's displeasure with sinful members of the community. The group itself is often the hero of Puritan writing, whose point of view is often collective. "We" and "they" figure as often as "I" and "he."

In addition to its strong communal sense, however, Puritanism was individualistic, at times defiantly so. While keeping society unified and making each man responsible for the welfare of his neighbors, Puritans wished to honor the claims of individual conscience. Governor John Winthrop attempted to draw the line between freedom and restraint by distinguishing natural from civil liberty. Natural liberty, one's liberty as a creature, is a liberty to do anything, the liberty of bears and wolves. Civil liberty, one's liberty as a member of society, is a liberty to do anything within the terms of God's covenant, the liberty of the regenerate. In drawing a further line between the governor and the governed, John Cotton articulated what became a popular Puritan argument: the people choose their leaders, but then are bound to obey them. The elected leader owes his allegiance only to the Word of God revealed in the Bible. The Word limits both his powers and the people's rights. While the leader serves the public good, this means the good described in Scripture rather than what the people may want for themselves. Government aims at doing right, whether popular or not.

How Puritan government and society influenced the later democratic tradition in America remains one of the more elusive questions in American cultural history. It is possible to point out resemblances between the two, yet Puritan social ideas resist being labelled "influences" on later American society because it is difficult to identify the means by which they were transmitted. Resemblances, however, do abound. So far as the social covenant attached virtue to simple meddling, Puritanism fostered a watchdog atmosphere that perhaps bequeathed to American life the smalltown snooping and public committees of investigation later reviled by writers like Sherwood Anderson and Arthur Miller. So far as it attached virtue to social concern, the view that we are each responsible for what happens in our societies is not different from the lesson that many have learned from the civil rights movement and the Vietnam war. One fact that obscures the relation between Puritan and later ideals of representative government is that Puritan government was representative only in a special way. The people (even then, not all of the people) chose their leader; afterward, the leader was responsible only to God. Here, in defining the aim of government as active moral leadership, Puritanism perhaps initiated a radical strain within the democratic tradition. One thinks of Thoreau's principle of the "majority of one," that the legitimacy of a government depends on its being morally right, and that a single man who is right constitutes a majority. Also, the Puritans did in their churches what later Americans did in town meetings, newspapers, and television debates. They aired momentous issues publicly. They shared with the later ideal of the democratic tradition an implicit faith in the public mind to understand issues of general concern. Most important of all, the Puritans wrestled very early, in both their political and religious theory, with a key problem of American civilization: how to grant the individual considerable autonomy while preserving a society.

The Puritans wished to accommodate not only the claims of the individual and of society, but also to reconcile, as Cotton said, "authority in magistrates, liberty in people, purity in the church." Puritan thinking about society began with religious principles, for the end toward which the individual and the group lived was the glorification of God. The Puritans' main theological interests are represented here in writings by two other influential and prominent ministers, THOMAS HOOKER (1586–1647) and THOMAS SHEPARD (1605–1649). Hooker arrived in Massachusetts, together with John Cotton, in 1633. Like Cotton, he took his M.A. at Cambridge (in 1611) and even before emigrating had established his reputation in England. He was ordained pastor at Newtown, but after some still-obscure difficulties with the Massachusetts authorities, he left the colony in 1636 and founded Hartford, Connecticut, which he virtually ruled. Hooker's close friend Thomas Shepard, another Cambridge graduate (1627), was the son of a grocer in Towcester, England. In 1635, as he wrote, he "saw the Lord departing from England when Mr. Hooker and Mr. Cotton were gone," and he escaped in disguise to New England. His lengthy treatise *The Sincere Convert*—praised and quoted by Jonathan Edwards—remained continually in print from 1641 to 1812.

The works of Hooker and Shepard amplify John Cotton's call for "purity in the church." For most Puritans, this meant returning the church to the form and ceremonies described in the New Testament and eliminating whatever forms had grown up since in Catholicism. Puritans thus renounced such Catholic practices as confession, last rites, prayer to saints—all of which they considered unscriptural. They found scriptural authority, however, for communion, baptism, fast days, and the preaching of sermons. They also rejected the Catholic form of church organization, of a hierarchy of priests, bishops, and cardinals culminating in the Pope. They replaced it with the Congregational design which Thomas Hooker pungently summarizes in the preface to his *Church Discipline*. Each church is free to follow its own ways, observe its own discipline, choose its own ministers. The visible church— those church members who have voting privileges and can be admitted to communion—is limited to persons who have had the mystical experience of grace. The question of who should be admitted to full church membership was one of the most divisive and explosive in all Puritan culture, since the church functioned as the heart of Puritan society, and in many cases to be excluded from the church was to be excluded from any privileged position in society at large. The Con- gregational ideal, we will see, was no sooner born than threatened. By denying the need for a church hierarchy, Puritanism had already gone far toward rejecting any intermediary authority between the believer and God. Some Puritans, such as Anne Hutchinson, questioned the need for even the Congregational church. Also, as fewer people after the first generation experienced grace, the church was threatened with extinction.

Not everything in Puritan religious thought was problematic, of course, least of all the concept of human nature. All Puritans believed in man's essential sinfulness. Man ineradicably wishes to order the world according to his own scheme instead of obeying God's. This essential corruption, as Shepard explains in *The Sincere Convert*, is man's legacy from Adam, for whose disordered spirit all men suffer. Taken as a command, the idea that we must all pay for the sin of Adam, the archetypal father, seems arbitrary. As a psychological description, however, original sin means that children imitate the behavior of their parents. Man suffers from a series of learned responses that he finds it hard, perhaps impossible, to break. The Puritans placed the idea of psychological determinism in a historical setting. Pursued far enough back, one's learned responses lead to the first disobedience of Adam. Man badly needs to undo the patterns of behavior he has been taught. Passed down from generation to generation throughout history, they have weakened man's understanding and affections. He can love only what he has been trained to love by a succession of fathers, each tainted with his ancestor's narrowness and weakness. After Freud, this view must seem more valid than, for instance, that of the framers of the American Constitution, with their confidence in man's ability to change and progress by virtue of his inherent goodness and sociability.

While all Puritans believed man's nature to be corrupt, Puritans disagreed on how this corruptness might be purged. One of the chief problems of existence for the Puritans was that man needs to love God, but that man cannot be taught to love. Man's very ability to love goodness has been poisoned by the whole of human history. How can man discard his current modes of understanding, re-program and re-educate himself to love goodness, when his very modes of perception, perverted, deny him the possibility of desiring or recognizing change? Affections, anyway, resist change. One who does not love fishing cannot make himself love fishing. He can fake it or talk himself into liking it—tie flies, rent a boat—all without loving fishing. Then how can man love God, when in his cells and synapses he does not love Him?

This breaking down of inherited, learned, tainted modes of perception is what the Puritans called grace. Commendably, they would settle for nothing halfway. They insisted on the real thing. Thinkers like Hooker and Shepard continually wrote to distinguish real love—grace—from deceptively similar counterfeits such as delusions, learned piousness, decency, and good works. No distinction was more important to them than the one between sanctification—pious behavior—and justification, the love of God. The Puritans approached the question of how man can be brought to love God subtly, vigorously, and endlessly. In its modern form, the question amounts to asking to what extent a man is responsible for his own feelings and actions. Then as now, the question brought forth a spectrum of answers. Its extremes were, on the one hand, that only God could change one's feelings and, on the other, that one could work toward changing his feelings himself. Cotton, for instance, believed that man could not work for grace, but must wait passively to receive it from God. Hooker, however, stressed the importance of preparatory activities and in *The Application of Redemption*, excerpted here, described the utility of sermonizing and meditation in the conversion experience.

Every answer came chained to some immense social consequences. For if grace, hence salvation, came from God alone, what need was there for a church, or for ministers, or for the Bible? The history of Puritanism can be seen as an effort to resolve this single question, whose presence can be felt in everything the Puritans ever wrote. Simply as a theological problem, grace entailed many related problems, which are discussed in some of the books listed in the bibliography—questions of baptism, free will, the nature of Christ, whether the few or the many are to be saved, the nature of divine love, and the question of a calling, of how a man is to live in the world and to regard his good works. Given the implications and the complexity of the problem, most Puritans sought a compromise that would protect God's sovereignty while encouraging the individual to act well. The Saint's paradoxical advice, already quoted, effects just such a compromise. The embodiment of this compromise in Puritan writing is that representative Puritan hero who appears in hundreds of treatises and poems: the poor doubting Christian. Humbly uncertain of his graciousness but not so uncertain that he despairs of it, he makes anxiety a way of life.

There is no overestimating the importance of the problem of grace in Puritan life. It swept up into itself all the other issues of Puritan society, including the very existence of that society and its form of organization.

ii Puritan Literature

Puritan religious thought largely determined Puritan literary thought also. Puritans who argued that grace could be worked for, highly valued the sermon. The sermon was a major literary form to colonial New Englanders, who often listened to sermons two or three times a week, two or three hours each time, and attentively. Like the related art of meditation, a sort of preaching to oneself, the sermon could prepare a man for grace by bringing him to a conviction of his own sinfulness. It did this not by affording an intellectual understanding of sin but, as Hooker says, by awakening the sinner to a lively perception, a true sight, of his own sinfulness. Hooker imagines the preacher as a physician (a popular Puritan comparison) who painfully lays his finger on the sore in order to heal. Shepard means sermons to be "axes and wedges . . . used to hew and break this rough, uneven, bold, yet professing age." Preachers like Shepard and Hooker knew that if they hoped to "hew and break," to "pinch the sluggard" and move his heart, they must avoid tired and conventional language. Translated into literary theory, the Puritan insistence on distinguishing mere notional understanding from genuine changes of feeling became a lofty hatred of clichés, cant, and any mere semblance of sincerity. The outstanding quality of the best Puritan writing is eloquence—a passionate honesty in the grip of a mighty theme.

Similarly, Puritan preachers who valued the sermon as a means of grace (and all preachers who wished to make God's word available) demanded that the sermon be easily understood. Hooker briefly expounds this Puritan ideal of the plain style in his *Preface*. The sermon, he says, must strike "the apprehension of the meanest." Other considerations than the desire to make God's word comprehensible justified the plain style. Literary style in the early seventeenth century had religious and political connotations. A heightened, elaborate, metaphysical style had become identified with Catholic and Anglican writers. Also, some Puritans felt that the plain style alone bespoke the conditions of their lives in the New World, "in the wildernesse," Hooker writes, "where curiosity is not studied." And most Puritans associated iconography with unscriptural religion; their insistence on a plain style forwarded their larger effort to strip the church of symbolism and embellishment.

Yet in literary theory as elsewhere, Puritans differed. "The meanest" to whose comprehension the preacher addressed himself, after all, varied from congregation to congregation. The lowest level of comprehension in a Boston congregation might be able to digest more complex ideas than the lowest level at Westfield. So the Boston preacher could serve up meatier substance more elaborately dressed. Most preachers divided their sermons into three or four parts: a statement of some biblical text, followed by a learned explication of the text, followed by a statement of the "use" or "application" of the doctrine to the sinner's own life. In the "use," preachers planned not merely to instruct the mind but to move the heart, and here they found rhythmic and verbal devices effective. Even ministers who insisted on the plain style were sometimes forced to admit, as Hooker does here, that the subject often dictates its own terms and that difficult subjects simply make difficult sermons. Indeed, Hooker's style is far more richly figured and imagistic than Cotton's. To read the following selections from Hooker, Cotton, and Shepard is to realize that the Puritans did not take the plain style as a rule.

Puritans applied the theory of the plain style to verse too, and just as flexibly. Puritan poets as well as preachers tolerated a heightened, figured style. The range of Puritan poetry takes in both the somberly plain style of Anne Bradstreet and the animated, embossed style of Edward Taylor. A literate and cultured group, the Puritans liked poetry, wrote a good deal of it, and thought it an important and legitimate use of language, largely because of its importance in the Old Testament. Generally, Puritan poets shunned the devices of classical literature because of their association with heathen deities, and very complicated metaphors because they drew the reader's attention away from the pious matter of the poem. These same poets freely used all of the poetic forms and devices of the Bible—acrostics, acronyms, types, anagrams, anastomasia, elegies and the like. The supreme importance which Puritans placed on reading and understanding the Bible—the source of all law—made illiteracy a kind of sin and made Puritanism preeminently a verbal culture.

Although Puritan New England bred many poets and poetasters, the range and quality of Puritan verse are typified here by a triumvirate of important writers—Anne Bradstreet, Michael Wigglesworth, and Edward Taylor. ANNE BRADSTREET (1612–1672), author of the first volume of poems written in America, *The Tenth Muse*, abandoned her comfortable and educated upper-middle-class life in England and came to Massachusetts in 1630. She was a woman of some stature in New England—the daughter of one governor and the wife of another—and in England, where her poems enjoyed some reputation. Her verse provides an inexhaustible insight into Puritan life, for the voice and personality that address us in it belong to the ideal Puritan wife. Her tone and manner declare the qualities Puritans expected their wives to have: love, piety, modesty, chasteness, devotion to family, quiet intelligence—and for all that, a clear acceptance of her sexual station and an unwillingness to place herself above men. Her habitual, typically Puritan mood is one of meditation and self-examination—an appropriate mood for a mature woman who wrote many of her best poems at about the age of fifty. As an ideal Puritan wife, her thoughts revolve about her family, which is both the subject of her verse and a metaphor for all experience. Many Puritans saw the family as a symbol of the structure of the universe. God governs earth and heaven as a father governs his family. At their most harmonious, relationships in state, church, and home repeat this divine familial order. Thus, in addressing her own family, Anne Bradstreet addresses the root of society and the universe at large.

Her verse treats nearly every side of family life: in-laws, furniture, temporary partings, child-rearing, not omitting sex. A celebrant, like

Milton, of "married chastity," she writes in one poem of her husband, called far away on business:

> My chilled limbs now numbed lie forlorn:
> Return, return, sweet sol, from Capricorn.
> In this dead time, alas, what can I more
> Than view those fruits which through thy heat I bore?

Anne Bradstreet's rather mournful longing for her husband's "heat" makes groundless the easy traditional assumption that the Puritans hated sex. They merely took sex very seriously. With Saint Augustine and many medieval thinkers, they saw it as a procreative act, hence the source of society and of all loving human relationships. Through sex, as Milton wrote, "Relations dear, and all the charities/ Of father, son, and brother first were known." Puritans did scorn promiscuous and sterile sex because it corrupted these relations and charities.

As an ideal Puritan wife, Anne Bradstreet also passes on to her children the lessons life has taught her—those of affliction and mutability. This world, Puritans were fond of saying, must be loved with "weaned affections," as a child loves the mother it must forsake. Anne Bradstreet combines the classical theme of *vanitas vanitatum*—all is vanity— with this Puritan theme of weaned affections. Her consuming, Shakespearean awareness of time and change plays a constant, affecting counterpoint to the children and husband she dotes on but must eventually leave. Her interest in death and time are no more bookish, however, than the omnipresent motto on Puritan tombstones: *memento mori*, remember death. Such a caution, kept always in mind, helped absorb the otherwise devastating shocks of a wilderness where through fire, cold, disease, or Indian attack, people died like flies. Only two of Cotton Mather's fifteen children survived him; on separate days within two weeks, his wife and three of his children died. It is to prepare psychologically for such shocks that, with the exultant morbidity of an Emily Dickinson, Anne Bradstreet depicts death in her poems as a welcome bridegroom.

The many-sided importance of the family in New England made inevitable the formation of a regional literary tradition distinct from English tradition. Because the Puritans considered their own families and those of their ancestors exalted subjects for literature, they more and more in their writing examined and praised the local scene, the local past, the life actually lived in New England. In some cases, this reverence for the family degenerated into mere ancestor worship and bed-warmer history; in others it produced the dynasties through which the New England culture perpetuated itself—such families as the Mathers, the Adamses, the Lowells, and most recently the Kennedys.

Although Anne Bradstreet designed many of her poems as instruction for her children, her poetic interests were more dramatic than didactic. One thoroughly didactic Puritan poet was MICHAEL WIGGLESWORTH (1631–1705), the author of several long works in verse and prose, including the most popular poem written in colonial America, *The Day of Doom*. Wigglesworth came to New England at the age of seven, graduated first in his class at Harvard (and returned as a tutor), then undertook the ministry of Malden, Massachusetts, where he was also a physician (although in frail health himself most of his life). The didactic purpose of *The Day of Doom* is to warn sinners about what inescapably awaits them on Judgment Day if they do not reform. Although Wigglesworth wrote a college oration praising eloquence, his poem epitomizes the plain style. He may have intended his undecorated language and simple ballad meter to compete with the secular, sometimes bawdy, ballads beginning to be hawked in New England in his time; but mostly he aimed at making his message memorable and easily understood by children. Fitly, the voice that addresses us in *The Day of Doom* belongs to the Puritan preacher. Indeed, Wigglesworth unfolds the poem as if it were a sermon: the biblical texts which he cites in the margin both authorize the didactic message of the verse and supply difficult texts which the verse explicates simply and palatably.

The Day of Doom is the Puritan *Divine Comedy*. Like Dante, Wigglesworth examines in series the various classes of sinners: those who thought they were saved simply because they took communion; those who acted well only to soothe their consciences, not to glorify God; "civil honest men"; the persecuted who feared to act as believers; the virtuous pagans; infants who died before baptism. The poem progresses by moving from the less to the more theologically perplexing cases, culminating in the discussion of predestination and infant damnation. The progress takes the form of a trial in which one accused sinner after another tries to justify his behavior. Each attempt is parried by the arguments of a rather Old Testament Christ—less a Sacrificer than a

Judge—whose legalistic logic at last wins the sinner's assent. In trying to justify God's ways, Christ reckons with a number of problems in the theory of grace. He resolves the problem of predestination versus free will much as does Milton's God, by distinguishing predestination from foreknowledge. God knows what will happen but does not cause it to happen. He foresees from the beginning of time the free choices man will make. God knows what man will do, yet man is responsible for doing it. If this justification is unsatisfying in its intellectual and emotional logic, it is because Wigglesworth conceives a God whose sovereignty depends on His total freedom in disposing human events, but whose freedom must be limited lest it appear arbitrary. The only answer for man is to live by the terms of the dilemma itself, neither overconfident of salvation nor despairing. Wigglesworth gives hope without being hopeful and strikes fear without mortifying.

Subtler answers to many of the same questions came from the greatest American Puritan poet, EDWARD TAYLOR (c. 1642–1729). At the age of twenty-six Taylor fled the Restoration of non-Puritan rule in England for Boston. He matriculated in the class of 1671 at Harvard, serving for a while as college butler and rooming with his lifelong friend Samuel Sewall. In 1671 he accepted what turned out to be a lifelong pastorate at the frontier village of Westfield, Massachusetts, a hundred miles remote from Boston. There he wrote much, in many forms, on many subjects: books on herbs and cordials, several difficult theological treatises, a long poem on the history of Protestantism, and a few dozen shorter poems. His two major poetic works are the great *Gods Determinations touching his Elect* and the *Preparatory Meditations*, a collection of more than two hundred poems which he worked on for forty-three years. During his lifetime he published only a few pages of his work, and in his will asked his descendants not to publish the rest. The first large selection of his poetry appeared only in 1939.

What makes Taylor the greatest American Puritan poet is both the subtlety of his theology and the poetic language he found for it. His language wears out whole vocabularies as it leaps with inspired surprise through law, science, cookery, gaming, theology, finance, perfumery, music, winemaking, barrelmaking, clothmaking—seeking God in a linguistic blizzard. Combining the rare theological skills of Jonathan Edwards and the passionate domestic vision of Anne Bradstreet, Taylor was able, in Emerson's phrase, to "domesticate culture" and to deal with the transcendental in terms of the near. In his works Puritanism reveals itself in the fullness of both its intellectual daring and its fond domesticity. To use one of Taylor's favorite words, the effect is "knottiness," a crabbed, unleavened intensity of vision that gives shape and accent to the Puritans' inmost feelings about existence. Taylor is also a difficult poet because of his difficult ambition: to forge the illogicalities of Puritan thought into a seamless defense of the Puritan way of life.

One of these illogicalities is the recurrent subject of Taylor's *Preparatory Meditations*, written to "prepare" him to give communion. These poems occasionally treat such abstruse matters as typology, but more often they explore the dilemmas arising from human depravity. Perhaps no other Puritan but Edwards insists so absolutely on man's innate corruption and conveys it so starkly. In his *Meditations* Taylor tries to fathom miraculously how this infinite depravity can merge in communion with the infinite beauty and goodness of God, and how— the corresponding rhetorical problem—the poet can ever praise God adequately. Each meditation means a fresh hunt for suitable language. The outpour of crisscrossing imagery—quite the opposite of the plain style—must be endless, because the effort to flesh God's beauty in the language of corrupt man must always be imperfect. How can stars, Taylor asks, woo lobster claws? How can man, the dungheap, canker, pustule, spider, weed, cockroach, ink, ever be joined with God, the jewel, gold, radiance, garden, perfume? He came closest to answering the question in his masterpiece, *Gods Determinations touching his Elect*.

If *The Day of Doom* is the Puritan *Divine Comedy*, *Gods Determinations* is the Puritan *Summa Theologica*. Through its plot and characters Taylor projects a synthesis of all the divergent elements in Puritan thought: grace and works, justice and mercy, Old and New Testaments, free will and determinism, Calvin and the Covenant. Taylor tasks himself with nothing less than explaining the bewildering Puritan God who "Frowns with a Smiling Face." His hero is the poor doubting Christian, burdened with "fears of fitness" for his salvation. Taylor probes his fears subtly and ingeniously to extricate the Christian's authentic self from the psychological tangle of wishes, delusions, and lies. The poem could be called a *psychomachia*, or mind drama, for it dramatizes the hero's state by representing contending subjective forces as contending characters. As in *The Day of Doom*, this psychic drama takes the form primarily of a "case," a legal "determination," a courtroom struggle in which one part of the fearful defendant's psyche tries another part. The trial has three parts, as suggested by Taylor's full title: (1) Gods Determinations touching his Elect; (2) The Elects Combat in their Conversion; (3) Coming up to God in Christ together with the Comfortable Effects thereof. The crucial section (which contains the opening quotation of this preface) begins with "Doubts from Satans Temptations Answered" and ends with "The Effect of this Discourse upon the second, and third Rancks." In these three hundred lines Taylor forces the mightily straining and opposed claims of Puritanism to a difficult resolution. Part Three follows, in which, the soul's doubts having been answered, images of marriage and harmony displace the earlier images of legal and military contest.

If this final harmony seems forced, it is because Taylor's answers to the poor Christian's doubts seem evasive. In Taylor's analysis, a tantalizing double bind paralyzes the soul. Humility and pride both mislead it. Humility makes the soul despair of God's mercy; pride makes it oblivious of God's vengeance. A conviction of sinfulness and a conviction of sinlessness are both similarly misleading. If the soul believes itself free from sin, it is hypocritical and belongs in hell; yet if the soul knows it is full of sin, it stands self-condemned. This cunning bind, the Saint points out, is the invention of Satan, who will badger the soul no matter what it feels:

> To proove thee Graceless he thy sins persues:
> To proove thee sinfull, doth thy Grace accuse.

If the soul claims graciousness, Satan accuses it of pride and hypocrisy; if the soul longs for graciousness, Satan insists on its sinfulness. By confounding the soul, Satan hopes to convince it "That God's a Heape of Contradictions high," which is to say that Puritanism makes no sense.

The way out of this bind is indicated in Taylor's chastely beautiful preface, with its Jobean mockery of wisdom. Here he ponders the paradox of all and nothing, the same paradox of the *Preparatory Meditations*. How can finite depraved man know infinite, holy God? In freeing the soul, the crucial section of the poem returns to this paradox. Man's understanding is necessarily imperfect. Man can never be filled with God because God is infinite and man is finite. Man, the Saint observes, desires God to come into him: "God, and His All, 's the Object of the

Will." Yet being finite, man cannot contain All: "What Mortall can contain immortall bliss"? Being finite, man can never be perfect. A physical law dooms him to doubt the reality of his graciousness. He can never be wholly gracious in the sense of being filled with the infinite God.

The only possible posture for the soul is the ambiguous one described in the preface, a state of hopeful doubt. This doubt itself, the Saint promises, will dissolve on Judgment Day. With it will come undone all the knotty riddles given men as rules by the God who "Frowns with a Smiling Face." Then the soul's

> . . . Wildred state will wane away, and hence
> These Crooked Passages will soon appear
> The Curious needlework of Providence,
> Embroidered with golden Spangles Cleare.
> Judge not this Web while in the Loom, but stay
> From judging it untill the judgment day.

Taylor's advice to "Judge not this Web" but to wait until the "Crooked Passages" (an apt description of the whole poem) will be straightened, provides a rather shaky start for the triumphal concluding images of marriage and harmony. Yet the agitated effect of the poem, explaining the unexplainable and defending the indefensible, faithfully records Puritan life, where the poor doubting Christian, caring and not caring, walks a slack rope over the infernal abyss, steadied only as he can balance, weight against weight, confidence and self-abasement, grace and works, mercy and justice; too much of one and he falls.

iii The Breakup of Organized Puritanism

Puritanism did, after not very long, fall. From about 1650 on, Puritan society grew more and more unsettled. By 1700 it was in such disarray that a synthesis such as the one Taylor attempted became necessary for its survival. Much of the trouble began with younger generations of Puritans who failed any more to experience the mystical state which the Puritans called grace. Brought up in the New World, their families prospering, the young had lost much of the social and religious zeal that activated the first settlers. The numbers of full church members, the Saints, dropped sharply; the churches began emptying out.

Various Puritans drew up proposals for extending the church franchise so as to admit to voting privileges those who had not yet experienced grace. The most famous of these was the Half-Way Covenant of 1662, which admitted to the church certain baptized persons who had not experienced grace but forbade them from taking communion. Even more boldly, Solomon Stoddard, the grandfather of Jonathan Edwards, proposed admitting everyone to communion. He redefined communion as a means of conversion rather than the privilege of the already converted. In such proposals, orthodox ministers like Taylor foresaw the imminent collapse of Puritanism. Taylor refused to admit to communion, thus to full voting privileges, anyone who had not had the traditional experience of grace. In effect, by writing *Gods Determinations*, Taylor was struggling not only to solve the problem of grace but to keep Puritanism alive. To appreciate how the two problems had become identical, one should read the poem together with Taylor's *Treatise on the Lords Supper*, excerpted here. Taylor hoped to meet the social crisis by prescribing a state of hopeful doubt as a sufficient qualification for communion. That way, both the new generation and the older one could remain in the fold without diluting the intensity of the church's piety. But the case was hopeless. The church would either insist on staying a church for mystics and continue emptying out, or it would admit the young and become a church for the decently behaved. The poem's rather tortured and unsatisfactory logic is the result of trying to bring the young back into the church without making membership automatic.

Wigglesworth's *Day of Doom*, too, is addressed not only to common sinners but to the generation of the 1660's which had slid back from the intense piety of the founders. Wigglesworth warns of the community's failure to maintain its solemn purpose and exhorts the new generation to persist in the original design. The literary form for this communal denunciation has been named the *jeremiad*. Perry Miller regarded the jeremiad, exemplified by *The Day of Doom* and implicitly by *Gods Determinations*, as the first distinctively American literary form. Within these denunciations of communal guilt and exhortations to communal virtue there grew a sense of a lost golden age in America, of an ideal early generation and the ideally excellent past ministers. In the jeremiad, as also in the elegy, Puritans began to express their sense of the richness and continuity of their lives in the New World. In these two forms more than in any others, one can trace the separation of American literature from the mainstream of English literature.

The increasing number of jeremiads after 1660 signifies the continued deterioration of Puritanism even as they denounce it. Many events and developments beside the backsliding of the young sped the breakup of organized Puritanism: the Restoration in England; the increasing influence of rationalistic thought; the growing prosperity of New England's rich; the challenge to clerical power by politicians, merchants, and even newspaper editors like Benjamin Franklin; the infiltration of Anglican groups into New England; a series of debilitating and expensive Indian wars that left a deflated currency; the establishment of a new charter in 1692 that drew New England more than ever before under the supervision of the crown. The Puritans' response to these changes can be seen in the following selections from Samuel Sewall, Cotton Mather, and Jonathan Edwards.

The versatility of the landowner and exporter SAMUEL SEWALL (1652–1730) placed him where he could observe these changes from the inside. After arriving from England at the age of nine, he graduated Harvard College in 1671. Discovering no gift in himself for theology, he entered business, married the daughter of the wealthiest man in Massachusetts, and soon became its wealthiest merchant himself. At various times he managed the Boston printing press and operated a bookstore, served on the Council, sat as a judge at the Salem witchcraft court, and eventually became chief justice of Massachusetts. He also led the singing in church, studied biblical prophecy, dabbled in verse, wrote against Negro slavery, and remained vigorous enough at sixty-eight to begin courting a new wife. This busy life—and such momentous events as the Salem trials and King Philip's War—he recorded in his important *Diary*, documenting the changes in Puritan society between 1673 and 1729.

The earlier Puritans also loved to study their own and others' lives. They were preoccupied with the inner life and watched it closely for signs of grace. In a few ways, Sewall's *Diary* differs little from theirs. He habitually draws spiritual lessons from the natural world, and, marking out his life in terms of funerals attended or missed, shares their fascinated, veritably Egyptian interest in death. Yet Sewall's *Diary* records a different world and records it in a different way. In the Boston it looks upon, a dancing master seeks employment and a brothel has already found it. Lewdness and profaneness exist, Sewall writes, such as "has hardly been heard of before." By 1700 the public life of Boston had become dramatically degraded from the ideal of the City on the Hill. As ministers learned to share their power with banking interests and merchants, the political atmosphere grew rank with bribery, threats, power plays, and infighting. Moreover, the essence of the older Puritan style, plain or not, was its gravity. Now the new backbiting spirit in Boston vented itself in comic and sometime bawdy ballads, broadsides, and parodies, and in Benjamin Franklin's *Dogood Papers* (represented in Part Two), with their attack on the traditional and customary New England ways, including such hallowed, but by now distastefully provincial, Puritan arts as the writing of elegies. The bantering air of Sewall's courtships reflects this coarsened tone of Puritan life. He calculates his marital prospects in terms of mortgages, slaves, gloves, and chocolates; the state of his soul adds little to the sum.

What was lost in grace and piety, however, was perhaps gained in good works and social benevolence. Sewall's public renunciation of his part in the witchcraft proceedings implies some tarnishing of the golden age, a sense that the older orthodoxy had not always been right, and had acted too harshly. His attack on slavery is only one expression of a new charitableness in Puritanism. Around 1700 charity and relief societies were formed all over Boston to help the poor, the orphaned, or the dispossessed. Sewall's *Selling of Joseph*, the first anti-slavery tract printed in America, reveals a change in Puritanism from being good within oneself to doing good in this world. (Not all Puritans turned this way, of course; Edward Taylor's works are a warning to turn back.) From the start of colonization, Puritans had owned slaves, and many merchants in Boston prospered on the slave trade. Sewall's arguments against slavery, like the comparable ones by Cotton Mather also included here, urge the unchristianity of slavery with only slightly greater emphasis than they deplore its impracticality. Most Puritans thought of the black man as possessing a soul no different from the white man's, and no less worthy of salvation. Yet the close familial organization of Puritan society denied the slave any place within it. In Sewall's *Diary*, in short, the grave inwardness of the earlier Puritans has become less grave and less inward.

But no writer illustrates the growing worldliness of Puritan society more colorfully, perhaps garishly, than COTTON MATHER (1663–1728).

Son of the famous Increase Mather and grandson of John Cotton, Mather incorporated a torrential energy that issued during his lifetime in more than four hundred books and treatises, several of them volumes long. While writing he cared for a large family, preached to the most prestigious congregation in America, kept up a vast correspondence at home and abroad, conducted scientific experiments, performed marriage ceremonies every few days, took sides in every conceivable political and religious squabble in Massachusetts, and, endlessly, did favors for as many people as he could enlist, particularly among the poor, whose financial lot he never escaped for very long, and always just barely. His need to involve himself in everything made him widely detested in Massachusetts. Abroad, his reputation was more favorable. The University of Glasgow awarded him an honorary Doctor of Divinity degree, and the scientists of the Royal Society made him a Fellow. In feeding his voracious interests, Mather reduced the mental distance separating America from Europe and ended the "cultural lag" that for a long time had kept current American fashions of thought similar to European fashions a generation earlier. Determined to stay abreast of the latest developments in European thought and culture, Mather was probably the best-informed man of his time in America.

This cosmopolitanism in Mather, and to a lesser degree in Sewall, is itself a novelty in Puritan life. Most earlier Puritans welcomed their separation from European culture, since it also isolated them from Europe's warfare and corruption. But Mather felt his talents suffocated by this parochialism. In breaking out of the rather cloistered world of the earlier Puritans, he left behind the obsessive concern with solving a few problems of great complexity. Although he wrote on everything, he wrote very little on theology. He did write constantly on religious subjects, but never with the analytical intent of Edward Taylor or Jonathan Edwards. In what is perhaps Mather's most typical work, *Bonifacius*, the theological-philosophical preoccupation of the earlier Puritans, the need to justify Puritanism, has suddenly disappeared.

To Mather, the art of doing good described in *Bonifacius* meant, in the largest sense, seeing to it that the great reformation begun by Calvin and Luther finally succeeded, and that all men became Reformed Christians. From this one concern flow his many, individual, specific instructions for doing good. *Bonifacius* makes clear, however, that Mather never confused doing good with graciousness, piousness with piety. While he clung to the exalted piety of the earlier Puritans, it is worth repeating, he abandoned the strenuous intellectual effort to explain and justify it. As the warning that concludes *Bonifacius* also makes clear, Mather expected a do-gooder to be spat upon, as he was. Indeed the central theme of Mather's existence, the motif that orders everything he wrote, is that, like Christ, every man must attempt to do good and must expect, like Christ, to be crucified for it. Expecting to be martyred for every breath he took, whether praying for the soul of his reckless son or gathering firewood for the poor, Mather has often been classified as a paranoid—or, what is worse, a pompous ass. Yet his idea of doing good grew out of the Puritan respect for conscience, the "majority of one," and in the corrupt political life of Boston around 1700, many of his fantasies sprang to life. He was defamed in the press, gossiped about all over Boston, and threatened with jail; his letters to others were intercepted; for pleading with the citizens of Boston to inoculate themselves against smallpox, he became the target of an assassin's bomb.

In science Mather saw a specially productive means for doing good. Earlier Puritans enjoyed scientific investigation and felt confident that no discovery about the physical world could clash with scriptural revelation. But Mather looked on science as a means of large-scale social benevolence, a means for curing disease, enriching agriculture, understanding the mind. Because the climate and topography of the New World opened unique possibilities for scientific study in America, it was in science (along with political theory) that colonial America most deeply influenced European thought. Only one product of Mather's interest was *Curiosa Americana*, represented here, a collection of lengthy communications on the American scene which he sent to the Royal Society in London. With William Byrd's *Histories*, Mather's *Curiosa* give the liveliest and most accurate descriptions of nature in early American literature. Although his scientific vision was tinted by do-goodism and the wish to master a gentlemanly accomplishment, Mather was neither more nor less credulous than the leading scientists of his time, with whom he corresponded. Much about Mather's life and personality remains problematic; to square his scientific interest with his printed defense of the Salem witchcraft trials seems especially so. Enough to say of this exceedingly complex biographical point that Mather's shallow understanding of other people and his reverence for his elders combined to force him into defending the trials. Privately he distrusted the trials and feared their consequences. Like the people he describes in the following selection, he considered "spectral representation"—the chief form of evidence offered at the trials—invalid.

But in no way does Mather illustrate the changes in Puritanism so clearly, and indeed garishly, as by his emergent nationalism. No writer before Mather is so intensely conscious of writing as an American or so preoccupied with seeing America. His introduction to *Parentator* (a life of his father) is among the earliest retorts by an American to foreign critics, especially Englishmen, who assume that every American lacks culture and is incapable of acquiring it. The exaggerated style and pompous tone of Mather's *Magnalia* exclaim that an American can equal any European in vastness of learning and personal *éclat*. Mather's performance in the *Magnalia* is both remarkable and dismaying. It is remarkable that any American in 1700 could have amassed so spectacularly much learning; *Magnalia* reads like a review book on the Vatican library. Yet Mather wears his learning much the same way as he signed his name "Doctor of Divinity" and "Fellow of the Royal Society"— as a title. His self-important style betrays the sense of cultural inferiority so long felt by American writers anxious to impress English readers with their cultivation—and so often ending in the overblown-ness and extravagance that characterize a whole epical strain of American writing from *Magnalia* to Joel Barlow's *Columbiad,* to *Moby Dick* and *Song of Myself,* to the works of Thomas Wolfe, William Faulkner, and Norman Mailer. The pretentious style of the *Magnalia* also marks how far Mather and some of his contemporaries had come from any earlier Puritan considerations of a plain style. With his vast learning, balanced sentences, consciousness of method, witty puns, and polylingual ornamentation, Mather appears in the book as a model of the eighteenth century gentleman, a type from a new age. In Mather, the Puritan as a historical figure is becoming the Puritan as a cultural phenomenon; the Puritan is shading off into someone puritanical.

The career of the greatest Puritan thinker, JONATHAN EDWARDS (1703–1758), outlasted the life of Puritanism as a form of social organization and witnessed its fall. Edwards' keen logic (which Bertrand Russell once compared to Aristotle's) sought written expression even during his boyhood in Connecticut, when he wrote precociously but precisely on insects and on the mind. He graduated from Yale in 1720, preached for a while in New York, returned to Yale for three years as a tutor, and in 1727 succeeded his grandfather, Solomon Stoddard, at the influential pulpit of Northampton. Although for the next two decades he shepherded his congregation through the religious revival known as the Great Awakening, they released him from his ministry after shrilly repudiating his conservative views on grace and communion. For a while he lived as a minister and missionary to the Indians in Stockbridge, Massachusetts, where he wrote some of his most profound works, including *The Freedom of the Will* and *The Nature of True Virtue*. In 1757 he was chosen president of the College of New Jersey, later Princeton, where the next year he died of a smallpox inoculation. After the Revolution, many Americans drew up lists of the great men America had produced, to assert the achievements of the infant republic and counter foreign attacks upon its genius. The two names most frequently listed are those of Benjamin Franklin and Jonathan Edwards.

Edwards' work can be judged in different ways: as philosophy, as literature, as religion, as an expression of the Enlightenment. His importance to Puritanism, however, was twofold: he tried to reverse its decline by accommodating it to the rationalistic eighteenth century, and he achieved the most brilliant intellectual solutions to its inherent problems. In the priority he gave to certain of those problems, and in the way he solved them, he closely resembles Edward Taylor. Like Taylor, he tried to invent a great synthesis of Puritan ideas. Unlike Taylor, he included the imposing truths about nature and man uncovered by the eighteenth-century philosophers, especially John Locke, whose works Edwards read while in college. It could be said that Edwards tried to revitalize Puritanism by answering its classic questions in terms of Locke. And Edwards was the last Puritan thinker to deal extensively with those problems in America.

As a figure in American history, Edwards' importance lies in his leadership during the revivals that "awakened" America, England, and Europe in the middle of the eighteenth century. In New England, the climax of the revivals came between 1739 and 1742. Edwards' sermons of the period do fume with the hellfire and brimstone that has come to be assigned, wrongly, to all Puritan preachers. The present volume includes his white-hot sermon *The Future Punishment of the Wicked*. At times it surpasses the better-known *Sinners in the Hands of an Angry God* by the vividness, the panicking actuality, of its imaginings of an eternity without God. For Edwards the spiritual world was as real as this one. The reader can share this reality because Edwards' scalding sermons and serene writings on heaven render the other world through sense experience. In the unspeakably awful hell promised the wicked, man lives forever, "full of fire"; in the rarified air of heaven, the saints, a thousand miles apart, can converse.

American historians still debate the significance of the revivals. Some regard them as a harbinger of the Revolution, a popular movement that all but destroyed the already weakened power of the clergy. To Edwards the revivals portended the total reformation of the world promised in Scripture. He believed, too, that the work of reformation had begun in America, in fact in New England. His essay *The Revival of Religion in New England* announces in revival terms what his grandson Timothy Dwight would call the "glorious contrast" between the corruption of Europe and the goodness of America—a theme of American writers from the Puritans to Hemingway. "The one continent has slain Jesus," Edwards saw, "the other will build his temple." Through the revivals the Puritan God who for so long had failed to speak to his City on the Hill spoke once more, commanding the city to re-arise.

But what rose again was only the old problem of grace. For many people the experience of conversion during the revivals was intense but quickly over. How, then, can one distinguish grace from its counterfeits? What is grace? Much of Edwards' thinking on these traditional, but now specially vexing, questions appears in his *Miscellanies*, the collection of random forays in logic from which he later developed his masterful treatises. Taking Locke's theory that all knowledge comes through the senses, Edwards argued that grace must depend upon a new, supernatural sense. This new mode of perception can come only from God. Can one then, as the earlier Puritans also asked, work toward achieving this state? How responsible is any man for his experience? In Edwards' time the problem demanded a surer resolution than ever before, not only because of the failure of many conversions to last, but also because of the spreading revival of the philosophy of Arminianism, which emphasized man's free will. If man did everything for himself, Edwards asked, what did God do?

Against the Arminians, Edwards argued in quasi-scientific, mechanistic terms. Every effect must have a cause; the will, too, must be caused, therefore cannot be free. Some outside cause must have determined the first act of will by the first man, since the will cannot have willed itself into existence. But if man's will is caused, how can he be held responsible for his acts, and how can he work for his salvation? Edwards attacked the problem by outflanking it. The problem only arises, he said, because of an inexact understanding of love. In love we both will and are will-less; we both love and are moved to love. As in mortal human love, in a state of grace—of loving God—we both consent and are compelled. God does it, and we do it too. Edwards' concept of gracious freedom recalls a nineteenth-century version of Protestant mysticism, the experiencing of what Emerson called the oversoul. In his poem "The Problem" Emerson described the mood of a cathedral architect:

> Art might obey, but not surpass.
> The passive Master lent his hand
> To the vast soul that o'er him planned . . . .

For Edwards, the person filled with gracious affections also freely "lends" himself while obeying the soul that "plans" and manipulates him. Man must work for grace even while passively receiving it.

Why then, as the earlier Puritans also asked, do we need Scripture, a church, a ministry, a society? Edwards solved this central problem of the New England theology, and the entire Puritan problem of freedom and restraint, by identifying love and knowledge as one thing. In a state of grace, he wrote, "here is by this light only given a due apprehension of the same truths that are revealed in the word of God." Edwards conceived of grace as an illumination of Scripture. Since grace cannot be experienced without a knowledge of Scripture, there can be no grace without a ministry to explain it, a church in which to teach it, a society to preserve it. An analogy may clarify his argument: a physicist contemplates a difficult problem in physics. At some moment he becomes inspired, and his inspiration allows him to solve the problem. The problem does not cause the inspiration, which comes from God. Yet without the problem there would be no inspiration. Similarly, without Scripture, church, and society, there would be no grace, although they do not cause grace. In a gracious state one beholds the universe as it really is, apart from the way one has been taught to perceive it, which means that at last one understands Scripture, the word of God. Grace for Edwards is the condition Edward Taylor withheld for Judgment Day, when God's "crooked passages" unknot. The gracious person accepts the crooked passages, loves without bewilderment the God who "frowns with a smiling face," perceives beauty in the difficult doctrines of Puritanism. He beholds in willing consent the actual nature of things. He loves a universe that exists not for his understanding, but for God.

But no measurement of Edwards' many achievements can omit the aesthetic dimension, the quiet formal beauty of his essays. He was a great writer. In his works an unyielding logic is the instrument by which a serenely sweet disposition precisely re-creates its unique vision of life. Indeed, the rock-ribbed delicacy of Edwards' style is itself but an expression of this vision. In grace, man beholds his place in the scheme of God's creation as he holds that whole infinitely complex scheme, its every nuance intact, in steady suspended view. Similarly, in Edwards' style—as in the music of his near-contemporary Johann Sebastian Bach —amid the steely orchestration and the insidious marshalling of themes, slight distinctions and definitions made ten or fifteen pages earlier wait their turn, always faintly there, to become the major note. Nuance with nuance, distinction with distinction combines, fuses in an irresistible confluence of truth until the height of argument, having shaped all that preceded it, glows and reverberates with all that preceded it, the inter-relatedness of every nuance glimpsed and heard, as in grace, but beyond analysis, the whole complex scheme, its every nuance intact, held in steady, suspended view.

Edwards' thoroughly organic language again calls to mind Emerson. Emerson too believed that language images forth the moral structure of the universe, that through using language man can become aware of the divinity within himself and without, that as Edwards says in the present essay on *Moral Government*, "all moral agents are *conversible* agents." The kinship between Edwards and Emerson is closer than a sharing of theories of language. It suggests that Puritanism grew into later American thought by way of a continued concern for authentic experience, for a man's being his most real self and able to discern his counterfeit selves. "Be it life or death," Thoreau said, "we crave only reality."

Although Edwards and other Puritans dedicated their freshest energies to finding that reality, that real self, we may feel that they failed. The truth, we may feel, ought to be starker, more direct than Edwards' slippery, labyrinthine arguments, or the blatant paradoxes of Edward

Taylor's Saint. What called into being the massive counterpointings of Edwards and the Puritans before him, however, was the need to reconcile the truth of self with a pragmatic need to live in an ordered world with others. The problem of how the self may express its nature while recognizing its communal obligations has continued to activate American thought and experience. If Edwards' answers fail, the attempts of later Americans to be themselves in company with others—whether whaling aboard the Pequod, hoeing potatoes at Brook Farm, or converging on the Woodstock Music Festival—have been no less tentative, ambiguous, or short-lived.

Yet the very effort makes Edwards and the Puritans interesting to us, and perhaps useful. Recent history forces us also to reckon with elusive questions of guilt, punishment, and moral responsibility, to find a definition of love that we can use. Puritanism was an extraordinary faith. It brought to public attention and for public discussion issues of intellectual and theological difficulty that before had been the preserve of schoolmen. It made every man responsible for understanding the rich intellectual problems surrounding his salvation and his life in the world. It is doubtful that the public life of any society has ever again been so intellectual and complex as it was in Puritan New England, or that the private lives of the members of any society have ever again been so honest and unsparing, or that the language of any society has ever again been so precise, demanded so much awareness of the problems of the past, insisted on the truth with so much passion.

The following are some important studies of Puritanism: Conrad Cherry, *The Theology of Jonathan Edwards* (New York, 1966); Everett Emerson, *John Cotton* (New York, 1965); Norman Grabo, *Edward Taylor* (New York, 1961); William Haller, *The Rise of Puritanism* (New York, 1938); Chadwick Hansen, *Witchcraft at Salem* (New York, 1969); Alan Heimert, *Religion and The American Mind: From the Great Awakening to the Revolution* (Cambridge, Mass., 1966); Harold Jantz, *The First Century of New England Verse* (repr. New York, 1962); Alan Ludwig, *Graven Images* (Puritan tombstone carving; Middletown, Conn., 1966); Perry Miller, *The New England Mind: The Seventeenth Century* (Cambridge, Mass., 1939); *The New England Mind: From Colony to Province* (Cambridge, Mass., 1953); *Jonathan Edwards* (New York,

1949); *Errand into the Wilderness* (Cambridge, Mass., 1953); Edmund Morgan, *The Puritan Family* (Boston, 1944); *The Puritan Dilemma* (Boston, 1958); Kenneth Murdock, *Increase Mather* (Cambridge, Mass., 1926); Norman Petit, *The Heart Prepared: Grace and Conversion in Puritan Spiritual Life* (New Haven, 1966); A. W. Plumstead, *The Wall and the Garden* (Puritan Election sermons; Minneapolis, 1968); Alan Simpson, *Puritanism in Old and New England* (Chicago, 1955); Williston Walker, *The Creeds and Platforms of Congregationalism* (New York, 1893); Larzer Ziff, *The Career of John Cotton: Puritanism and the American Experience* (Princeton, 1962).

JOHN COTTON

(1584–1652)

The first selection below is taken from *Gods Promise to His Plantation*. As suggested in the Introduction to Part One, Cotton was giving the Puritans Biblical justifications for the action they were about to take—sailing for the new land. Since the Bible was the authority for the Puritans, they needed to feel that their actions were sanctioned by it. Cotton, then, reminded them of God's promises concerning the placing of a people and their establishment in a new land. In the next selection, Cotton's ideas on the issue of separation of church and state become more apparent as he again appeals to Biblical authority.

From *Gods Promise to His Plantation**

> *Moreover I will appoint a place for my people Israell, and I will plant them, that they may dwell in a place of their owne, and move no more. (2 Sam. 7. 10.)*

In the beginning of this chapter we reade of *Davids* purpose to build God an house, who thereupon consulted with *Nathan* about it, one Prophet standing in neede of anothers help in such waightie matters. *Nathan* incourageth the King unto this worke, verse 3. God the same night meetes *Nathan* and tells him a contrary purpose of his: Wherein God refuseth *Davids* offer, with some kind of earnest and vehement dislike, *verse 4, 5:* Secondly, he refuseth the reason of *Davids* offer, from his long silence. For foure hundred yeares together he spake of no such thing, unto any of the Tribes of *Israel* saying, *Why build you not me an house?* in 6. 7. verses.

Now lest *David* should be discouraged with this answer, the Lord bids *Nathan* to shut up his speech with words of encouragement, and so he remoues his discouragement two wayes:

* Old South Leaflets No. 53.

32

First, by recounting his former favours dispensed unto *David.* Secondly, by promising the continuance of the like or greater: and the rather, because of this purpose of his. And five blessings God promiseth unto *David*, and his, for his sake.

The first is in the 10. verse: *I will appoint a place for my people Israell.*

Secondly, seeing it was in his heart to build him an house, God would therefore, *build him an house renowned forever*, verse 11.

Thirdly, that he would accept of an house from *Solomon*, verse 12.

Fourthly, hee will be a Father to his sonne, vers. 14. 15.

Fifthly, that he will *establish the throne of his house for ever.*

In this 10 verse is a double blessing promised:

First, the designment of a place for his people.

Secondly, a plantation of them in that place, from whence is promised a threefold blessing.

First, they shall dwell there like Free-holders in a place of their owne.

Secondly, hee promiseth them firme and durable possession, they shall move no more.

Thirdly, they shall have peaceable and quiet resting there, The sonnes of wickedness shall afflict them no more: which is amplified by their former troubles, as before time.

From the appointment of a place for them, which is the first blessing, you may observe this note,

The placing of a people in this or that Countrey is from the appointment of the Lord.

This is evident in the Text, and the Apostle speakes of it as grounded in nature, *Acts* 17. 26. *God hath determined the times before appointed, and the bounds of our habitation. Dut. 2 chap. 5. 9.* God would not have the *Israelites* meddle with the *Edomites*, or the *Moabites*, because he had given them their land for a possession. God assigned out such a land for such a posterity, and for such a time.

QUESTION: Wherein doth this worke of God stand in appointing a place for a people?

ANSWER: First, when God espies or discovers a land for a people, as in *Ezek.* 20. 6. he brought them into a land that he had espied for them: And that is, when either he gives them to discover it themselves, or heare of it discovered by others, and fitting them.

Secondly, after he hath espied it, when he carrieth them along to it, so that they plainly see a providence of God leading them from one Country to another: As in *Exod.* 19. 4. *You have seene how I have borne you as on Eagles wings, and brought you unto my selfe.* So that though they met with many difficulties, yet hee carried them high above them all, like an eagle, flying over seas and rockes, and all hindrances.

Thirdly, when he makes roome for a people to dwell there, as in *Psal.* 80. 9. *Thou preparedst roome for them.* When *Isaac* sojourned among the *Philistines*, he digged one well, and the *Philistines* strove for it, and he called it *Esek.* and he digged another well, and for that they strove also, therefore he called it *Sitnah:* and he removed thence, and digged an other well, and for that they strove not, and he called it *Rohoboth*, and said, *For now the Lord hath made roomee for us, and we shall be fruitfull in the Land.* Now no *Esek*, no *Sitnah*, no quarrel or contention, but now he sits downe in *Rohoboth* in a peaceable roome.

Now God makes room for a people 3 wayes:

First, when he casts out the enemies of a people before them by lawfull warre with the inhabitants, which God cals them unto: as in *Ps.* 44. 2. *Thou didst driue out the heathen before them.* But this course of warring against others, & driving them out without provocation, depends upon speciall Commission from God, or else it is not imitable.

Secondly, when he gives a forreigne people favour in the eyes of any native people to come and sit downe with them either by way of purchase, as *Abraham* did obtaine the field of *Machpelah;* or else when they give it in courtesie, as *Pharaoh* did the land of *Goshen* unto the sons of *Jacob*.

Thirdly, when hee makes a Countrey though not altogether void of inhabitants, yet voyd in that place where they reside. Where there is a vacant place, there is liberty for the sonne of *Adam* or *Noah* to come and inhabite, though they neither buy it, nor aske their leaves. . . . If therefore any sonne of *Adam* come and finde a place empty, he hath liberty to come, and fill, and subdue the earth there. This Charter was renewed to *Noah, Gen.* 9. 1. *Fulfill the earth and multiply:* So that it is free from that comon Grant for any to take possession of vacant Countries. Indeed no Nation is to drive out another without speciall Commission from heaven, such as the Israelites had, unless the Natives do unjustly wrong them, and will not recompence the wrongs done in peaceable fort, & then they may right themselves by lawfull war, and subdue the Countrey unto themselves.

This placeing of people in this or that Countrey, is from Gods soveraignty over all the earth, and the inhabitants thereof: as in *Psal.* 24. 1. *The earth is the Lords, and the fulnesse thereof.* And in *Ier.* 10. 7. God is there called, *The King of Nations:* and in *Deut.* 10. 14. Therefore it is meete he should provide a place for all Nations to inhabit, and haue all the earth replenished. Onely in the Text here is meant some more speciall appointment, because God tells them it by his owne mouth; he doth not so with other people, he doth not tell the children of *Sier*, that hee hath appointed a place for them: that is,

He gives them the land by promise; others take the land by his providence, but Gods people take the land by promise: And therefore the land of *Canaan* is called a land of promise. Which they discerne, first, by discerning themselves to be in Christ, in whom all the promises are yea, and amen.

Secondly, by finding his holy presence with them, to wit, when he plants them in the holy Mountaine of his Inheritance: *Exodus.* 15. 17. And that is when he giveth them the liberty and purity of his Ordinances. It is a land of promise, where they have provision for soule as well as for body. *Ruth* dwelt well for outward respects while shee dwelt in *Moab*, but when shee cometh to dwell in *Israel*, shee is said to come under the wings of God: *Ruth* 2. 12. When God wrappes us in with his Ordinances, and warmes us with the life and power of them as with wings, there is a land of promise.

This may teach us all where we doe now dwell, or where after wee may dwell, be sure you looke at every place appointed to you, from the hand of God: wee may not rush into any place, and never say to God, By your leave; but we must discerne how God appoints us this place. There is poore comfort in sitting down in any place, that you cannot say, This place is appointed me of God. Canst thou say that God spied out this place for thee, and there hath setled thee above all hinderances? didst thou finde that God made roome for thee either by lawfull descent, or purchase, or gift, or other warrantable right? Why then this is the place God hath appointed thee; here hee hath made roome for thee, he hath placed thee in *Rehoboth*, in a peaceable place: This we must discerne, or els we are but intruders upon God. And when wee doe withall discerne, that God giveth us these outward blessings from his love in Christ, and maketh comfortable provision as well for our soule as for our bodies, by the meanes of grace, then doe we enjoy our present possession as well by gracious promise, as by the common, and just, and bountifull providence of the Lord. Or if a man doe remove, he must see that God hath espied out such a Countrey for him.

Secondly, though there be many difficulties yet he hath given us hearts to overlook them all, as if we were carried upon eagles wings.

And thirdly, see God making roome for us by some lawfull means.

QUESTION: But how shall I know whether God hath appointed me such a place, if I be well where I am, what may warrant my removeall?

ANSWER: There be foure or five good things, for procurement of any of which I may remove. Secondly, there be some evill things, for avoiding of any of which wee may transplant our selves. Thirdly, if withall we find some speciall providence of God concurring in either of both concerning our selves, and applying general grounds of removall to our personall estate.

First, wee may remove for the gaining of knowledge. Our Saviour commends it in the Queene of the south, that she came from the utmost parts of the earth to heare the wisdom of *Solomon: Matth.* 12. 42. And surely with him she might have continued for the same end, if her personall calling had not recalled her home.

Secondly, some remove and travaile for merchandize and gaine-sake; *Daily bread may be sought from farre, Prov.* 31. 14. Yea our Saviour approveth travaile for Merchants, *Matth.* 13. 45, 46. when hee compareth a Christian to a Merchantman seeking pearles: For he never fetcheth a comparison from any unlawfull thing to illustrate a thing lawfull. The comparison from the unjust Steward, and from the Theefe in the night, is not taken from the injustice of the one, or the theft of the other; but from the wisdome of the one, and the sodainnesse of the other; which in themselves are not unlawfull.

Thirdly, to plant a Colony, that is, a company that agree together to remove out of their owne Country, and settle a Citty or commonwealth elsewhere. Of such a Colony wee reade in *Acts* 16. 12. which God blessed and prospered exceedingly, and made it a glorious Church. Nature teacheth Bees to doe so, when as the hive is too full, they seeke abroad for new dwellings: So when the hive of the Common wealth is so full, that Tradesmen cannot live one by another, but eate up one another, in this case it is lawfull to remove.

Fourthly, God alloweth a man to remove, when he may employ his Talents and gift better elsewhere, especially when where he is, he is not bound by any speciall engagement. Thus God sent *Ioseph* before to preserve the Church: *Iosephs* wisedome and spirit was not fit for a shepheard, but for a Counsellour of State, and therefore God sent him into *Egypt. To whom much is given of him God will require the more: Luk* 12. 48.

Fifthly, for the liberty of the Ordinances. 2 *Chron.* 11. 13, 14, 15. When *Ieroboam* made a desertion from *Iudah*, and set up golden Calves to worship, all that were well affected, both Priests and people, sold their possessions, and came to *Ierusalem* for the Ordinances sake. This case was of seasonable use to our fathers in the dayes of Queene *Mary;* who removed to *France* and *Germany* in the beginning of her Reign, upon Proclamation of alteration of religion, before any persecution began.

Secondly, there be evills to be avoyded that may warrant removeall. First, when some grievous sinnes overspread a Country that threaten desolation. *Mic.* 2. 6 to 11 verse: When the people say to them that prophecie, *Prophecie not;* then verse 10. *Arise then, this is not your rest.* Which words though they be a threatning, not a commandement; yet as in a threatning a wise man foreseeth the plague, so in the threatning he seeth a commandement, to hide himselfe from it. This case might have been of seasonable use unto them of the *Palatinate*, when they saw their Orthodox Ministers banished, although themselues might for a while enjoy libertie of conscience.

Secondly, if men be overburdened with debts and miseries, as *Davids* followers were; they may then retire out of the way (as they retired to *David* for safety) not to defraud their creditors (for *God is an avenger of such things*, 1 *Thess.* 4. 6.) but to gaine further opportunity to discharge their debts, and to satisfie their Creditors. 1 *Sam.* 22. 1, 2.

Thirdly, in case of persecution, so did the Apostle in *Acts* 13. 46, 47.

Vse. 2. Secondly, this may teach us in every place where God appoints us to sit downe, to acknowledge him as our Landlord. The earth is the Lords and the fullnesse thereof; his are our Countries, our Townes, our houses; and therefore let us acknowledge him in them all. The Apostle makes this use of it amongst the *Athenians, Acts* 17. 26, 27. *He hath appointed the times and places of our habitation; that we might seeke and grope after the Lord.* There is a threefold use thaat we are to make of it, as it appeareth there; Let us seek after the Lord, why? Because if thou commest into an house thou wilt aske for the owner of it: And so if thou commest into a forreigne land, and there findest an house and land provided for thee, wilt thou not enquire, where is the Landlord? where is that God that gave me this house and land? He is missing, and therefore seek after him.

Secondly, thou must feele after him, grope after him by such sensible things, strive to attaine the favour of your Landlord, and labour to be obedient to him that hath given you such a place.

Thirdly, you must labour to finde him in his Ordinances, in prayer and in Christian communion. These things I owe him as my Landlord, and by these I find and enjoy him. This use the very Pagans were to make of their severall Plantations: And if you knew him before, seeke him yet more, and feele after him till you find him in his Ordinances, and in your consciences.

Vse. 3. Thirdly, when you have found God making way and roome for you, and carrying you by his providence into any place, learne to walke thankfully before him, defraud him not of his rent, but offer yourselves unto his service: Serve that God, and teach your children to serve him, that hath appointed you and them the place of your habitation.

2 Observation. *A people of Gods plantation shall enjoy their owne place with safety and peace.*

This is manifest in the Text: I will plant them and what followes from thence? They shall dwell in their owne place; But how? Peaceably, they shall not be moved any more. Then they shall dwell safely, then they shall live in peace. The like promise you reade of in *Psal.* 89. 21, 22. *The enemie shall not exact upon them any more. And in Psal.* 92. 13. *Those that be planted in the house of the Lord, shall flourish in the Courts of our God. Gods plantation is a florishing plantation, Amos* 9. 15.

QUESTION: What is it for God to plant a people?

ANSWER: It is a Metaphor taken from young Impes; I will plant them, that is, I will make them to take roote there; and that is, where they and their soyle agree well together, when they are well and sufficiently provided for, as a plant suckes nourishment from the soyle that fitteth it.

Secondly, When hee causeth them to grow as plants doe, in *Psal.* 80. 8, 9, 10. 11. When a man growes like a tree in tallnesse and strength, to more firmnesse and eminency, then hee may be said to be planted.

Thirdly, When God causeth them to *fructifie. Psal.* 1. 5.

Fourthly, When he establisheth them there, then he plants, and rootes not up.

But here is something more especiall in this planting; for they were planted before in this land, and yet he promiseth here againe, that he will plant them in their owne land; which doth imply, first, That whatever former good estate they had already, he would prosper it, and increase it.

Secondly, God is said to plant a people more especially, when they become *Trees of righteousnesse, Isay* 61. 3: That they may be called trees of righteousnesse, the planting of the Lord. So that there is implyed not onely a continuance of their former good estate, but that hee would make them a good people, a choice generation: which he did, first, by planting the Ordinances of God amongst them in a more glorious manner, as he did in *Salomons* time.

Vse. 1. To exhort all that are planted at home, or intend to plant abroad, to looke well to your plantation, as you desire that the sonnes of wickednesse may not afflict you at home, nor enemies abroad, looke that you be right planted, and then you need not to feare, you are safe enough: God hath spoken it, I will plant them, and they shall not be moved, neither shall the sonnes of wickednesse afflict them any more.

QUESTION: What course would you have us take?

ANSWER: Have speciall care that you ever have the Ordinances planted amongst you, or else never looke for security. As soone as Gods Ordinances cease, your security ceaseth likewise; but if God plant his Ordinances among you, feare not, he will mainetaine them. *Isay* 4. 5, 6. *Vpon all their glory there shall be a defence;* that is, upon all Gods Ordinances: for so was the Arke called *the Glory of Israel,* 1 *Sam.* 4. 22.

Secondly, have a care to be implanted into the Ordinances, that the word may be ingrafted into you, and you into it: If you take rooting in the ordinances, grow up thereby, bring forth much fruite, continue and abide therein, then you are vineyard of red wine, and the Lord will keepe you, *Isay* 27. 2. 3. that no sonnes of violence shall destroy you. Looke into all the stories whether divine or humane, and you shall never finde that God ever rooted out a people that had the Ordinances planted amongst them, and themselves planted into the Ordinances: never did God suffer such plants to be plucked up; on all their glory shall be a defence.

Thirdly, be not unmindfull of our *Ierusalem* at home, whether you leave us, or stay at home with us. *Oh pray for the peace of Ierusalem, they shall prosper that love her. Psal.* 122. 6. *They shall all be confounded and turned backe that hate Sion, Psal.* 129. 5. As God continueth his presence with us, (blessed be his name) so be ye present in spirit with us, though absent in body: Forget not the wombe that bare you and the brest that gave you sucke. Even ducklings hatched under an henne, though they take the water, yet will still have recourse to the wing that hatched them: how much more should chickens of the same feather, and yolke? In the amity and unity of brethren, the Lord hath not onely promised, but commanded a blessing, even life forevermore: *Psal.* 133. 1, 2.

Fourthly, goe forth, every man that goeth, with a publick spirit, looking not on your owne things onely, but also on the things of others: *Phil.* 2. 4. This care of universall helpfullnesse was the prosperity of the first Plantation of the Primitive Church, *Acts* 4. 32.

Fifthly, have a tender care that you looke well to the plants that spring from you, that is, to your children, that they doe not degenerate as the Israelites did; after which they were vexed with afflictions on every hand. How came this to passe? *Ier.* 2. 21. *I planted them a noble Vine, holy, a right seede, how then art thou degenerate into a strange Vine before mee?* Your Ancestours were of a noble divine spirit, but if they suffer their children to degenerate, to take loose courses, then God will surely plucke you up: Otherwise if men have a care to propagate the Ordinances and Religion to their children after them, God will plant them and not roote them up. For want of this, the seede of the repenting *Ninivites* was rooted out.

Sixthly, and lastly, offend not the poore Natives, but as you partake in their land, so make them partakers of your precious faith: as you reape their temporalls, so feede them with your spiritualls: winne them to the love of Christ, for whom Christ died. They never yet refused the Gospell, and therefore more hope they will now receive it. Who knoweth whether God have reared this whole Plantation for such an end:

Vse. 2. Secondly, for consolation to them that are planted by God in any place, that finde rooting and establishing from God, this is a cause of much encouragement unto you, that what hee hath planted he will maintaine, every plantation his right hand hath not planted shalbe rooted up, but his owne plantation shall prosper, & flourish. When he promiseth peace and safety, what enemies shalstbe able to make the promise of God of none effect? Neglect not walls, and bulwarkes, and fortifications for your owne defence; but

ever let the name of the Lord be your strong
Tower; and the word of his Promise the
Rocke of your refuge. His word
that made heaven and earth
will not faile, till heaven
and earth be no more
Amen.

(1630)

From *Copy of a Letter from Mr. Cotton to Lord Say and Seal in the year 1636* *

Right Honourable, . . .

I am very apt to believe, what Mr. Perkins[1] hath, in one of his prefatory pages to his golden chaine, that the word, and scriptures of God doe conteyne a short *upoluposis*, or platforme, not onely of theology, but also of other sacred sciences, (as he calleth them) attendants, and handmaids thereunto, which he maketh ethicks, eoconomicks, politicks, church-government, prophecy, academy. It is very suitable to Gods all-sufficient wisdome, and to the fulnes and perfection of Holy Scriptures, not only to prescribe perfect rules for the right ordering of a private mans soule to everlasting blessednes with himselfe, but also for the right ordering of a mans family, yea, of the commonwealth too, so farre as both of them are subordinate to spiritual ends, and yet avoide both the churches usurpation upon civill jurisdictions, *in ordine ad spiritualia,*[2] and the commonwealths invasion upon ecclesiasticall administrations, *in ordine* to civill peace, and conformity to the civill state. Gods institutions (such as the government of church and of commonwealth be) may be close and compact, and co-ordinate one to another, and yet not confounded. God hath so framed the state of church government and ordinances, that they may be compatible to any commonwealth, though never so much disordered in his frame. But yet when a commonwealth hath liberty to mould his owne frame (*scripturæ plenitudinem adoro*)[3] I conceyve the scripture hath given full direction for the right ordering of the same, and

---

* From *Puritan Political Ideas*, edited by Edmund S. Morgan, copyright © 1965 by The Bobbs-Merrill Company, Inc.

[1] William Perkins (1558–1602), English Calvinist divine.

[2] In order towards things spiritual.

[3] I speak of the plenitude of Scripture.

that, in such sort as may best mainteyne the *euexia*[4] of the church. Mr. Hooker doth often quote a saying out of Mr. Cartwright (though I have not read it in him) that noe man fashioneth his house to his hangings, but his hangings to his house. It is better that the commonwealth be fashioned to the setting forth of Gods house, which is his church: than to accommodate the church frame to the civill state. Democracy, I do not conceyve that ever God did ordeyne as a fitt government eyther for church or commonwealth. If the people be governors, who shall be governed? As for monarchy, and aristocracy, they are both of them clearly approoved, and directed in scripture, yet so as referreth the soveraigntie to himselfe, and setteth up Theocracy in both, as the best forme of government in the commonwealth, as well as in the church.

The law, which your Lordship instanceth in [that none shall be chosen to magistracy among us but a church member] was made and enacted before I came into the country; but I have hitherto wanted sufficient light to plead against it. 1st. The rule that directeth the choice of supreame governors, is of like aequitie and weight in all magistrates, that one of their brethren (not a stranger) should be set over them, Deut. 17. 15. and Jethroes counsell to Moses was approved of God, that the judges, and officers to be set over the people, should be men fearing God, Exod. 18. 21. and Solomon maketh it the joy of a commonwealth, when the righteous are in authority, and their mourning when the wicked rule, Prov. 29. 21. Jab 34. 30. Your Lordship's feare, that this will bring in papal excommunication, is just, and pious: but let your Lordship be pleased againe to consider whether the consequence be necessary. *Turpius ejicitur quam non admittitur:*[5] non-membership may be a just cause of non-admission to the place of magistracy, but yet, ejection out of his membership will not be a just cause of ejecting him out of his magistracy. A godly woman, being to make choice of an husband, may justly refuse a man that is eyther cast out of church fellowship, or is not yet receyved into it, but yet, when shee is once given to him, shee may not reject him then, for such defect. Mr. Humfrey was chosen for an assistant (as I heare) before the colony came over hither: and, though he be not as yet joyned into church fellowship (by reason of the unsetlednes of the congregation where he liveth) yet the commonwealth doe still continue his magistracy to him, as knowing he waiteth for oppertunity of enjoying church fellowship shortly.

When your Lordship doubteth, that this corse will draw all things under the determination of the church, *in ordine ad spiritualia* (seeing the church is to determine who shall be members, and none but a member may have to

[4] Vigor.
[5] More unseemly to be ejected than not to be admitted.

doe in the government of a commonwealth) be pleased (I pray you) to conceyve, that magistrates are neyther chosen to office in the church, nor doe governe by directions from the church, but by civill lawes, and those enacted in generall corts, and executed in corts of justice, by the governors and assistants. In all which, the church (as the church) hath nothing to doe: onely, it prepareth fitt instruments both to rule, and to choose rulers, which is no ambition in the church, nor dishonor to the commonwealth, the apostle, on the contrary, thought it a great dishonor and reproach to the church of Christ, if it were not able to yield able judges to heare and determine all causes amongst their brethren, 1 Cor. 6. 1. to 5. which place alone seemeth to me fully to decide this question: for it plainely holdeth forth this argument: It is a shame to the church to want able judges of civill matters (as v. 5.) and an audacious act in any church member voluntarily to go for judgment, otherwhere than before the saints (as v. 1.) then it will be noe arrogance nor folly in church members, nor prejudice to the commonwealth, if voluntarily they never choose any civill judges, but from amongst the saints, such as church members are called to be. But the former is cleare: and how then can the latter be avoyded. If this therefore be (as your Lordship rightly conceyveth one of the maine objections if not the onely one) which hindereth this commonwealth from the entertainment of the propositions of those worthy gentlemen, wee intreate them, in the name of the Lord Jesus, to consider, in meeknes of wisdome, it is not any conceite or will of ours, but the holy counsell and will of the Lord Jesus (whom they seeke to serve as well as wee) that overruleth us in this case: and we trust will overrule them also, that the Lord onely may be exalted amongst all his servants. What pittie and griefe were it, that the observance of the will of Christ should hinder good things from us!

But your Lordship doubteth, that if such a rule were necessary, then the church estate and the best ordered commonwealth in the world were not compatible. But let not our Lordship so conceyve. For, the church submitteth itselfe to all the lawes and ordinances of men, in what commonwealth soever they come to dwell. But it is one thing, to submit unto what they have noe calling to reforme: another thing, voluntarily to ordeyne a forme of government, which to the best discerning of many of us (for I speake not of myselfe) is expressly contrary to rule. Nor neede your Lordship feare (which yet I speake with submission to your Lordships better judgment) that this corse will lay such a foundation, as nothing but a mere democracy can be built upon it. Bodine[6] confesseth, that though it be *status popularis*, where a people choose their owne governors; yet the government is not a democracy, if it be administred, not by the people, but by the governors, whether one (for

6 Jean Bodin (1530–1596), French political theorist.

then it is a monarchy, though elective) or by many, for then (as you know) it is aristocracy. In which respect it is, that church government is justly denied (even by Mr. Robinson) to be democratical, though the people choose their owne officers and rulers.

Nor neede wee feare, that this course will, in time, cast the commonwealth into distractions, and popular confusions. For (under correction) these three things doe not undermine, but doe mutually and strongly mainteyne one another (even those three which wee principally aime at) authority in magistrates, liberty in people, purity in the church. Purity, preserved in the church, will preserve well ordered liberty in the people, and both of them establish well-ballanced authority in the magistrates. God is the author of all these three, and neyther is himselfe the God of confusion, nor are his wayes the wayes of confusion, but of peace. . . . (1636)

THOMAS HOOKER

(1586–1647)

In the first selection below, Hooker argues for the appropriateness of his plain language style before coming to the main argument. In that argument he asserts that each congregation has its own power to do certain things and that no higher church authority can usurp that power. (See the Introduction, p. 9, for an explanation of the membership issue.) In the other selection from Hooker's writings, two central issues are discussed. The function of the minister and the function of meditation were important problems to the Puritan, since both were part of the conversion experience. Hooker's description of these functions can help us to understand the places of the minister and of meditation in the Puritan world.

From the Preface to *Survey of the Summe of Church Discipline**

. . . THAT the discourse comes forth in such a homely dresse and course habit, the Reader must be desired to consider, It comes out of the wildernesse, where curiosity is not studied. Planters if they can provide cloth to go warm, they leave the cutts[1] and lace to those that study to go fine.

As it is beyond my skill, so I professe it is beyond my care to please the nicenesse of mens palates, with any quaintnesse of language. They who covet more sauce then meat, they must provide cooks to their minde. It was a cavill cast upon Hierom,[2] that in his writings he was Ciceronianus non Christianus: My rudenesse frees me wholly from this exception, for being Λόγῳ Ἰδιώτης,[3] as the Apostle hath it, if I would, I could not lavish out in the loosenesse of language, and as the case stands, if I could answer any mans desire in that daintinesse of speech, I would not do the matter that

---

* *Old South Leaflets No. 55.*
[1] Fashion, style.
[2] St. Jerome (*c.* 347–419), Church Father.
[3] Ignorant of the Word.

Injury which is now under my hand: Ornari res ipsa negat.[4] The substance and solidity of the frame is that, which pleaseth the builder, its the painters work to provide varnish.

If the manner of the discourse should occasion any disrellish in the apprehension of the weaker Reader, because it may seem too Logicall, or Scholasticall, in regard of the terms I use, or the way of dispute that I proceed in, in some places: I have these two things to professe,

1. That plainesse and perspicuity, both for matter and manner of expression, are the things, that I have conscientiously indeavoured in the whole debate: for I have ever thought writings that come abroad, they are not to dazle, but direct the apprehension of the meanest, and I have accounted it the chiefest part of Iudicious learning, to make a hard point easy and familiar in explication. Qui non vult intelligi, debet negligi.[5]

2. The nature of the subject that is under my hand, is such, that I was constrained to accommodate and conform my expressions more or lesse, in some kinde of sutablenesse thereunto: for in some passages of the dispute, the particulars in their very rise and foundation, border so neer upon the principles of Logick: (as whether Ecclesia Catholica visibilis, was to be attended, as a Totum universale, or Integrale) that either I must resolve to say nothing, or to speak (though as sparingly as I could of such things) as the quality of the things did require. And let any man make a triall, and I do much mistake my self, but he will be neccessitated to take the same course, if he speaks to the cause. If the Reader shall demand how far this way of Church-proceeding receives approbation by any common concurrence amongst us: I shall plainly and punctually expresse my self in a word of truth, in these following points, viz.

Visible Saints are the only true and meet matter, whereof a visible Church should be gathered, and confœderation is the form.

The Church as Totum essentiale, is, and may be, before Officers.

There is no Presbyteriall Church (*i.e.* A Church made up of the Elders of many Congregations appointed Classickwise, to rule all those Congregations) in the N.T.

A Church Congregationall is the first subject of the keys.[6]

Each Congregation compleatly constituted of all Officers, hath sufficient power in her self, to exercise the power of the keyes, and all Church discipline, in all the censures thereof.

Ordination is not before election.

[4] "The need for decoration argues a weak structure."
[5] "Who does not wish to be intelligible should be passed over."
[6] Keys: ecclesiastical authority, including preaching and the administration of sacraments.

There ought to be no ordination of a Minister at large, Namely, such as should make him Pastour without a People.

The election of the people hath an instrumentall causall vertue under Christ, to give an outward call unto an Officer.

Ordination is only a solemn installing of an Officer into the Office, unto which he was formerly called.

Children of such, who are members of Congregations, ought only to be baptized.

The consent of the people gives a causall vertue to the compleating of the sentence of excommunication.

Whilst the Church remains a true Church of Christ, it doth not loose this power, nor can it lawfully be taken away.

Consociation of Churches should be used, as occasion doth require.

Such consociations and Synods have allowance to counsell and admonish other Churches, as the case may require.

And if they grow obstinate in errour or sinfull miscarriages, they should renounce the right hand of fellowship with them.

But they have no power to excommunicate. . . . (1648)

From *The Application of Redemption**

Doct. *A plain and particular application of special sins by the ministry of the word is a special means to bring the soul to a sight of, and sorrow for them.*

Plain application and powerful conviction go together. *Let the house of Israel know that God hath made him Lord and Christ whom ye have crucified;* you are the men I mean, this is your sin I mention. Thus our Saviour the great Prophet of His Church, who spake as never man spake and best knew how to deal with deceitful hearts; he layeth his finger upon the sore, and mark how he pincheth with particulars, as his ordinary manner of dispensation was to the churches: *Rev. 3.2. I know thy works, thou hast a name to be alive but thou art dead.* I say thou art hypocritical, and I know what I say, and I tell thee openly what I know: thou hast a form of profession but thou hast no heart nor life nor power of religion in thy course; He that could not err in what he did teach, he teacheth what ministers should do in their dispensations. And there was nothing more usual with our Saviour, than to point out particular sins and sinners: *We be to you Scribes, Pharisees, Hypocrites, Math. 23.* and therefore he doth not closely and covertly, as it were, give a kind of intimation, afar off, what he would, and leave men to pick and search out his meaning, but tells them their own in English as we say, plucks them

* *The Application of Redemption* (London, 1656).

out by the pole, goes not behind the door to tell men their faults, but gives in testimony against their sin and that to their teeth; Luke 16.15. when the Pharisees in an impudent manner began to mock at him, he lets fly point blank, *You are they that justify yourselves, but the Lord knows your hearts.* Yea, it was the charge he gives to all his prophets when they were to deal with the Jews and to dispense his counsels unto them, Hos. 2.1.2. *Plead with your mother, plead, tell her she is not my wife. Plead* is a law term, call her by name, summon her into the court of conscience, follow the suit against her, lay the charge and plead the action against her particular sins. Thus Stephen, Acts 7.51. *Ye stiff-necked and hard-hearted, ye have always resisted the Holy Ghost; as your fathers did, so do ye.* So the Apostle frequently, Acts 4.10.11. *be it known to you and to all the people of Israel, that in the name of Jesus Christ etc. whom ye have crucified, This is the stone refused by you builders,* you are the men, and this is your evil.

The Reasons shall be touched in a word.

Reason 1. *The place and duty of a minister requires this,* who hath a special charge, and therefore should have a particular care to foresee, and so to prevent the particular and special evils, which he perceives to blemish the Christian course, and endanger the spiritual comforts of the people under his guidance, and of whose safety he must give an account; and this will not be done unless a man single out the persons and set home their sins in special. The steward is not only to know the several conditions of the persons in the family, but to provide a portion suitable for each, if ever the safety of the whole be provided for; and the cordials for the weak, milk for the little ones, and stronger meat for those who are of able strength. The skill of the physician and the only way to cure a settled and inward distemper as the dropsy or falling sickness, is not to give the patient an ordinary purge, a common receipt; that every quack-salver will do and no good at all. But he must have that wisdom to hit the humor, and to provide ingredients that will suit the temper of the party and the particular nature of the disease. So it is the part of a skillful minister to hit the humor of the heart of a sinner, to make a receipt on purpose to meet with the particular distemper such as will work upon, or sluggishness, pride, hypocrisy, perverseness, and as the medicine doth upon the spleen or choler. . . .

Reason 2. *The necessity of sinners requires this.* For this manner of the delivery of the truth, it awakens and stirs up the mind and heart of the hearer to a more serious attention to that which is spoken, and settles the heart upon a more thorough consideration of himself and his ways, unto both which the soul of a sinner, rocked as it were asleep in the security of a sinful course, is loath to come, not willing to hear anything that would trouble him in his sins, and very ready to lay aside the consideration of that he hears in that behalf. Whereas particular application provokes to the practice of both, calls a man by name as it were, that he must come to his answer; he cannot avoid it; it will not suffer him to make an escape before he give in his answer. This flings in the light so full into men's faces that it forceth them to look about them. General truths generally do little good. That which is spoken to all is spoken to none at all. No man heeds more than needs he must to such things he hath little heart unto, or takes little delight in. An indictment or attachment without a name, read, published, and proclaimed in the face of the world, no man is either troubled at it, or reclaimed by it; but when the name is recorded, and the man challenged, it makes him bethink himself how to get a surety, or pay the debt, or prevent the danger. So is it with a general reproof: no man will own it, and therefore no man reforms by it, or is forced to seek out. . . . It's not enough that we be stirring in the house and people be up; but we must knock at men's doors, bring a candle to their bed-sides, and pinch the sluggard, and then if he have any life he will stir. While the ministers of the Lord are preaching and publishing the mind and counsel of God in the assemblies, there is some stirring in God's house; but yet the secure person sits and sleeps on the stool as the sluggard in his bed, unless some special application pinch him to the quick. Then he begins to look up and ask, who is there? So it was with David, *thou art the man* did prevail more with him than all the parable, 2 Sam. 12. As the noise of a piece afar off makes the fowl listen, but one scattered shot that falls upon the wing or leg makes them cry and stir. All the common discourse came not near David, but *thou art the man*; three words like three small shot awakened him with a witness.

Reason 3. *The nature of the Word calls for this manner of dispensation as that which suits and serves best for the end and work of it.* It makes it hit sooner, and pierce more deeply and prevailingly into the heart. The speech of the minister and his words are like darts and arrows; the right and particular applying them is the level carriage of them to the heart, and so they hit unavoidably, and fasten strongly thereupon. General discourses are like arrows shot a cock-height at all adventures without aim, and so without success or special profit, or powerful work upon the hearer; men come and go away not touched, not troubled, not affected with anything. The word is compared to a sword, the explication is like the drawing of it. So the truth in the naked nature and virtue of it comes to be discovered; but the flourishing of the sword will never do the deed. But he that handles it suitable to the end and work of it, he must follow the blow if he purpose to force his enemy either to fly or yield. So it is with the truth: down-right blows put sometimes the most cunning fencer past his sense; so these cunning hypocrites beyond all their shifts. See how the woman of Sammaria, John 4.18.19. put off our

Saviour with fond cavils, saucey and contemptuous speeches, until our Saviour met with her in particular, *Go call thy husband*; she answers, *I have no husband*; our Saviour comes within her, *Thou hast had five husbands, and he whom thou now hast is not thine husband, in that thou sayest right*, thou poor sinful adulteress. Then she fell before our Saviour. It is in a man's spiritual as it is with a man's outward estate. The bond lies forfeited, and the careless debtor or bankrupt he looks not out to pay. He hears the news of a writ out for him, but sees none to arrest, and therefore he grows fearless. But when the sergeant arrests him, and drags him to prison, you will not provide for your debt to pay, provide then to go to prison, that makes him begin to send to friends to gather up his debts, sell his commodities, crave bail and surety. So it is with careless prodigal sinners which suffer their souls and salvations to lie forfeit, and yet look not out, until some particular word meet and make an arrest upon the soul, and the minister by his commission, like the sergeant, seizeth upon him: you will not forsake your sins, you must therefore perish in your sins. He then begins to bethink himself what to do.

Use 1. We here see the reason why there is so little good done by the ministry of the Word upon the hearts of ungodly men. Many hypocrites lie skulking under the covers of deceit, and are not discovered; many proud hearts not humbled, but go on in their sturdy distempers; many sleepers sit and snort in their security, and go hood-winked down to destruction, and see nothing before they sink into the pit. We do not knock at men's doors; we do not bring the light to their bed-sides; we do not pinch them indeed with sharp and particular reproofs, and those set on to purpose; we do not put them beyond their sense; we do not keep them under the arrest of some conviction, so that they cannot make an escape, but each carnal reason rescues them from the hold of some common truths that happily are delivered. Oh we level not, we hit not, we apply not the Word to home, so particularly as the occasions, conditions, corruptions of men require; and therefore it prevails not with that power, finds not that success which otherwise it might. Common reproofs are like the confused noise in the ship when the mariners were rowing Jonah to the shore, notwithstanding all which Jonah lies and sleeps under hatches; but when they go down to him and laid hold upon him, and awakened him with a witness, *Arise thou sluggard, and call upon thy God, lest we all perish*, Jonah. 1.5. he then began to bethink himself where he was, and what he had done; and then remembered that though he had feared and served the God of Heaven, yet by his rebellion he had departed away from him. So here, all the while we take up men's minds, and exercise their ears and thoughts with some hovering discourses, and common words of course, *We are all sinners, in many things we offend all, all flesh is frail*; but I hope better things of you; I hope there is none such amongst you.

These daubing discourses and roving reproofs, toothless, powerless dispensations, like arrows shot a cock-height, they touch not, trouble not, and in the issue profit no man at all. They come proud and stubborn and perverse and careless; they sit so and return so, day after day and year after year. But you should shake up a sinner, go down under the hatches to Jonah, set upon the hearts of men in particular, *Awake thou sluggard.* Thou a master of a family and teachest not, instructest not those that are under thee? Thou a servant, yet stubborn and perverse, and submits not to those that are set over thee in the Lord? Art thou a wife and dost not reverence and obey with fear him whom God hath made thy head and guide? Art thou a member of a Christian congregation, and hast the name of Christ called upon thee, and art thou treacherous to the Covenant of Christ, opposest the government and spirit of Christ, and despisest the ordinances of the Lord Jesus? Awake you careless masters and rebellious servants, perverse wives, treacherous and faithless members; know that your religion is vain and yourselves also while these distempers rest in your bosom; call upon your own hearts for humiliation and repentance, and unto God for mercy that you perish not. . . .

Use 2. Here see the reason why the best preaching finds the least and worst acceptance at the hands of rebellious sinners, that which works, and troubles most, that they most distaste, that which gives the least quiet to them, to that they give the least respect and liking; like children they love raw fruit which will breed worms and sickness, rather than worm-seed, though that would prevent both. So men love raw and windy discourses to please sinful humors, and corrupt hearts, rather than some bitter and particular reproofs which would make them sound in the faith. Ahab will nourish *four hundred false prophets at his table,* feed them with dainties, and make choice provision for them, that they may feed his humor, and speak good things to him, when he is not able to abide the sight, scarce to hear the name, of Micaiah the prophet of the Lord, who would speak the counsel of the Lord without fear and partiality. I Kings 22. So they in Isai. 30.10. *They say to the seers, see not; and to the prophets, prophecy not unto us right things, prophesy smooth things,* such as might suit their sensual appetites, and would down without chewing. And it's strange to see when such men have told a grave tale, and vented a heartless, toothless discourse, neither pith nor power in it, I say, it's strange to see what admiration and esteem such carnal hearts will set upon such persons and expressions: great their parts, prudence, and discretion: Oh how sweet and seasonable their discourse, how glad to hear, and how un-weariable to attend such. And all the while they may sit and sleep in their sinful condition, and neither have their consciences awakened nor their corruption discovered. Squeamish stomachs had rather take sugar-sops a whole week together than a bitter portion one day. This is the disease which

Paul complains of as incident to the last age of the world, and therefore adviseth his Scholar Timothy, 2. Tim. 4.2,3. *To be instant in season, out of season, convince, rebuke, exhort, for the time will come that men will not endure sound doctrine; but according to their proper lusts, having itching ears, will heap to themselves teachers.* Itching ears must be scratched, not boxed.

Second part of exhortation. The exhortation to the people is that as ever you desire to see your sins and have your hearts brought to sorrow for them, you must desire it and delight in it, that you may have the light brought home to your souls in way of particular application to your own sins. There is no means so effectual as this; therefore desire God that your minister may take such pains that they may speak to your consciences.

Take three considerations here.

1. Weigh sadly that when the minister speaks in way of application so as to discover thy sins, he doth no more than he may, nay no more than he should in point of conscience; his life lies at stake if he should not deal plainly and faithfully, and therefore know it's unreasonable for thee to quarrel with the minister, or wish that he speaks when he hath the word for his warrant in what he does.

2. Look at the good of the dispensation of an ordinance and overlook the tartness of it. As some would not see but drink of the physic, minding the wholesomeness and bearing with the unpleasantness of it for the present. As it's wearisome to the surgeon to be raking in the sore, so it is to the minister; but it is for thy good, and the sore, though it be painful and cross to thy carnal affection, yet thou shouldest take contentment in such a dispensation of the word as is such an effectual means of thy good.

3. When thou findest thy heart skittish, consider that an under quiet taking in sharp reproof; it's a sound argument of the sincerity of thy heart and truth of thy love to God and his Word. When a man begins to be shaken in his comforts, and a sharp and keen reproof comes home to a man, to force him to see and be humbled and reform his evil ways, if he can willingly receive and yield himself to such a reproof, it's a sign his heart is sincere in the sight of God, when he says as they did Zach. 13.6. *these are the wounds I received in the house of my friends.*

WHEN THEY HEARD THIS

We heard before that application and special discovery of our particular corruptions, what force it had to break the heart. We have here yet a second means couched in the manner of the speech expressed in the text. The word is read in the participle, and carries a kind of indefinite endeavor with it, a bent of mind about that which was heard. *In hearing they heard it,* and when the sermon was over, and they had received the message of the Lord delivered by the Apostle, when they (happily) were departed, yet that word departed not out of their ears and hearts. They heard it over again, they mused upon it, it stuck by them, their thoughts recollect afresh upon the consideration thereof, it pressed heavy upon their hearts. Conviction brings the sin, application lays it; meditation settles it upon the heart, that it sinks under it as unsupportable.

Hence then the Doctrine is,

Doct. *Through Meditation of sins applied, is a special means to break the heart of a sinner.*

As men that are stoned and pressed to death, while the stones are few that are cast, and the weight not great, may be they are not broken, not yet their lives hazarded, but while they still continue flinging and adding to the number and weight, their bones break and their lives fail under the over-bearing pressure that is put upon them. A serious thought and right apprehension and application of a sin toucheth and troubleth the sinner; but daily meditation flings in one terror after another, and follows the soul with fresh consideration of yet more sin, and yet more evil, and that more heinous and yet more dangerous beyond all apprehension and imagination; so that a sinner is stoned to death as it were, and breaks under the burden of it. Thus the repenting Church Lam. 3.19.20. *In remembering mine affliction, the wormwood and the gall, my soul hath them still in remembrance and is humbled in me*, in remembering I remembered they were daily musing and continually poring, and that made them pierce inwardly. Look, as it is in the body, so it is in the soul; meat minced if never chewed and digested, it never nourisheth. A potion prepared and given, if not retained and kept in the stomach, it never purgeth or worketh kindly for cure. So here in the soul, application carves out a fit potion of truth to the sinner; but meditation is that which digests it and makes good blood of it. Application compounds the potion; a particular reproof which is keen in the working brings it home; but meditation retains it, that so it may work kindly and put forth the proper powerful effect for the loosening of those loathesome lusts, which are like noisome and corrupt humors, which threaten the death and ruin of the soul. . . .

For explication we shall

1. Show what this meditation is.

2. Apply the general doctrine to the particular occasion, and see how this helps forward this work. Then,

3. We shall make use.

What Meditation is. For the first. *Meditation is a serious intention of the mind whereby we come to search out the truth, and settle it effectually upon the heart.*

1. *An intention of the mind*; when one puts forth the strength of their

understanding about the work in hand, takes it as an especial task whereabout the heart should be taken up and that which will require the whole man, and that to the bent of the best ability he hath, so the word is used, Jos. 1.8. *thou shalt not suffer the Word to depart out of thy mind, but thou shalt meditate therein day and night,* when either the Word would depart away or our corruptions would drive it away, meditation lays hold upon it and will not let it go, but exerciseth the strength of the attention of his thoughts about it, makes a business of it as that about which he might do his best, and yet falls short of what he should do in it. So David when he would discover where the stream and overflowing strength of his affections vented themselves, he points at this practice as that which employs the mind to the full. Psal. 119.97. *O how I love thy law, it is my meditation all the day,* love is the great wheel of the soul that sets all on going, and how doth that appear? it is my meditation day and night; the word in the original signifieth to swim, a man spreads the breadth of his understanding about that work, and lays out himself about the service wherein there is both difficulty and worth.

Serious. Meditation is not a flourishing of a man's wit, but hath a set bout at the search of the truth, beats his brain as we use to say, hammers out a business, as the goldsmith with his metal, he heats it and beats it, turns it on this side and then on that, fashions it on both that he might frame it to his mind; meditation is hammering of a truth or point propounded, that he may carry and conceive the frame and compass in his mind, not salute a truth as we pass by occasionally but solemnly entertain it into our thoughts; not look upon a thing presented as a spectator or passenger that goes by; but lay other things aside, and look at this as the work and employment for the present to take up our minds. It's one thing in our diet to take a snatch and away, another thing to make a meal, and sit at it on purpose until we have seen all set before us and we have taken our fill of all, so we must not cast an eye or glimpse at the truth by some sudden or flighty apprehension, a snatch and away, but we must make a meal of musing. Therefore, the Psalmist makes it the main trade that a godly man drives, professedly opposite to the carriage of the wicked, whether in his outward or inward work, in his disposition or expression of himself in his common practice; whereas they walk in the corrupt counsels of their own hearts, stand in the way of sinners, not only devise what is naught, but practice and persevere in what they have devised, and sit in the seat of the scorners; a blessed man his road in which he travels, his set trade, *he meditates in the law of God day and night*: that is the counsel in which he walks, the way in which he stands, the seat in which he sits. Look at this work as a branch of our Christian calling, not that which is left to our liberty, but which is of necessity to be attended and that in good earnest as a Christian duty, which God requires, not a little available to our spiritual welfare.

The end is doubly expressed in the other part of the description.

1. *The searching of the truth.*
2. *The effectual settling of it upon the heart.*

The search of the truth: meditation is a coming in with the truth or any cause that comes to hand, that we may enquire the full state of it before our thoughts part with it, so that we see more of it or more clearly and fully than formerly we did; this is one thing in that of the prophet Hos. 6.8. *then shall ye know if you follow on to know*, when we track the footsteps of the truth, in all the passages, until we have viewed the whole progress of it, from truth to truth, from point to point. *This it is to dig for wisdom*, Prov. 2.2. When men have found a mine or a vein of silver, they do not content themselves, to take that which is uppermost and next at hand within sight which offers itself upon the surface of the earth, but they dig further as hoping to find more, because they see somewhat. So meditation rests not in what presents itself to our consideration, but digs deeper, gathers in upon the truth, and gains more of it then did easily appear at the first, and this it doth.

1. *When it recalls things formerly past, sets them in a present view before our consideration and judgment.* Meditation sends a man's thought afar off, calls over and revives the fresh apprehension of things done long before, marshals them all in rank together, brings to mind such things which were happily quite out of memory, and gone from a man, which might be of great use and special help to discover our condition according to the quality of it; maybe conscience starts the consideration of but one sin, but meditation looks abroad, and brings to hand many of the same, and of the like kind and that many days past and long ago committed. This distemper now sticks upon a man and brings him under the arrest of conscience and the condemnation thereof. But, says meditation, let me mind you of such and such sins at such and such times, in such and such companies, committed and multiplied both more and worse than those that now appear so loathsome and so troublesome to you; meditation is as it were the register and remembrancer, that looks over the records of our daily corruptions, and keeps them upon file, and brings them into court and fresh consideration, Job 13.26. *Thou makest me to possess the sins of my youth.* This makes a man to renew the sins of his youth, makes them fresh in our thoughts, as though new done before our eyes. This interpreters make the meaning of that place, Job 14.17. *My transgression is sealed up in a bag, and thou sewest up mine iniquity*; though God do thus, yet He doth it by this means in the way of His providence, i.e., by recounting and recalling our corruptions to mind, by serious

meditation we sew them all up together, we look back to the lineage and pedigree of our lusts, and track the abominations of our lives, step by step, until we come to the very nest where they are hatched and bred, even of our original corruption, and body of death, where they had their first breath and being, links all our distempers together from our infancy to our youth, from youth to riper age, from thence to our declining days. So David, from the vileness of his present lusts is led to the wickedness *in which he was warmed*, Psal. 51.5. This was typed out in the old law by *the chewing of the cud*; meditation calls over again those things that were past long before, and not within a man's view and consideration.

2. Meditation *takes a special survey of the compass of our present condition, and the nature of those corruptions that come to be considered*: it's the traversing of a man's thoughts, the coasting of the mind and imagination into every crevice and corner, pries into every particular, takes a special view of the borders and confines of any corruption or condition that comes to be scanned, Psal. 119.59. *I considered my ways, and turned my feet unto thy testimonies*; he turned them upside down, looked through them as it were; a present apprehension peeps in as it were through the crevice or keyhole, looks in at the window as a man passeth by; but meditation lifts up the latch and goes into each room, pries into every corner of the house, and surveys the composition and making of it, with all the blemishes in it. Look as the searcher at the seaport, or customhouse, or ships, satisfies himself not to overlook carelessly in a sudden view, but unlocks every chest, rummages every corner, takes a light to discover the. darkest passages. So is it with meditation, it observes the woof and web of wickedness, the full frame of it, the very utmost selvage and outside of it, takes into consideration all the secret conveyances, cunning contrivements, all bordering circumstances that attend the thing, the consequences of it, the nature of the causes that work it, the several occasions and provocations that lead to it, together with the end and issue that in reason is like to come of it, Dan. 12.4. *Many shall run to and fro, and knowledge shall increase*: meditation goes upon discovery, toucheth at every coast, observes every creek, maps out the daily course of a man's conversation and disposition.

3. The second end of meditation is, *it settles effectually upon the heart*. It's not the pashing of the water at a sudden push, but the standing and soaking to the root, that loosens the weeds and thorns, that they may be plucked up easily. It's not the laying of oil upon the benumbed part, but the chafing of it in, that suppleth the joints, and easeth the pain. It is so in the soul: application lays the oil of the Word that is searching and savory, meditation chafeth it in, that it may soften and humble the hard and stony heart; application is like the conduit or channel that brings the stream of the truth upon the

soul; but meditation stops it as it were, and makes it soak into the heart, that so our corruptions may be plucked up kindly by the roots.

This settling upon the heart appears in a threefold work.

1. *It affects the heart with the truth attended,* and leaves an impression upon the spirit answerable to the nature of the thing which is taken into meditation: II Pet. 2.8. it's said of Lot, *in seeing and hearing, he vexed his righteous soul.* Many saw and heard the hideous abominations, and were not touched nor affected therewith. No more had he been, but that he vexed and troubled his own righteous soul, because he was driven to a daily consideration of them which cut him to the quick. The word is observable, it signifies to try by a touchstone, and to examine, and then upon search to bring the soul upon the rack: therefore the same word is used, Matt. 14.24. *The ship was tossed by the waves;* the consideration of the abominations of the place raised a tempest of trouble in Lot's righteous soul. This the wise man calls laying to the heart, Eccles. 7.1,2. *It's better to go to the house of mourning than to the house of laughter; for this is the end of all men, and the living will lay it to his heart.* When the spectacle of misery and mortality is laid in the grave, yet savory meditation lays it to a man's heart, and makes it real there in the work of it. The goldsmith observes that it is not the laying of the fire, but the blowing of it that melts the metal. So with meditation, it breathes upon any truth that is applied, and that makes it really sink and soak into the soul; and this is the reason why in an ordinary and common course of providence, and God's dealing with sinners (leaving His own exceptions to His own good pleasure), that the most men in the time and work of conversion have that scorn cast upon them, *that they grow melancholy.* And it's true thus far in the course of ordinary appearance; the Lord usually never works upon the soul by the ministry of the Word to make it effectual, but He drives the sinner to sad thoughts of heart, and makes him keep an audit in his own soul by serious meditation, and pondering of his ways; otherwise the Word neither affects thoroughly, nor works kindly upon him.

2. *It keeps the heart under the heat and authority of the truth that it's taken up withal, by constant attendance of his thoughts.* Meditation keeps the conscience under an arrest, so that it cannot make an escape from the evidence and authority of the truth, so that there is no way, but either to obey the rule of it, or else be condemned by it. But escape it cannot. Meditation meets and stops all the evasions and sly pretenses the false-hearted person shall counterfeit. If a man should deny his fault, and himself guilty, meditation will evidence it beyond all gainsaying by many testimonies which meditation will easily call to mind; remember ye not in such and such a place: upon such an occasion, you gave way to your wicked heart to do thus and thus; you know it, and God knows it, and I have recorded it. If the sinner would lessen his

fault, meditation aggravates it; or if he seem to slight it, and look at it as a matter of no moment, yet meditation will make it appear, there is greater evil in it, and greater necessity to bestow his thoughts upon it than he is aware of.

Hence it is meditation lays siege unto the soul, and cuts off all carnal pretenses that a wretched self-deceiving hypocrite would relieve himself by; and still lies at the soul, this you did, at that time, in that place, after that manner; so that the soul is held fast prisoner, and cannot make an escape; but as David said, Psal. 51.3. *My sins are ever before me.* Consideration keeps them within view, and will not suffer them to go out of sight and thoughts; and therefore it is Paul joins those two together, I Tim. 3.15. *Meditate in these things, and be in them.*

3. It provokes a man (by a kind of overbearing power) to the practice of that with which he is so affected: a settled and serious meditation of anything, is as the setting open of the floodgates, which carries the soul with a kind of force and violence, to the performance of what he so bestows his mind upon; as a mighty stream let out turns the mill. Phil. 4.9. *Think of these things, and do them:* thinking men are doing men. Psal. 39.3. *While I was thus musing, the fire brake out, and I spake:* the busy stirring of meditation is like the raising of a tempest in the heart, that carries out all the actions of the man by an uncontrollable command. *I considered my ways, and turned my feet unto thy statutes:* right consideration, brings in a right reformation with it.

(1656)

THOMAS SHEPARD

(1605–1649)

Modern readers may consider Shepard's writing among the clearest and most understandable of the early period. Discussing sin, redemption, ways to heaven and ways to hell, Shepard dwells upon issues and problems central to the Puritan theology for the individual. In effect, Shepard tells each man why he is damned and how he can be saved. To understand this selection is to begin to understand the fears and preoccupations of the people for whom Shepard wrote.

From *The Sincere Convert**

That All Mankind is Fallen by Sin from that Glorious Estate he was made in, into a most Woful and Miserable Condition

1. EVERY man living is born guilty of Adam's sin. Now, the justice and equity of God, in laying this sin to every man's charge, though none of Adam's posterity personally committed it, appears thus:—

First. If Adam standing, all mankind had stood, then it is equal, that he falling, all his posterity should fall. All our estates were ventured in this ship; therefore, if we should have been partakers of his gains, if he had continued safe, it is fit we should be partakers of his loss too.

But, secondly. We are all in Adam, as a whole country in a parliament man; the whole country doth what he doth. And although we made no particular choice of Adam to stand for us, yet the Lord made it for us; who, being goodness itself, bears more good will to man than he can or could bear to himself; and being wisdom itself, made the wisest choice, and took the wisest course for the good of man. For this made most for men's safety and quiet; for if he had stood, all fear of losing our happy estate had vanished;

* John A. Albro, ed., *The Works of Thomas Shepard* (Boston, 1853).

whereas, if every man had been left to stand or fall for himself, a man would ever have been in fear of falling.

And again: this was the sure way to have all men's states preserved; for having the charge of the estates of all men that ever should be in the world, he was the more pressed to look the more about him, and so to be more watchful, that he be not robbed, and so undo and procure the curses of so many thousands against him. Adam was the head of mankind, and all mankind naturally are members of that head; and if the head invent and plot treason, and the head practice treason against the king or state, the whole body is found guilty, and the whole body must needs suffer. Adam was the poisoned root and cistern of all mankind: now, the branches and streams being in the root and spring originllay, they therefore are tainted with the same poisoned principles. If these things satisfy not, God hath a day coming wherein he will reveal his own righteous proceedings before men and angels. (Rom. ii. 4.)

O that men would consider this sin, and that the consideration of it could humble people's hearts! If any mourn for sin, it is for the most part for other foul actual sins; few for this sin that first made the breach, and began the controversy betwixt God and man. Next unto the sin against the Holy Ghost, and contempt of the gospel, this is the greatest sin that crieth loudest in God's ears for vengeance, day and night, against a world of men. For now men's sins are against God in their base and low estates; but this sin was committed against Jehovah, when man was at the top of his preferment. Rebellion of a traitor on a dunghill is not so great as of a favorite in court. Little sins against light are made horrible. No sin, by any man committed, was ever against so much light as Adam had. This sin was the first that ever displeased God. Drunkenness deprives God of the glory of sobriety; whoring, of chastity; but this sin darkens the very sun, defaces all the image of God, the glory of man, and the glory of God in man; this is the first sin ever did thee mischief. This sin, like a captain, hath gathered together all those troops and swarms of sins that now take hold upon thee. Thank this sin for a hard heart thou so much complainest of; thank this sin for that hellish darkness that overspreads thee. This hath raised Satan, death, judgment, hell, and heaven against thee.

That the Lord Jesus Christ is the Only Means of Redemption and Deliverance out of this Estate.

"IN whom we have redemption through his blood," (Eph. i. 7,) which plainly demonstrates that

"Jesus Christ is the only means of man's redemption and deliverance out of his bondage and miserable estate."

And this is the doctrine I shall now insist upon.

When the Israelites were in bondage and misery, he sends Moses to deliver them. When they were in Babylon, he stirred up Cyrus to open the prison gates to them; but when all mankind is under spiritual misery, he sends the Lord Jesus, God and man, to redeem him. (Acts iv. 12.)

QUESTION. How doth Christ redeem men out of this misery?

ANSWER. By paying a price for them. (1 Cor. vi. ult.) God's mercy will be manifested in saving some, and his justice must be satisfied by having satisfaction or price made and paid for man's sin. Hence Christ satisfieth God's justice,—

First. By standing in the room of all them whom mercy decreeth to save. A surety standeth in the room of a debtor. (Heb. vii. 22.) As the first Adam stood in the room of all mankind fallen, so Christ standeth in the room of all men rising, or to be restored again.

Secondly. By taking from them in whose room he stood the eternal guilt of all their sins, and by assuming the guilt of all those sins unto himself. (2 Cor. v. 22.) Hence Luther said Christ was the greatest sinner by imputation.

Thirdly. By bearing the curse and wrath of God kindled against sin. God is holy, and when he seeth sin sticking only by imputation to his own Son, he will not spare him, but his wrath and curse must he bear. (Gal. iii. 13.) Christ drinks up the cup of all the elect at one draught, which they should have been sipping and drinking, and tormented with, millions of years.

Fourthly. By bringing into the presence of God perfect righteousness, (Rom. v. 21;) for this also God's justice required perfection, conformity to the law, as well as (perfect satisfaction) suffering for the wrong offered to the Lawgiver. Justice thus requiring these four things, Christ satisfies justice by performing them, and so pays the price.

1. Christ is a Redeemer by strong hand. The first redemption by price is finished in Christ's person, at his resurrection; the second is begun by the Spirit in man's vocation, and ended at the day of judgment; as money is first paid for a captive in Turkey, and then because he can not come to his own prince himself, he is fetched away by strong hand.

Here is encouragement to the vilest sinner, and comfort to the self-succorless and lost sinner, who have spent all their money, their time and endeavors upon those duties and strivings that have been but poor physicians to them. O, look up here to the Lord Jesus, who can do that cure for thee in a moment which all creatures can not do in many years. What bolts, what strong fetters, what unruly lusts, temptations, and miseries art thou locked into? Behold, the Deliverer is come out of Sion, having satisfied justice, and paid a price to ransom poor captives, (Luke iv. 18;) with the keys of heaven, hell, and thy unruly heart in his hand, to fetch thee out with great mercy and strong hand. Who knows but thou poor prisoner of hell, thou poor captive of the devil, thou poor shackled sinner, mayest be one whom he is come for? O, look up to him, sigh to heaven for deliverance from him, and be glad and rejoice at his coming!

This strikes terror to them, that though there is a means of deliverance, yet they lie in their misery, never groan, never sigh to the Lord Jesus for deliverance; nay, that rejoice in their bondage, and dance to hell in their bolts; nay, that are weary of deliverance; that sit in the stocks when they are at prayers; that come out of the church, when the tedious sermon runs somewhat beyond the hour, like prisoners out of a jail, that despise the Lord Jesus, when he offers to open the doors, and so let them out of that miserable estate. O, poor creatures! is there a means of deliverance, and dost thou neglect, nay, despise it? Know it, that this will cut thine heart one day, when thou art hanging in thy gibbets in hell, to see others standing at God's right hand, redeemed by Christ: thou mightest have had share in their honor; for there was a Deliverer come to save thee, but thou wouldest have none of him. O, thou wilt lie yelling in those everlasting burnings, and tear thy hair, and curse thyself: From hence might I have been delivered, but I would not. Hath Christ delivered thee from hell, and hath he not delivered thee from thine alehouse? Hath Christ delivered thee from Satan's society, when he hath not delivered thee from thy loose company yet? Hath Christ delivered thee from burning, when thy fagots, thy sins, grow in thee? Is Christ's blood thine, that makest no more account of it, nor feelest no more virtue from it, than in the blood of a chicken? Art thou redeemed? Dost thou hope by Christ to be saved, that didst never see, nor feel, nor sigh under thy bondage? O, the devils will keep holiday (as it were) in hell, in respect of thee, who shalt mourn under God's wrath, and lament. O, there was a means to deliver us out of it, but thou shalt mourn forever for thy misery. And this will be a bodkin at thine heart one day, to think there was a Deliverer, but I, wretch, would none of him. Here, likewise, is matter of reproof to such as seek to come out of this misery from and by themselves. If they be ignorant, they hope to be saved by their good meaning and prayers. If civil, by paying all they owe, and doing as they would be done by, and by doing nobody any harm. If they be troubled about their estates, then they lick themselves whole by their mourning, repenting, and reforming. O, poor stubble, canst thou stand before this consuming fire without sin? Canst thou make thyself a Christ for thyself? Canst thou bear and come from under an infinite wrath? Canst thou bring in perfect righteousness into the presence of God? This Christ must do, else he could not satisfy and redeem. And if thou canst not do thus, and hast no Christ, desire and pray that heaven and earth shake till thou hast worn thy tongue to the stumps; endeavor as much as thou canst, and others commend thee for a diligent Christian; mourn in some wilderness till doomsday; dig thy grave there with thy nails; weep buckets full of hourly tears, till thou canst weep no more; fast and pray till thy skin and bones cleave together; promise and purpose with full resolution to be better; nay, reform thy head, heart, life, and tongue, and some, nay, all sins; live like an angel; shine like a sun; walk up and down the world like a distressed pilgrim going to another country, so that all Christians commend and admire thee; die ten thousand deaths; lie at the fireback in hell so many millions of years as there be piles of grass on the earth, or sands upon the sea shore, or stars in heaven, or motes in the sun; I tell thee, not one spark of God's wrath against thy sin shall be, can be, quenched by all these duties, nor by any of these sorrows, or tears; for these are not the blood of Christ. Nay, if all the angels and saints in heaven and earth should pray for thee, these can not deliver thee, for they are not the blood of Christ. Nay, God, as a Creator, having made a law, will not forgive one sin without the blood of Christ; nay, Christ's blood will not do it neither, if thou dost join never so little that thou hast or dost unto Jesus Christ, and makest thyself or any of thy duties copartners with Christ in that great work of saving thee. Cry out, therefore, as that blessed martyr did, None but Christ, none but Christ. . . .

That Those that are Saved are Saved with Very Much Difficulty.

Doctrine 2. That those that are saved are saved with much difficulty; or it is a wonderful hard thing to be saved.

The gate is strait, and therefore a man must sweat and strive to enter; both the entrance is difficult, and the progress of salvation too. Jesus Christ is not got with a wet finger. It is not wishing and desiring to be saved will bring men to heaven; hell's mouth is full of good wishes. It is not shedding a tear at a sermon, or blubbering now and then in a corner, and saying over thy prayers, and crying God mercy for thy sins, will save thee. It is not, Lord, have mercy upon us, will do thee good. It is not coming constantly to church. These are easy matters. But it is a tough work, a wonderful hard matter, to be saved. (1 Pet. iv. 18.) Hence the way to heaven is compared to a race, where a man must put forth all his strength, and stretch every limb, and all to get forward. Hence a Christian's life is compared to wrestling. (Eph. vi. 12.) All the policy and power of hell buckle together against a Christian; therefore he must look to himself, or else he falls. Hence it is compared to fighting. (2 Tim. iv. 7.) A man must fight against the devil, the world, himself, who shoot poisoned bullets in the soul, where a man must kill or be killed. God hath not lined the way to Christ with velvet, nor strewed it with rushes. He will never feed a slothful humor in man, who will be saved if Christ and heaven would drop into their mouths, and if any would bear their charges thither. If Christ might be bought for a few cold wishes and lazy desires, he would be of small reckoning amongst men, who would say, Lightly come, lightly go. Indeed, Christ's yoke is easy in itself; and when a man is got into Christ, nothing is so sweet; but for a carnal, dull heart, it is hard to draw in it; for

There are four strait gates which every one must pass through before he can enter into heaven.

1. There is the strait gate of humiliation. God saveth none but first he humbleth them. Now, it is hard to pass through the gates and flames of hell; for a heart as stiff as a stake to bow; as hard as a stone to bleed for the least prick; not to mourn for one sin, but all sins; and not for a fit, but all a man's lifetime. O, it is hard for a man to suffer himself to be loaden with sin, and pressed to death for sin, so as never to love sin more, but to spit in the face of that which he once loved as dearly as his life. It is easy to drop a tear or two, and be sermon sick; but to have a heart rent for sin and from sin, this is true humiliation; and this is hard.

2. The strait gate of faith. (Eph. i. 19.) It is an easy matter to presume, but hard to believe in Christ. It is easy for a man that was never humbled to believe and say, It is but believing; but it is a hard matter for a man humbled, when he sees all his sins in order before him, the devil and conscience roaring upon him, and crying out against him, and God frowning upon him, now to call God Father, is a hard work. Judas had rather be hanged than believe. It is hard to see a Christ as a rock to stand upon, when we are overwhelmed with sorrow of heart for sin. It is hard to prize Christ above ten thousand worlds of pearl; it is hard to desire Christ, and nothing but Christ; hard to follow Christ all the day long, and never to be quiet till he is got in thine arms, and then with Simeon to say, "Lord, now lettest thou thy servant depart in peace."

3. The strait gate of repentance. It is an easy matter for a man to confess himself to be a sinner, and to cry to God forgiveness until next time; but to have a bitter sorrow, and so to turn from all sin, and to return to God, and all the ways of God, which is true repentance indeed, this is hard.

4. The strait gate of opposition of devils, the world, and a man's own self, who knock a man down when he begins to look toward Christ and heaven.

Hence learn, that every easy way to heaven is a false way, although ministers should preach it out of their pulpits, and angels should publish it out of heaven.

Now, there are nine easy ways to heaven, (as men think,) all which lead to hell.

1. The common broad way, wherein a whole parish may all go abreadth in it; tell these people they shall be damned, their answer is, Then woe to many more besides me.

2. The way of civil education, whereby many wild natures are by little and little tamed, and like wolves are chained up easily while they are young.

3. Balaam's way of good wishes, whereby many people will confess their ignorance, forgetfulness, and that they can not make such shows as others do, but they thank God their hearts are as good, and God for his part accepts (say they) the will for the deed. And, "My son, give me thy heart;" the heart is all in all, and so long they hope to do well enough. Poor deluded creatures thus think to break through armies of sins, devils, temptations, and to break open the very gates of heaven with a few good wishes; they think to come to their journey's end without legs, because their hearts are good to God.

4. The way of formality, whereby men rest in the performance of most or of all external duties without inward life. (Mark i. 14.) Every man must have some religion, some fig leaves to hide their nakedness. Now, this religion must be either true religion or the false one; if the true, he must either take up the power of it,—but that he will not, because it is burdensome,—or the form of it; and this being easy, men embrace it as their God, and will rather lose their lives than their religion thus taken up. This form of religion is the easiest religion in the world; partly because it easeth men of trouble of conscience, quieting that: Thou hast sinned, saith conscience, and God is offended; take a book, and pray, keep thy conscience better, and bring thy Bible with thee; now, conscience is silent, being charmed down with the form of religion, as the devil is driven away (as they say) with holy water; partly, also, because the form of religion credits a man, partly because it is easy in itself; it is of a light carriage, being but the shadow and picture of the substance of religion; as now, what an easy matter it is to come to church! They hear (at least outwardly) very attentively an hour and more, and then to turn to a proof, and to turn down a leaf: here is the form. But now to spend Saturday night, and all the whole Sabbath day morning, in trimming the lamp, and in getting oil in the heart to meet the bridegroom the next day, and so meet him in the word, and there to tremble at the voice of God, and suck the breast while it is open; and when the word is done, to go aside privately, and there to chew upon the word, there to lament with tears all the vain thoughts in duties, deadness in hearing, this is hard, because this is the power of godliness, and this men will not take up: so for private prayer; what an easy matter is it for a man to say over a few prayers out of some

devout book, or to repeat some old prayer, got by heart since a child, or to have two or three short-winded wishes for God's mercy in the morning and at night! this form is easy. But now to prepare the heart by serious meditation of God and man's self, before he prays, then to come to God with a bleeding, hunger-starved heart, not only with a desire, but with a warrant, I must have such or such a mercy, and there to wrestle with God, although it be an hour or two together for a blessing, this is too hard; men think none do thus, and therefore they will not.

5. The way of presumption, whereby men, having seen their sins, catch hold easily upon God's mercy, and snatch comforts before they are reached out unto them. There is no word of comfort, in the book of God, intended for such as regard iniquity in their hearts, though they do not act it in their lives. Their only comfort is, that the sentence of damnation is not yet executed upon them.

6. The way of sloth, whereby men lie still, and say, God must do all. If the Lord would set up a pulpit at the alehouse door, it may be they would hear oftener. If God will always thunder, they will always pray; if strike them now and then with sickness, God shall be paid with good words and promises enough, that they will be better if they live; but, as long as peace lasts, they will run to hell as fast as they can; and, if God will not catch them, they care not, they will not return.

7. The way of carelessness, when men, feeling many difficulties, pass through some of them, but not all, and what they can not get now, they feed themselves with a false hope they shall hereafter; they are content to be called precisians, and fools, and crazy brains, but they want brokenness of heart, and they will pray (it may be) for it, and pass by that difficulty; but to keep the wound always open, this they will not do; to be always sighing for help, and never to give themselves rest till their hearts are humbled, that they will not: "These have a name to live, yet are dead."

8. The way of moderation, or honest discretion, (Rev. iii. 16,) which, indeed, is nothing but lukewarmness of the soul; and that is, when a man contrives, and cuts out such a way to heaven as he may be hated of none, but please all, and so do any thing for a quiet life, and so sleep in a whole skin. The Lord saith, "He that will live godly must suffer persecution." No, not so, Lord. Surely, (think they,) if men were discreet and wise, it would prevent a great deal of trouble and opposition in good courses; this man will commend those that are most zealous, if they were but wise; if he meet with a black-mouthed swearer, he will not reprove him, lest he be displeased with him; if he meet with an honest man, he will yield to all he saith, that so he may commend him; and when he meets them both together,

they shall be both alike welcome (whatever he thinks) to his house and table, because he would fain be at peace with all men.

9, and lastly. The way of self-love, whereby a man, fearing terribly he shall be damned, useth diligently all means whereby he shall be saved. Here is the strongest difficulty of all, to row against the stream, and to hate a man's self, and then to follow Christ fully.   (1640)

ANNE BRADSTREET

(c. 1612–1672)

Just as Shepard clarifies basic elements of theology through his prose, Anne Bradstreet presents quite simply many Puritan attitudes in her poetry. In the Prologue to *The Tenth Muse* she justifies her writing of poetry without elevating herself out of her accepted position; in "Childhood" she assumes the persona of a child, thereby revealing something of what it was to be a Puritan child; in "To my Dear and loving Husband" she is wife; in the next poem, mother; in the next, author. In short, her poetry holds glimpses of the roles a woman at such a time and place might have. "To My Dear Children" illustrates the same characteristics in her prose as she describes her life and her faith. The *Meditations*, like the poetry, presents through fresh images her interpretations and knowledge of Puritan doctrine. In Anne Bradstreet's prose and poetry, Puritan belief can be seen embedded within a human and humane sensibility. Ideas that might otherwise seem sterile and cold are here presented with the warmth of human reality.

Prologue to *The Tenth Muse**

1.

To sing of Wars, of Captains, and of Kings,
Of Cities founded, Common-wealths begun,
For my mean pen are too superiour things:
Or how they all, or each their dates have run
Let Poets and Historians set these forth,
My obscure Lines shall not so dim their worth.

* All selections from *The Works of Anne Bradstreet*, ed. John Harvard Ellis (Charlestown, 1867), slightly revised by the editor.

2.

But when my wondring eyes and envious heart
Great *Bartas*[1] sugar'd lines, do but read o're
Fool I do grudg the Muses did not part
'Twixt him and me that overfluent store;   10
A *Bartas* can, do what a *Bartas* will
But simple I according to my skill.

3.

From school-boyes tongue no rhet'rick we expect
Nor yet a sweet Consort from broken strings,
Nor perfect beauty, where's a main defect:
My foolish, broken, blemish'd Muse so sings
And this to mend, alas, no Art is able,
'Cause nature, made it so irreparable.

4.

Nor can I, like that fluent sweet tongu'd Greek,
Who lisp'd at first, in future times speak plain   20
By Art he gladly found what he did seek
A full requital of his, striving pain
Art can do much, but this maxime's most sure
A weak or wounded brain admits no cure.

5.

I am obnoxious to each carping tongue
Who says my hand a needle better fits,
A Poets pen all scorn I should thus wrong,
For such despite they cast on Female wits:
If what I do prove well, it won't advance,
They'l say it's stoln, or else it was by chance.   30

---

[1] Guillaume Salluste Du Bartas (1544–1590), French poet admired and often imitated by the Puritans.

6.

But sure the Antique Greeks were far more mild
Else of our Sexe, why feigned they those Nine
And poesy made, *Calliope's* own Child;
So 'mongst the rest they placed the Arts Divine,
But this weak knot, they will full soon untie,
The Greeks did nought, but play the fools & lye.

7.

Let Greeks be Greeks, and women what they are
Men have precedency and still excell,
It is but vain unjustly to wage warre;
Men can do best, and women know it well   40
Preheminence in all and each is yours;
Yet grant some small acknowledgement of ours.

8.

And oh ye high flown quills that soar the Skies,
And ever with your prey still catch your praise,
If e're you daigne these lowly lines your eyes
Give Thyme or Parsley wreath, I ask no bayes,
This mean and unrefined ure of mine
Will make you glistring gold, but more to shine.   (1650)

From *The Four Ages of Man*

Childhood

Ah me! conceived in sin and born with sorrow,
A nothing, here today and gone tomorrow,
Whose mean beginning blushing can't reveal,
But night and darkness must with shame conceal.

My mother's breeding sickness I will spare,
Her nine months weary burthen not declare.
To show her bearing pains, I should do wrong,
To tell those pangs which can't be told by tongue:
With tears into the world I did arrive;
My mother still did waste as I did thrive,   10
Who yet with love and all alacrity,
Spending, was willing to be spent for me.
With wayward cries I did disturb her rest,
Who sought still to appease me with the breast:
With weary arms she danced and *By By* sung,
When wretched I ingrate had done the wrong.
When infancy was past, my childishness
Did act all folly that it could express,
My silliness did only take delight
In that which riper age did scorn and slight.   20
In rattles, baubles and such toyish stuff,
My then ambitious thoughts were low enough:
My highborn soul so straitly was confin'd,
That its own worth it did not know nor mind:
This little house of flesh did spacious count,
Through ignorance all troubles did surmount;
Yet this advantage had mine ignorance,
Freedom from envy and from arrogance.
How to be rich or great I did not cark,[1]
A baron or a duke ne'er made my mark,   30
Nor studious was kings' favours how to buy,
With costly presents or base flattery:
No office coveted wherein I might
Make strong myself and turn aside weak right:
No malice bear to this or that great peer,
Nor unto buzzing whisperers gave ear:
I gave no hand nor vote for death or life,
I'd nought to do 'twixt King and people's strife.
No statist I, nor martialist in th' field;
Where e'er I went mine innocence was shield.   40
My quarrels not for diadems did rise,
But for an apple, plum, or some such prize:

[1] Care.

My strokes did cause no blood, no wounds or scars,
My little wrath did end soon as my wars:
My duel was no challenge nor did seek
My foe should weltring in his bowels reek.
I had no suits at law neighbours to vex,
Nor evidence for lands did me perplex.
I feared no storms, nor all the wind that blows,
I had no ships at sea, nor freights to lose.   50
I feared no drought nor wet, I had no crop,
Nor yet on future things did set my hope.
This was mine innocence, but ah! the seeds
Lay raked up of all the cursed weeds
Which sprouted forth in mine ensuing age,
As he can tell that next comes on the stage:
But yet let me relate before I go
The sins and dangers I am subject to,
Stained from birth with *Adam's* sinful fact,
Thence I began to sin as soon as act: 60
A perverse will, a love to what's forbid,
A serpent's sting in pleasing face lay hid:
A lying tongue as soon as it could speak,
And fifth commandment do daily break.
Oft stubborn, peevish, sullen, pout and cry,
Then nought can please, and yet I know not why.
As many are my sins, so dangers too;
For sin brings sorrow, sickness, death, and woe:
And though I miss the tossings of the mind,
Yet griefs in my frail flesh I still do find.   70
What gripes of wind mine infancy did pain,
What tortures I in breeding teeth sustain?
What crudities my stomach cold hath bred,
Whence vomits, flux, and worms have issued?
What breaches, knocks, and falls I daily have,
And some perhaps I carry to my grave;
Sometimes in fire, sometimes in water fall,
Strangely preserved, yet mind it not at all:
At home, abroad my danger's manifold,
That wonder 'tis, my glass till now doth hold.   80
I've done; unto my elders I give way,
For 'tis but little that a child can say.   (1650)

To my Dear and loving Husband[1]

If ever two were one, then surely we.
If ever man were lov'd by wife, then thee;
If ever wife was happy in a man,
Compare with me ye women if you can.
I prize thy love more then whole Mines of gold,
Or all the riches that the East doth hold.
My love is such that Rivers cannot quench,
Nor ought but love from thee, give recompence.
Thy love is such I can no way repay,
The heavens reward thee manifold I pray.   10
Then while we live, in love lets so persever,
That when we live no more, we may live ever.   (undated)

Before the Birth of one of her Children

All things within this fading world hath end,
Adversity doth still our joyes attend;
No tyes so strong, no friends so dear and sweet,
But with deaths parting blow is sure to meet.
The sentence past is most irrovocable,
A common thing, yet oh inevitable;
How soon, my Dear, death may my steps attend,
How soon't may be thy Lot to lose thy friend,
We both are ignorant, yet love bids me
These farewell lines to recommend to thee,   10
That when that knot's untyd that made us one,
I may seem thine, who in effect am none.
And if I see not half my dayes that's due,
What nature would, God grant to yours and you;
The many faults that well you know I have,
Let be interr'd in my oblivious grave;
If any worth or virtue were in me,
Let that live freshly in thy memory
And when thou feel'st no grief, as I no harms,
Yet love thy dead, who long lay in thine arms: 20

---

[1] Anne Bradstreet's husband was Simon Bradstreet (1603–1697), governor of the colony. Her father, Thomas Dudley, served as governor for four terms.

And when thy loss shall be repaid with gains
Look to my little babes my dear remains.
And if thou love thy self, or loved'st me
These O protect from stepdame's injury.
And if chance to thine eyes shall bring this verse,
With some sad sighs honour my absent Herse;
And kiss this paper for thy love's dear sake,
Who with salt tears this last Farewell did take. (undated)

The Author to her Book

Thou ill-form'd offspring of my feeble brain,
Who after birth did'st by my side remain,
Till snatcht from thence by friends, less wise then true
Who thee abroad, expos'd to publick view,
Made thee in raggs, halting to th'press to trudg,
Where errors were not lessened (all may judg)
At thy return my blushing was not small,
My rambling brat (in print) should mother call,
I cast thee by as one unfit for light,
Thy Visage was so irksome in my sight;   10
Yet being mine own, at length affection would
Thy blemishes amend, if so I could:
I wash'd thy face, but more defects I saw,
And rubbing off a spot, still made a flaw.
I stretcht thy joynts to make thee even feet,
Yet still thou run'st more hobling then is meet;
In better dress to trim thee was my mind,
But nought save home-spun Cloth, i'th' house I find
In this array, 'mongst Vulgars mayst thou roam
In Criticks hands, beware thou dost not come;   20
And take thy way where yet thou art not known,
If for thy Father askt, say, thou hadst none:
And for thy Mother, she alas is poor,
Which caus'd her thus to send thee out of door.   (undated)

To My Dear Children

This book by any yet unread,
I leave for you when I am dead,
That being gone, here you may find
What was your living mother's mind.
Make use of what I leave in love,
And God shall bless you from above.
                                        A. B.

My dear children,

I, knowing by experience that the exhortations of parents take most effect when the speakers leave to speak, and those especially sink deepest which are spoke latest, and being ignorant whether on my death bed I shall have opportunity to speak to any of you, much less to all, thought it the best, whilst I was able, to compose some short matters (for what else to call them I know not) and bequeath to you, that when I am no more with you, yet I may be daily in your remembrance (although that is the least in my aim in what I now do), but that you may gain some spiritual advantage by my experience. I have not studied in this you read to show my skill, but to declare the Truth, not to set forth myself, but the glory of God. If I had minded the former, it had been perhaps better pleasing to you, but seeing the last is the best, let it be best pleasing to you.

The method I will observe shall be this: I will begin with God's dealing with me from my childhood to this day. In my young years, about 6 or 7 as I take it, I began to make conscience of my ways, and what I knew was sinful, as lying, disobedience to parents, etc., I avoided it. If at any time I was overtaken with the like evils, it was a great trouble. I could not be at rest 'till by prayer I had confessed it unto God. I was also troubled at the neglect of private duties, though too often tardy that way. I also found much comfort in reading the Scriptures, especially those places I thought most concerned my condition, and as I grew to have more understanding, so the more solace I took in them.

In a long fit of sickness which I had on my bed I often communed with my heart, and made my supplication to the most High who set me free from that affliction.

But as I grew up to be about 14 or 15 I found my heart more carnal, and sitting loose from God, vanity and the follies of youth take hold of me.

About 16, the Lord laid His hand sore upon me and smote me with the smallpox. When I was in my affliction, I besought the Lord and confessed my pride and vanity and He was entreated of me, and again restored me. But I rendered not to Him according to the benefit received.

After a short time I changed my condition and was married, and came into this country, where I found a new world and new manners, at which my heart rose. But after I was convinced it was the way of God, I submitted to it and joined to the church at Boston.

After some time I fell into a lingering sickness like a consumption, together with a lameness, which correction I saw the Lord sent to humble and try me and do me good: and it was not altogether ineffectual.

It pleased God to keep me a long time without a child, which was a great grief to me and cost me many prayers and tears before I obtained one, and after him gave me many more, of whom I now take the care, that as I have brought you into the world, and with great pains, weakness, cares, and fears brought you to this, I now travail in birth again of you till Christ be formed in you.

Among all my experiences of God's gracious dealings with me I have constantly observed this, that He never suffered me long to sit loose from Him, but by one affliction or other hath made me look home, and search what was amiss; so usually thus it hath been with me that I have no sooner felt my heart out of order, but I have expected correction for it, which most commonly hath been upon my own person in sickness, weakness, pains, sometimes on my soul, in doubts and fears of God's displeasure, and my sincerity towards Him; sometimes He hath smote a child with sickness, sometimes chastened by losses in estate, and these times (through His great mercy) have been the times of my greatest getting and advantage; yea, I have found them the times when the Lord hath manifested the most love to me. Then have I gone to searching and have said with David, "Lord search me and try me, see what ways of wickedness are in me, and lead me in the way everlasting," and seldom or never but I have found either some sin I lay under which God would have reformed, or some duty neglected which He would have performed. And by His help I have laid vows and bonds upon my soul to perform His righteous commands.

If at any time you are chastened of God, take it as thankfully and joyfully as in greatest mercies, for if ye be His, ye shall reap the greatest benefit by it. It hath been no small support to me in times of darkness when the Almighty hath hid His face from me, that yet I have had abundance of sweetness and refreshment after affliction and more circumspection in my walking after I have been afflicted. I have been with God like an untoward child, that no longer than the rod has been on my back (or at least in sight) but I have been apt to forget Him and myself, too. Before I was afflicted I went astray, but now I keep Thy statutes.

I have had great experience of God's hearing my prayers, and returning comfortable answers to me, either in granting the thing I prayed for, or else in satisfying my mind without it, and I have been confident it hath been from Him, because I have found my heart through His goodness enlarged in thankfulness to Him.

I have often been perplexed that I have not found that constant joy in my pilgrimage and refreshing which I supposed most of the servants of God have, although He hath not left me altogether without the witness of His holy spirit, who hath oft given me His word and set to His seal that it shall be well with me. I have sometimes tasted of that hidden manna that the world knows not, and have set up my Ebenezer, and have resolved with myself that against such a promise, such tastes of sweetness, the gates of hell shall never prevail. Yet have I many times sinkings and droopings, and not enjoyed that felicity that sometimes I have done. But when I have been in darkness and seen no light, yet have I desired to stay myself upon the Lord.

And when I have been in sickness and pain, I have thought if the Lord would but lift up the light of His countenance upon me, although He ground me to powder, it would be but light to me; yea, oft have I thought were I in hell itself and could there find the love of God toward me, it would be a heaven. And could I have been in heaven without the love of God, it would have been a hell to me, for in truth it is the absence and presence of God that makes heaven or hell.

Many times hath Satan troubled me concerning the verity of the Scriptures, many times by atheism how I could know whether there was a God; I never saw any miracles to confirm me, and those which I read of, how did I know but they were feigned? That there is a God my reason would soon tell me by the wondrous works that I see, the vast frame of the heaven and the earth, the order of all things, night and day, summer and winter, spring and autumn, the daily providing for this great household upon the earth, the preserving and directing of all to its proper end. The consideration of these things would with amazement certainly resolve me that there is an Eternal Being.

But how should I know He is such a God as I worship in Trinity, and such a Saviour as I rely upon? Though this hath thousands of times been suggested to me, yet God hath helped me over. I have argued thus with myself. That there is a God, I see. If ever this God hath revealed himself, it must be in His word, and this must be it or none. Have I not found that operation by it that no human invention can work upon the soul, hath not judgments befallen divers who have scorned and contemned it, hath it not been preserved through all ages maugre all the heathen tyrants and all of the enemies who have opposed it? Is there any story but that which shows the beginnings of times, and how the world came to be as we see? Do we not know the prophecies in it fulfilled which could not have been so long foretold by any but God Himself?

When I have got over this block, then have I another put in my way, that admit this be the true God whom we worship, and that be his word, yet why may not the Popish religion be the right? They have the same God, the same Christ, the same word. They only interpret it one way, we another.

This hath sometimes stuck with me, and more it would, but the vain fooleries that are in their religion together with their lying miracles and cruel persecutions of the saints, which admit were they as they term them, yet not so to be dealt withal.

The consideration of these things and many the like would soon turn me to my own religion again.

But some new troubles I have had since the world has been filled with blasphemy and sectaries, and some who have been accounted sincere Christians have been carried away with them, that sometimes I have said, "Is there faith upon the earth?" and I have not known what to think. But then I have remembered the words of Christ that so it must be, and if it were possible, the very elect should be deceived. "Behold," saith our Saviour, "I have told you before." That hath stayed my heart, and I can now say, "Return, O my Soul, to thy rest, upon this rock Christ Jesus will I build my faith; and if I perish, I perish." But I know all the Powers of Hell shall never prevail against it. I know whom I have trusted, and whom I have believed, and that He is able to keep that I have committed to His charge.

Now to the King, immortal, eternal, and invisible, the only wise God, be honor, and glory for ever and ever! Amen.

This was written in much sickness and weakness, and is very weakly and imperfectly done; but if you can pick any benefit out of it, it is the mark which I aimed at.

For Deliverance from a Fever

When sorrows had begirt me round,
And pains within and out,
When in my flesh no part was found,
Then didst Thou rid me out.
My burning flesh in sweat did boil,
My aching head did break;
From side to side for ease I toil,
So faint I could not speak.
Beclouded was my soul with fear
Of Thy displeasure sore,   10
Nor could I read my evidence
Which oft I read before.
Hide not Thy face from me! I cried,
From burnings keep my soul;
Thou know'st my heart, and hast me tried:
I on Thy mercies roll.
O heal my soul, Thou know'st I said,
Though flesh consume to nought,
What though in dust it shall be laid,
To glory 't shall be brought.   20
Thou heard'st, Thy rod Thou didst remove
And spared my body frail,
Thou show'st to me Thy tender love,
My heart no more might quail.
O, praises to my mighty God,
Praise to my Lord, I say,
Who hath redeemed my soul from pit:
Praises to Him for aye!   (*c.* 1656)

From *Meditations, Divine and Moral*

1.

THERE is no object that we see, no action that we do, no good that we enjoy, no evil that we feel or fear, but we may make some spiritual advantage of all; and he that makes such improvement is wise as well as pious.

5.

It is reported of the peacock that, priding himself in his gay feathers, he ruffles them up; but spying his black feet, he soon lets fall his plumes. So he that glories in his gifts and adornings should look upon his corruptions, and that will damp his high thoughts.

9.

Sweet words are like honey: a little may refresh, but too much gluts the stomach.

30.

Yellow leaves argue want of sap, and gray hairs want of moisture; so dry and sapless performances are symptoms of little spiritual vigor.

31.

Iron till it be thoroughly heat, is uncapable to be wrought; so God sees good to cast some men into the furnace of affliction, and then beats them on his anvil into what frame he pleases.

36.

Sore laborers have hard hands, and old sinners have brawny consciences.

38.

Some children are hardly weaned; although the teat be rubbed with wormwood or mustard, they will either wipe it off, or else suck down sweet and bitter together. So is it with some Christians: let God embitter all the sweets of this life, that so they might feed upon more substantial food, yet they are so childishly sottish that they are still hugging and sucking these empty breasts, that God is forced to hedge up their way with thorns, or lay affliction on their loins, that so they might shake hands with the world before it bid them farewell.

62.

As man is called the little world, so his heart may be called the little commonwealth: his more fixed and resolved thoughts are like to inhabitants; his slight and flitting thoughts are like passengers that travel to and fro continually. Here is also the great court of justice erected, which is always kept by conscience, who is both accuser, excuser, witness, and judge; whom no bribes can pervert, nor flattery cause to favor, but as he finds the evidence, so he absolves or condemns. Yea, so absolute is this court of judicature, that there is no appeal from it—no, not to the court of Heaven itself—for if our conscience condemn us, he, also, who is greater than our conscience, will do it much more. But he that would have boldness to go to the throne of grace to be accepted there, must be sure to carry a certificate from the court of conscience, that he stands right there.   (1664)

. . . *some verses upon the burning of our house, July 10th, 1666*

In silent night when rest I took,
For sorrow neer I did not look,
I waken'd was with thundring nois
And Piteous shrieks of dreadfull voice.
That fearfull sound of fire and fire,
Let no man know is my Desire.
I, starting up, the light did spye,
And to my God my heart did cry
To strengthen me in my Distresse
And not to leave me succourlesse.   10
Then coming out beheld a space,
The flame consume my dwelling place.
And, when I could no longer look,

I blest his Name that gave and took,
That layd my goods now in the dust:
Yea so it was, and so 'twas just.
It was his own: it was not mine;
Far be it that I should repine.
He might of All justly bereft,
But yet sufficient for us left.   20
When by the Ruines oft I past,
My sorrowing eyes aside did cast,
And here and there the places spye
Where oft I sate, and long did lye.
Here stood that Trunk, and there that chest;
There lay that store I counted best:
My pleasant things in ashes lye,
And them behold no more shall I.
Under thy roof no guest shall sitt,
Nor at thy Table eat a bitt.   30
No pleasant tale shall 'ere be told,
Nor things recounted done of old.
No Candle 'ere shall shine in Thee,
Nor bridegroom's voice ere heard shall bee.
In silence ever shalt thou lye;
Adeiu, Adeiu; All's vanity.
Then streight I gin my heart to chide,
And did thy wealth on earth abide?
Didst fix thy hope on mouldring dust,
The arm of flesh didst make thy trust?   40
Raise up thy thoughts above the skye
That dunghill mists away may flie.
Thou hast an house on high erect,
Fram'd by that mighty Architect,
With glory richly furnished,
Stands permanent tho: this bee fled.
It's purchaséd, and paid for too
By him who hath enough to doe.
A Prise so vast as is unknown,
Yet, by his Gift, is made thine own.   50
Ther's wealth enough, I need no more;
Farewell my Pelf, farewell my Store.
The world no longer let me Love,
My hope and Treasure lyes Above.   (1666)

As Weary Pilgrim

As weary pilgrim, now at rest,
  Hugs with delight his silent nest,
His wasted limbs, now lie full soft
  That mirey steps, have trodden oft,
Blesses himself, to think upon
  His dangers past, and travails done.
The burning sun no more shall heat,
  Nor stormy rains, on him shall beat.
The briars and thorns no more shall scratch,
  Nor hungry wolves at him shall catch.   10
He erring paths no more shall tread,
  Nor wild fruits eat, instead of bread.
For waters cold he doth not long
  For thirst no more shall parch his tongue.
No rugged stones his feet shall gall,
  Nor stumps nor rocks cause him to fall.
All cares and fears, he bids farewell
  And means in safety now to dwell.
A pilgrim I, on earth, perplexed
  With sins with cares and sorrows vext,   20
By age and pains brought to decay,
  And my clay house mold'ring away.
Oh how I long to be at rest
  And soar on high among the blest.
This body shall in silence sleep
  Mine eyes no more shall ever weep
No fainting fits shall me assail
  Nor grinding pains my body frail
With cares and fears ne'er cumb'red be
  Nor losses know, nor sorrows see.   30
What though my flesh shall there consume,
  It is the bed Christ did perfume,
And when a few years shall be gone,
  This mortal shall be clothed upon.
A corrupt carcass down it lies,
  A glorious body it shall rise.
In weakness and dishonor sown,
  In power 'tis raised by Christ alone.

Then soul and body shall unite
   And of their Maker have the sight.   40
Such lasting joys shall there behold
   As ear ne'er heard nor tongue e'er told.
Lord make me ready for that day,
   Then come dear Bridegroom come away.   (1669)

MICHAEL WIGGLESWORTH

(1631–1705)

In the Introduction (pp. 15–16), the editor summarizes the content of the poem, states its purpose, and comments on its method. Since this didactic poem was intended to be read by children, the simple narrative line can easily be followed. On the Day of Doom, the Judgment Day, the saved go to Heaven, while the damned try to argue their way into Heaven. Embedded in their arguments is the theology that assures their damnation. While these arguments are not simple, they present the Puritan beliefs in a vivid way.

From *The Day of Doom**

1.

The security of the World before Christs coming to judgment.
Luk. 12:19

Still was the night, Serene and Bright,
    when all Men sleeping lay;
Calm was the season, and carnal reason
    thought so 'twould last for ay.
Soul, take thine ease, let sorrow cease,
    much good thou hast in store:
This was their Song, their Cups among,
    the Evening before.

* Kenneth B. Murdock, ed., *The Day of Doom* (New York, 1929).

84

2.

Wallowing in all kind of sin,
　　vile wretches lay secure:　　　　　　10
The best of men had scarcely then
　　their Lamps kept in good ure.　　　*Mat.* 25:5
Virgins unwise, who through disguise
　　amongst the best were number'd,
Had clos'd their eyes; yea, and the wise
　　through sloth and frailty slumber'd.

3.

Like as of old, when Men grow bold
　　God's threatnings to contemn,　　*Mat.* 24:37, 38
Who stopt their Ear, and would not hear,
　　when Mercy warned them:　　　　　20
But took their course, without remorse,
　　till God began to powre
Destruction the World upon
　　in a tempestuous showre.

4.

They put away the evil day,
　　And drown'd their care and fears,
Till drown'd were they, and swept away
　　by vengeance unawares:
So at the last, whilst Men sleep fast　　1 *Thes.* 5:3
　　in their security,　　　　　　　　30
Surpriz'd they are in such a snare
　　as cometh suddenly.

5.

For at midnight brake forth a Light,　　*The Suddenness,*
　　which turn'd the night to day,　　*Majesty, &*
And speedily an hideous cry　　　　　*Terror of Christ's*
　　did all the world dismay.　　　　　*appearing.*
Sinners awake, their hearts do ake,　　*Mat.* 25:6
　　trembling their loynes surprizeth;　　2 *Pet.* 3:10
Amaz'd with fear, by what they hear,
　　each one of them ariseth.　　　　　40

6.

They rush from Beds with giddy heads,
    and to their windows run,
Viewing this light, which shines more bright
Mat. 24:29, 30   then doth the Noon-day Sun.
Straightway appears (they see't with tears)
    the Son of God most dread;
Who with his Train comes on amain
    To Judge both Quick and Dead.

7.

Before his face the Heav'ns gave place,
2 *Pet.* 3:10   and Skies are rent asunder,   50
With mighty voice, and hideous noise,
    more terrible than Thunder.
His brightness damps heav'ns glorious lamps
    and makes them hide their heads,
As if afraid and quite dismay'd,
    they quit their wonted steads.

8.

Ye sons of men that durst contemn
    the Threatnings of Gods Word,
How cheer you now? your hearts, I trow,
    are thrill'd as with a sword.   60
Now Atheist blind, whose brutish mind
    a God could never see,
Dost thou perceive, dost now believe,
    that Christ thy Judge shall be?

9.

Stout Courages, (whose hardiness
    could Death and Hell out-face)
Are you as bold now you behold
    your Judge draw near apace?
They cry, no, no: Alas! and wo!
    our Courage all is gone: 70
Our hardiness (fool hardiness)
    hath us undone, undone.

10.

No heart so bold, but now grows cold
   and almost dead with fear:
No eye so dry, but now can cry,   *Rev.* 6:16
   and pour out many a tear.
Earths Potentates and pow'rful States,
   Captains and Men of Might
Are quite abasht, their courage dasht
   at this most dreadful sight.   80

11.

Mean men lament, great men do rent
   their Robes, and tear their hair:
They do not spare their flesh to tear   *Mat.* 24:30
   through horrible despair.
All Kindreds wail: all hearts do fail:
   horror the world doth fill
With weeping eyes, and loud out-cries,
   yet knows not how to kill.

12.

Some hide themselves in Caves and Delves,   *Rev.* 6:15, 16
   in places under ground: 90
Some rashly leap into the Deap,
   to scape by being drown'd:
Some to the Rocks (O sensless blocks!)
   and woody Mountains run,
That there they might this fearful sight,
   and dreaded Presence shun.

13.

In vain do they to Mountains say,
   Fall on us, and us hide
From Judges ire, more hot than fire,
   for who may it abide?   100
No hiding place can from his Face,
   sinners at all conceal,
Whose flaming Eyes hid things doth 'spy,
   and darkest things reveal.

14.

The Judge draws nigh, exalted high
    upon a lofty Throne,
Mat. 25:31

Amidst the throng of Angels strong,
    lo, Israel's Holy One!
The excellence of whose presence
    and awful Majesty,   110
Amazeth Nature, and every Creature,
    doth more than terrify.

15.

Rev. 6:14   The Mountains smoak, the Hills are shook,
    the Earth is rent and torn,
As if she should be clean dissolv'd,
    or from the Center born.
The Sea doth roar, forsakes the shore,
    and shrinks away for fear;
The wild Beasts flee into the Sea,   120
    so soon as he draws near.

16.

Whose Glory bright, whose wondrous might,
    whose Power Imperial,
So far surpass whatever was
    in Realms Terrestrial;
That tongues of men (nor Angels pen)
    cannot the same express,
And therefore I must pass it by,
    lest speaking should transgress.

17.

1 *Thes.* 4:16
Resurrection
of the Dead.
Joh. 5:28, 29

Before his Throne a Trump is blown,
    Proclaiming th' Day of Doom: 130
Forthwith he cries, *Ye Dead arise,*
    and unto Judgment come.
No sooner said, but 'tis obey'd;
    Sepulchers open'd are:
Dead Bodies all rise at his call,
    and's mighty power declare.

38.

All silence keep, both Goats and Sheep,
  before the Judge's Throne;
With mild aspect to his Elect
  then spake the Holy One: 140
My sheep draw near, your Sentence hear,
  which is to you no dread,
Who clearly now discern, and know
  your sins are pardoned.

*The Saints
cleared &
justified.*

39.

'Twas meet that ye should judged be,
  that so the world may spy
No cause of grudge, when as I Judge
  and deal impartially.
Know therefore all, both great and small,
  the ground and reason why   150
These Men do stand at my right hand,
  and look so cheerfully.

2 Cor. 5:10
Eccles. 3:17
Joh. 3:18

40.

These Men be those my Father chose
  before the worlds foundation,
And to me gave, that I should save
  from Death and Condemnation.
For whose dear sake I flesh did take,
  was of a Woman born,
And did inure my self t'indure,
  unjust reproach and scorn.   160

Joh. 17:6
Eph. 1:4

41.

For them it was that I did pass
  through sorrows many one:
That I drank up that bitter Cup,
  which made me sigh and groan.
The Cross his pain I did sustain;
  yea more, my Fathers ire
I underwent, my Blood I spent
  to save them from Hell fire.

Rev. 1:5

42.

Thus I esteem'd, thus I redeem'd
   all these from every Nation,   170
That they may be (as now you see)
   a chosen Generation.
What if ere-while they were as vile,

Eph. 2:1, 3   and bad as any be,
And yet from all their guilt and thrall
   at once I set them free?

43.

My grace to one is wrong to none:
Mat. 20:13, 15   none can Election claim,
Rom. 9:20, 21
Amongst all those their souls that lose,
   none can Rejection blame.   180
He that may chuse, or else refuse,
   all men to save or spill,
May this Man chuse, and that refuse,
   redeeming whom he will.

44.

Isa. 53:4, 5, 11   But as for those whom I have chose
   Salvations heirs to be,
I underwent their punishment,
   and therefore set them free;
I bore their grief, and their relief
   by suffering procur'd,   190
That they of bliss and happiness
   might firmly be assur'd.

45.

Acts 13:48   And this my grace they did imbrace,
Jam. 2:18   believing on my Name;
Heb. 12:7
Mat. 19:29 Which Faith was true, the fruits do shew
   proceeding from the same:
Their Penitence, their Patience,
   their Love and Self-denial
In suffering losses, and bearing Crosses,
   when put upon the tryal.   200

46.

Their sin forsaking, their chearful taking
   my yoke, their Charity
Unto the Saints in all their wants,
   and in them unto me,
These things do clear, and make appear
   their Faith to be unfaigned,
And that a part in my desert
   and purchase they have gained.

1 Joh. 3:3
Mat. 25:39, 40

47.

Their debts are paid, their peace is made,
   their sins remitted are;
Therefore at once I do pronounce,
   and openly declare
That Heav'n is theirs, that they be Heirs
   of Life and of Salvation!
Nor ever shall they come at all
   to Death or to Damnation.

210 *Isa.* 53:11, 12
Rom. 8:16, 17,
33, 34
Joh. 3:18

48.

Come, Blessed Ones, and sit on Thrones,
   Judging the World with me:
Come, and possess your happiness,
   and bought felicitie.
Henceforth no fears, no care, no tears,
   no sin shall you annoy,
Nor any thing that grief doth bring:
   Eternal Rest enjoy.

Luk. 22:29, 30
Mat. 19:28

220

49.

You bore the Cross, you suffered loss
   of all for my Names sake:
Receive the Crown that's now your own;
   come, and a Kingdom take.
Thus spake the Judge; the wicked grudge,
   and grind their teeth in vain;
They see with groans these plac't on Thrones
   which addeth to their pain:

Mat. 25:34
*They are placed on
Thrones to joyn
with Christ in
judging the wicked.*

230

50.

That those whom they did wrong and slay,
    must now their judgment see!
Such whom they slighted, and once despighted,
    must now their Judges be!
Thus 'tis decreed, such is their meed,
1 Cor. 6:2   and guerdon glorious!
With Christ they sit, Judging is fit
    to plague the Impious.   240

51.

The wicked
brought to the Bar.   The wicked are brought to the Bar,
Rom. 2:3, 6, 11   like guilty Malefactors,
That oftentimes of bloody Crimes
    and Treasons have been Actors.
Of wicked Men, none are so mean
    as there to be neglected:
Nor none so high in dignity,
    as there to be respected.

52.

Rev. 6:15, 16   The glorious Judge will priviledge
Isa. 30:33   nor Emperour, nor King: 250
But every one that hath mis-done
    doth into Judgment bring.
And every one that hath mis-done,
    the Judge impartially
Condemneth to eternal wo,
    and endless misery.

53.

Thus one and all, thus great and small,
    the Rich as well as Poor,
And those of place as the most base,
    do stand the Judge before.   260
There are arraign'd, and there detain'd,
    before Christ's Judgment-seat
With trembling fear, their Doom to hear,
    and feel his angers heat.

54.

There Christ demands at all their hands
    a strict and strait account
Of all things done under the Sun,
    whose number far surmount
Man's wit and thought: yet all are brought
    unto this solemn Tryal;
And each offence with evidence,
    so that there's no denial.

Eccles. 11:9 &
12:14

270

55.

There's no excuses for their abuses,
    since their own Consciences
More proof give in of each Man's sin,
    than thousand Witnesses,
Though formerly this faculty
    had grosly been abused,
Men could it stifle, or with it trifle,
    when as it them accused.

280

56.

Now it comes in, and every sin
    unto Mens charge doth lay:
It judgeth them, and doth condemn,
    though all the world say nay.
It so stingeth and tortureth,
    it worketh such distress,
That each Man's self against himself,
    is forced to confess.

57.

It's vain, moreover, for Men to cover
    the least iniquity:
The Judge hath seen, and privy been
    to all their villany.
He unto light, and open sight
    the works of darkness brings:
He doth unfold both new and old,
    both known and hidden things.

Secret sins and
290 *works of darkness*
brought to light.
Psal. 139:2, 4, 12
Rom. 2:16

58.

Eccles. 12:14

All filthy facts, and secret acts,
   however closly done,
And long conceal'd, are there reveal'd
   before the mid-day Sun.   300
Deeds of the night shunning the light,
   which darkest corners sought,
To fearful blame, and endless shame,
   are there most justly brought.

92.

*Civil honest mens
pleas.
Luk.* 18:11

Then were brought nigh a Company
   of Civil honest Men,
That lov'd true dealing, and hated stealing,
   ne'r wrong'd their Bretheren;
Who pleaded thus, Thou knowest us
   that we were blameless livers;   310
No Whoremongers, no Murderers,
   no quarrellers nor strivers.

93.

Idolaters, Adulterers,
   Church-robbers we were none,
Nor false-dealers, no couzeners,
   but paid each man his own.
Our way was fair, our dealing square,
   we were no wastful spenders,
No lewd toss-pots, no drunken sots,
   no scandalous offenders.   320

94.

We hated vice, and set great price,
   by vertuous conversation:
And by the same we got a name,
   and no small commendation.

1 *Sam.* 15:22

Gods Laws express that righteousness,
   is that which he doth prize;
And to obey, as he doth say,
   is more than sacrifice.

95.

Thus to obey, hath been our way;
   let our good deeds, we pray,   330
Find some regard and some reward
   with thee, O Lord, this day.
And whereas we transgressors be,   *Eccles.* 7:20
   of *Adam's* Race were none,
No not the best, but have confest
   themselves to have mis-done.

96.

Then answered unto their dread,   *Are taken off &*
   the Judge: True Piety   *rendred invalid.*
God doth desire and eke require   *Deut.* 10:12
   no less than honesty.   *Tit.* 2:12
Justice demands at all your hands   340 *Jam.* 2:10
   perfect Obedience:
If but in part you have come short,
   that is a just offence.

97.

On Earth below, where men did ow
   a thousand pounds and more,
Could twenty pence it recompence?
   could that have clear'd the score?
Think you to buy felicity
   with part of what's due debt?   350
Or for desert of one small part,
   the whole should off be set?

98.

And yet that part, whose great desert
   you think to reach so far
For your excuse, doth you accuse,
   and will your boasting mar.
However fair, however square,   *Luk.* 18:11, 14
   your way and work hath been,
Before mens eyes, yet God espies
   iniquity therein.   360

99.

1 *Sam.* 16:7
2 *Chron.* 25:2

God looks upon th' affection
    and temper of the heart;
Not only on the action,
    and the external part.
Whatever end vain men pretend,
    God knows the verity;
And by the end which they intend
    their words and deeds doth try.

100.

Heb. 11:6

Without true Faith, the Scripture saith
    God cannot take delight   370
In any deed, that doth proceed
    from any sinful wight.

1 *Cor.* 13:1, 2, 3

And without love all actions prove
    but barren empty things.
Dead works they be, and vanitie,
    the which vexation brings.

101.

Nor from true faith, which quencheth wrath,
    hath your obedience flown:
Nor from true love, which wont to move
    Believers, hath it grown.   380
Your argument shews your intent,
    in all that you have done:
You thought to scale Heav'ns lofty Wall
    by Ladders of your own.

102.

Rom. 10:3

Your blinded spirit, hoping to merit
    by your own Righteousness,
Needed no Saviour, but your behaviour,
    and blameless carriages;
You trusted to what you could do,
    and in no need you stood: 390
Your haughty pride laid me aside,
    and trampled on my Blood.

103.

All men have gone astray, and done,
   that which Gods Laws condemn:
But my Purchase and offered Grace
   all men did not contemn.
The *Ninevites*, and *Sodomites*,
   had no such sin as this:
Yet as if all your sins were small,
   you say, All did amiss.

Rom. 9:30, 32
Mat. 11:23, 24
& 12:41

400

104.

Again you thought and mainly sought
   a name with men t' acquire;
Pride bare the Bell, that made you swell,
   and your own selves admire.
Mean fruit it is, and vile, I wiss,
   that springs from such a root:
Vertue divine and genuine
   wonts not from pride to shoot.

Mat. 6:5

105.

Such deeds as your are worse than poor;
   they are but sins guilt over
With silver dross, whose glistering gloss
   can them no longer cover.
The best of them would you condemn,
   and ruine you alone,
Although you were from faults so clear,
   that other you had none.

410

Prov. 26:23
Mat. 23:27

106.

Your Gold is brass, your silver dross,
   your righteousness is sin:
And think you by such honesty
   eternal life to win?
You much mistake, if for its sake
   you dream of acceptation;
Whereas the same deserveth shame,
   and meriteth Damnation.

Prov. 15:8
Rom. 3:20

420

130.

Others plead for
Pardon both from
Gods mercy and
justice.
Psal. 78:38

Others Argue, and not a few,
　　is not God gracious?
His Equity and Clemency
　　are they not marvellous?
Thus we believ'd; are we deceiv'd?
　　cannot his mercy great,　　　　　　　　430
(As hath been told to us of old)
　　asswage his angers heat?

131.

2 *Kings* 14:26

How can it be that God should see
　　his Creatures endless pain,
Or hear the groans and rueful moans,
　　and still his wrath retain?
Can it agree with Equitie?
　　can mercy have the heart
To recompence few years offence
　　with Everlasting smart?　　　　　　　　440

132.

Can God delight in such a sight
　　as sinners misery?
Or what great good can this our blood
　　bring unto the most High?

Psal. 30:9
Mic. 7:18

Oh, thou that dost thy Glory most
　　in pard'ning sin display!
Lord, might it please thee to release,
　　and pardon us this day?

133.

Unto thy Name more glorious fame
　　would not such mercy bring?　　　　　　450
Would not it raise thine endless praise,
　　more than our suffering?
With that they cease, holding their peace,
　　but cease not still to weep;
Grief ministers a flood of tears,
　　in which their words do steep.

134.

But all too late, grief's out of date,
    when life is at an end.
The glorious King thus answering,
    all to his voice attend: 460 *They answered.*
God gracious is, quoth he, like his
    no mercy can be found;
His Equity and Clemency
    to sinners do abound.

135.

As may appear by those that here   *Mercy that now*
    are plac'd at my right hand;   *shines forth in the*
Whose stripes I bore, and clear'd the score,   *vessels of Mercy.*
    that they might quitted stand.   *Mic.* 7:18
For surely none, but God alone,   *Rom.* 9:23
    whose Grace transcends mens thought,   470
For such as those that were his foes
    like wonders would have wrought.

136.

And none but he such lenitee   *Did also long wait*
    and patience would have shown   *upon such as*
To you so long, who did him wrong,   *abused it.*
    and pull'd his judgments down.   *Rom.* 2:4
How long a space (O stiff neck'd race)   *Hos.* 11:4
    did patience you afford?
How oft did love you gently move,
    to turn unto the Lord?   480

137.

With Cords of love God often strove   *Luk.* 13:34
    your stubborn hearts to tame: *The day of Grace*
Nevertheless your wickedness,   *now past.*
    did still resist the same.
If now at last Mercy be past
    from you for evermore,
And Justice come in Mercies room,
    yet grudge you not therefore.

138.

If into wrath God turned hath
   his long long suffering,   490

Luk. 19:42, 43
Jude 4
And now for love you vengeance prove,
   it is an equal thing.
Your waxing worse, hath stopt the course
   of wonted Clemency:
Mercy refus'd, and Grace misus'd,
   call for severity.

139.

Rom. 2:5, 6
Isa. 1:24
Amos 2:13
Gen. 18:25
It's now high time that ev'ry Crime
   be brought to punishment:
Wrath long contain'd, and oft restrain'd,
   at last must have a vent: 500
Justice severe cannot forbear
   to plague sin any longer,
But must inflict with hand most strict
   mischief upon the wronger.

140.

Mat. 25:3, 11, 12
Prov. 1:28, 29, 30
In vain do they for Mercy pray,
   the season being past,
Who had no care to get a share
   therein, while time did last.
The man whose ear refus'd to hear
   the voice of Wisdoms cry,   510
Earn'd this reward, that none regard
   him in this misery.

141.

It doth agree with equity,
   and with Gods holy Law,

Isa. 5:18, 19
Gen. 2:17
Rom. 2:8, 9
That those should dye eternally
   that death upon them draw.
The Soul that sins damnation wins,
   for so the Law ordains;
Which Law is just, and therefore must
   such suffer endless pain.   520

142.

Eternal smart is the desert,
　ev'n of the least offence;
Then wonder not if I allot
　to you this Recompence:
But wonder more, that since so sore
　and lasting plagues are due
To every sin, you liv'd therein,
　who well the danger knew.

Rom. 6:23
2 Thes. 1:8, 9

143.

God hath no joy to crush or 'stroy,
　and ruine wretched wights,
But to display the glorious Ray
　of Justice he delights.
To manifest he doth detest,
　and throughly hate all sin,
By plaguing it as is most fit,
　this shall him glory win.

Ezek. 33:11
Exod. 34:7
& 14:17
530 *Rom.* 9:22

144.

Then at the Bar arraigned are
　an impudenter sort,
Who to evade the guilt that's laid
　upon them, thus retort;
How could we cease thus to transgress?
　how could we Hell avoid,
Whom Gods Decree shut out from thee,
　and sign'd to be destroy'd?

*Some pretend they
were shut out from
Heaven by Gods
Decree.*
540 *Rom.* 9:18, 19

145.

Whom God ordains to endless pains,
　by Law unalterable,
Repentance true, Obedience new,
　to save such are unable:
Sorrow for sin, no good can win,
　to such as are rejected;
Ne can they grieve, nor yet believe,
　that never were elected.

Heb. 22:17
550 *Rom.* 11:7, 8

146.

Of Man's fall'n Race, who can true Grace,
    or Holiness obtain?
Who can convert or change his heart,
    if God withhold the same?
Had we apply'd our selves, and try'd
    as much as who did most
God's love to gain, our busie pain
    and labour had been lost.   560

147.

Their pleas
taken off.
Luk. 13:27
2 *Pet.* 1:9, 10
compared with
Mat. 19:6

Christ readily makes this Reply,
    I damn you not because
You are rejected, or not elected,
    but you have broke my Laws:
It is but vain your wits to strain,
    the end and means to sever:
Men fondly seek to part or break
    what God hath link'd together.

148.

Acts 3:19
& 16:31
* 1 *Sam.* 2:15
Joh. 3:19
Joh. 5:40
2 *Thes.* 2:11, 12

Whom God will save, such he will have,
    the means of life to use: 570
Whom he'll pass by, shall chuse to dy,
    and ways of life refuse.
He that fore-sees, and foredecrees,
    in wisdom order'd has,
That man's free-will electing ill,
    shall bring his will to pass.

149.

Ezek. 33:11, 12, 13
Luk. 13:34
Prov. 8:33, 36

High God's Decree, as it is free,
    so doth it none compel
Against their will to good or ill,
    it forceth none to Hell.   580
They have their wish whose Souls perish
    with Torments in Hell-fire,
Who rather chose their Souls to lose,
    than leave a loose desire.

150.

God did ordain sinners to pain
  and I to Hell send none,
But such as swerv'd, and have deserv'd
  destruction as their own,
His pleasure is, that none from bliss
  and endless happiness   590
Be barr'd, but such as wrong'd him much
  by wilful wickedness.

Gen. 2:17
Mat. 25:41, 42
Ezek. 18:20

151.

You, sinful Crew, no other knew
  but you might be elect;
Why did you then your selves condemn?
  why did you me reject?
Where was your strife to gain that life
  which lasteth evermore?
You never knock'd, yet say God lock'd
  against you Heav'ns door.   600

2 Pet. 1:10
Acts 13:46
Luk. 13:24

152.

'Twas no vain task to knock, to ask,
  whilst life continued.
Whoever sought heav'n as he ought,
  and seeking perished?
The lowly meek who truly seek
  for Christ, and for Salvation,
There's no Decree whereby such be
  ordain'd to Condemnation.

Mat. 7:7, 8

Gal. 5:22, 23

153.

You argue then: But abject men,
  whom God resolves to spill,   610
Cannot repent, nor their hearts rent;
  ne can they change their will.
Not for his *Can* is any man
  adjudged unto Hell:
But for his *Will* to do what's ill,
  and nilling to do well.

Joh. 3:19

154.

I often stood tend'ring my Blood
    to wash away your guilt:
And eke my Spright to frame you right,
    lest your Souls should be spilt.   620

Joh. 5:40   But you vile Race, rejected Grace,
    when Grace was freely proffer'd:
No changed heart, no heav'nly part
    would you, when it was offer'd.

155.

Who wilfully the Remedy,
    and means of life contemned,
Cause have the same themselves to blame,

Joh. 15:22, 24   if now they be condemned.
Heb. 2:3   You have your selves, you and none else,
Isa. 66:3, 4   your selves have done to dy.   630
You chose the way to your decay,
    and perisht wilfully.

166.

Then to the Bar, all they drew near
    who dy'd in Infancy,
And never had or good or bad
    effected pers'nally,
But from the womb unto the tomb
    were straightway carried,
(Or at the last e're they transgrest)
    who thus began to plead: 640

167.

Ezek. 18:2   If for our own transgression,
    or disobedience,
We here did stand at thy left-hand
    just were the Recompence:
But *Adam's* guilt our souls hath spilt,
    his fault is charg'd on us;
And that alone hath overthrown,
    and utterly undone us.

168.

Not we, but he, ate of the Tree,
   whose fruit was interdicted: 650
Yet on us all of his sad Fall,
   the punishment's inflicted.
How could we sin that had not been,
   or how is his sin our,
Without consent, which to prevent,
   we never had a pow'r?

169.

O great Creator, why was our Nature
   depraved and forlorn?
Why so defil'd, and made so vild
   whilst we were yet unborn?   660
If it be just, and needs we must
   transgressors reck'ned be,
Thy Mercy, Lord, to us afford,
   which sinners hath set free.   *Psal.* 51:5

170.

Behold we see *Adam* set free,
   and sav'd from his trespass,
Whose sinful Fall hath split us all,
   and brought us to this pass.
Canst thou deny us once to try,
   or Grace to us to tender,   670
When he finds grace before thy face,
   that was the chief offender?

171.

Then answered the Judge most dread,   *Their Argument*
   God doth such doom forbid,   *taken off.*
That men should dye eternally   *Ezek.* 18:20
   for what they never did.   *Rom.* 5:12, 19
But what you call old *Adam's* Fall,
   and only his Trespass,
You call amiss to call it his,
   both his and yours it was.   680

172.

He was design'd of all Mankind
   to be a publick Head,
A common Root, whence all should shoot,
   and stood in all their stead.

1 Cor. 15:48, 49

He stood and fell, did ill or well,
   not for himself alone,
But for you all, who now his Fall,
   and trespass would disown.

173.

If he had stood, then all his brood
   had been established   690
In Gods true love, never to move,
   nor once awry to tread:
Then all his Race, my Father's Grace,
   should have enjoy'd for ever,
And wicked Sprights by subtile sleights
   could them have harmed never.

174.

Would you have griev'd to have receiv'd
   through *Adam* so much good,
As had been your for evermore,
   if he at first had stood?   700
Would you have said, we ne'r obey'd,
   nor did thy Laws regard;
It ill befits with benefits,
   us, Lord, so to reward?

175.

Since then to share in his welfare,
   you could have been content,
You may with reason share in his treason,
   and in the punishment.

Rom. 5:12
Psal. 51:5
Gen. 5:3

Hence you were born in state forlorn,
   with Natures so depraved: 710
Death was your due, because that you
   had thus your selves behaved.

176.

You think if we had been as he,
   whom God did so betrust,
We to our cost would ne're have lost   *Mat.* 23:30, 31
   all for a paltry Lust.
Had you been made in *Adam's* stead,
   you would like things have wrought,
And so into the self-same wo,
   your selves and yours have brought.   720

177.

I may deny you once to try,   *Rom.* 9:15, 18
   or Grace to you to tender,   *The free gift.*
Though he finds Grace before my face,   *Rom.* 5:15
   who was the chief offender:
Else should my Grace cease to be Grace;
   for it should not be free,
If to release whom I should please,
   I have no libertee.

178.

If upon one what's due to none
   I frankly shall bestow,   730
And on the rest shall not think best,
   compassions skirts to throw,
Whom injure I? will you envy,
   and grudge at others weal?
Or me accuse, who do refuse
   your selves to help and heal?

179.

Am I alone of what's my own,   *Mat.* 20:15
   no Master or no Lord?
Or if I am, how can you claim,
   what I to some afford?   740
Will you demand Grace at my hand,
   and challenge what is mine?
Will you teach me whom to set free,
   and thus my Grace confine?

180.

Psal. 58:3
Rom. 6:23
Gal. 3:10
Rom. 8:29, 30
& 11:7
Rev. 21:27
Luk. 12:48

You sinners are, and such a share
    as sinners may expect,
Such you shall have; for I do save
    none but mine own Elect.
Yet to compare your sin with their,
    who liv'd a longer time,   750
I do confess yours is much less,
    though every sin's a crime.

181.

Mat. 11:22
*The wicked all
convinced and
put to silence.*
Rom. 3:19
Mat. 22:12

A crime it is, therefore in bliss
    you may not hope to dwell;
But unto you I shall allow
    the easiest room in Hell.
The glorious King thus answering,
    they cease, and plead no longer:
Their Consciences must needs confess
    his Reasons are the stronger.   760

201.

*The Judge
pronounceth the
Sentence of
condemnation.*
Mat. 25:41

*Ye sinful wights, and cursed sprights,
    that work Iniquity,
Depart together from me for ever
    to endless Misery;
Your portion take in yonder Lake,
    where Fire and Brimstone flameth:
Suffer the smart, which your desert
    as it's due wages claimeth.*

202.

Oh piercing words more sharp than swords!
    what, to depart from *Thee*,   770

The terrour of it.

Whose face before for evermore
    the best of Pleasures be!
What? to depart (unto our smart)
    from thee *Eternally:*
To be for aye banish'd away,
    with *Devils* company!

203.

What? to be sent to *Punishment*,
    and flames of *Burning Fire*,
To be surrounded, and eke confounded
    with Gods *Revengful ire*.   780
What? to abide, not for a tide
    these Torments, but for *Ever:*
To be released, or to be eased,
    not after years, but *Never*.

204.

Oh, *fearful Doom*! now there's no room
    for hope or help at all:
Sentence is past which aye shall last,
    Christ will not it recall.
There might you hear them rent and tear
    the Air with their out-cries: 790
The hideous noise of their sad voice
    ascendeth to the Skies.

205.

They wring their hands, their caitiff-hands   *Luk.* 13:28
    and gnash their teeth for terrour;
They cry, they roar for anguish sore,
    and gnaw their tongues for horrour.
But get away without delay,
    Christ pitties not your cry:
Depart to Hell, there may you yell,
    and roar Eternally.   800 *Prov.* 1:26

206.

That word, *Depart*, maugre their heart,   *It is put in*
    drives every wicked one,   *Execution.*
With mighty pow'r, the self-same hour,
    far from the Judge's Throne.   *Mat.* 25:46
Away they're chaste by the strong blast
    of his Death-threatning mouth:
They flee full fast, as if in haste,
    although they be full loath.

207.

As chaff that's dry, and dust doth fly
    before the Northern wind: 810
Right so are they chased away,
    and can no Refuge find.

Mat. 13:41, 42   They hasten to the Pit of Wo,
    guarded by Angels stout;
Who to fulfil Christ's holy will,
    attend this wicked Rout.

208.

HELL.
Mat. 25:30   Whom having brought, as they are taught,
Mark 9:43   unto the brink of Hell,
Isa. 30:33   (That dismal place far from Christ's face,
Rev. 21:8   where Death and Darkness dwell: 820
Where Gods fierce Ire kindleth the fire,
    and vengeance feeds the flame
With piles of Wood, and Brimstone Flood,
    that none can quench the same,)

209.

Wicked Men
and Devils cast into   With Iron bands they bind their hands,
it for ever.   and cursed feet together,
Mat. 22:13 &   And cast them all, both great and small,
25:46   into that Lake for ever.
Where day and night, without respite,
    they wail, and cry, and howl   830
For tort'ring pain, which they sustain
    in Body and in Soul.

210.

Rev. 14:10, 11   For day and night, in their despight,
    their torments smoak ascendeth.
Their pain and grief have no relief,
    their anguish never endeth.
There must they ly, and never dy,
    though dying every day:
There must they dying ever ly,
    and not consume away.   840

211.

Dy fain they would, if dy they could,
  but Death will not be had;
God's direful wrath their bodies hath
  for ev'r Immortal made.
They live to ly in misery,
  and bear eternal wo;
And live they must whilst God is just,
  that he may plague them so. (1662)

EDWARD TAYLOR

(c. 1642–1729)

Taylor is considered the best of the Puritan poets. While his work lacks the simplicity of Anne Bradstreet's, it has many other admirable qualities. The intensity, the range of imagery, the scope of the vision, the substance of the doctrine—these and much more account for its excellence. The *Meditations* further our understanding of the Puritan view of the depravity of man. *Gods Determinations* can be seen as one of the significant works of Christian literature. There Taylor presents the crucial problems of the nature of God and man and their reconciliation. A careful reading will be helped by the bracketed notes. Some readers find it useful to read at least once for the content and again to study the poetic devices; such a division is arbitrary but necessary. The *Treatise Concerning the Lord's Supper* may at first seem similar to the *Meditations,* but, as pointed out in the Introduction, the problem is essentially political and reminds us once more of the primacy and urgency of theological problems in Puritan life. See the Introduction (pp. 16–19) for a lengthy discussion of the Puritan thought contained in the poetry.

From *Preparatory Meditations before my Approach to the Lords Supper**

6. ANOTHER MEDITATION AT THE SAME TIME.

> Am I thy Gold? Or Purse, Lord, for thy Wealth;
>   Whether in mine, or mint refinde for thee?
> Ime counted so, but count me o're thyselfe,
>   Lest gold washt face, and brass in Heart I bee.
>   I Feare my Touchstone touches when I try
>   Mee, and my Counted Gold too overly.

* All poems from Donald Stanford, ed., *The Poems of Edward Taylor* (New Haven, 1960).

Am I new minted by thy Stamp indeed?
  Mine Eyes are dim; I cannot clearly see.
Be thou my Spectacles that I may read
  Thine Image, and Inscription stampt on mee.   10
  If thy bright Image do upon me stand
  I am a Golden Angell[1] in thy hand.

Lord, make my Soule thy Plate: thine Image bright
  Within the Circle of the same enfoile.
And on its brims in golden Letters write
  Thy Superscription in an Holy style.
  Then I shall be thy Money, thou my Hord:
  Let me thy Angell bee, bee thou my Lord.   (undated)

19. MEDITATION. PHIL. 2.9. GOD HATH HIGHLY EXALTED HIM.

Looke till thy Looks look Wan, my Soule; here's ground.
  The Worlds bright Eye's dash't out: Day-Light so brave
Bemidnighted; the sparkling sun, palde round
  With flouring Rayes lies buri'de in its grave
  The Candle of the World blown out, down fell.
  Life knockt a head by Death: Heaven by Hell.

Alas! this World all filld up to the brim
  With Sins, Deaths, Divills, Crowding men to Hell.
For whose reliefe Gods milkwhite Lamb stept in
  Whom those Curst Imps did worry, flesh, and fell.   10
  Tread under foot, did Clap their Wings and so
  Like Dunghill Cocks over their Conquourd, Crow.

Brave Pious Fraud; as if the Setting Sun:
  Dropt like a Ball of Fire into the Seas,
And so went out. But to the East come, run:
  You'l meet the morn Shrinde with its flouring Rayes.
  This Lamb in laying of these Lyons dead;
  Drank of the brooke: and so lift up his Head.

---

[1] A seventeenth-century coin.

Oh! sweet, sweet joy! These Rampant Fiends befoold:
    They made their Gall his Winding sheete; although   20
They of the Heart-ach dy must, or be Coold
    With Inflamation of the Lungs, they know.
    He's Cancelling the Bond, and making Pay:
    And Ballancing Accounts: its Reckoning day.

See, how he from the Counthouse shining went,
    In Flashing Folds of Burnisht Glory, and
Dasht out all Curses from the Covenant
    Hath Justices Acquittance in his hand
    Pluckt out Deaths Sting, the Serpents Head did mall
    The Bars and Gates of Hell he brake down all.   30

The Curse thus Lodgd within his Flesh, and Cloyde,
    Can't run from him to his, so much he gave.
And like a Gyant he awoke, beside,
    The Sun of Righteousness rose out of's Grave.
    And setting Foot upon its neck I sing
    Grave, where's thy Victory? Death, Where's thy Sting?   (1686)

47. MEDITATION ON MATT. 25.21.
ENTER THOU INTO THE JOY OF THY LORD.

Strang, strang indeed. It rowell doth my heart
    With pegs of Greefe, and tents of greatest joy:
When I wore Angells Glory in each part
    And all my skirts wore flashes of rich die
    Of Heavenly Colour, hedg'd in with rosie Reechs,[1]
    A spider spit its Vomit on my Cheeks.

This ranckling juyce bindg'd[2] in its cursed stain
    Doth permeat both Soul and Body: soile
And drench each Fibre, and infect each grain.
    Its ugliness swells over all the ile.   10
    Whose stain'd mishapen bulk's too high, and broad
    For th'Entry of the narrow gate to God.

[1] Odors.
[2] Swollen.

Ready to burst, thus, and to burn in hell:
    Now in my path I finde a Waybred³ spring
Whose leafe drops balm that doth this venom quell
    And juyce's a Bath, that doth all stains out bring
    And sparkling beauty in the room convay.
    Lord feed me with this Waybred Leafe, I pray.

My stain will out: and swelling swage apace.
    And holy Lusters on my shape appeare.   20
All Rosie Buds: and Lilly flowers of grace
    Will grace my turfe with sweet sweet glory here.
    Under whose shades Angells will bathing play
    Who'l guard my Pearle to glory, hous'd in clay.

Those Gates of Pearle, porter'd with Seraphims,
    On their carbuncle joynts will open wide.
And entrance give me where all glory swims
    In to the Masters Joy, e're to abide.
    O sweet sweet thought. Lord take this praise though thin.
    And when I'm in't Ile tune an higher pin.   (1692)   30

5. MEDITATION ON GAL. 3.16. AND TO THY SEED WHICH IS CHRIST.

Art thou, Lord, Abraham's Seed, and Isaac too?
    His Promisd Seed? That One and Only Seed?
How can this bee? Paul certainly saith true.
    But one Seed promisd. Sir this Riddle read.
    Christ is the Metall: Isaack is the Oar.
    Christ is the Pearle, in Abraham's tread therefore.

Christ's Antitype Isaac his Type up spires
    In many things, but Chiefly this because
This Isaac, and the Ram caught in the briars
    One Sacrifice, fore shew by typick laws   10
    Christs Person, all Divine, joynd whereto's made
    Unperson'd Manhood, on the Altar's laid.

³ Plantain, a medicinal herb.

The full grown Ram, provided none knows how,
    Typing Christ's Manhood, made by God alone
Caught in the brambles by the horns, must bow,
    Under the Knife: The manhoods Death, and Groan.
    Yet Isaac's leaping from the Altar's bed,
    Foretold its glorious rising from the Dead.

But why did things run thus? For Sin indeed,
    No lesser price than this could satisfy.   20
Oh costly Sin! this makes mine intraills bleed.
    What fills my Shell, did make my Saviour die.
    What Grace then's this of God, and Christ that stills
    Out of this Offering into our tills?

Lord with thine Altars Fire, mine Inward man
    Refine from dross: burn out my sinfull guise
And make my Soul thine Altars Drippen pan
    To Catch the Drippen of thy Sacrifice.
    This is the Unction thine receive; the which
    Doth teach them all things of an happy pitch.   30

Thy Altars Fire burns not to ashes down
    This Offering. But it doth roast it here.
This is thy Roastmeate cooked up sweet, brown,
    Upon thy table set for Souls good cheer.
    The Drippen, and the meate are royall fair
    That fatten Souls, that with it welcomd are.

My Trencher, Lord, with thy Roast Mutton dress:
    And my dry Bisket in thy Dripping Sap.
And feed my Soul with thy Choice Angell Mess:
    My heart thy Praise, Will, tweedling Larklike tap.   40
    My florid notes, like Tenderills of Vines
    Twine round thy Praise, plants sprung in true Love's Mines.
                                  (1694)

150. MEDITATION. CANT. 7.3.
THY TWO BREASTS ARE LIKE
TWO YOUNG ROES THAT ARE TWINS.

My Blessed Lord, how doth thy Beautious Spouse
    In Stately Stature rise in Comliness?
With her two breasts like two little Roes that browse
    Among the lillies in their Shining dress
    Like stately milke pailes ever full and flow
    With spirituall milke to make her babes to grow.

Celestiall Nectar Wealthier far than Wine
    Wrought in the Spirits brew house and up tund
Within these Vessells which are trust up fine
    Likend to two pritty neate twin Roes that run'd   10
    Most pleasently by their dams sides like Cades[1]
    And suckle with their milk Christs Spirituall Babes.

Lord put these nibbles then my mouth into
    And suckle me therewith I humbly pray,
Then with this milk thy Spirituall Babe I'st grow,
    And these two milke pails shall themselves display
    Like to these pritty twins in pairs round neate
    And shall sing forth thy praise over this meate.   (1719)

[1] Pets.

From *Gods Determinations touching his Elect: and The Elects Combat in their Conversion, and Coming up to God in Christ together with the Comfortable Effects thereof*

From *The Poetical Works of Edward Taylor*, ed. Thomas H. Johnson (Princeton Paperback, 1966). Copyright Rockland, 1939; Princeton University Press, 1943. Reprinted by permission of Princeton University Press. The text followed here is that of the Yale University Press, with their permission.

THE PREFACE

Infinity, when all things it beheld
In Nothing, and of Nothing all did build,
Upon what Base was fixt the Lath, wherein
He turn'd this Globe, and rigalld it so trim?
Who blew the Bellows of his Furnace Vast?
Or held the Mould wherein the world was Cast?
Who laid its Corner Stone? Or whose Command?
Where stand the Pillars upon which it stands?
Who Lac'de and Fillitted the earth so fine,
With Rivers like green Ribbons Smaragdine?[1]   10
Who made the Sea's its Selvedge, and its locks
Like a Quilt Ball within a Silver Box?
Who Spread its Canopy? Or Curtains Spun?
Who in this Bowling Alley bowld the Sun?
Who made it always when it rises set
To go at once both down, and up to get?
Who th'Curtain rods made for this Tapistry?
Who hung the twinckling Lanthorns in the Sky?
Who? who did this? or who is he? Why, know
Its Onely Might Almighty this did doe.   20
His hand hath made this noble worke which Stands
His Glorious Handywork not made by hands.
Who spake all things from nothing; and with ease
Can speake all things to nothing, if he please.
Whose Little finger at his pleasure Can
Out mete ten thousand worlds with halfe a Span:

---

[1] Resembling emerald.

Whose Might Almighty can by half a looks
Root up the rocks and rock the hills by th'roots.
Can take this mighty World up in his hande,
And shake it like a Squitchen[2] or a Wand.   30
Whose single Frown will make the Heavens shake
Like as an aspen leafe the Winde makes quake.
Oh! what a might is this Whose single frown
Doth shake the world as it would shake it down?
Which All from Nothing fet, from Nothing, All:
Hath All on Nothing set, lets Nothing fall.
Gave All to nothing Man indeed, whereby
Through nothing man all might him Glorify.
In Nothing then imbosst the brightest Gem
More pretious than all pretiousness in them.   40
But Nothing man did throw down all by Sin:
And darkened that lightsom Gem in him.
    That now his Brightest Diamond is grown
    Darker by far than any Coalpit Stone.

[Before God, Justice and Mercy debate man's fate. How can he be both punished for his sin, as Justice requires, and forgiven for it, as Mercy requires? Called to account for his fallen state, man explains that Eve tempted him.]

GODS SELECTING LOVE IN THE DECREE

    Man in this Lapst Estate at very best,
A Cripple is and footsore, sore opprest,
Can't track Gods Trace but Pains, and pritches prick
Like poyson'd splinters sticking in the Quick.
Yet jims in th'Downy path with pleasures spread
As 'twas below him on the Earth to tread.
Can prance, and trip within the way of Sin,
Yet in Gods path moves not a little wing.

[2] Piece of bark used in grafting?

        Almighty this foreseing, and withall
That all this stately worke of his would fall   10
Tumble, and Dash to pieces Did in lay
Before it was too late for it a Stay.
Doth with his hands hold, and uphold the same.
Hence his Eternall Purpose doth proclaim.
Whereby transcendently he makes to shine
Transplendent Glory in his Grace Divine.
Almighty makes a mighty sumptuous feast:
Doth make the Sinfull Sons of men his guests.
But yet in speciall Grace he hath to some,
(Because they Cripples are, and Cannot come)   20
He sends a Royall Coach forth for the same,
To fetch them in, and names them name by name.
A Royall Coach whose scarlet Canopy
O're silver Pillars, doth expanded ly:
All bottomed with purest gold refin'de,
And inside o're with lovely Love all linde.
Which Coach indeed you may exactly spy
All mankinde splits in a Dicotomy.
    For all ride to the feast that favour finde.
    The rest do slite the Call and stay behinde.   30

    O! Honour! Honour! Honours! Oh! the Gain!
And all such Honours all the saints obtain.
It is the Chariot of the King of Kings:
That all who Glory gain, to glory brings.
Whose Glory makes the rest, (when spi'de) beg in.
Some gaze and stare. Some stranging at the thing.
Some peep therein; some rage thereat, but all,
Like market people seing on a stall,
Some rare Commodity Clap hands thereon
And Cheapen't hastily, but soon are gone.   40
For hearing of the price, and wanting pay
Do pish thereat, and Coily pass away.
So hearing of the terms, whist, they'le abide
At home before they'l pay so much to ride.
But they to whom its sent had rather all,
Dy in this Coach, than let their journey fall.
They up therefore do get, and in it ride
Unto Eternall bliss, while down the tide

The other scull unto eternall woe;
By letting slip their former journey so.   50
For when they finde the Silver Pillars fair
The Golden bottom pav'de with Love as rare,
To be the Spirits sumptuous building cleare,
When in the Soul his Temple he doth reare
And Purple Canopy to bee (they spy)
All Graces Needlework and Huswifry;
Their stomachs rise: these graces will not down.
They think them Slobber Sawces: therefore frown.
They loath the same, wamble keck,[3] heave they do:
Their Spleen thereat out at their mouths they throw,   60
Which while they do, the Coach away doth high
Wheeling the Saints in't to eternall joy.
    These therefore and their journey now do come
    For to be treated on, and Coacht along.

[Satan rages against the souls who have chosen to be saved. The souls explain that they first sided with Satan only "Through weakeness, not rebellion." Christ offers grace to all who oppose Satan. Hearing this, Satan renews his assault.]

FIRST SATANS ASSAULT AGAINST THOSE THAT FIRST CAME UP TO MERCYS TERMS.

SATAN

Soon ripe, soon rot. Young Saint, Old Divell. Loe
Why to an Empty Whistle did you goe?
What Come Uncalld? And Run unsent for? Stay
Its Childrens Bread: Hands off: out, Dogs, away.

SOUL

It's not an Empty Whistle: yet withall,
And if it be a Whistle, then a Call:
A Call to Childrens Bread, which take we may.
Thou onely art the Dog whipt hence away.

---

[3] Feel nauseated.

SATAN

If I then you: for by Apostasy
You are the Imps of Death as much as I.   10
And Death doth reign o're you through Sin: you see,
As well as Sin doth reign to Death in mee.

SOUL

It is deni'd: Gods Mercy taking place,
Prepared Grace for us, and us for Grace.
And Graces Coach in Grace hath fetcht us in,
Unto her Feast. We shall not dy in Sin.

SATAN

If it be so, your sins are Crucifide:
Which if they be, they struggl'd when they di'de.
It is not so with you: you judge before
You felt them gird, you'de got them out of Doore.   20

SOUL

Mercy the Quartermaster speedily,
Did stifle Sin, and still its hidious Cry,
Whose Knife at first stuck in its heart to th'head:
That sin, before it hard did sprunt, fell dead.

SATAN

A mere Delusion! Nature shows that life
Will strugle most upon the bloody Knife
And so will Sin. Nay Christ doth onely Call,
And offer ease to such as are in thrall.

SOUL

He offer'd unto mee, and I receiv'd
Of what hee wrought, I am not yet bereav'd.   30
Though Justice set Amercement[4] on mee
Mercy hath took it off, and set me free.

SATAN

Is Mercy impudent? or Justice blinde?
I am to make distraint on thee Designd.
The North must wake before the South proves Kind.
The Law must breake before the Gospell binde.

[4] Penalty or fine.

SOUL

But Giliads Balm, like Balsom heald my wound
Makes not the Patient sore, yet leaves him sound.
The Gospell did the Law prevent: my heart
Is therefore dresst from Sin: and did not smart.   40

SATAN

A likely thing! Oh shame! presume on Grace!
Here's Sin in Grain: it hath a Double Face.
Come, Come with mee I'le shew your Outs, and Inns,
Your Inside, and your out: your Holy things.
     For these I will anatomize then see,
     Believe your very Eyes, believe not mee.

THE SOUL ACCUSED IN ITS SERVING GOD

When thou dost go to serve thy God, behold
What greate Distractions do thy Soule infold?
How thy Religious Worship's much abusde?
And with Confusion greate thy Soul's amus'de?
What thoughts to God on Errand dost thou send
That have not Sin therein, or in the End?
In Holy-Waters I delight to fish
For then I mudd them, or attain a Dish,
Of Holy things. I oft have Chiefest part,
And Cutting: nay do Carve the fat, and heart.   10
For in Gods worship still thy heart doth cling
Unto and follows toyish Earthly things.
And what thou offer'st God his Holy Eye
Sees, is an Offering of Hypocrisy.
And if thou saw'st no hell, nor heaven; I see,
My Soule for thine, thy Soule and mine agree.
What then's thy Love to God, and Piety?
Is it not selfish? And Comes in by th'by?
For selfe is all thine aim; not God thine end:
And what Delight hath he in such a friend?   20
Lip Love is little else, but such a ly,
As makes the matter but Hypocrisy.

What's thy Repentance? Can'st thou come and show
By those salt Rivers which do Ebb, and Flow
By th'motion of that Ocean Vast within,
Of pickled sorrow rising for thy Sin?
For Sin prooves very Costly unto all.
It cost Saint Peter bitter tears, and Paul.
Thy joy is groundless, Faith is false, thy Hope
Presumption, and Desire is almost broke.   30
Zeale Wildfire is, thy Pray'res are sapless most,
Or like the Whistling of some Dead mans Ghost:
Thy Holy Conference is onely like
An Empty Voice that tooteth through a pipe.
Thy Soule doth peep out at thine Eares, and Eyes
To bless those bawbles that are earthly toyes.
But when Gods Words in at those Windows peepe
To kiss thy Soul, thy Soul lies dead asleep.
Examine but thy Conscience, her reply,
Will suite hereto: For Conscience dare not ly.   40
When did thine Eyes run down for sin as sin,
That thus thy heart runs up with joy to sing?
   Thy sins do sculk under a flowrisht[5] paint.
   Hence thou a Sinner art, or I a Saint.

SOUL

Well, Satan, well: with thee I'le parle no more.
But do adjure thee hence: begone therefore.
If I as yet was thine, I thus do say
I from thy flag would quickly fly away.
   Begone therefore; to him I'le send a groane
   Against thee drawn, who makes my heart his Throne.   50

THE SOULS GROAN TO CHRIST FOR SUCCOUR

Good Lord, behold this Dreadfull Enemy
   Who makes me tremble with his fierce assaults,
I dare not trust, yet feare to give the ly,
   For in my soul, my soul finds many faults.
   And though I justify myselfe to's face:
   I do Condemn myselfe before thy Grace.

[5] Flowery.

He strives to mount my sins, and them advance
  Above thy Merits, Pardons, or Good Will
Thy Grace to lessen, and thy Wrath t'inhance
  As if thou couldst not pay the sinners bill.   10
  He Chiefly injures thy rich Grace, I finde
  Though I confess my heart to sin inclin'de.

Those Graces which thy Grace enwrought in mee,
  He makes as nothing but a pack of Sins.
He maketh Grace no grace, but Crueltie,
  Is Graces Honey Comb, a Comb of Stings?
  This makes me ready leave thy Grace and run.
  Which if I do, I finde I am undone.

I know he is thy Cur, therefore I bee
  Perplexed lest I from thy Pasture stray.   20
He bayghs, and barks so veh'mently at mee.
  Come rate this Cur, Lord, breake his teeth I pray.
  Remember me I humbly pray thee first.
  Then halter up this Cur that is so Curst.

CHRISTS REPLY

Peace, Peace, my Hony, do not Cry,
My Little Darling, wipe thine eye,
  Oh Cheer, Cheer up, come see.
Is anything too deare, my Dove,
Is anything too good, my Love
  To get or give for thee?

If in the severall thou art
This Yelper fierce will at thee bark:
  That thou art mine this shows.
As Spot barks back the sheep again   10
Before they to the Pound are ta'ne,
  So he and hence 'way goes.

But yet this Cur that bayghs so sore
Is broken tootht, and muzzled sure,
   Fear not, my Pritty Heart.
His barking is to make thee Cling
Close underneath thy Saviours Wing.
   Why did my sweeten start?

And if he run an inch too far,
I'le Check his Chain, and rate the Cur.   20
   My Chick, keep clost to mee.
The Poles shall sooner kiss, and greet
And Paralells shall sooner meet
   Than thou shalt harmed bee.

He seeks to aggrivate thy sin
And screw them to the highest pin,
   To make thy faith to quaile.
Yet mountain Sins like mites should show
And then these mites for naught should goe
   Could he but once prevaile.   30

I smoke thy sins upon the Head.
They Dead'ned are, though not quite dead:
   And shall not rise again.
I'l put away the Guilt thereof,
And purge its Filthiness cleare off:
   My Blood doth out the stain.

And though thy judgment was remiss
Thy Headstrong Will too Willfull is.
   I will Renew the same.
And though thou do too frequently   40
Offend as heretofore hereby
   I'l not severly blaim.

And though thy senses do inveagle
Thy Noble Soul to tend the Beagle,
   That t'hunt her games forth go.
I'le Lure her back to me, and Change
Those fond Affections that do range
   As yelping beagles doe.

Although thy sins increase their race,
And though when thou hast sought for Grace,   50
   Thou fallst more than before
If thou by true Repentence Rise,
And Faith makes me thy Sacrifice,
   I'l pardon all, though more.

Though Satan strive to block thy way
By all his Stratagems he may:
   Come, come though through the fire.
For Hell that Gulph of fire for sins,
Is not so hot as t'burn thy Shins.
   Then Credit not the Lyar.   60

Those Cursed Vermin Sins that Crawle
All ore thy Soul, both Greate, and small
   Are onely Satans own:
Which he in his Malignity
Unto thy Souls true Sanctity
   In at the doors hath thrown.

And though they be Rebellion high,
Ath'ism or Apostacy:
   Though blasphemy it bee:
Unto what Quality, or Sise   70
Excepting one, so e're it rise.
   Repent, I'le pardon thee.

Although thy Soule was once a Stall
Rich hung with Satans nicknacks all;
   If thou Repent thy Sin,
A Tabernacle in't I'le place
Fild with Gods Spirit, and his Grace.
   Oh Comfortable thing!

I dare the World therefore to show
A God like me, to anger slow: 80
   Whose wrath is full of Grace.
Doth hate all Sins both Greate, and small:
Yet when Repented, pardons all.
   Frowns with a Smiling Face.

As for thy outward Postures each,
Thy Gestures, Actions, and thy Speech,
   I Eye and Eying spare,
If thou repent. My Grace is more
Ten thousand times still tribled ore
   Than thou canst want, or ware.   90

As for the Wicked Charge he makes,
That he of Every Dish first takes
   Of all thy holy things.
Its false, deny the same, and say,
That which he had he stool away
   Out of thy Offerings.

Though to thy Griefe, poor Heart, thou finde
In Pray're too oft a wandring minde,
   In Sermons Spirits dull.
Though faith in firy furnace flags,   100
And Zeale in Chilly Seasons lags.
   Temptations powerfull.

These faults are his, and none of thine
So far as thou dost them decline.
   Come then receive my Grace.
And when he buffits thee therefore
If thou my aid, and Grace implore
   I'le shew a pleasant face.

But still look for Temptations Deep,
Whilst that thy Noble Sparke doth keep   110
   Within a Mudwald Cote.
These White Frosts and the Showers that fall
Are but to whiten thee withall.
   Not rot the Web they smote.

If in the fire where Gold is tride
Thy Soule is put, and purifide
   Wilt thou lament thy loss?
If silver-like this fire refine
Thy Soul and make it brighter shine:
   Wilt thou bewaile the Dross?   120

Oh! fight my Field: no Colours fear:
I'l be thy Front, I'l be thy reare.
   Fail not: my Battells fight.
Defy the Tempter, and his Mock.
Anchor thy heart on mee thy Rock.
   I do in thee Delight.

[Satan accuses the outright rebels against God and the Worldly. After bemoaning their unworthiness for salvation, these two "Rankes" seek counsel of "the Pious Wise," i.e., the Saints. They learn that the elect also felt unworthy and that sin may be redeemed by Repentance. But the soul must be patient. Finite man can never be completely happy or completely certain: "What Mortall can contain immortall bliss . . ."]

DOUBTS FROM SATANS TEMPTATIONS ANSWERED

SOUL
But oh the Tempter harries me so fast
And on me falls to make me fall at last.
Had I but Grace surely I might repell
His firy Darts that dart on fire from hell.

SAINT
If you had none, he never would bestow
Such darts upon you Grace to overthrow.
The Bullets shot are blinde, the fowlers eye
Aims at the marke before he lets them fly.

SOUL
But he bewilders me: I scarce can finde
But lose myselfe again within my minde.
My thoughts are Laberryntht, I can't enjoyn
And thereof the rest to discipline.

SAINT
I once was thus. The Crooked Serpent old
Doth strive to hinder what he can't withhold.
And where he cannot keep from Grace, he's loath,
To keep from keeping Saving Grace from Growth.

   10

SOUL

But if a Pious thought appeare, I finde
It's brambled in the briers of my minde.
Or in those brambles lost, or slinks away:
But Viprous thoughts do in these thickets stay.   20
With these I pest'red am in Duty so,
I doubt I undo all thereby I do.

SAINT

First Satan envies each Choice thought: then hee
To murder it, or make't short winded bee
Doth raise a Fog, or fude of thoughts most vile
Within the soul; and darkens all that ile.
And when he cannot hinder pray're he'le strive
To spoil the same, but still hold on, and thrive.

SOUL

But yet I feare there oft lurks secretly
Under each Duty done Hypocrisy.   30
I finde no heart unto the Wayes of Grace.
It's but their End my heart would fain imbrace.

SAINT

Why give you Credit to your deadly foe?
He turns ore ery stone Grave t'overthrow.
He'l fight on both sides Grace, Grace to destroy.
To ruinate your Souls Eternally.
He makes some thus red mad on mischiefe grow
And not to matter what they say, or do.
He makes Civility to pass for Grace,
With such as hunt riches hot senting trace.   40
To such as God doth Call, he doth reply
That all their Grace is but Hypocrisy.

Contrarily, a Refuge strong to make
For e'ry sin, he doth this method take.
He tells the Doubting soul, this is no Sin,
Until he Diveth over head therein.
But then to breake his Heart he doth reply:
That done is Sin, He sinned willingly.
He to the Sinner saith, Great Sins are small,

Small Sins he telleth him, are none at all.   50
And so to such there is no sin: for why
Great sins are small, Small None. But oh but eye
If God awakes a Soul, he doth begin
To make him count indifferent things as Sin,
Nay Lawfull things wanting a Circumstance
Or having one too much although by Chance.
And thus he doth involve the doubting soule
In dismall doubts and makes it fear to rowle,
Himselfe on Christ for fear it should presume.
But if he doth he quickly turns his tune   60
And doth accuse, because he did not take
As soon as mercy did an offer make.
Oh! see the Craft the Serpent old doth use
To hopple⁶ souls in Sin, and Sin to Choose.
One while he terms true Grace a morall thing.
One while morality a splendid Sin.

SOUL
You shew the matter as the matter is
But shew me how in such a Case as this,
T'repell the Tempter, and the field t'obtain,
To Chaff away the Chaff and Choose the grain.   70

SAINT
Perform the Duty, leave th'event unto
His Grace that doth both in, and outside know.
Beg pardon for your Sins: bad thoughts defy,
That are Cast in you by the Enemy.
Approove yourselfe to God, and unto his
And beg a pardon where you do amiss.
If wronged go to God for right, and pray
Hard thoughted Saints black thoughted thoughts away.
Renew your acts of Faith: believe in him,
Who died on the Cross to Cross out Sin.   80
Allow not any Sin: and if you sin
Through frailty, Faith will a new pardon bring.
Do all Good Works, work all good things you know
As if you should be sav'd for doing so.

⁶ Fetter the legs of an animal.

Then undo all you've done, and it deny
And on a naked Christ alone rely.
Believe not Satan, Unbelieve his tales
Lest you should misbelieve the Gospell bales.
   Do what is right, and for the right Contend.
   Make Grace your way, and Glory'l be your End.   90

[The Saint describes more of "Satans Sophestry." Satan encourages sin
and smugness, and raises doubts. He tries to make man think that "God's
a Heape of Contradictions high."]

DIFFICULTIES ARISING FROM UNCHARITABLE CARIAGES OF CHRISTIANS.

When these assaults proove vain, the Enemy
   One Saint upon another oft doth set,
To make each fret like to Gum'd Taffity,
   And fire out Grace thus by a Chafe or Fret.
   Uncharitable Christians inj'rous are:
   Two Freestons rubd together each do ware.

When Satan jogs the Elbow of the one
   To Spleenish Passions which too oft doth rise,
For want of Charity, or hereupon
   From some Uncharitable harsh Surmise,   10
   Then the Poore Doubting Soul is oft oppresst,
   By hard Reflections from an harder breast.

Th'Uncharitable Soul oft thus reflects,
   After each Birth a second birth doth Come.
Your Second Birth no Second Birth ejects.
   The Babe of Grace then's strangld in the Womb.
   There's no new Birth born in thy Soul thou'lt find
   If that the after Birth abide behinde.

The Babe of Grace, thinks he, 's not born its sure.
   Sins Secundine[7] is not as yet out Cast.   20
The Soul no Bracelet of Graces pure
   Doth ware, while wrapt in nature's slough so fast.
   And thus he doth for want of Charity,
   The wounded wound Uncharitably.

[7] Placenta.

And thus some Child of God, when led awry
  By Satan, doth with Satan take a part,
Against some Child of God, whom frowardly
  He by Reflections harsh wounds thus in heart.
  Pough! Here's Religion! Strange indeed! Quoth hee.
  Grace makes a Conscience of things here that bee.   30

Grace Conscious makes one how to spend ones time
  How to perform the Duties of one's place
Not onely in the things which are Divine;
  But in the things which ware a Sublime Face.
  Do you do so? And order good persue?
  Don't Earth and Heaven interfer in you?

Will God accept the service if the time
  Is stolen from our Calling him to pay?
What will he yield that Sacrifice his shine,
  That from anothers Altar's stole away?   40
  God and our Callings Call: and th'Sacrifice
  Stole from our Callings Altar he defies.

Yet if it falls on worldly things intense
  Its soon scourgd then with whips of Worldliness:
It gives to many, nay to all, offence
  And gathers to itselfe great penciveness.
  Intense on God, or on the world, all's one.
  The Harmless Soule is hardly thought upon.

Such Traps, and Wilds as these are, Satan sets,
  For to intrap the Innocent therein: 50
These are his Wyers, Snares, and tangling Nets,
  To hanck, and hopple harmless souls in Sin.
  If in such briars thou embrambled light
  Call on the Mighty God with all thy might.

On God in Christ Call hard: For in him hee
  Hath Bowells melting, and Expanded arms:
Hath sweet imbraces, Tender mercy free
  Hath Might Almighty too to save from harms.
  Into his Dove streakt Downy bosom fly,
  In Spite of Spite, or Spiters Enmity.   60

These are Gods Way-Marks thus inscrib'd; this hand
    Points you the way unto the Land Divine,
The Land of Promise, Good Immanuels Land.
    To New Jerusalem above the line.
    Ten thousand times thrice tribled blesst he is,
    That walketh in the suburbs here of bliss.

His Wildred state will wane away, and hence
    These Crooked Passages will soon appeare
The Curious needlework of Providence,
    Embrodered with golden Spangles Cleare.   70
    Judge not this Web while in the Loom, but stay
    From judging it untill the judgment day.

For while its foiled up the best Can see
    But little of it, and that little too
Shews weather beaten but when it shall bee
    Hung open all at once, Oh beautious shew!
    Though thrids run in, and out, Cross snarld and twinde
    The Web will even be enwrought you'l finde.

If in the golden Meshes of this Net
    (The Checkerwork of Providence) you're Caught   80
And Carride hence to Heaven, never fret:
    Your Barke shall to an Happy Bay be brought.
    You'l se both Good and Bad drawn up hereby,
    These to Hells Horrour, those to Heavens Joy.

Fear not Presumption then, when God invites:
    Invite not Fear, when that he doth thee Call:
Call not in Question whether he delights
    In thee, but make him thy Delight, and all.
    Presumption lies in Backward Bashfulness,
    When one is backward though a bidden Guest.   90

[The second and third Ranks detect "Cloudy Pillars of Perfume" and feel themselves exalted. Christ befriends the soul and arrays it as a bride. The soul, entering the garden of Church-Fellowship, makes Covenant with God.]

THE JOY OF CHURCH FELLOWSHIP RIGHTLY ATTENDED.

In Heaven soaring up, I dropt an Eare
   On Earth: and oh! sweet Melody:
And listening, found it was the Saints who were
   Encoacht for Heaven that sang for Joy.
   For in Christs Coach they sweetly sing;
   As they to Glory ride therein.

Oh! joyous hearts! Enfir'de with holy Flame!
   Is speech thus tassled with praise?
Will not your inward fire of Joy contain;
   That it in open flames doth blaze?   10
   For in Christs Coach Saints sweetly sing,
   As they to Glory ride therein.

And if a string do slip, by Chance, they soon
   Do screw it up again: whereby
They set it in a more melodious Tune
   And a Diviner Harmony.
   For in Christs Coach they sweetly sing
   As they to Glory ride therein.

In all their Acts, publick, and private, nay
   And secret too, they praise impart.   20
But in their Acts Divine and Worship, they
   With Hymns do offer up their Heart.
   Thus in Christs Coach they sweetly sing
   As they to Glory ride therein.

Some few not in; and some whose Time, and Place
   Block up this Coaches way do goe
As Travellers afoot, and so do trace
   The Road that gives them right thereto
   While in this Coach these sweetly sing
   As they to Glory ride therein.   30

(Undated. 1685? 1700?)

From *Treatise Concerning the Lord's Supper**

TOUCHING the things sought after, as sin/grace.

As touching sin, and here I lay these things down; you must not draw up any positive conclusion that this wedden garment is not yours in that you find:

1. The being of sin in you. It is the work we are always to attend upon, to strive against sin. We are always to be putting sin to death. We are always to be purifying ourselves from all filthiness both of flesh and spirit. But though we must do this always, and must not make any league with these unclean beasts, yet they will be as the Canaanites in the land, and as vermin in the house till the house tumble down. As the ill humors in the body will abide till this earthly tabernacle be dissolved, so will the being of sin continue in us so long as we continue at home in the body: yea, and more, we shall find these vermin crawling in our souls ofttimes, as worms in our bowels, infesting our thoughts and sometimes crawling out in our discourse, and flyblowing our works, both civil and sacred concerns. So that our best service will appear unto us as an unclean thing, and all our righteousness as a filthy rag or a menstruous cloth. If therefore thou findest it thus with thee, and thy soul be humbled hereat, and engaged in truth against the same, thou art not to conclude that the wedden garment is not thine. For then thou wilt never find the wedden garment on if it cannot be on till these things be not to be found. For they are common to the best of God's saints.

2. An inclination in you unto unwarrantable things. The inclination will hanker after forbidden fruit so long as the soul is sanctified but in part. So long as thou art in the body, thou wilt have a body of sin in thee, and so long as the body of sin is in thee, so long thou wilt have the inclination vexing of thee thus. For the law in the members will be warring, the flesh will be lusting against the spirit. There will be a tendence to rebellion attending the being of the Old Man. There is a spiritual war that you are entered upon. The New Man having took possession in the soul and dethroned the Old Man, the Old Man is raising forces against the New. The old serpent comes to help his old friend, and besieges the soul with a whole army of assaults to sin, and is shooting his fireballs, and casting his bombs over the walls into the city to set all on fire. The confederates within incline the soul, or otherwise move some inclinations and desires after the enemies' prosperity. But the spiritual watch in the soul makes discovery of the same, and the regenerate part apprehends this inclination moving after the enemy, and taketh the same, and chastiseth it, labors against it, and bewails its treachery

* Norman S. Grabo, ed., *Edward Taylor's Treatise Concerning the Lord's Supper* (East Lansing, Mich., 1966).

before God. Yet though this darkens the evidence, thou art not to conclude hence that thou hast not the wedden garment. For these things are consistent with the wedden garment. Therefore you may not draw up a negative conclusion from this inclination. There was the serpent in paradise, as well as the Tree of Life.

3. A multitude of carnal thoughts, or worldly ploddings about the things of this life. This is a burden to the spirit of a child of God. Oh! I am so thronged with carnal thoughts, I know not what to make of myself. I find I am called to set mine affection on things above, and not on things upon the earth, and Christ saith, "take no thought for tomorrow, but let tomorrow take thought for itself" (Matt. 6: *ult.*), and David saith, "when I awake I am still with thee." But alas, I find it otherwise with me. I am overrun with evil and carnal thoughts. Where I have one thought of spiritual concerns, I have twenty laid out upon the things of the world. Truly this is the condition of God's children here in this life. While we have these bodies of clay to look after, and are betrusted with the concerns of families, towns, and public duties in our hands, they necessitate our thoughts; so that we lay out a great deal of our contemplative substance all the day long upon them, and are constrained to put off spiritual concerns with some transient ejaculatory thoughts. But as for this matter, I say, you are not to draw up your conclusion in this case from these thoughts. For while we are in the flesh this is the fruit of our labor. I doubt not but it is thus with many a thousand of the choicest of God's children that are singled out by Him to eminent service for Him that the managing of the concerns of their particular callings are so circumstanced with difficulties and attendants, which with the circumstances of their personal refreshment summon, maybe, out from them a thousand thoughts for one bestowed upon spiritual things, save in a transient way. So that it is not safe to conclude in this case, from the thoughts of thy heart laid out upon secular concerns, that thou hast not this wedden garment. Of all the enjoyments of this world, the enjoyment of this temporary life is enjoyment of the choicest thing. But yet I doubt not but persons lay out an hundred thoughts upon the concerns of the world for one upon the life immediately. So a tender mother: how tender is she of her little babe, yet doubtless the number of her thoughts, if she be not a person that hath the world disht up to her without her concerning of herself therein, spends more thoughts in ordering the affairs of her family, than she lays out upon her child. So that is not a right arguing from the multitudes of thoughts but from the strength of the desires in this matter. But thus I close up this head about sin.

As touching grace, there are several considerations that are to be made, touching which, simply considered, it is not safe to draw up any conclusion, and yet God's people are very apt to do it to their own discouragement; and they are such as these:

A plain discovery of the truth of repentance as evangelical. While the soul doth not repent, it is impenitent; while it is impenitent, it hath nothing of the wedden garment. But now it finds repentance so much against the grain of flesh and blood that it is at a loss whether it hath anything thereof, and so not being well enlightened in the gospel nature of repentance, it is at a loss whether that its turning from sin be any more than a moral work, and hence it is in the stocks, and cannot get out. Hence it is ready to judge it hath not the wedden garment. Now hereupon it is not safe to conclude negatively that thou hast it not. For this is unhopeful, it being very sildom seen that the impenitent are thus concerned with repentance.

A real evidence of the truth of grace. The desire of a child of God is so vehement and strongly carried out after the truth of sanctifying grace that occasions great fear lest it should take up with counterfeit coin instead of true gold, and his sight and knowledge being so dim and weak, especially as to the applicatory use of it, that it cannot ofttimes make but an uncertain and feeble conjecture in this matter; and many fears cloud the soul, and many things contrary to it appear strong. Hence if the soul draw up its conclusions from the present condition that it's in, while thus in the difficulties, it will either conclude that it hath or it hath not the wedden garment without grounds. For until it comes to better discovery than its clouded state admits of, it hath not sufficient evidence to raise any conclusion upon. He may find more than enough to make him fear and hardly enough to uphold hope; and although there is more ground to hope than to fear, yet if he draw up any conclusion while in this state, doubtless it will be that he hath not the wedden garment, because he cannot find clear evidences that he hath any real grace.

The truth of saving faith: this carries with it an interest in Christ of a saving nature; and therefore where this is, there the wedden garment is. Now while the soul is in the dark touching this, and finds the actings of faith so feeble, and so obstructed by fear as that he doubts greatly whether his faith be any more than a moral persuasion, or a presumptuous confidence, he is not able to come to any rational conclusion in this matter: it is not safe to draw up any conclusion merely from the present judgment. You must endeavor after better light, for you may not from your present difficult appearance conclude negatively, that the wedden garment is not yours. Whereas probably by other things it may undoubtedly be evidenced to be yours. But I will proceed no further here touching this first head of things sought after.

As touching the knowledge gained by your trial, it is requisite some things be laid in here to help ye. For often persons' expectations go beyond the thing, and so they have not what they would have when they have done their search, and so sit down either in the midst of discouragements, or in a dull stupidity or carelessness. And therefore, here I might have laid in some special considerations in order to a suitable capacity of trying, as that you must well inform yourselves about the nature of grace out of the Word: clear the sight of your souls by this eye salve of the Spirit (Rev. 3:18). This is necessary, for the blind are no competent judges of beauteous colors. And also I might here add that you should wholly surrender yourselves up unto the conclusion that is made of your case by the Word and the light that thence informs your judgment: let no forestalling conceptions prejudice the same: remove all before the evidence that the impartial trial brings in upon you. And to help hereunto, I come to set before your consideration some things touching the knowledge arrived at by the trial negatively/affirmatively.

Negatively, you must not look that your trial will bring you to such a conclusion as hands in:

A knowledge of assurance. It is a duty in all to make after assurance. Rather give diligence to make your calling and election sure, and Paul saith (2 Cor. 5:1, 6, 8): "We know that if this earthly tabernacle be dissolved, we have an house, not made with hands: eternal in the heavens." But this is a jewel that the crown of every Christian is not studded with, and therefore though you are to strive for this knowledge of assurance, yet, though your trials may not hand in this knowledge, you may have that that is sufficient in order to the present duty. For the wedden garment is of a larger donation than the knowledge of assurance. You may easier come to be sure that you have it not, if you have it not, than that you have it, if you have it.

A knowledge of infallibility. *Humanum est errare.* It is proper to men while here to be mistaken, though it be *per accidens:* our conclusions are syllogistical: these always are births teemed out of the womb of the weaker sex, and therefore are not above a possibility of being mistakes. But yet the wedden garment doth not consist in such a knowledge. Nor is such a knowledge of it made necessary to the discovery of it. It's possible to attain to such a knowledge, for if there be a certainty of it attained, it is infallible. Yet I may have a certainty of it, and may lose it again. For the Apostle saith that where there is knowledge, it shall fail (1 Cor. 13:8), or vanish away; and though your knowledge be not a knowledge of assurance, yet it may be a knowledge of infallibility. For the infallibleness of it lies in the truth of the knowledge of the thing known and not in the assurance that the soul hath within itself that he knows it. And yet the infallibility is not the essential property of that knowledge that you are to accept of as the effect of your search after this wedden garment. For although you are to endeavor after a knowledge of infallibility, yet if you attain unto a knowledge of probability, you are to build upon it.

A knowledge of an extraordinary revelation. We are in the way of ordinary dispensations, and therefore are not to expect extraordinary communications; the wedden garment is attained unto by ordinary means, and therefore ordinary means are sufficient to discover the attainment thereof. An ordinary call makes it your duty to approach to the wedden: hence no extraordinary discovery of your preparation for it is to be expected. The thing is a thing of an ordinary knowledge, and calls for no extraordinary discovery. Thus far negatively.

Affirmatively, and here I assert that although we are not to rest in any attainments, yet as to this matter before us, so far as is sufficient to make us welcome guests at the Lord's Table, or this wedden feast, a probable knowledge that this wedden garment is ours is that which we are thankfully to accept of as a matter that makes a large requital of us for all our trial. Now this probable knowledge is such as is come at by arguments drawn out of the fabric of the thing and its circumstances confirmed by light of scripture, reason, and the testimony of God's Spirit therein unto conscience, sealing up the same, and although many a child of God is so low in his intellectuals, as that he is not able to run his collections of arguments methodically through the frame of the thing, yet he can by the assistance of God's Spirit common to all God's children, gather up some scripture testimonies to the case in hand that the Spirit of God hath set home unto their soul, and in which they find the testimony of the Spirit given them that they are inable to say to God (Job 10:7): "Thou knowest that I am not wicked." Nay, and with Peter to make this appeal to the Almighty (John 21:15, 16, 17): "Thou knowest that I love thee." And it's observed that the Spirit of God in conversion doth not observe method, but some single sentence of a sermon, whether well methoded, or of a more loose discourse, He singles out, and sets home upon the soul to its conversion. Now then, to return to the matter before us, that the knowledge of probability touching this wedden garment that it is the soul's, is that which is sufficient to give him a warrantable approach unto the wedden supper, I shall thus establish.

That knowledge is a good and warrantable ground for thy approach to the wedden feast that is a good ground for thy hope in Christ to stand upon. For a grounded hope is sufficient in this case. For it lays hold upon the promises of God. Christ dwells in the soul by hope. It is the instrument of communicating much of the love of God to the soul. Hence it makes not

ashamed. Nay, by hope, we are saved. Hence a well grounded hope is sufficient warrant to approach. But the knowledge of probability that the wedden
garment is ours, is a good and warrantable ground for hope in the Lord Christ
to stand on. No man can deny this with any shew of reason. For this knowledge takes the soul's case as confirmed by scripture evidence, in the strength
of reason, and as attested to by the influences of God's own Spirit in conscience. Hence hope hath a foundation to stand upon, and such as will break
in pieces all the waves of opposition that beat against it. . . .   (*c.* 1708)

SAMUEL SEWALL

(1652–1730)

Through her poetry Anne Bradstreet gives us one view of every day Puritan life; Sewall presents quite another. Sewall records his introspection—a typical Puritan activity—and he notes his attitudes toward Negroes, his courting his encounters, and so forth. The selections from the *Diary,* then, enable us to see more of the daily life of the Puritans of Sewall's time and give some evidence of a shift toward a less restricted view in this world. The anti-slavery tract, *The Selling of Joseph,* also suggest a broader view of the world than that exhibited by earlier Puritans.

From the *Diary of Samuel Sewall**

FEBRUARY 16, 1677. Brewed my wife's groaning beer.

March 16. Dr. Alcock dies about midnight. Note: Mrs. Williams told us presently after duties how dangerously ill he was, and to get John to go for his grandmother. I was glad of that information, and resolved to go and pray earnestly for him; but going into the kitchen, fell into discourse with Tim about metals, and so took up the time. The Lord forgive me and help me not to be so slack for time to come, and so easy to disregard and let die so good a resolution.

January 13, 1677.[1] Giving my chickens meat, it came to my mind that I gave them nothing save Indian corn and water, and yet they eat it and thrived very well, and that that food was necessary for them, how mean soever, which much affected me and convinced what need I stood in of spiritual food, and that I should not nauseate daily duties of prayer etc.

March 1679. Note. I have been of a long time loathe to enter into strict

---

* *Diary of Samuel Sewall*, 3 vols., *Collections of the Massachusetts Historical Society*, 5th ser., V–VII (1878–1882), modernized by the editor.

[1] *Sic.* The chronology of the *Diary* seems to err here.

bonds with God. . . . And on Saturday Goodman Walker came in, who used to be very familiar with me. But he said nothing of my coming into the Church, nor wished God to show me grace therein, at which I was almost overwhelmed, as thinking that he deemed me unfit for it. And I could hardly sit down to the Lord's Table. But I feared that if I went away I might be less fit next time, and thought that it would be strange for me who was just then joined to the Church, to withdraw, wherefore I stayed. But I never experienced more unbelief. I feared at least that I did not believe that there was such a one as Jesus Christ, and yet was afraid that because I came to the ordinance without belief, that for the abuse of Christ I should be stricken dead; yet I had some earnest desires that Christ would, before the ordinance were done, though it were when he was just going away, give me some glimpse of himself; but I perceived none. Yet I seemed then to desire the coming of the next sacrament day, that I might do better, and was stirred up hereby dreadfully to seek God, who many times before had touched my heart by Mr. Thacher's praying and preaching more than now. The Lord pardon my former grieving of His Spirit, and circumcise my heart to love Him with all my heart and soul.

June 20, 1685. Carried my wife to Dorchester to eat cherries, raspberries, chiefly to ride and take the air. The time my wife and Mrs. Flint spent in the orchard, I spent in Mr. Flint's study, reading Calvin on the Psalms etc.

November 12, 1685. . . . the ministers of this town come to the Court and complain against a dancing master who seeks to set up here and hath mixed dances, and his time of meeting is Lecture-Day; and 'tis reported he should say that by one play he could teach more divinity than Mr. Willard or the Old Testament. Mr. Moodey said 'twas not a time for New England to dance. Mr. Mather struck at the root, speaking against mixed dances.

January 24, 1686. Friday night and Saturday were extreme cold, so that the harbor frozen up, and to the Castle. This day so cold that the sacramental bread is frozen pretty hard, and rattles sadly as broken into the plates.

September 3, 1686. Mr. Shrimpton, Capt. Lidget and others come in a coach from Roxbury about 9 o'clock or past, singing as they come, being inflamed with drink. At Justice Morgan's they stop and drink healths, curse, swear, talk profanely and bawdily, to the great disturbance of the town and grief of good people. Such high-handed wickedness has hardly been heard of before in Boston.

October 24, 1686. A man swoons in our meeting-house and falls down, which makes much disturbance; yet Mr. Willard breaks not off preaching.

December 25, 1687. Just as morn-exercise ends, Mr. Cotton Mather's child dies; yet he preaches at Charlestown in the afternoon. . . .

March 19, 1691. Mr. C. Mather preaches the lecture from Mat. 24., and appoint his portion with the hypocrites. In his proem said, *Totus mundus agit histrionem.*[2] Said one sign of a hypocrite was for a man to strain at a gnat and swallow a camel. Sign in's throat discovered him. To be zealous against an innocent fashion, taken up and used by the best of men, and yet make no conscience of being guilty of great immoralities. Tis supposed means wearing of perriwigs; said would deny themeselves in anything but parting with an opportunity to do God service, that so might not offend good Christians. Meaning, I suppose, was fain to wear a perriwig for his health. I expected not to hear a vindication of perriwigs in Boston pulpit by Mr. Mather.

April 11, 1692. Went to Salem, where, in the meeting-house, the persons accused of witchcraft were examined; was a very great assembly; 'twas awful to see how the afflicted persons were agitated.

August 19, 1692. This day George Burrough, John Willard, John Procter, Martha Carrier and George Jacobs were executed at Salem, a very great number of spectators being present. Mr. Cotton Mather was there, Mr. Sims, Hale, Noyes, Cheever, etc. All of them said they were innocent, Carrier and all. Mr. Mather says they all died by a righteous sentence. Mr. Burrough, by his speech, prayer, protestation of his innocence, did much move unthinking persons, which occasions their speaking hardly concerning his being executed.

November 6, 1692. Joseph threw a knop of brass and hit his sister Betty on the forehead, so as to make it bleed and swell; upon which, and for his playing at prayer-time, and eating when return thanks, I whipped him pretty smartly. When I first went in (called by his grandmother) he sought to shadow and hide himself from me behind the head of the cradle, which gave me the sorrowful remembrance of Adam's carriage.

March 9, 1693. Joseph puts his grandmother and mother in great fear by swallowing a bullet, which for a while stuck in his throat. He had quite got it down before I knew what the matter was. This day in the afternoon, one of Mr. Holyoke's twins falls into the well and is drowned, nobody but a Negro being at home; was a very lovely boy of about four years old. Saturday, March 11, about sunset he is buried. When I come home from the funeral, my wife shows me the bullet Joseph swallowed, which he voided in the orchard. The Lord help us to praise Him for his distinguishing favor.

January 13, 1696. When I came in, past seven at night, my wife met me in the entry and told me Betty had surprised them. I was surprised with the abruptness of the relation. It seems Betty Sewall had given some signs of dejection and sorrow; but a little after dinner she burst out into an amazing

---

[2] The whole world is playing a role.

cry, which caused all the family to cry too. Her mother asked the reason; she gave none. At last said she was afraid she should go to Hell, her sins were not pardoned. She was first wounded by my reading a sermon of Mr. Norton's, about the 5th of January. Text John 7.34. Ye shall seek me and shall not find me. And those words in the sermon John 8. 21. Ye shall seek me and shall die in your sins, ran in her mind, and terrified her greatly. And staying at home January 12, she read out of Mr. Cotton Mather, Why hath Satan filled thy heart, which increased her fear. Her mother asked her whether she prayed. She answered yes, but feared her prayers were not heard because her sins not pardoned. . . . The Lord bring light and comfort out of this dark and dreadful cloud, and grant that Christ's being formed in my dear child may be the issue of these painful pangs.

December 24, 1696. Sam. recites to me in Latin, Mat. 12. from the 6th to the end of the 12th v. The 7th verse did awfully bring to mind the Salem tragedy.

January 14, 1697. Copy of the bill I put up on the Fast-day, giving it to Mr. Willard as he passed by, and standing up at the reading of it, and bowing when finished; in the afternoon.

Samuel Sewall, sensible of the reiterated strokes of God upon himself and family; and being sensible, that as to the guilt contracted upon the opening of the late commission of oyer and terminer at Salem (to which the order for this day relates) he is, upon many accounts, more concerned than any that he knows of, desires to take the blame and shame of it, asking pardon of men, and especially desiring prayers that God, who has an unlimited authority, would pardon that sin and all other his sins, personal and relative; And according to His infinite benignity, and sovereignty, not visit the sin of him, or of any other, upon himself or any of his, nor upon the land; but that He would powerfully defend him against all temptations to sin, for the future, and vouchsafe him the efficacious, saving conduct of His Word and Spirit.

December 21, 1699. Went to lecture, wearing my black cap.[3]

June 19, 1700. Having been long and much dissatisfied with the trade of fetching Negroes from Guinea, at last I had a strong inclination to write something about it; but it wore off. At last reading Bayne, Ephes., about servants, who mentions blackamoors, I began to be uneasy that I had so long neglected doing anything. When I was thus thinking, in came brother Belknap to show me a petition he intended to present to the General Court for the freeing a Negro and his wife who were unjustly held in bondage. And there is a motion by a Boston committee to get a law that all importers

[3] Sewall was worried about balding, which made him cold.

of Negroes shall pay 40s. per head, to discourage the bringing of them. And Mr. C. Mather resolves to publish a sheet to exhort masters to labor their conversion. Which makes me hope that I was called of God to write this apology for them. Let His blessing accompany the same.

June 10, 1701. Having last night heard that Josiah Willard had cut off his hair (a very full head of hair) and put on a wig, I went to him this morning. Told his mother what I came about, and she called him. I inquired of him what extremity had forced him to put off his own hair and put on a wig? He answered, none at all. But said that his hair was straight, and that it parted behind. Seemed to argue that men might as well shave their hair off their head as off their face. I answered men were men before they had hair on their faces (half of mankind have never any). God seems to have ordained our hair as a test, to see whether we can bring our minds to be content to be at his finding, or whether we would be our own carvers, Lords, and come no more at Him. . . . He seemed to say would leave off his wig when his hair was grown. I spake to his father of it a day or two after. He thanked me that had discoursed his son, and told me that when his hair was grown to cover his ears he promised to leave off his wig.

October 20. 1701. [*sic*] Mr. Cotton Mather came to Mr. Wilkins's shop and there talked very sharply against me as if I had used his father worse than a Neger; spake so loud that people in the street might hear him. Then went and told Sam, that one pleaded much for Negroes, and he had used his father worse than a Negro, and told him that was his father.

October 9, 1701. I sent Mr. Increase Mather a haunch of very good venison; I hope in that I did not treat him as a Negro.

November 10, 1706. This morning Tom Child, the painter, died.

> Tom Child had often painted death,
> But never to the life, before:
> Doing it now, he's out of breath;
> He paints it once, and paints no more.

September 10, 1707. Midweek, sentenced a woman that whipped a man, to be whipped; said a woman that had lost her modesty was like salt that had lost its savor; good for nothing but to be cast to the dunghill. Seven or eight joined together called the man out of his bed, guilefully praying him to show them the way. Then by help of a Negro youth, tore off his clothes and whipped him with rods, to chastise him for carrying it harshly to his wife.

February 12, 1708. I prayed God to accept me in keeping a private day of prayer with fasting. . . . I kept it upon the third day February 10, 1708 in the upper chamber at the northeast end of the house, fastening the shutters next the street—Perfect what is lacking in my faith and in the faith of my dear yokefellow. Convert my children, especially Samuel and Hannah; provide rest and settlement for Hannah; recover Mary, save Judith, Elizabeth, and Joseph; requite the labor of love of my kinswoman Jane Tappin, give her health, find out rest for her. . . . Steer the government in this difficult time, when the Governor and many others are at so much variance. . . . Revive the business of religion at Natick. . . . Save the town, college, province from invasion of enemies, open, secret, and from false brethren; defend the purity of worship. Save Connecticut, bless their new Governor. Save the reformation under New York government. Reform all the European plantations in America: Spanish, Portuguese, English, French, Dutch. Save this new world, that where sin hath abounded, grace may superabound; that CHRIST, who is stronger, would bind the strong man and spoil his house; and order the Word to be given, Babylon is fallen. Save our Queen, lengthen out her life and reign. Save France, make the proud helper stoop, save all Europe; save Asia, Africa, Europe, and America. These were general heads of my meditation and prayer, and through the bounteous grace of GOD, I had a very comfortable day of it.

December 23, 1714. Dr. C. Mather preaches excellently from Ps. 37. Trust in the Lord etc. only spake of the sun being in the center of our system. I think it inconvenient to assert such problems.

June 22, 1716. I essayed June 22 to prevent Indians and Negroes being rated with horses and hogs, but could not prevail.

October 19, 1717. Called Dr. C. Mather to pray, which he did excellently in the dining room, having suggested good thoughts to my wife before he went down. After, Mr. Wadsworth prayed in the chamber when 'twas supposed my wife took little notice. About a quarter of an hour past four, my dear wife expired in the afternoon, whereby the chamber was filled with a flood of tears. God is teaching me a new lesson: to live a widower's life. Lord help me to learn; and be a sun and shield to me, now so much of my comfort and defense are taken away.

July 7, 1718. Cousin Moody went with me into the new Hall, read the history of Rebekah's courtship, and prayed with me respecting my widowed condition.

July 25, 1718. Visit Mrs. Denison; she invites me to eat. I give her two cases with a knife and fork in each; one turtle shell tackling; the other long, with ivory handles, squared, cost 4s. 6d.

November 1, 1718. . . . visited Mrs. Denison. Sat in the chamber next Major Bowls. I told her 'twas time now to finish our business. Asked her what I should allow her; she not speaking, I told her I was willing to give her two hundred and fifty pounds per annum during her life, if it should please God to take me out of the world before her. She answered she had better keep as she was than give a certainty for an uncertainty; she should pay dear for dwelling at Boston.

November 28, 1718. . . . speak with Mrs. Denison. . . . She asked me if I would drink, I told her yes. She gave me cider, apples, and a glass of wine; gathered together the little things I had given her and offered them to me; but I would take none of them. Told her I wished her well, should be glad to hear of her welfare. She seemed to say she should not again take in hand a thing of this nature. . . . My bowels yearn towards Mrs. Denison; but I think God directs me in His Providence to desist.

April 1, 1719. In the morning I dehorted Samuel Hirst and Grindal Rawson from playing idle tricks because 'twas first of April; they were the greatest fools that did so. New England men came hither to avoid anniversary days, the keeping of them, such as the 25th of December.

September 21, 1719. I gave Mrs. Tilly a little book entitled *Ornaments for the Daughters of Sion*. I gave it to my dear wife August 28, 1702.

October 29, 1719. Thanksgiving-day. Between 6 and 7 Brother Moodey and I went to Mrs. Tilley's, and about 7 or 8 were married by Mr. J. Sewall in the best room below stairs. . . . Distributed cake. Mrs. Armitage introduced me into my bride's chamber after she was a-bed. I thanked her that she had left her room in that chamber to make way for me, and prayed God to provide for her a better lodging. So none saw us after I went to bed. Quickly after our being a-bed my bride grew so very bad she was fain to sit up in her bed; I rose to get her petticoats about her. I was exceedingly amazed, fearing lest she should have died. Through the favor of God she recovered in some considerable time of her fit of the tissick, spitting, partly blood.

May 26, 1720. NB. Went to bed after 10; about 11 or before, my dear wife was oppressed with a rising of phlegm that obstructed her breathing. I arose and lighted a candle, made Scipio give me a basin of water (he was asleep by the fire), called Philadelphia, Mr. Cooper, Mayhew. About midnight my dear wife expired to our great astonishment, especially mine. May the Sovereign Lord pardon my sin, and sanctify to me this very extraordinary, awful dispensation.

October 1, 1720. I went to Madam Winthrop's just at 3. Spake to her, saying my loving wife died so soon and suddenly, 'twas hardly convenient for me to think of marrying again; however, I came to this resolution, that I would not make my court to any person without first consulting with her.

October 3, 1720. Waited on Madam Winthrop again; 'twas a little while before she came in. . . . By and by in came Mr. Airs, Chaplain of the Castle, and hanged up his hat, which I was a little startled at, it seeming as if he was to lodge there. At last Madam Winthrop came too. After a considerable time, I went up to her and said, if it might not be inconvenient I desired to speak with her. . . . I prayed that Katharine[4] might be the person assigned for me. She instantly took it up in the way of denial, as if she had catched at an opportunity to do it, saying she could not do it before she was asked. Said that was her mind unless she should change it, which she believed she could not; could not leave her children.

October 6, 1720. Madam seemed to harp upon the same string. Must take care of her children; could not leave that house and neighborhood where she had dwelt so long. I told her she might do her children as much or more good by bestowing what she laid out in housekeeping, upon them. Said her son would be of age the 7th of August. I said it might be inconvenient for her to dwell with her daughter-in-law, who must be mistress of the house. I gave her a piece of Mr. Belcher's cake and ginger-bread wrapped up in a clean sheet of paper.

October 11, 1720. I writ a few lines to Madam Winthrop to this purpose: ". . . I pray GOD to keep you, and give you a joyful entrance upon the Two Hundred and Twenty Ninth year of Christopher Columbus his discovery."

October 12, 1720. Mrs. Anne Cotton came to door ('twas before 8) said Madam Winthrop was within, directed me into the little room, where she was full of work behind a stand; Mrs. Cotton came in and stood. Madam Winthrop pointed to her to set me a chair. Madam Winthrop's countenance was much changed from what 'twas on Monday, looked dark and lowering. At last the work (black stuff or silk) was taken away, I got my chair in place, had some converse, but very cold and indifferent to what 'twas before. Asked her to acquit me of rudeness if I drew off her glove. Inquiring the reason, I told her 'twas great odds between handling a dead goat and a living lady. Got it off. . . . Told her the reason why I came every other night was lest I should drink too deep draughts of pleasure. She had talked of canary, her kisses were to me better than the best canary. Explained the expression concerning Columbus.

October 17, 1720. In the evening I visited Madam Winthrop, who treated me courteously, but not in clean linen as sometimes. She said she did not know whether I would come again, or no. I asked her how she could so impute inconstancy to me. (I had not visited her since Wednesday night, being unable to get over the indisposition received by the treatment received that night, and *I must* in it seemed to sound like a made piece of formality.)

October 19, 1720. Was courteous to me, but took occasion to speak pretty

---

[4] I.e., Madam Winthrop.

earnestly about my keeping a coach. I said 'twould cost £100 per annum; she said 'twould cost but £40. Spake much against John Winthrop, his false-heartedness.

October 20, 1720. She spake something of my needing a wig. Asked me what her sister said to me. I told her, she said if her sister were for it, she would not hinder it. But I told her, she did not say she would be glad to have me for her brother. Said, I shall keep you in the cold, and asked her if she would be within tomorrow night, for we had had but a running feat. She said she could not tell whether she should, or no. I took leave. As were drinking at the Governor's, he said: In England the ladies minded little more than that they might have money, and coaches to ride in. I said, And New-England brooks its name.

October 21, 1720. After a good while, and clapping the garden door twice or thrice, she came in. I mentioned something of the lateness; she bantered me, and said I was later. She received me courteously. I asked when our proceedings should be made public; she said they were like to be no more public than they were already. Offered me no wine that I remember. I rose up at 11 a-clock to come away, saying I would put on my coat; she offered not to help me. I prayed her that Juno might light me home; she opened the shutter and said 'twas pretty light abroad; Juno was weary and gone to bed. So I came home by starlight as well as I could.

October 24, 1720. I told her it did not lie in my lands to keep a coach. If I should, I should be in danger to be brought to keep company with her neighbor Brooker (he was a little before sent to prison for debt). Told her I had an antipathy against those who would pretend to give themselves; but nothing of their estate. I would a proportion of my estate with my self. And I supposed she would do so. As to a perriwig, my best and greatest friend, I could not possibly have a greater, began to find me with hair before I was born, and had continued to do so ever since, and I could not find in my heart to go to another.

November 7, 1720. I went to Madam Winthrop; found her rocking her little Katie in the cradle. I excused my coming so late (near eight). She set me an armed chair and cushion, and so the cradle was between her armed chair and mine. Gave her the remnant of my almonds; she did not eat of them as before, but laid them away. I said I came to inquire whether she had altered her mind since Friday, or remained of the same mind still. She said, thereabouts. I told her I loved her, and was so fond as to think that she loved me. She said had a great respect for me. I told her I had made her an offer, without asking any advice; she had so many to advise with that 'twas a hindrance. The fire was come to one short brand besides the block, which brand was set up in end; at last it fell to pieces, and no recruit was made. . . . I did not bid her draw off her glove as sometime I had done. Her dress was not so clean as sometime it had been. Jehovah jireh!

November 11, 1720. Went not to Madam Winthrop's.

March 5, 1721. Just as I sat down in my seat, one of my fore-teeth in my under jaw came out, and I put it in my pocket. This old servant and daughter of music[5] leaving me does thereby give me warning that I must shortly resign my head. The Lord help me to do it cheerfully!

The Selling of Joseph*

A MEMORIAL

"For as much liberty is in real value next unto life: None ought to part with it themselves, or deprive others of it, but upon most mature consideration."

THE numerousness of slaves at this day in the province, and the uneasiness of them under their slavery, hath put many upon thinking whether the foundation of it be firmly and well laid; so as to sustain the vast weight that is built upon it. It is most certain that all men, as they are the sons of Adam, are coheirs; and have equal right unto liberty, and all other outward comforts of life. "God hath given the earth [with all its commodities] unto the sons of Adam," Psal. cxv. 16. "And hath made of one blood, all nations of men, for to dwell on all the face of the earth, and hath determined the times before appointed, and the bounds of their habitation: That they should seek the Lord. Forasmuch then as we are the offspring of God," etc. Acts xvii. 26, 27, 29. Now although the title given by the last Adam doth infinitely better men's estates, respecting God and themselves; and grants them a most beneficial and inviolable lease under the broad seal of heaven, who were before only tenants at will: yet through the indulgence of God to our first parents after the fall, the outward estate of all and every of their children remains the same, as to one another. So that originally and naturally there is no such thing as slavery. Joseph was rightfully no more a slave to his brethren, than they were to him; and they had no more authority to sell him than they had to slay him. And if they had nothing to do to sell him, the Ishmaelites bargaining with them, and paying down twenty pieces of silver, could not make a title. Neither could Potiphar have any better interest in him than the Ishmaelites

---

[5] Sewall led the singing in church.

* Trent and Wells, eds., *Colonial Prose and Poetry* (New York, 1929).

had. Gen. xxxvii. 20, 27, 28. For he that shall in this case plead alteration of property, seems to have forfeited a great part of his own claim to humanity. There is no proportion between twenty pieces of silver and liberty. The commodity itself is the claimer. If Arabian gold be imported in any quantities, most are afraid to meddle with it, though they might have it at easy rates, lest if it should have been wrongfully taken from the owners, it should kindle a fire to the consumption of their whole estate. 'Tis pity there should be more caution used in buying a horse, or a little lifeless dust, than there is in purchasing men and women: whenas they are the offspring of God, and their liberty is,

——*Auro pretiosior omni.*[1]

And seeing God hath said, "He that stealeth a man and selleth him, or if he be found in his hand, he shall surely be put to death." Exod. xxi. 16. This law being of everlasting equity, wherein man-stealing is ranked among the most atrocious of capital crimes, what louder cry can there be made of that celebrated warning,

Caveat emptor![2]

And all things considered, it would conduce more to the welfare of the province, to have white servants for a term of years, than to have slaves for life. Few can endure to hear of a negro's being made free; and indeed they can seldom use their freedom well; yet their continual aspiring after their forbidden liberty renders them unwilling servants. And there is such a disparity in their conditions, color and hair, that they can never embody with us and grow up into orderly families, to the peopling of the land: but still remain in our body politic as a kind of extravasate blood. As many negro men as there are among us, so many empty places there are in our train bands, and the places taken up of men that might make husbands for our daughters. And the sons and daughters of New England would become more like Jacob and Rachel, if this slavery were thrust quite out of doors. Moreover, it is too well known what temptations masters are under, to connive at the fornication of their slaves; lest they should be obliged to find them wives or pay their fines. It seems to be practically pleaded that they might be lawless; 'tis thought much of, that the law should have satisfaction for their thefts and other immoralities; by which means, holiness to the Lord is more rarely

---

[1] "More precious than all gold."
[2] "Buyer, beware!"

engraven upon this sort of servitude. It is likewise most lamentable to think how, in taking negroes out of Africa and selling of them here, that which God has joined together men do boldly rend asunder; men from their country, husbands from their wives, parents from their children. How horrible is the uncleanness, immorality, if not murder, that the ships are guilty of that bring great crowds of these miserable men and women! Methinks, when we are bemoaning the barbarous usage of our friends and kinsfolk in Africa, it might not be unseasonable to inquire whether we are not culpable in forcing the Africans to become slaves among ourselves. And it may be a question whether all the benefit received by negro slaves will balance the account of cash laid out upon them; and for the redemption of our own enslaved friends out of Africa. Besides all the persons and estates that have perished there.

OBJECT 1. These blackamoors are of the posterity of Cham, and therefore are under the curse of slavery. Gen. ix. 25, 26, 27.

ANSWER. Of all offices, one would not beg this, viz., uncalled for, to be an executioner of the vindictive wrath of God; the extent and duration of which is to us uncertain. If this ever was a commission, how do we know but that it is long since out of date? Many have found it to their cost, that a prophetical denunciation of judgment against a person or people would not warrant them to inflict that evil. If it would, Hazael might justify himself in all he did against his master, and the Israelites, from II. Kings viii. 10, 12.

But it is possible that, by cursory reading, this text may have been mistaken. For Canaan is the person cursed three times over, without the mentioning of Cham. Good expositors suppose the curse entailed on him, and that this prophecy was accomplished in the extirpation of the Canaanites, and in the servitude of the Gibeonites. *Vide pareum.* Whereas the blackamoors are not descended of Canaan, but of Cush. Psal. lxviii. 31. "Princes shall come out of Egypt (Mizraim) Ethiopia (Cush) shall soon stretch out her hands unto God." Under which names, all Africa may be comprehended; and their promised conversion ought to be prayed for. Jer. xiii. 23. "Can the Ethiopian change his skin?" This shows that black men are the posterity of Cush, who time out of mind have been distinguished by their color. And for want of the true, Ovid assigns a fabulous cause of it:

> *Sanguine tum credunt in corpora summa vocato*
> *Æthiopum populos nigrum traxisse colorem.*
> Metamorph. lib. 2.[3]

[3] Probably *Metamorphoses* II, ". . . men think, the people/ of Africa turned black, since the blood was driven/ By that fierce heat to the surface of their bodies." (Rolfe Humphries).

OBJECT 2. The *nigers* are brought out of a pagan country into places where the gospel is preached.

ANSWER. Evil must not be done, that good may come of it. The extraordinary and comprehensive benefit accruing to the church of God, and to Joseph personally, did not rectify his brethren's sale of him.

OBJECT 3. The Africans have wars one with another: our ships bring lawful captives taken in those wars.

ANSWER. For aught is known, their wars are much such as were between Jacob's sons and their brother Joseph. If they be between town and town, provincial or national, every war is upon one side unjust. An unlawful war can't make lawful captives. And by receiving, we are in danger to promote and partake in their barbarous cruelties. I am sure, if some gentlemen should go down to the Brewsters to take the air and fish, and a stronger party from Hull should surprise them and sell them for slaves to a ship outward bound, they would think themselves unjustly dealt with; both by sellers and buyers. And yet 'tis to be feared we have no other kind of title to our *nigers*. "Therefore all things whatsoever ye would that men should do to you, do ye even so to them: for this is the law and the prophets." Matt. vii. 12.

OBJECT 4. Abraham had servants bought with his money, and born in his house.

ANSWER. Until the circumstances of Abraham's purchase be recorded, no argument can be drawn from it. In the meantime charity obliges us to conclude that he knew it was lawful and good.

It is observable that the Israelites were strictly forbidden the buying or selling one another for slaves. Levit. xxv. 39, 46. Jer. xxxiv. 8–22. And God gaged his blessing in lieu of any loss they might conceive they suffered thereby. Deut. xv. 18. And since the partition wall is broken down, inordinate self-love should likewise be demolished. God expects that Christians should be of a more ingenuous and benign frame of spirit. Christians should carry it to all the world, as the Israelites were to carry it one towards another. And for men obstinately to persist in holding their neighbors and brethren under the rigor of perpetual bondage, seems to be no proper way of gaining assurance that God has given them spiritual freedom. Our blessed Saviour has altered the measures of the ancient love-song, and set it to a most excellent new tune, which all ought to be ambitious of learning. Matt. v. 43, 44. John xii. 34. These Ethiopians, as black as they are, seeing they are the sons and daughters of the first Adam, the brethren and sisters of the last Adam, and the off-spring of God, they ought to be treated with a respect agreeable.

(1700)

COTTON MATHER

(1663–1728)

The range of Mather's writings can only be suggested by the selections that follow. The excerpts from the *Magnalia* exemplify one of Mather's most famous (or perhaps infamous) interests—witchcraft. They provide us with some insight into the minds of those who believed in witches and in the imperative Puritan need for driving them out. Yet Mather also could show humanity, as in *The Negro Christianized,* where he pleads his case for the Negro. (Compare Sewall's *The Selling of Joseph.*) Doing good, the subject of his *Bonifacius,* shows a new emphasis in Puritan thought. The elaborate theological analyses and defenses were giving way to a more ethical view and one more familiar to twentieth century readers. The account from the *Curiosa* exemplifies Mather's interest in science. The Puritans, unlike some subsequent Christian sects, did not see science as opposed to religion, although to us Mather's science may seem less sophisticated than his theology. Mather's defensiveness in the selection from the *Parentator* was a position he was accustomed to, but the excerpt also shows his belief in himself and in the coming nation.

From *Magnalia Christi Americana**

16. ABOUT the time of our Blessed Lord's coming to reside on Earth, we read of so many *possessed with Devils,* that it is commonly thought the *Number* of such miserable *Energumens*[1] was then encreased above what has been usual in other Ages; and the *Reason* of that Increase has been made a Matter of some Enquiry. Now though the *Devils* might herein design by *Preternatural Operations* to blast the *Miracles* of our Lord Jesus Christ, which point they gained among the Blasphemous *Pharisees;* and the *Devils* might herein also design a Villanous *Imitation* of what was coming to pass

* Kenneth B. Murdock, ed., *Cotton Mather: Selections* (New York, 1926).

[1] Persons possessed by devils. [This and the following notes are from Murdock's edition.]

155

in the *Incarnation* of our Lord Jesus Christ, wherein *God* came to *dwell in Flesh;* yet I am not without suspicion, that there may be something further in the Conjecture of the Learned *Bartholinus* hereupon, who says, It was *Quod judæi præter modum, Artibus Magicis dediti Dæmonem Advocaverint,* the *Jews,* by the frequent use of *Magical Tricks,* called in the *Devils* among them.

It is very certain, there were hardly any People in the World grown more fond of *Sorceries,* than that unhappy People: The *Talmuds* tell us of the little *Parchments* with Words upon them, which were their common *Amulets,* and of the *Charms* which they mutter'd over *Wounds,* and of the various *Enchantments* which they used against all sorts of Disasters whatsoever. It is affirmed in the *Talmuds,* that no less than Twenty-four Scholars in one School were killed by *Witchcraft;* and that no less than *Fourscore* Persons were Hanged for *Witchcraft* by one Judge in one Day. The *Gloss* adds upon it, *That the Women of* Israel *had generally fallen to the Practice of Witchcrafts;* and therefore it was required, that there should be still chosen into the Council one skilful in the *Arts of Sorcerers,* and able thereby to discover who might be guilty of those *Black Arts* among such as were accused before them.

Now the Arrival of Sir *William Phips* to the Government of *New-England,* was at a time when a Governour would have had Occasion for all the Skill in *Sorcery,* that was ever necessary to a *Jewish Councellor;* a time when Scores of poor People had newly fallen under a prodigious *Possession of Devils,* which it was then generally thought had been by *Witchcrafts* introduced. It is to be confessed and bewailed, that many Inhabitants of *New-England,* and Young People especially, had been led away with little *Sorceries,* wherein they *did secretly those things that were not right against the Lord their God;* they would often cure Hurts with *Spells,* and practise detestable Conjurations with *Sieves,* and *Keys,* and *Pease,* and *Nails,* and *Horse-shoes,* and other Implements, to learn the things for which they had a forbidden and impious Curiosity. Wretched Books had stoln into the Land, wherein Fools were instructed how to become able Fortune-Tellers: Among which, I wonder that a blacker Brand is not set upon that Fortune-Telling Wheel, which that Sham-Scribler, that goes under the Letters of *R. B.* has promised in his *Delights for the Ingenious,* as an *honest and pleasant Recreation:*[2] And by these Books, the Minds of many had been so poisoned, that they studied this *Finer Witchcraft,* until, 'tis well, if some of them were not betray'd into what is Grosser, and more Sensible and Capital. Although these *Diabolical Divinations* are more ordinarily committed perhaps all over the *whole*

[2] Nathaniel Crouch, using the initials R. B., published his *Delights for the Ingenious* in London in 1684.

World, than they are in the Country of *New-England*, yet, that being a Country Devoted unto the Worship and Service of the Lord JESUS CHRIST above the *rest of the World*, *He* signalized his Vengeance against these Wickednesses, with such extraordinary Dispensations as have not been often seen in other places.

The *Devils* which had been so play'd withal, and, it may be, by some few Criminals more Explicitly engaged and imployed, now broke in upon the Country, after as astonishing a manner as was ever heard of. Some Scores of People, first about *Salem*, the Centre and First-Born of all the Towns in the Colony, and afterwards in several other places, were Arrested with many *Preternatural Vexations* upon their Bodies, and a variety of cruel Torments, which were evidently inflicted from the *Dæmons*, of the *Invisible World*. The People that were *Infected* and *Infested* with such *Dæmons*, in a few Days time arrived unto such a *Refining Alteration* upon their Eyes, that they could see their Tormentors; they saw a *Devil* of a Little *Stature*, and of a Tawny *Colour*, attended still with *Spectres* that appeared in more Humane Circumstances.

These *Tormentors* tendred unto the afflicted a *Book*, requiring them to *Sign* it, or to *Touch* it at least, in token of their consenting to be Lifted in the Service of the *Devil*; which they refusing to do, the *Spectres* under the Command of that *Blackman*, as they called him, would apply themselves to Torture them with prodigious Molestations.

The afflicted Wretches were horribly *Distorted* and *Convulsed;* they were *Pinched* Black and Blue: *Pins* would be run every where in their Flesh; they would be *Scalded* until they had *Blisters* raised on them; and a Thousand other things before Hundreds of Witnesses were done unto them, evidently *Preternatural:* For if it were *Preternatural* to keep a rigid *Fast* for *Nine*, yea, for *Fifteen* Days together; or if it were *Preternatural* to have one's Hands *ty'd* close together with a *Rope* to be plainly seen, and then by *unseen Hands* presently pull'd up a great way from the Earth before a Croud of People; such *Preternatural* things were endured by them.

But of all the *Preternatural* things which befel these People, there were none more *unaccountable* than those, wherein the prestigious *Dæmons* would ever now and then cover the most *Corporeal* things in the World with a *Fascinating Mist* of *Invisibility*. As now; a Person was cruelly assaulted by a *Spectre*, that, she said, run at her with a *Spindle*, though no Body else in the room could see either the *Spectre* or the *Spindle:* At last, in her Agonies, giving a snatch at the *Spectre*, she pulled the *Spindle* away; and it was no sooner got into her Hand, but the other Folks then present beheld that it was indeed a Real, Proper, Iron *Spindle;* which when they locked up very safe, it was nevertheless by the *Dæmons* taken away to do farther Mischief.

Again, a Person was haunted by a most abusive *Spectre*, which came to her, she said, with a *Sheet* about her, though seen to none but her self. After she had undergone a deal of Teaze from the Annoyance of the *Spectre*, she gave a violent *Snatch* at the *Sheet* that was upon it; where-from she tore a Corner, which in her Hand immediately was beheld by all that were present, a palpable Corner of a *Sheet:* And her Father, which was now holding of her, *catch'd*, that he might *keep* what his Daughter had so strangely seized; but the *Spectre* had like to have wrung his Hand off, by endeavouring to wrest it from him: However he still held it; and several times this odd Accident was renewed in the Family. There wanted not the *Oaths* of good credible People to these particulars.

Also, it is well known, that these wicked *Spectres* did proceed so far as to steal several Quantities of Money from divers People, part of which Individual Money was dropt sometimes out of the Air, before sufficient *Spectators*, into the Hands of the Afflicted, while the *Spectres* were urging them to subscribe their *Covenant with Death*. Moreover, *Poisons* to the Standers-by, wholly *Invisible*, were sometimes forced upon the Afflicted; which when they have with much Reluctancy swallowed, they have *swoln* presently, so that the common Medicines for *Poisons* have been found necessary to relieve them: Yea, sometimes the *Spectres* in the *struggles* have so dropt the *Poisons*, that the Standers-by have smelt them, and view'd them, and beheld the *Pillows* of the miserable stained with them.

Yet more, the miserable have complained bitterly of *burning Rags* run into their forceably distended *Mouths;* and though no Body could see any such *Clothes*, or indeed *any Fires* in the Chambers, yet presently the *scalds* were seen plainly by every Body on the Mouths of the Complainers. and not only the *Smell*, but the *Smoke* of the Burning sensibly fill'd the Chambers.

Once more, the miserable exclaimed extreamly of *Branding Irons* heating at the Fire on the Hearth to mark them; now though the Standers-by could see no *Irons*, yet they could see distinctly the *Print* of them in the Ashes, and *smell* them too as they were carried by the *not-seen Furies*, unto the Poor Creatures for whom they were intended; and those Poor Creatures were thereupon so *Stigmatized* with them, that they will bear the *Marks* of them to their Dying Day. Nor are these the *Tenth Part* of the *Prodigies* that fell out among the Inhabitants of *New-England*.

Flashy People may *Burlesque* these Things, but when Hundreds of the most sober People in a Country, where they have as much *Mother-Wit* certainly as the rest of Mankind, know them to be *True*, nothing but the absurd and froward Spirit of *Sadducism*[3] can Question them. I have not yet

---

[3] The spirit of the Sadducees, who denied the existence of angels and spirits.

mentioned so much as one Thing that will not be justified, if it be required by the *Oaths* of more considerate Persons than any that can ridicule these odd *Phænomena*.

But the worst part of this astonishing *Tragedy* is yet behind; wherein Sir *William Phips*, at last being dropt, as it were from the *Machin of Heaven*, was an Instrument of easing the Distresses of the Land, now *so darkned by the Wrath of the Lord of Hosts*. There were very worthy Men upon the Spot where the *assault from Hell* was first made, who apprehended themselves call'd from the *God of Heaven*, to sift the business unto the bottom of it; and indeed, the continual *Impressions*, which the outcries and the havocks of the *afflicted People* that lived nigh unto them caused on their Minds, gave no little Edge to this Apprehension.

The Persons were Men eminent for *Wisdom* and *Virtue*, and they went about their enquiry into the matter, as *driven* unto it by a *Conscience* of Duty to God and the World. They did in the first Place take it for granted, that there are *Witches*, or wicked Children of Men, who upon *Covenanting* with, and *Commissioning* of *Evil Spirits*, are attended by their Ministry to accomplish the things desired of them: To satisfie them in which Perswasion, they had not only the *Assertions* of the *Holy Scripture*; Assertions, which the *Witch-Advocates* cannot evade without Shifts, too foolish for any *Prudent*, or too profane for any *Honest* Man to use; and they had not only the well-attested *Relations* of the gravest Authors from *Bodin* to *Bovet*, and from *Binsfeld* to *Bromhal* and *Baxter*; to deny all which, would be as reasonable as to turn the Chronicles of all Nations into Romances of *Don Quixot* and the *Seven Champions;* but they had also an *Ocular Demonstration* in one, who a little before had been executed for *Witchcraft*, when *Joseph Dudley*, Esq; was the Chief Judge. There was one whose *Magical Images* were found, and who *confessing her Deeds*, (when a Jury of Doctors returned her *Compos Mentis*) actually shewed the whole Court, by what *Ceremonies* used unto them, she directed her *Familiar Spirits* how and where to Cruciate[4] the Objects of her Malice; and the Experiments being made over and over again before the whole Court, the *Effect* followed exactly in the Hurts done to People at a distance from her. The Existence of such *Witches* was now taken for granted by those good Men, wherein so far the generality of reasonable Men have thought *they ran well;*[5] and they soon received the *Confessions* of some *accused* Persons to confirm them in it; but then they took one thing more for granted, wherein 'tis now as generally thought they *went out of the Way*. The Afflicted People vehemently accused several

4 Torment.
5 I.e., they were right.

Persons in several Places, that the *Spectres* which afflicted them, did exactly resemble *them;* until the Importunity of the Accusations did provoke the Magistrates to examine them. When many of the *accused* came upon their Examination, it was found, that the *Dæmons* then a thousand ways abusing of the poor *afflicted* People, had with a marvellous exactness *represented* them; yea, it was found, that many of the *accused*, but casting their Eye on the *afflicted*, the *afflicted*, though their Faces were never so much another way, would fall down and lye in a sort of a Swoon, wherein they would continue, whatever Hands were laid upon them, until the Hands of the *accused* came to touch them, and *then* they would revive immediately: And it was found, that various kinds of *natural Actions*, done by many of the *accused* in or to their own Bodies, as *Leaning, Bending, Turning* Awry, or *Squeezing* their Hands, or the like, were presently attended with the like things *preternaturally* done upon the Bodies of the *afflicted*, though they were so far asunder, that the *afflicted* could not at all observe the *accused*.

It was also found, that the Flesh of the Afflicted was often *Bitten* at such a rate, that not only the *Print of Teeth* would be left on their *Flesh*, but the very *Slaver* of Spittle too: And there would appear just such a *set of Teeth* as was in the *accused*, even such as might be clearly distinguished from other Peoples. And usually the *afflicted* went through a terrible deal of seeming Difficulties from the tormenting *Spectres*, and must be long waited on, before they could get a Breathing Space from their *Torments* to give in their Testimonies.

Now many good Men took up an Opinion, That the *Providence* of God would not permit an *Innocent Person* to come under such a *Spectral Representation;* and that a concurrence of so many Circumstances would prove an *accused* Person to be in a *Confederacy* with the *Dæmons* thus afflicting of the Neighbours; they judged, that except these things might amount unto a *Conviction*, it would scarce be possible ever to *Convict* a *Witch;* and they had some *Philosophical Schemes* of *Witchcraft*, and of the Method and Manner wherein *Magical Poisons* operate, which further supported them in their Opinion.

Sundry of the *accused* Persons were brought unto their *Trial*, while this Opinion was yet prevailing in the Minds of the *Judges* and the *Juries*, and perhaps the most of the People in the Country, then mostly Suffering; and though against some of them that were Tried there came in so much *other Evidence* of their Diabolical Compacts that some of the most *Judicious*, and yet *Vehement* Opposers of the Notions then in Vogue, publickly declared, *Had they themselves been on the Bench, they could not have Acquitted them;*

nevertheless, divers were Condemned, against whom the *chief Evidence* was founded in the *Spectral Exhibitions*. . . .

On the other Part, there were many Persons of great Judgment, Piety and Experience, who from the beginning were very much dissatisfied at these Proceedings; they feared lest the *Devil* would get so far into the *Faith* of the People, that for the sake of many *Truths*, which they might find him telling of them, they would come at length to believe all his *Lies*, whereupon what a Desolation of *Names*, yea, and of *Lives* also, would ensue, a Man might without much *Witchcraft* be able to Prognosticate; and they feared, lest in such an extraordinary Descent of *Wicked Spirits* from their *High Places* upon us, there might such *Principles* be taken up, as, when put into *Practice*, would unavoidably cause the *Righteous to perish with the Wicked*, and procure the Blood-shed of Persons like the *Gibeonites*, whom some learned Men suppose to be under a false Pretence of *Witchcraft*, by *Saul* exterminated.

However uncommon it might be for *guiltless Persons* to come under such unaccountable Circumstances, as were on so many of the Accused, they held *some things there are, which if suffered to be Common, would subvert Government, and Disband and Ruin Humane Society, yet God sometimes may suffer such Things to evene, that we may know thereby how much we are beholden to him for that restraint which he lays upon the Infernal Spirits, who would else reduce a World into a* Chaos. . . .

In fine, the Country was in a dreadful *Ferment*, and wise Men foresaw a long Train of Dismal and Bloody Consequences. Hereupon they first advised, that the *afflicted* might be kept asunder in the closest Privacy; and one particular Person (whom I have cause to know) in pursuance of this Advice, offered himself singly to provide Accommodations for any *six* of them, that so the Success of more than ordinary *Prayer* with *Fasting*, might, with *Patience*, be *experienced*, before any other Courses were taken.[6]

And Sir *William Phips* arriving to his Government, after this *ensnaring horrible Storm* was begun, did consult the neighbouring Ministers of the Province, who made unto his Excellency and the Council a return, (drawn up at their desire by Mr. *Mather* the Younger[7] as I have been inform'd) wherein they declared.

We judge, that in the Prosecution of these and all such Witchcrafts, *there is*

[6] Mather here refers to himself.

[7] Cotton Mather. The "as I have been inform'd" is part of his attempt to retain his anonymity, since the life of Phips was first published with no author's name. When it appeared in the *Magnalia*, Mather was known as its author, but he did not alter the phrasing of the original edition.

need of a very Critical and Exquisite Caution: Lest by too much Credulity for things received only upon the Devil's Authority, *there be a Door opened for a long Train of miserable Consequences, and Satan get an Advantage over us; for* we should not be Ignorant of his Devices.

As in complaints upon Witchcrafts, *there may be Matters of* Enquiry, *which do not amount unto Matters of* Presumption; *and there may be Matters of* Presumption, *which yet may not be reckoned Matters of* Conviction; *so 'tis necessary that all Proceedings thereabout be managed with an* exceeding Tenderness *towards those that may be complained of; especially if they have been Persons formerly of an* unblemished Reputation.

When the first Enquiry *is made into the Circumstances of such as may lye under any just Suspicion of* Witchcrafts, *we could wish that there may be admitted as little as is possible of such* Noise, Company, *and* Openness, *as may too hastily expose them that are Examined; and that there may nothing be used as a* Test *for the Trial of the Suspected, the lawfulness whereof may be doubted among the People of God: But that the Directions given by such judicious Writers as* Perkins *and* Bernard, *be consulted in such a Case.*

Presumptions, *whereupon Persons may be committed, and much more* Convictions, *whereupon Persons may be condemned as guilty of* Witchcrafts, *ought certainly to be more considerable, than barely the* accused *Persons being* represented *by a* Spectre *to the afflicted: Inasmuch as it is an undoubted and a notorious Thing, that a* Dæmon *may, by God's Permission, appear even to ill Purposes in the shape of an* Innocent, *yea, and a* Virtuous *Man: Nor can we esteem* Alterations *made in the* Sufferers, *by a* look *or* touch *of the* accused, *to be an infallible Evidence of Guilt; but frequently liable to be abused by the Devil's* Legerdemains.

We know not whether some remarkable Affronts *given to the* Devils, *by our dis-believing of those Testimonies whose whole Force and Strength is from* them *alone, may not put a Period unto the Progress of a direful Calamity begun upon us, in the* accusation *of so many Persons, whereof, we hope, some are yet* clear from the great Transgression *laid unto their Charge.* . . .

Now upon a Deliberate Review of these things, his Excellency first *Reprieved,* and then *Pardoned* many of them that had been Condemned; and there fell out several strange things that caused the Spirit of the Country to run as vehemently upon the *Acquitting* of all the *accused,* as it by mistake ran at first upon the *Condemning* of them. Some that had been zealously of the Mind, that the *Devils* could not in the *Shapes* of good Men afflict other Men, were terribly Confuted, by having their own *Shapes,* and the *Shapes* of their most intimate and valued Friends, thus abused. And though more than twice Twenty had made such voluntary, and harmonious, and uncontroulable Confessions, that if they were all *Sham,* there was therein the greatest Violation made by the Efficacy of the *Invisible World*, upon the *Rules of Understanding Humane Affairs*, that was ever seen since *God made Man upon the Earth*, yet they did so recede from their *Confessions*, that it was very clear, some of them had been hitherto, in a sort of a *Præternatural Dream*, wherein they had said *of themselves*, they *knew not what themselves*.

In fine, The last Courts that sate upon this *Thorny Business*, finding that it was impossible to Penetrate into the whole Meaning of the things that had happened, and that so many *unsearchable Cheats* were interwoven into the *Conclusion* of a Mysterious Business, which perhaps had not crept thereinto at the *Beginning* of it, they *cleared* the *accused* as fast as they *Tried* them; and within a little while the *afflicted* were most of them delivered out of their *Troubles* also: And the Land had Peace restored unto it, by the *God of Peace, treading Satan under Foot. Erasmus*, among other Historians, does tell us, that at a Town in *Germany*, a *Dæmon* appearing on the Top of a Chimney, threatned that he would set the Town on *Fire*, and at length scattering some Ashes abroad, the whole Town was presently and horribly Burnt unto the Ground.

Sir *William Phips* now beheld such *Dæmons* hideously scattering *Fire* about the Country, in the Exasperations which the Minds of Men were on these things rising unto; and therefore when he had well Canvased a *Cause*, which perhaps might have puzzled the Wisdom of the wisest Men on Earth to have managed, without any *Error* in their Administrations, he thought, if it would be any *Error* at all, it would certainly be the *safest* for him to put a stop unto all future Prosecutions, as far as it lay in him to do it.

He did so, and for it he had not only the Printed Acknowledgments of the *New-Englanders*, who publickly thanked him, *As one of the Tribe of* Zebulun, *raised up from among themselves, and* Spirited *as well as* Commissioned *to be the* Steers-man *of a Vessel befogg'd in the* Mare Mortuum[8] *of* Witchcraft, *who now so happily* steered *her Course, that she escaped Shipwrack, and was safely again Moored under the Cape of* Good Hope; *and cut asunder the* Circæan *Knot of Enchantment, more difficult to be Dissolved than the famous* Gordian *one of Old. . . .* (1702)

8 Dead sea.

From *The Negro Christianized**

IT is a Golden Sentence that has been sometimes quoted from Chrysostom,[1] that *for a man to know the Art of Alms, is more than for a man to be crowned with the Diadem of Kings. But to convert one soul unto God, is more than to pour out Ten Thousand Talents into the Baskets of the Poor.* Truly, to raise a Soul from a dark state of ignorance and wickedness, to the knowledge of God and the belief of Christ, and the practice of our Holy and Lovely Religion, 'tis the noblest work that ever was undertaken among the children of men. An opportunity to endeavor the Conversion of a Soul, from a life of sin, which is indeed a woeful death, to fear God, and love Christ, and by a religious life to escape the Paths of the Destroyer, it cannot but be acceptable to all that have themselves had in themselves experience of such a conversion. And such an opportunity there is in your hands, O all you that have any NEGROES in your Houses; an opportunity to try whether you may not be the happy Instruments of converting the blackest instances of blindness and baseness into admirable candidates for Eternal Blessedness. Let not this opportunity be lost; if you have any concern for souls, your own or others; but make a trial, whether by your means, the most bruitish of creatures upon earth may not come to be disposed, in some degree, like the Angels of Heaven, and the Vassals of Satan become the Children of God. Suppose these wretched Negroes to be the offspring of Cham[2] (which yet is not so very certain) yet let us make a trial whether the CHRIST who *dwelt in the Tents of Shem* have not some of His Chosen among them. Let us make a trial whether they that have been scorched and blackened by the sun of Africa may not come to have their minds healed by the more benign Beams of the Suns of Righteousness.

It is come to pass by the Providence of God, without which there comes nothing to pass, that poor NEGROES are cast under your government and protection. You take them into your Families; you look on them as part of your Possessions; and you expect from their service a support, and perhaps an increase, of your other Possessions. How agreeable would it be, if a religious master or mistress thus attended, would now think with themselves! *Who can tell but that this poor creature may belong to the Election of God! Who can tell but that God may have sent this poor creature into my hands, that so one of the Elect may by my means be called, and by my instruction be made wise unto Salvation! The glorious God will put an unspeakable Glory upon me if it may be so!* The considerations that would move you to teach your

---

* *The Negro Christianized* (Boston, 1706).
[1] Saint John Chrysostom (*c.* 347–407), Greek Church Father.
[2] Ham, second-born son of Noah.

Negroes the Truths of the Glorious Gospel, as far as you can, and bring them, if it may be, to live according to those Truths, a Sober, and a Righteous, and a Godly Life—they are innumerable. And, if you would after a reasonable manner consider the pleas which we have to make on the behalf of God, and of the Souls which He has made, one would wonder that they should not be Irresistible. *Show yourselves men,* and let *Rational Arguments* have their force upon you, to make you treat, not as brutes but as men those *Rational Creatures* whom God has made your Servants. . . .

Be assured, Sirs, your Servants will be the Better Servants for being made Christian Servants. To Christianize them aright will be to fill them with all Goodness. Christianity is nothing but a very mass of Universal Goodness. Were your Servants well tinged with the spirit of Christianity, it would render them exceeding dutiful unto their Masters, exceeding patient under their Masters, exceeding faithful in their business, and afraid of speaking or doing anything that may justly displease you. It has been observed that those Masters who have used their Negroes with most of humanity, in allowing them all the comforts of life that are necessary and convenient for them (who have remember that by the Law of God, even an ass was to be relieved when sinking under his burden, and an ox might not be muzzled when treading out the corn; and that a just man will regard the life of the beast, he will much more allow the comforts of life to and not [hide?] himself from his own flesh) have been better served, had more work done for them, and better done, than those Inhuman Masters who have used their Negroes worse than their Horses. And those Masters, doubtless, who use their Negroes with most of Christianity, and use most pains to inform them in, and conform them to, Christianity, will find themselves no losers by it. . . . But many Masters whose Negroes have greatly vexed them, with miscarriages, may do well to examine whether Heaven be not chastising of them for their failing in their duty about their Negroes. Had they done more to make their Negroes the knowing and willing Servants of God, it may be God would have made their Negroes better Servants to them. Sirs, you may read your Sin in the Punishment.

And now, what Objection can any man living have, to retund the force of these Considerations? Produce thy cause, O Impiety, *Bring forth thy strong reasons,* and let all men see what Idle and silly cavils are thy best Reasons against this Work of God.

It has been cavilled by some that it is questionable whether the Negroes have Rational Souls or no. But let that Bruitish insinuation be never whispered any more. Certainly, their discourse will abundantly prove that they have Reason. Reason shows itself in the design which they daily act upon. The vast improvement that Education has made upon some of them argues there is a Reasonable Soul in all of them. . . . They are Men, and not Beasts, that you have bought, and they must be used accordingly. 'Tis true, they are barbarous. But so were our own Ancestors. The Britons were in many things as barbarous, but a little before our Saviour's nativity, as the Negroes are at this day, if there be any credit in Caesar's *Commentaries*. Their complexion sometimes is made an argument why nothing should be done for them. A gay sort of argument! As if the great God went by the Complexion of Men in His Favors to them! As if none but Whites might hope to be favored and accepted with God! Whereas it is well known that the Whites are the least part of Mankind. The biggest part of Mankind, perhaps, are Copper-colored, a sort of Tawnies. And our English that inhabit some climates do seem growing apace to be not much unlike unto them. As if, because a people, from the long force of the African sun and soil upon them (improved, perhaps, to further degrees by maternal imagination, and other accidents) are come at length to have the small fibers of their veins, and the blood in them, a little more interspersed through their Skin, than other people, this must render them less valuable to Heaven than the rest of Mankind? Away with such trifles! The God who *looks on the Heart* is not moved by the color of the Skin, is not more propitious to one Color than another. Say rather, with the Apostle Acts 10. 34, 35. *Of a truth I perceive, that God is no respecter of persons, but in every nation he that feareth Him and worketh righteousness is accepted with Him.* Indeed their Stupidity is a discouragement. It may seem unto as little purpose to teach as to wash an Ethiopian. But the greater their Stupidity, the greater must be our Application. If we can't learn them so much as we would, let us learn them as much as we can. A little divine Light and Grace infused into them will be of great account. And the more difficult it is to fetch such forlorn things up out of the perdition whereinto they are fallen, the more laudable is the undertaking. There will be the more of a Triumph if we prosper in the undertaking. Let us encourage ourselves from that word Mat. 3. 9. *God is able of these stones to raise up children unto Abraham.*

Well, but if the Negroes are Christianized they will be baptised, and their baptism will presently entitle them to their freedom; so our money is thrown away.

Man, if this were true, that a Slave bought with thy Money were by thy means brought unto *the Things that accompany Salvation,* and thou shouldest from this time have no more Service from him, yet thy Money were not thrown away. That man's Money will perish with him who had rather the Souls in his family should perish than that he should lose a little Money. And suppose it were so, that baptism gave a legal title to freedom. Is there no guarding against this inconvenience? You may by sufficient indentures keep off the things which you reckon so inconvenient. But it is all a mistake. There is no such thing. What Law is it that sets the baptized slave at liberty? Not the Law of Christianity, that allows of Slavery. Only it wonderfully dulcifies and mollifies and moderates the circumstances of it. Christianity directs a Slave, upon his embracing the Law of the Redeemer, to satisfy himself *That he is the Lord's Free-man*, tho' he continues a Slave. It supposes (Col. 3. 11.) that there are *bond* as well as *free* among those that have been Renewed in the *Knowledge and Image of Jesus Christ*. Will the Canon-law do it? No, the Canons of numberless Councils mention *the Slaves of Christians* without any contradiction. Will the Civil Law do it? No: tell, if you can, any part of Christendom wherein Slaves are not frequently to be met withal. But is not Freedom to be claimed for a baptised Slave, by the English Constitution? The English Laws about Villains or Slaves will not say so; for by those laws, they may be granted for Life, like a lease, and passed over with a manner, like other goods or chattels. And by those laws, the Lords may seize the bodies of their Slaves even while a writ . . . is depending. These English laws were made when the Lords and the Slaves were both of them Christians, and they stand still unrepealed. If there are not now such Slaves in England as formerly, it is from the Lords more than from the Laws. The baptised then are not thereby entitled unto the Liberty. Howbeit, if they have arrived unto such a measure of Christianity that *none can forbid Water for the Baptising of them*, it is fit that they should enjoy those comfortable circumstances with us which are due to them, not only as the Children of Adam, but also as our Brethren, on the same level with us in the expectations of a blessed immortality through the Second Adam. Whatever slaughter the assertion may make among the pretensions which are made unto Christianity, yet while the sixteenth chapter of Matthew is in the Bible, it must be asserted: the Christian who cannot so far deny himself, can be no Disciple of the Lord JESUS CHRIST. But, O Christian, thy Slave will not serve thee one jot the worse for that *Self-denial*.   (1706)

From *Bonifacius**

7. To the title of GOOD WORKS there do belong, those *essays to do good*, which are now urged for. To produce them, the *first* thing, and indeed the ONE thing, that is *needful*, is, a glorious work of GRACE on the soul, renewing and quickening of it, and *purifying* of the sinner, and rendering him *zealous of good works:* a *workmanship of God* upon us, *creating* us over again, by JESUS CHRIST, *for good works*. And then, there is needful, what will necessarily follow upon such a *work:* that is, a *disposition* to *do good works* upon true, genuine, generous, and evangelical *principles*. Those *principles* are to be *stated*, before we can go any further; when they are *active*, we shall go a great deal further.

It is in the first place, to be taken for granted: that the *end* for which we do *good works* must not be, to afford the matter of our *justification*, before the Law of the holy GOD. Indeed, no *good works* can be done by any man until he be *justified*. Until a man be united unto the glorious CHRIST, who is *our life*, he is a *dead man*. And, I pray, what *good works* to be expected from such a man? They will all be *dead works*. For, "Severed from me ye can do nothing," saith our SAVIOUR. The *justification of a* sinner, *by faith, before good works, and in order to them*, is one of those truths, which may say to the Popish innovations, "With us are the gray-headed, and very aged men, much elder than thy Father." It was an old maxim of the faithful, *Bona opera sequuntur justificatum, non præcedunt justificandum.*[1] It is the *righteousness* of the *good works* done by our Saviour and *Surety*, not our own, that *justifies* us before God, and answers the demands of HIS LAW upon us. We do by *faith* lay hold on those *good works* for our *justifying righteousness* before we arrive to do our own. 'Tis not our *faith* itself, either as doing of *good works*, or as being itself one of them, which entitles us to the *justifying righteousness* of our Saviour. But it is *faith*, only *as* renouncing of our own righteousness, and relying on that of our Saviour, provided for the *chief of sinners*, by which we are *justified*. Sir, all your attempts at *good works* will come to nothing, till a *justifying faith* in your Saviour, shall carry you forth unto them. This was the divinity of the ancients; *Jerome* has well expressed it: *Sine Christo omnis virtus est in vitie.*[2] Nevertheless; first, you are to look upon it, as a glorious truth of the Gospel, that the *moral law* (which prescribes and requires *good works*) must by every Christian alive be made the *rule* of his life. *Do we make void the Law through faith? God forbid. Yea, we establish the Law.*

---

* David Levin, ed., *Bonifacius: An Essay Upon the Good* (Cambridge, Mass., 1966). Notes below from Levin's edition.

[1] Good works follow justification; they do not precede justification.

[2] Without Christ, all virtue is vice.

The *rule*, by which we are to *glorify* God, is given us in the law of *good works*, which we *enjoy* (I will express it *so!*) in the *Ten Commandments*. It is impossible for us, to be released from all obligations to glorify God by a conformity to this *rule;* sooner shall we cease to be creatures. The *conformity* to that rule in the *righteousness*, which our Saviour by His obedience to it, has *brought in*, to *justify* us, has forever *magnified the Law, and made it honorable*. Though our Saviour has furnished us, with a perfect and spotless *righteousness*, when His obedience to the *Law*, is placed unto our account; yet it is a *sin* for us at all to fall short in our own obedience to the *Law:* we must always loathe and judge ourselves for the *sin*. We are not under the *Law* as a *covenant of works*. Our own exactness in doing of *good works*, is not now the *condition* of our *entering into life. Woe unto us if it were!* But still, the *Covenant of Grace* holds us to it, as our *duty;* and if we are in the *Covenant of Grace*, we shall make it our *study*, to *do* those *good works* which once were the terms of our *entering into life. Manet lex tota pietatis;*[3] that was the divinity in *Tertullian's* days! There must be such an esteem for the *law* of *good works* retained forever in all the *justified: a law* never to be abrogated; never to be abolished! And then, secondly, though we are *justified* by a *precious faith* in the *righteousness of God our Saviour*, yet good works are demanded of us, to *justify* our *faith;* to *demonstrate*, that it is indeed that *precious faith. A justifying faith* is a *jewel*, which may be *counterfeited*. But now the *marks* of a *faith*, which is no counterfeit, are to be found in the *good works* whereto a servant of God is inclined and assisted by his *faith*. It is by a *regenerating work* of the Holy Spirit, that *faith* is wrought in the souls of the chosen people. Now the same *work* of God, and of *grace*, which does in a *regeneration* dispose a man to make his flight by *faith*, unto the *righteousness* of his only Saviour, will also dispose him to the *good works* of a *Christian life*. And the same *faith* which goes to the Saviour for a part in His *righteousness*, will also go to Him, for an heart and strength to do the *good works*, which are *ordained, that we should walk in them*. If our *faith* be not such a *faith*, 'tis a *lifeless* one, and it will not bring to *life. A workless faith* is a *worthless faith*. My friend, suppose thyself standing before the *Judgment-seat* of the glorious LORD. A needful, a prudent, supposal; it ought to be a very *frequent* one. The *Judge* demands, "What hast thou to plead, for a portion in the blessedness of the righteous?" The plea must be:

"O my glorious Judge, Thou hast been my sacrifice. Oh! Judge of all the earth, give poor dust and ashes leave to say, 'My righteousness is on the bench. Surely in the Lord I have my righteousness. O my Saviour, I have received it, I have secured it, upon Thy gracious offer of it.' "

The *Judge* proceeds:

[3] The entire law of duty (or obedience to God) remains.

"But what hast thou to plead, that thy faith should not be rejected, as the faith and hope of the hyprocrite?"

Here the plea must be:

"Lord, my faith was Thy work. It was a faith which disposed me to all the good works of Thy holy religion. My faith sanctified me. It carried me to Thee, O my Saviour, for grace to do the works of righteousness. It embraced that for my Lord as well as for my Saviour. It caused me with sincerity to love and keep Thy commandments; with assiduity to serve the interests of Thy Kingdom in the world." Thus you have *Paul* and *James* reconciled. Thus you have *good works* provided for. The aphorism of the physician, is, *Per brachium fit judicium de corde*. The *doings* of men are truer and surer indications, than all their *sayings*, of what they are *within*. But there is yet a further consideration, upon which you must be *zealously affected* for them. You must consider *good works*, as the *way* to, yea, as a *part* of, the *great salvation*, which is purchased and intended for you by your blessed Saviour. Without an *holy heart* you can't be fit for an *holy heaven; meet for the inheritance of the holy ones* in that *light*, which admits no *works of darkness* where none but *good works* are done for eternal ages. But an *holy heart* will cause a man to do *good works* with all his heart. The motto on the gates of the Holy City is: None But the Lovers of Good Works to Enter Here. . . .

8. It is to be feared, that we too seldom *inquire* after our Opportunities to Do Good. Our *opportunities to do good* are our Talents. An awful account must be rendered unto the great GOD, concerning our use of the Talents, wherewith He has entrusted us, in these precious *opportunities*. We do not *use* our *opportunities*, many times because we do not *know* what they are; and many times, the reason why we do not *know*, is because we do not *think*. Our *opportunities to do good*, lie by unregarded, and unimproved, and so 'tis but a mean account that can be given of them. We *read* of a thing, which we *deride* as often as we behold: *there is, that maketh himself poor, and yet has great riches*. It is a thing too frequently exemplified, in our *opportunities to do good*, which are some of our most valuable *riches*. Many a man seems to reckon himself destitute of those *talents;* as if there were *nothing* for him to do: he pretends he is not in a condition to *do* any *good. Alas! poor man; what can he do?* My friend, *think* again; *think* often. *Inquire* what your *opportunities* are. You will doubtless find them, to be more than you were *aware* of. *Plain men dwelling in tents*, persons of a very *ordinary character*, may in a way of bright piety, prove persons of *extraordinary usefulness*. . . . I have read of a pious *Weaver*, of whom some eminent persons would say, "Christ walked as it were alive upon the Earth in that man." And a world of *good* was done by that man. A mean *mechanic*, who can tell what an *engine* of *good* he may be, if humbly and wisely applied unto it!

This then is the next PROPOSAL. Without abridging yourselves of your *occasional thoughts* on the question, often every day, *What good may I do?*, state a *time* now and then for more *deliberate thoughts* upon it. Can't you find a *time* (suppose once a week, yea, and how agreeably, on the *Lord's* day) to take that question into your consideration: WHAT IS THERE THAT I MAY DO, FOR THE SERVICE OF THE GLORIOUS LORD, AND FOR THE WELFARE OF THOSE, FOR WHOM I OUGHT TO BE CONCERNED? Having implored the *direction* of God, who is the *Father of Lights*, and the Author and Giver of *good thoughts*, *consider* on the matter, in the various aspects of it. *Consider* till you have *resolved* on something. The *resolutions* which you *take up*, immediately *write down*. Examine what *precept* and what *promise*, you can find in the Word of God, that may countenance the intentions, in these your *memorials*. Look over the *memorials* at proper seasons afterwards, to see how far you have proceeded in the execution of them. The advantages of these *reserved* and *revised* MEMORIALS, no *rhetoric* will serve to commend them, no *arithmetic* to number them. There are some *animals*, of whom we say, "They do not know their own strength." *Christians*, why should you be *they?*

Chapter Eight: *Physicians*

. . . *Physicians* are even overstocked with opportunities, to help the *poor*, and heal them for nothing. It was a noble saying of *Cicero, Nil habet Fortuna melius, quam ut possis, neque natura Praestantius, quam ut velis, servare plures.*[4] But I will set before you an higher consideration, than what a pagan *Kirker* was ever acquainted with. Sirs, the more charity, and compassion, and condescension you treat the *poor* withal, the more will you arrive to, *the greatest of all glories:* I say, the *greatest* and *highest* of all glories!—I mean, an imitation of your admirable SAVIOUR. You will readily say, *Quod decuit* CHRISTUM, *cur mihi turpe putem?*[5] In comparison of this consolation, it will be a small thing to say unto you, that your coming among the *poor*, will be like the descent of the angel of *Bethesda* unto them. We will not presume to prescribe unto you, what *good* you shall do to the *poor*, and by what generous actions you shall *take their infirmities and bear their sicknesses*. Only we enter an objection against your taking any *fees* for your *visits* on the *Lord's-Days;* because, the *time* is none of *yours;* 'tis the *Lord's!*

When we consider how much the *lives* of men are in the *hands* of God;

[4] Fortune can give you nothing better than the power, and Nature nothing more excellent than the desire, to save (or serve) many people.

[5] Why do I consider shameful to me that which was worthy of Christ?

and what a dependence we have on the *God of our health* for our cure, when we have lost it; and what strange and strong *proofs* we have had, of *angels* by their communications or operations contributing to the cure of the diseases wherewith *mortals* have been oppressed (whereof I can myself relate astonishing instances!); and the marvelous efficacy of *prayer* for the recovery of a *sick brother, who has not sinned a sin unto death;* what better thing is there to be recommended unto a *physician*, who desires to *do good*, than this: *Good Sir, be a man of prayer.* In your daily and secret *prayer* carry every one of your *patients* by name (as you would your own children) unto the glorious *Lord our Healer*, for His healing *mercies:* place them as far as your *prayer* will do it, under the *beams* of the *Sun of Righteousness.* And as any *new case* of your patients may occur, especially if there be any difficulty in it, why should you not make your particular and solicitous applications to Heaven for direction! *O Lord, I know that the way of man is not in himself, nor is it in man that walketh, to direct his steps;* no, nor in man that healeth, to perform his cures. *Hippocrates* advised physicians, that when they visited their patients, they should consider, whether there might not be, *divinum quiddam in morbo.*[6] Truly, in some sense, there is ever so, and it should be considered. What an *heavenly life* might you lead, if your business may be carried on with as many visits to *Heaven*, as you make unto your *patients!* One *Jacob Tzaphalon*, a famous Jew in the former century, published at *Venice*, a book entitled *Precious Stones.* There are several *prayers* in the book; and among them a pretty long one, *for physicians when they go to visit their patients.* When the Psalmist says, "Thou hast made me wiser than my enemies"; it may be read, "Thou hast made me wise from my Enemies." We should learn *wisdom* from them; *fas est, et ab hoste!*[7]—O *Christianity*, certainly thou wilt outdo *Judaism* in thy devotions!

We read, "Heaviness in the heart of man makes it stoop, but a good word makes it glad." We read, "A cheerful heart doth good like a medicine, but a broken spirit drieth the bones." And *Baglivi* is not the only physician, who has made the observation, "That a great part of our diseases, either do rise from, or are fed by, a *weight of cares* lying on the *minds* of men. Diseases that seem *incurable*, are easily cured by agreeable conversation. *Disorders* of the *mind*, first bring diseases on the *stomach;* and so the whole mass of blood gradually becomes infected. And as long as the *passions* of the *mind* continue, the *diseases* may indeed change their *forms*, but they rarely quit the patients." *Tranquillity of mind* will do strange things, towards the relief of *bodily maladies.* 'Tis not without reason, that *Hoffmann*, in his dissertation, *Des Moyens de Vivre Longtemps*, does insist on *tranquillity of mind* as the chief

---

[6] Something divine in sickness.
[7] It is right, even from the enemy!

among the *ways to live long;* and that this is the cause why we read, "The fear of the Lord tendeth to life." They that have practiced *the art of curing by expectation*, have made an experiment of what the *mind* will do towards the cure of the *body*. By practicing *the art of curing by consolation*, you may carry on the experiment. I propound then, let the *physician* with all possible ingenuity of *conversation*, find out, what matter of *anxiety*, there may have been upon the mind of his *patient;* what there is, that has made his life *uneasy* to him. Having discovered the *burden*, let him use all the ways he can devise to take it off. Offer him such *thoughts*, as may be the best *anodynes* for his distressed mind; especially, the *right thoughts of the righteous*, and the ways to a composure upon *religious principles*. Give him a *prospect*, if you can, of some *deliverance* from his distresses, or some *abatement* of them. Raise in him as *bright thoughts* as may be, and scatter the *clouds*, remove the *loads*, which his mind is perplexed withal: especially, by representing and magnifying the *mercy* of GOD in CHRIST unto him. It is possible, Sir, that you may in this way also, find our [out?] *obliging occasions* to exercise abundance of *goodness*, in doing yourself, or in bringing others to do, *kindnesses* for the miserable. . . .

THE CONCLUSION

. . . I hope, you have more discretion, than to imagine, that because you are never *weary of well-doing*, therefore you should be universally *well-spoken of*. No; 'twill be just the contrary. To *do well*, and to *hear ill*, is the common experience, and ought to be our constant expectation. For this most *unreasonable* thing, there are very many *reasons*. 'Twill be impossible to *do much good*, but some or other will count themselves *hurt* by what you do. You will unavoidably serve some *interests*, which others are indisposed unto. 'Tis also in the nature of *madmen*, to take up strange prejudices against their *best friends;* to be set against none so much as *them*. Now, we may everywhere see those, concerning whom we are told, *madness is in their hearts*. It will appear in their being unaccountably prejudiced, against those that most of all seek to *do good* unto them. Then, *he teareth me in his wrath who hateth me; he gnasheth upon me with his teeth, mine enemy sharpeneth his eyes upon me!* Then, to *skorakizing* a *benefactor*, for nothing in the world but because he would have been so! He shall be honored, as the *Lindians* worshipped *Hercules*, by *cursing*, and throwing of *stones*. The *wrath* of God, against a sinful and woeful world, has likewise its operation in this grievous matter. If men always upon *intentions* and *inventions* to do *good*, were so generally beloved and esteemed as they might be, they would be *instruments* of doing more *good*, than the justice of Heaven, can yet allow to be done for *such* a world. *The world is not worthy* of them, nor of that *good* that is endeavored by them. To deprive the world of that *good*, they must be left unto a strange *aversion* for those men that would fain do it. This cripples them, fetters them, defeats their excellent purposes! Nor is the *Devil* idle on this occasion. A man who shall *do much good*, will therein do much *harm* unto the empire of the *Devil*. It would be much, if the *Devil* should not *seek to devour*, or take an exquisite revenge upon such *men of God.* Except God lay an uncommon restraint upon that *wicked one*, such is the *power of the Adversary*, and such an *energy* the *Devil* has upon the minds of multitudes, that he will notably and bitterly *revenge* himself upon any notable *doer of good;* and procure him a *troop* of enemies, three volleys of obloquies. But, O servant of God, *by Him thou wilt run through a troop; by thy God thou wilt leap over a wall.* We may be so far from wondering, that *wicked men* are violently disaffected unto a man who does abundance of *good*, and spread as many stories, and write as many libels, to his disadvantage, as ever the incomparable *Calvin* suffered from them; we may rather wonder that the *Devil* does not make this world hotter than a *Babylonish furnace* for him; too hot for his abiding in it. Sirs, if you will *do much*, 'tis very likely that the *Devil* may sometimes raise upon your opportunities to *do good*, such an *horrible tempest*, as may threaten a total ruin unto them. You may fear that you see your *serviceableness*, the *apple of your eye struck out;* you may be driven to prayers, to tears, to *fasting often* in secret places; prostrate in the dust, you must *offer up your supplications, with strong crying and tears*, to Him that is *able to save* your opportunities from *death;* you must cry out, "O deliver my soul (my serviceableness), from the sword, my darling (my serviceableness), from the power of the Dog!". . . . (1710)

*

From *Curiosa Americana**

Sir,

. . . A better dish than that [locusts] you would have in our pigeons, a bird which in almost everything resembles your turtle-doves, only that it is a little bigger. The numbers of these that visit us in their seasons are such that I am almost afraid of giving you a true report of them, lest you should imagine a Palephatus were imposing his incredibles upon you. Yet it will a little answer the intention of the correspondence wherewith you favor me, if I do report something of them.

I affirm to you, then, that sometimes we have mighty flocks of these pigeons flying over us, thousands in a flock, the best part of a mile square occupied

---

* MS draft, Massachusetts Historical Society, modernized by the editor.

by a flock, these passing along, the welkin in a manner obscured and covered with them; and several hours have run out before the appearance of these birds thus making the best of their way have been over. They have been frequently sold for two pence or three pence a dozen, tho' two or three of them, roast or boiled or broiled, may make a meal for a temperate man; yea, they are sometimes killed in such plenty that the country-people feed their hogs with them. One of my neighbors has killed no fewer than two and thirty dozen at one shot.

Gentlemen have complained unto me that they have lit in such numbers on their trees as to break down the limbs thereof, and spoil their orchards. They will sometimes roost at night in such numbers among our thickets, that our people, with no other weapons than sticks and poles, kill thousands of them.

One worthy person of my acquaintance had a descent of them in his neighborhood, in the month of December, a very unusual time of the year, while there was yet no snow, but many acorns, on the ground; which, 'tis thought, might then draw them thither. At their lighting on a place of thick woods, the *front* wheeled about, the *flanks* wheeled inward, and *rear* came up (Sir, he was a Captain who gave me the written relation!) and pitched as near to the center as they could find any limb, or twig, or bush to seize upon. Yea, they sat upon one another like bees, till a limb of a tree would seem near as big as a horse. 'Tis incredible to tell how large and strong and many limbs were broken down by this new burden upon them. The breaking of them was heard at a mighty distance. The birds filled more than half a mile about from the center; and the noise they made was like the roaring of the sea. The night was dark; but this gentleman and his sons, with guns, and some other less noxious tools, laid in among them, and some they took alive with their hands, and in the morning found the number of their slain to be one hundred and three dozen, besides what some other people had carried away.

A few days ago, I was at the table of a superior gentleman, relating some of these things. And one, whose veracity was not to be disputed, said he had a story that would cap all of mine; for (said he) "I have catched no less than two hundred dozens of pigeons, in less than two minutes of time, and all in one trap!" The pleasant mention of this whetstone on the occasion, obliged the gentleman immediately to explain himself, and add: "Such a number broke into my barn, and but by shutting the doors I had them all at my mercy. . . ."

Heartily and forever at your service, (1713)

From *Parentator**

I AM no pretender to what some have been commended for, The Art of good Narrative. And therefore, as for the style of this narrative, I will make no excuses, till you, *Gentlemen-Critics*, first can show your patent for your criticizing, and who constituted *You* to be Censors for the rest of mankind, and until you are better agreed among yourselves upon the Rules of Criticizing. For I cannot learn that there are any two of you, but what are intolerably severe and cruel in your censures upon one another. I acknowledge that I am too liable to an infirmity of salting my sentences now and then with short, instructive, and unforced Intermixtures of something or other that I have read of; but as I was upon reforming it, I stumbled upon a passage in a letter of Mons. Tournefort unto the Lord Pontchartrain, *You gave me leave to insert some touches of erudition, to heighten the subjects treated of; and I fancy such additions will make them the less tiresome.* However, having exhibited the lives of about seventy ministers, all published in one volume, and the characters of near twenty more, at several times in more separate publications, it can't well be expected that I should be very liberal in dealing out those intermixed embellishments which make a narrative less tedious to the Sons of Erudition; or have my speech seasoned with so many grains of salt as it use to be. And yet I can truly say, I have studiously laid aside that care of embellishing; I have dropped a world of what some would count ornaments, which while I was writing offered themselves unto my mind, resolving upon a plain, simple, honest narrative of matters which alone would by being so remarkable afford a continual feast unto the readers. . . .

By having mentioned a book (that is to say, the *Magnalia* CHRISTI *Americana*) whereto this may pass for an appendix, I think I have here a proper occasion to take some notice of the fate which it has met withal. For the very same thing in the heavens above us is by some called the Milky Way, and by others called the Crooked Serpent.

The Book being written with a variety of Projection and Contrivance to serve that Real, Vital, Solid PIETY which seems now almost wholly to have left the earth . . . and give some account of Men and Things which cannot be given without exposing the Persecuting Spirit of some that hate to be reformed, I could not be so weak as to imagine that impious people, or such as are no better than mere formalists in religion, would forbear their invectives against it, and their endeavors to bring all possible contempt upon it. The Introduction to the History sufficiently foretold it, and also signified how much the breast of the Author, *Trebly Oak'd and Brass'd*, was prepared for it.

* *Parentator* (Boston, 1724).

I cannot but wonder at the kind reception which that work has found in Scotland and in Ireland, and in many parts of England; and the compliments which I have received upon it (even equal to what a Sallust could have had from his Milton) from as *Competent Judges of Writing* as any of them whose malice against the design of the work has disposed them to decry it. It would be a trespass upon the laws of Modesty in me to recite them; and I must ask pardon if I do so far trespass as to let the world know just this one little part of my Buckler: that the famous and acute Mr. Alsop, in an assembly of ministers, when some were proposing to make an abridgement of that History, said upon it: *It is a very improper proposal. 'Tis impossible to abridge it! You injure it if you go to do it. There is nothing superfluous in it; instead of talking about epitomizing it, go do as I have done: read all of it no less than twice over. No man that has a relish for piety or variety can ever be weary of reading it. . . .*

But it is no wonder at all to me, that the poor book has met with some that have thought it proper to let the world see that they look upon it as an object for their Enmity. And among these none has more signalized the Enmity, or more put the Third Chapter of Genesis in execution, than one John Oldmixon, in a book entitled, *The English Empire in America. . . .*

. . . Oldmixon's chief rage is at the Church-History of a country, which also Dr. Mather[1] was in some regards much of a Father to. And of his Church History, to pass by his grin, that the book is *cramm'd full of— Acrostics;* whereas, Reader, if thou find so much as one Acrostic in all the Book—let the Book be treated as *The English Empire in America* is like to be! I say, to pass by this, the Accuser would have it believed that *the Church-History is very trivial in the matter of it.* Yes, by all means! The Marvellous Works of GOD in producing and maintaining and afflicting and relieving of colonies in a matchless manner, formed upon the noble intentions of pure and undefiled religion; the wise measures taken by the best of men to establish that religion, and the bright patterns of living up to it seen in the lives of such men; and as choice materials as a Church History can be composed of—there are *Trivial Matters!* Come then, let us go to Master Oldmixon for *Important Matters.* It is a trouble unto me to descend unto anything so ludicrous, but it is he and not I that must answer for it. In his History, wherein he rails at ours, you shall find whole pages consecrated unto long, long tiresome relations of some that he singles out as *the more curious events;* he calls 'em so. These *curious events* are, "That a couple of starved Indians (at Hudson's Bay) went a-fishing—and then, a hunting—and met with only two moose—and—how 'twas—and how the geese flying away to the southward, in October, the people there (such their sagacity!) knew that

[1] Increase Mather (Cotton's father), the subject of *Parentator.*

hard weather was approaching—and in November (Marvellous!) it snowed —And then—a long tedious narrative, how they catched partridges (not woodcocks!) yet (an exploit that should be told unto future generations) four men in a week's time killed six and twenty—and then (a terrible thing happened, as much to be remembered as the Sicilian earthquake) in December, a boy had his feet hurt with the frost—and a hundred more such *curious events*, is this History set off withal. These it seems are the Important Matters, that are most worthy of a room in History. A Church-History furnished as aforesaid, has only *trivial matters* for you!

. . . I do here publicly make this declaration: In reading eighty-six pages of what this wretched and worse than careless writer has given us about New England, I noted down with my pen the more gross, evident, and notorious falsehoods which I observed in it, omitting many lesser matters which cannot be justified. And casting up the number, of these falsehoods I found them to be above the number of eighty-seven. These falsehoods are many of them the more inexcusable because the History of New England which he decries with so much foolish malignity had in those very points given him a truer information. And for many of them, 'tis impossible for him to find any author but his own Romantic Brain. O Palephatus, thou hast nothing so incredible. Unhappy collection! In which there are so often more lies than pages! Miserable age! How do thy Historians put upon thee!

I suppose this is that Oldmixon who wrote a play called *Amyntas*, whereof the late writer of the History of the more celebrated Play-writers has left this upon lasting record: *it met with ill success*. And it is a pity he should succeed any better in writing of English Empires. I am not alone in my complaints of this miserable romancer, who even in an Old Irish family of quality would scarce have been thought worthy to supply the office of a story-teller. The ingenious Beverly in his well-composed History of Virginia declares that he found Oldmixon's account of that country (just as I found his account of New England) so very faulty, that he laid aside all thoughts of correcting it, it being bad beyond all possibility of amending it. He stigmatizes him as a *faithless and a fruitless* historian, and says, *It would make a book larger than his own to expose his errors*. And indeed, as he has dealt with New England and with Virginia, so his dealings with New York are such that when any gentleman of the province will please to oblige their country with a True History of it, he will certainly join with us in just castigations upon such a *Wretched Scribbler*. But I have now done with him!

Reader, I am heartily sorry that thou shouldest find such a creature chained at the porch, when thou art entering into a structure where thirty-four articles, like so many Apartments, will afford thee, I hope, some agreeable entertainment. . . . (1724)

JONATHAN EDWARDS

(1703–1758)

The last of the Puritan writers in this text is often cited as a source for Puritan beliefs. Ironically, he was the last Puritan writer to treat Puritan issues significantly. In the *Thoughts on the Revival of Religion in New England*, Edwards wrote of the contrast between the old Europe and the new America, a theme that runs through American literature from its beginning to the present. The excerpt from *The Future Punishment of the Wicked Unavoidable and Intolerable* shows the vivid imagery Edwards could create to realize hell for his listeners while he explained doctrinal matters to them. The selection from the *Miscellanies*, as explained in the Introduction (p. 27), exemplifies Edwards' approach to the traditional Puritan questions. Compelling, rigorous logic is employed to persuade an audience of truth. Combining this logic with such vivid imagery as that of hell in the preceding selection is one of Edwards' remarkable literary achievements. "On the Medium of Moral Government—particularly Conversation" can be quite difficult for the new reader of colonial literature until he comes upon such central passages as those in sections 13 and 25 and until he comprehends the "conversation" Edwards examines. The relations between reason and emotion constitute an important part of the excerpt and an important concern for Edwards and for his twentieth-century readers.

From *Thoughts on the Revival of Religion in New England**

. . . IT is not unlikely that this work of God's Spirit, that is so extraordinary and wonderful, is the dawning, or at least, a prelude of that glorious work of God, so often foretold in Scripture, which in the progress and issue of it shall renew the world of mankind. If we consider how long since, the things foretold, as what should precede this great event have been accomplished; and how long this event has been expected by the church of God, and thought to be nigh by the most eminent men of God in the church;

* *The Works of President Edwards*, vol. 3 (New York, 1843).

and withal consider what the state of things now is, and has for a considerable time been, in the church of God, and world of mankind, we cannot reasonably think otherwise, than that the beginning of this great work of God must be near. And there are many things that make it probable that this work will begin in America. It is signified that it shall begin in some very remote part of the world, that the rest of the world have no communication with but by navigation, in Isa. lx. 9: "Surely the Isles will wait for me, and the ships of Tarshish first, to bring my sons from far." It is exceeding manifest that this chapter is a prophecy of the prosperity of the church, in its most glorious state on earth, in the latter days; and I cannot think that any thing else can be here intended but America, by the isles that are afar off, from whence the first born sons of that glorious day shall be brought. Indeed by *the isles*, in prophecies of gospel times, is very often meant *Europe*: it is so in prophecies of that great spreading of the gospel that should be soon after Christ's time, because it was far separated from that part of the world where the church of God had, until then been, by the sea. But this prophecy cannot have respect to the conversion of Europe, in the time of that great work of God, in the primitive ages of the Christian church; for it was not fulfilled then: the isles and ships of Tarshish, thus understood, did not wait for God first; that glorious work did not begin in Europe, but in Jerusalem, and had for a considerable time, been very wonderfully carried on in Asia, before it reached Europe. And as it is not that work of God that is chiefly intended in this chapter, but that more glorious work that should be in the latter ages of the Christian church, therefore some other part of the world is here intended by the Isles, that should be as Europe then was, far separated from that part of the world where the church had before been, by the sea, and with which it can have no communication but by the ships of Tarshish. And what is chiefly intended is not the British Isles, nor any Isles near the other continent; for they are spoken of as at a great distance from that part of the world where the church had till then been. This prophecy therefore seems plainly to point out America, as the first fruits of that glorious day.

God has made as it were two worlds here below, the old and the new (according to the names they are now called by), two great habitable continents, far separated one from the other; the latter is but newly discovered, it was formerly wholly unknown, from age to age, and is as it were now but newly created: it has been, until of late, wholly the possession of Satan, the church of God having never been in it, as it has been in the other continent, from the beginning of the world. This new world is probably now discovered, that the new and most glorious state of God's church on earth might commence there; that God might in it begin a new world in a spiritual respect, when he creates the *new heavens* and *new earth*.

God has already put that honor upon the other continent, that Christ was born there literally, and there made the *purchase of redemption:* so, as Providence observes a kind of equal distribution of things, it is not unlikely that the great spiritual birth of Christ, and the most glorious *application of redemption* is to begin in this: as the elder sister brought forth Judah, of whom came Christ, and so she was the mother of Christ: but the younger sister, after long barrenness, brought forth Joseph and Benjamin, the beloved children. Joseph, that had the most glorious apparel, the coat of many colors, who was separated from his brethren, and was exalted to such glory out of a dark dungeon, and fed and saved the world, when ready to perish with famine, and was as a fruitful bough by a well, whose branches ran over the wall, and was blessed with all manner of blessings and precious things, of heaven, and earth, through the good will of him that dwelt in the bush; and was, as by the horns of a unicorn, to push the people together, to the ends of the earth, i.e., conquer the world. See Gen. xlix. 22, &c., and Deut. xxxiii. 13, &c. And Benjamin, whose mess was five times so great as that of any of his brethren, and to whom Joseph, the type of Christ, gave wealth and raiment far beyond all the rest. Gen. xlv. 22.

The other continent hath slain Christ, and has from age to age shed the blood of the saints and martyrs of Jesus, and has often been as it were deluged with the church's blood: God has therefore probably reserved the honor of building the glorious temple to the daughter, that has not shed so much blood, when those times of the peace, and prosperity, and glory of the church shall commence, that were typified by the reign of Solomon.

The Gentiles first received the true religion from the Jews: God's church of ancient times had been among them, and Christ was of them: but that there might be a kind of equality in the dispensations of Providence, God has so ordered it, that when the Jews come to be admitted to the benefits of the evangelical dispensation, and to receive their highest privileges of all, they should receive the gospel from the Gentiles. Though Christ was of them, yet they have been guilty of crucifying him; it is therefore the will of God, that that people should not have the honor of communicating the blessings of the kingdom of God in its most glorious state, to the Gentiles, but on the contrary, they shall receive the gospel in the beginning of that glorious day, from the Gentiles. In some analogy to this, I apprehend God's dealings will be with the two continents. America has received the true religion of the old continent; the church of ancient times has been there, and Christ is from thence; but that there may be an equality, and inasmuch as that continent has crucified Christ, they shall not have the honor of communicating religion in its most glorious state to us, but we to them.

The old continent has been the source and original of mankind, in several respects. The first parents of mankind dwelt there; and there dwelt Noah and his sons; and there the second Adam was born, and was crucified and rose again: and it is probable that, in some measure to balance these things, the most glorious renovation of the world shall originate from the new continent, and the church of God in that respect be from hence. And so it is probable that that will come to pass in spirituals, that has in temporals, with respect to America; that whereas till of late, the world was supplied with its silver and gold and earthly treasures from the old continent, now it is supplied chiefly from the new, so the course of things in spiritual respects will be in like manner turned.

And it is worthy to be noted that America was discovered about the time of the reformation, or but little before: which reformation was the first thing that God did towards the glorious renovation of the world, after it had sunk into the depths of darkness and ruin, under the great antichristian apostasy. So that as soon as this new world is (as it were) created, and stands forth in view, God presently goes about doing some great thing to make way for the introduction of the church's latter day glory, that is to have its first seat in, and is to take its rise from that new world.

It is agreeable to God's manner of working, when he accomplishes any glorious work in the world, to introduce a new and more excellent state of his church, to begin his work where his church had not been till then, and where was no foundation already laid, that the power of God might be the more conspicuous; that the work might appear to be entirely God's, and be more manifestly a creation out of nothing; agreeably to Hos. i. 10: "And it shall come to pass that in the place where it was said unto them, ye are not my people, there it shall be said unto them, ye are the sons of the living God." When God is about to turn the earth into a Paradise, he does not begin his work where there is some good growth already, but in a wilderness, where nothing grows, and nothing is to be seen but dry sand and barren rocks; that the light may shine out of darkness, and the world be replenished from emptiness, and the earth watered by springs from a droughty desert; agreeably to many prophecies of Scripture, as Isa. xxxii. 15: "Until the Spirit be poured from on high, and the wilderness become a fruitful field." And chap. xli. 18, "I will open rivers in high places, and fountains in the midst of the valleys; I will make the wilderness a pool of water, and the dry land springs of water: I will plant in the wilderness the cedar, the shittah tree, and the myrtle and oil tree: I will set in the desert the fir tree, and the pine, and the box tree together;" and chap. xliii. 20, "I will give waters in the wilderness, and rivers in the desert, to give drink to my people, my chosen." And many other parallel Scriptures might be mentioned.

I observed before, that when God is about to do some great work for his church, his manner is to begin at the lower end; so when he is about to renew the whole habitable earth, it is probable that he will begin in this utmost, meanest, youngest and weakest part of it, where the church of God has been planted last of all; and so the first shall be last, and the last first; and that will be fulfilled in an eminent manner in Isa. xxiv. 16, "From the uttermost part of the earth have we heard songs, even glory to the righteous."

There are several things that seem to me to argue, that when the Sun of Righteousness, the sun of the new heavens and new earth, comes to rise, and *come forth as the bridegroom* of his church, *rejoicing as a strong man to run his race, having his going forth from the end of heaven, and his circuit to the end of it, that nothing may be hid from the light and heat of it,* that the sun shall rise in the west, contrary to the course of this world, or the course of things in the old heavens and earth. The course of God's providence shall in that day be so wonderfully altered in many respects, that God will as it were change the course of nature, in answer to the prayers of his church; as God changed the course of nature, and caused the sun to go from the West to the East, when Hezekiah was healed, and God promised to do such great things for his church, to deliver it out of the hand of the king of Assyria, by that mighty slaughter by the angel; which is often used by the prophet Isaiah, as a type of the glorious deliverance of the church from her enemies in the latter days: the resurrection of Hezekiah, the king and captain of the church (as he is called 2 Kings xx. 5), as it were from the dead, is given as an earnest of the church's resurrection and salvation, Isa. xxxviii. 6, and is a type of the resurrection of Christ. At the same time there is a resurrection of the sun, or coming back and rising again from the west, whither it had gone down; which is also a type of the Sun of Righteousness. The sun was brought back ten degrees; which probably brought it to the meridian. The Sun of Righteousness has long been going down from east to west; and probably when the time comes of the church's deliverance from her enemies, so often typified by the Assyrians, the light will rise in the west, until it shines through the world, like the sun in its meridian brightness.

The same seems also to be represented by the course of the waters of the sanctuary, Ezek. xlvii., which was from west to east; which waters undoubtedly represent the Holy Spirit, in the progress of his saving influences, in the latter ages of the world: for it is manifest that the whole of those last chapters of Ezekiel, are concerning the glorious state of the church that shall then be.

And if we may suppose that this glorious work of God shall begin in any part of America, I think if we consider the circumstances of the settlement of New England, it must needs appear the most likely of all American colonies, to be the place whence this work shall principally take its rise.

And if these things are so, it gives more abundant reason to hope that what is now seen in America, and especially in New England, may prove the dawn of that glorious day: and the very uncommon and wonderful circumstances and events of this work, seem to me strongly to argue that God intends it as the beginning or forerunner of something vastly great.

I have thus long insisted on this point, because if these things are so, it greatly manifests how much it behooves us to encourage and promote this work, and how dangerous it will be to forbear so to do. . . . (1740)

"On Heaven" from *Miscellaneous Observations**

182. *Heaven.* How ravishing are the proportions of the reflexions of rays of light, and the proportion of the vibrations of the air! and without doubt God can contrive matter so that there shall be other sort of proportions that may be quite of a different kind, and may raise another sort of pleasure in the sense, and in a manner to us now inconceivable, that shall be vastly more ravishing and exquisite. And in all probability the abode of the saints after the resurrection will be so contrived by God that there shall be external beauties and harmonies altogether of another kind from what we perceive here, and probably those beauties will appear chiefly in the bodies the man Christ Jesus, and of the saints. Our animal spirits will also be capable of immensely more fine and exquisite proportions in their motions, than now they are, being so gross; but how much more ravishing will the exquisite spiritual proportions be that shall be seen in minds, in their acts between one spiritual act and another, between one disposition and another, and between one mind and another, and between all their minds and Christ Jesus, and particularly between the man Christ Jesus and the Deity, and among the persons of the Trinity, the supreme harmony of all! And it is out of doubt with me that there will be immediate intellectual views of minds, one of another, and of the Supreme mind, more immediate, clear, and sensible than our views of bodily things with bodily eyes. In this world we behold spiritual beauties only mediately by the intervention of our senses, in perceiving those external actions which are the effects of spiritual proportion. Hereby the ravishingness of the beauty is much obscured, and our sense of it flattened and deadened; but when we behold the beauties of mind more immediately than now we do the colours of the rainbow, how ravishing will it be! All that there wants in order to such an intellectual view, is that a clear and sensible apprehension of what is in mind should be raised in our own mind

* *Works of President Edwards*, vol. 8 (New York, 1830).

constantly according to such and such laws; for it is no other way that we perceive with our bodily eyes, or perceive by any of our senses.

Then also our capacities will be exceedingly enlarged, and we shall be able to apprehend, and to take in more extended and compounded proportions. We see that the narrower the capacity the more simple must the beauty be to please: thus, in proportion of sounds, the birds and brute creatures are most delighted with simple music, and in the proportion confined to a few notes; so little children are not able to perceive the sweetness of very complex tunes where respect is to be had to the proportion of a great many notes together, in order to perceive the sweetness of the tune; then perhaps we shall be able fully and easily to apprehend the beauty, or where respect is to be had to thousands of different ratios at once to make up the harmony. Such kind of beauties, when fully perceived, are far the sweetest.

188. *Heaven.* The best, most beautiful, and most perfect way that we have of expressing a sweet concord of mind to each other is by music. When I would form in my mind ideas of a society in the highest degree happy, I think of them as expressing their love, their joy, and the inward concord, and harmony, and spiritual beauty of their souls, *by sweetly singing to each other.* But if in heaven minds will have an *immediate* view of one another's dispositions without any such intermediate expression, how much sweeter will it be! But to me it is probable that the glorified saints, after they have again received their bodies, will have ways of expressing the concord of their minds by some other emanations than sounds, of which we cannot conceive, that will be vastly more proportionate, harmonious, and delightful than the nature of sounds is capable of; and the music they will make will be in a measure capable of modulations in an infinitely more nice, exact, and fine proportion than our gross airs, and with organs as much more adapted to such proportions.

198. *Happiness.* How soon do earthly lovers come to an end of their discoveries of each other's beauty! how soon do they see all that is to be seen! Are they united as near as possible, and have communion as intimate as possible? How soon do they come to the most endearing expressions of love that it is possible to give, so that no new ways can be invented, given, or received. And how happy is that love in which there is an eternal progress in all those things wherein new beauties are continually discovered, and more and more loveliness, and in which we shall for ever increase in beauty ourselves; where we shall be more capable of finding out and giving, and shall receive more and more endearing expressions of love for ever; our union will become more close, and communion more intimate!

263. *Heaven.* If the saints after the resurrection shall see by light, and speak and hear by sounds, it is probable that the medium will be infinitely finer,

and more adapted to a distant and exact representation, so that a small vibration in sound, though the undulations may proportionally decrease according to the distance from their rise or fountain, yet may be conveyed infinitely farther with exactness before they begin to be confused and lost through the sluggishness of the medium, or through the bulk, the roughness, or tenaciousness of the particles, and the conveyance may likewise be with far greater swiftness. The organs also will be immensely more exquisitely perceptive, so that perhaps a vibration a thousand times less than can now be perceived by the ear, may be distinctly and easily perceived by them; and yet the organs may be far more able to bear a very strong vibration than ours in this state; and through niceness of the organ they shall be able to distinguish in the greatest multitude of sounds according to their distance and direction, more exactly by the ear than we do visible objects by the eye; and we know not how far they may clearly hear one another's discourses. So the eye may be so much more sensible, and the medium of vision (the rays) so much more exquisite, that for aught we know they may distinctly see the beauty of one another's countenances and smiles, and hold a delightful and most intimate conversation at a thousand miles distance. . . . (Undated)

From *The Future Punishment of the Wicked Unavoidable and Intolerable**

EZEKIEL XXII. 14.—Can thine heart endure, or can thine hands be strong in the days that I shall deal with thee? I the Lord have spoken it, and will do it.

THUS impenitent sinners will be able neither to shun the punishment threatened, nor to deliver themselves from it, nor to find any relief under it.
I come now,
IV. To show, that neither will they be able to bear it. Neither will their hands be strong to deliver themselves from it, nor will their hearts be able to endure it. It is common with men, when they meet with calamities in this world, in the first place to endeavor to shun them. But if they find, that they cannot shun them, then after they are come, they endeavor to deliver themselves from them as soon as they can; or at least, to order things so, as to deliver themselves in some degree. But if they find that they can by no means

* Clarence Faust and Thomas Johnson, eds., *Jonathan Edwards Representative Selections* (reprinted New York, 1962).

deliver themselves, and see that the case is so that they must bear them; then they set themselves to bear them: they fortify their spirits, and take up a resolution, that they will support themselves under them as well as they can. They clothe themselves with all the resolution and courage they are masters of, to keep their spirits from sinking under their calamities.

But it will be utterly in vain for impenitent sinners to think to do thus with respect to the torments of hell. They will not be able to endure them, or at all to support themselves under them: the torment will be immensely beyond their strength. What will it signify for a worm, which is about to be pressed under the weight of some great rock, to be let fall with its whole weight upon it, to collect its strength, to set itself to bear up the weight of the rock, and to preserve itself from being crushed by it? Much more in vain will it be for a poor damned soul, to endeavor to support itself under the weight of the wrath of Almighty God. What is the strength of man, who is but a worm, to support himself against the power of Jehovah, and against the fierceness of his wrath? What is man's strength, when set to bear up against the exertions of infinite power? Matt. xxi. 44, "Whosoever shall fall on this stone shall be broken; but on whomsoever it shall fall, it will grind him to powder."

When sinners hear of hell torments, they sometimes think with themselves: Well, if it shall come to that, that I must go to hell, I will bear it as well as I can: as if by clothing themselves with resolution and firmness of mind, they would be able to support themselves in some measure; when, alas! they will have no resolution, no courage at all. However they shall have prepared themselves, and collected their strength; yet as soon as they shall begin to feel that wrath, their hearts will melt and be as water. However before they may seem to harden their hearts, in order to prepare themselves to bear, yet the first moment they feel it, their hearts will become like wax before the furnace. Their courage and resolution will be all gone in an instant; it will vanish away like a shadow in the twinkling of an eye. The stoutest and most sturdy will have no more courage than the feeblest infant: let a man be an infant, or a giant, it will be all one. They will not be able to keep alive any courage, any strength, any comfort, any hope at all.

I come now as was proposed,

V. To answer an inquiry which may naturally be raised concerning these things.

INQUIRY. Some may be ready to say, If this be the case, if impenitent sinners can neither shun future punishment, nor deliver themselves from it, nor bear it; then what will become of them?

ANSWER. They will wholly sink down into eternal death. There will be that sinking of heart, of which we now cannot conceive. We see how it is with the body when in extreme pain. The nature of the body will support itself for a considerable time under very great pain, so as to keep from wholly sinking. There will be great struggles, lamentable groans and panting, and it may be convulsions. These are the strugglings of nature to support itself under the extremity of the pain. There is, as it were, a great lothness in nature to yield to it; it cannot bear wholly to sink.

But yet sometimes pain of body is so very extreme and exquisite, that the nature of the body cannot support itself under it; however loth it may be to sink, yet it cannot bear the pain; there are a few struggles, and throes, and pantings, and it may be a shriek or two, and then nature yields to the violence of the torments, sinks down, and the body dies. This is the death of the body. So it will be with the soul in hell; it will have no strength or power to deliver itself; and its torment and horror will be so great, so mighty, so vastly disproportioned to its strength, that having no strength in the least to support itself, although it be infinitely contrary to the nature and inclination of the soul utterly to sink; yet it will sink, it will utterly and totally sink, without the least degree of remaining comfort, or strength, or courage, or hope. And though it will never be annihilated, its being and perception will never be abolished, yet such will be the infinite depth of gloominess that it will sink into, that it will be in a state of death, eternal death.

The nature of man desires happiness; it is the nature of the soul to crave and thirst after well-being; and if it be under misery, it eagerly pants after relief; and the greater the misery is, the more eagerly doth it struggle for help. But if all relief be withholden, all strength overborne, all support utterly gone; then it sinks into the darkness of death.

We can conceive but little of the matter; we cannot conceive what that sinking of the soul in such a case is. But to help your conception, imagine yourself to be cast into a fiery oven, all of a glowing heat, or into the midst of a glowing brick-kiln, or of a great furnace, where your pain would be as much greater than that occasioned by accidentally touching a coal of fire, as the heat is greater. Imagine also that your body were to lie there for a quarter of an hour, full of fire, as full within and without as a bright coal of fire, all the while full of quick sense; what horror would you feel at the entrance of such a furnace! And how long would that quarter of an hour seem to you! If it were to be measured by a glass, how long would the glass seem to be running! And after you had endured it for one minute, how overbearing would it be to you to think that you had it to endure the other fourteen!

But what would be the effect on your soul, if you knew you must lie there enduring that torment to the full for twenty-four hours! And how much greater would be the effect, if you knew you must endure it for a whole year; and how vastly greater still, if you knew you must endure it for a thousand years! O then, how would your heart sink, if you thought, if you knew, that you must bear it forever and ever! That there would be no end! That after millions of millions of ages, your torment would be no nearer to an end, than ever it was; and that you never, never should be delivered!

But your torment in hell will be immensely greater than this illustration represents. How then will the heart of a poor creature sink under it! How utterly inexpressible and inconceivable must the sinking of the soul be in such a case!

This is the death threatened in the law. This is dying in the highest sense of the word. This is to die sensibly; to die and know it; to be sensible of the gloom of death. This is to be undone; this is worthy of the name of destruction. This sinking of the soul under an infinite weight, which it cannot bear, is the gloom of hell. We read in Scripture of the blackness of darkness; this is it, this is the very thing. We read in Scripture of sinners being lost, and of their losing their souls: this is the thing intended; this is to lose the soul: they that are the subjects of this are utterly lost. . . . (1741)

From *Miscellanies**

71. *Free will.* 'Tis very true that God requires nothing of us as condition of eternal life but what is in our own power, and yet 'tis very true at the same time that it's an utter impossible thing that ever man should do what is necessary in order to salvation, nor do the least towards it, without the almighty operation of the Holy Spirit of God—yea, except everything be entirely wrought by the Spirit of God. True and saving faith in Christ is not a thing out of the power of man, but infinitely easy. 'Tis entirely in a man's power to submit to Jesus Christ as a savior if he will. But the thing is, is [it] man's will that he should will it, except God works it in him? To will it, as to do it, depends on a man's will and not on his power; and however easy the thing be and however much in a man's power, 'tis an impossibility that he should ever do it except he wills it, because submission to Christ is a willing. There are many things that are entirely in our power, of which things yet it may be said that 'tis an impossibility they should be, because of our dispositions. Perhaps some may say that 'tis a contradiction to say that that is in our power which yet 'tis an impossibility they [i.e., it] should be. 'Tis according to what they mean by being in our power. I mean this: that that is in our power which we can do when we please, and I think those

* Harvey Townsend, ed., *The Philosophy of Jonathan Edwards from His Private Note-books* (Eugene, Ore., 1955).

mean very improperly who mean otherwise. Now it is no contradiction to say that we can do such a thing when we please, and yet that 'tis an impossibility that it should be what we please. And, although it may be the easiest thing in the world, yet it is not contradictory to say that it is impossible that we should please to do it, except God works it in us, according as I have explained. It is altogether in a man's power, when he has a cup of poison offered to him, whether he will drink it or no, and yet by reason of the man's internal disposition—the ideas and notions of things that he then has—it may be an impossibility that he should will to drink it. If a man who is a servant, exceeding wicked, debauched, and licentious, who has it offered to him whether he will choose a man of most exemplary holiness and strict piety for his master and submit to his government, it is perfectly (in my sense) in the servant's power whether he will take him for his master and governor or no; and yet it may be an impossible thing that it should be as long as the servant has such and such inclination and desire, judgment, and ideas.

The world has got into an exceeding wrong and confused way of talking about will and power, not knowing what they mean by them. They say man can will such a thing and man can't will it, which is dreadful confusion. When we say a man can't will such a thing, the notion that is raised in our mind by such an expression is that the man might heartily and truly desire to will it but could not; that is, he truly willed to will it but could not; that is, he truly willed it but could not will it. I am sure that when we say a man can or cannot do such a thing we don't mean that he wills or does not will it. We say, and truly often, he can do such a thing when yet he wills it not; and yet 'tis an impossibility that he should do when he wills it not. But you'll say he could will it if he would. 'Tis most certainly true if he does will it he can will it. And you'll say, if he does not will it, he can will it. I say 'tis true things may so happen, circumstances or ideas may so fall, as to cause him to will it, but it is no act of his own power that he wills it, though it be necessary there should be a capacity, because will is the first spring of the voluntary exertions of the active power in man and the cause of it. And therefore, 'tis impossible that active power should cause the will to spring, except the effect causes its own cause, however we are compelled, unavoidably, thus to express—that of ourselves we can do nothing, that we have no power— and however this manner of expression, as well as the contrary, carries often a wrong idea in the mind; so that all that men do in real religion is entirely their own act and yet every tittle is wrought by the Spirit of God. Neither do I contradict myself by saying that all that men do in religion is entirely their own act. I mean that everything they do, they themselves do, which I suppose none will contradict. 'Tis the exertion of their own power.

530. *Love to God.* Self-love. Whether or no a man ought to love God more than himself. Self-love, taken in the most extensive sense, and love to God are not things properly capable of being compared one with another; for they are not opposites or things entirely distinct, but one enters into the nature of the other. Self-love is a man's love of his own pleasure and happiness and hatred of his own misery, or rather, 'tis only a capacity of enjoyment or suffering; for to say a man loves his own happiness or pleasure is only to say that he delights in what he delights; and to say he that hates his own misery is only to say that he is grieved or afflicted in his own affliction. So that self-love is only a capacity of enjoying or taking delight in anything. Now surely 'tis improper to say that our love to God is superior to our general capacity of delighting in anything. Proportionable to our love to God is our disposition to delight in His good. Now our delight in God's good can't be superior to our own general capacity of delighting in anything or, which is the same thing, our delight in God's good can't be superior to our love to delight in general; for proportionately as we delight in God's good, so shall we love that delight. A desire of and delight in God's good is love to God, and love to delight is self-love. Now the degree of delight in a particular thing and the degree of love to pleasure, or delight in general, ben't properly comparable one with another; for they are not entirely distinct, but one enters into the nature of the other. Delight in a particular thing includes a love to delight in general. A particular delight in anything can't be said to be superior to love to delight in general; for always in proportion to the degree of delight is the love a man hath to the delight, for he loves greater delight more or less, in proportion as it is greater. If he did not love it more, it would not be a greater delight to him. Love of benevolence to any person is an inclination to their good. But evermore equal to the inclination or desire anyone has of another's good is the delight he has in that other's good if it be obtained, and the uneasiness if it be not obtained. But equal to that delight is a person's love to that delight, and equal to that uneasiness is his hatred of that uneasiness. But love to our own delight or hatred of our own uneasiness is self-love, so that no love to another can be superior to self-love as most extensively taken.

Self-love is a man's love to his own good. But self-love may be taken in two senses, or any good may be said to be a man's own good in two senses. 1. Any good whatsoever that a man any way enjoys, or anything that he takes delight in—it makes it thereby his own good whether it be a man's own proper and separate pleasure or honor, or the pleasure or honor of another. Our delight in it renders it our own good in proportion as we delight in it. 'Tis impossible that a man should delight in any good that is not his own, for to say that would be to say that he delights in that in which he does not delight. Now take self-love for a man's love to his own good in this more general sense—and love to God can't be superior to it. But secondly, a person's good may be said to be his own good as 'tis his proper and separate good, which is his and what he has delight in directly and immediately. Love to good that is a man's own, in this sense, is what is ordinarily called self-love. And superior to this, love to God can and ought to be.

Self-love is either simple, mere self-love, which is a man's love to his own proper, single, and separate good, and is what arises simply and necessarily from the nature of a perceiving, willing being—it necessarily arises from that without the supposition of any other principle. I therefore call it simple self-love because it arises simply from that principle, viz., the nature of a perceiving, willing being. Self-love, taken in this sense, and love to God are entirely distinct and don't enter one into the nature of the other at all. 2. There is a compounded self-love which is exercised in the delight that a man has in the good of another—it is the value that he sets upon that delight. This I call compounded self-love because it arises from a compounded principle. It arises from the necessary nature of perceiving and willing being, whereby he takes his own pleasure or delight, but not from this alone; but it supposes also another principle that determines the exercise of this principle —a certain principle uniting this person with another that causes the good of another to be its good, and makes that to become delight which otherwise cannot. The first arises simply from his own being, whereby that which agrees immediately and directly with his own being is his good, though it arises also from a principle uniting him to another being, whereby the good of that other being does in a sort become his own. This second sort of self-love is not entirely distinct from love to God, but enters into its nature.

Corollary. Hence, 'tis impossible for any person to be willing to be perfectly and finally miserable for God's sake, for this supposes love to God is superior to self-love in the most general and extensive sense of self-love, which enters into the nature of love to God. It may be possible that a man may be willing to be deprived of all his own proper, separate good for God's sake. But then he is not perfectly miserable, but happy in the delight that he hath in God's good. For he takes greater delight in God's good, for the sake of which he parts with his own, than he did in his own. So that the man is not perfectly miserable; he is not deprived of all delight, but he is happy. He has greater delight in what is obtained for God than he had in what he has lost of his own, so that he has only exchanged a lesser joy for a greater. But if a man is willing to be perfectly miserable for God's sake, then he is willing to part with all his own separate good, but he must be willing also to be deprived of that which is indirectly his own, viz., God's good, which supposition is inconsistent with itself; for to be willing to be deprived of this latter sort of good is opposite to that principle of love to God itself, from whence such a willingness is supposed to arise. Love to God, if it be superior to any other principle, will make a man forever unwilling, utterly and finally, to be deprived of that part of his happiness which he has in God's being blessed and glorified, and the more he loves Him, the more unwilling he will be. So that this supposition, that a man can be willing to be perfectly and utterly miserable out of love to God, is inconsistent with itself.

Note. That love of God, which we have hitherto spoke of, is a love of benevolence only. But this is to be observed, that there necessarily accompanies a love of benevolence a love of appetite or complacence, which is a disposition to desire or delight in beholding the beauty of another, and a relation to or union with him. Self-love, in its most general extent, is very much concerned in this, and is not entirely distinct from it. The difference is only this: that self-love is a man's desire of, or delight in, his own happiness. This love of complacence is a placing of his happiness, which he thus desires and delights in, in a particular object. This sort of love, which is always in proportion to a love of benevolence, is also inconsistent with a willingness to be utterly miserable for God's sake; for if the man is utterly miserable, he is utterly excluded [from] the enjoyment of God. But how can man's love of complacence towards God be gratified in this? The more a man loves God, the more unwilling will he be to be deprived of this happiness.

238. *Trinity.* Those ideas which we call ideas of reflection, all ideas of the acts of the mind (as the ideas of thought, of choice, love, fear, etc.)—if we diligently attend to our own minds we shall find they are not properly representations but are, indeed, repetitions of these very things, either more fully or more faintly. They, therefore, are not properly ideas. Thus, 'tis impossible to have an idea of thought or of an idea, but it will [be] that same idea repeated. So if we think of love, either of our past love that is now vanished, or of the love of others which we have not, we either so frame things in our imagination that we have for a moment a love to that thing or to something we make represent it, or we excite for a moment that love which we have, and suppose it in another place; or we have only an idea of the antecedents, concomitants, and effects of loving and suppose something unseen, and govern our thoughts about [it] as we have learned how by experience and habit. Let anyone try himself in a particular instance and diligently observe. So if we have an idea of a judgment, not our own, we have the same ideas that are the terms of the proposition repeated in our own minds, and as being something in our own minds that is really our judgment, and suppose it there; that is, we govern our thought about it as if it were there, if we have a distinct idea of that judgment, or else we have only an

idea of the attendants and effects of that judgment, and supply the name and our actions about it as we have habituated ourselves. And so, certainly, it is in all our spiritual ideas. They are the very same things repeated, perhaps very faintly and obscurely, and very quick and momentaneously, and with many new references, suppositions, and translations; but if the idea be perfect, it is only the same thing absolutely over again.

Now if this be certain, as it seems to me to be, then it's quite clear that, if God doth think of Himself and understand Himself with perfect clearness, fullness, and distinctness, that idea He hath of Himself is absolutely Himself again, and is God perfectly to all intents and purposes. That which God knowest of the divine nature and essence is really and fully the divine nature and essence again. So that, by God's thinking of Himself, the deity must certainly be generated. This seems exceeding clear to me. God doubtless understands Himself in the most perfect sense; for therein His infinite understanding chiefly consists. And He understands Himself at all times perfectly, without intermission or succession in His thought.

When we have the idea of another's love to a thing, if it be the love of a man to a woman that we are unconcerned about, we neither love in such cases nor have generally any proper idea at all of his love. We only have an idea of his actions that are the effects of love, as we have found by experience, and of those external things which belong to love and which appear in case of love. Or if we have any idea of it, it is either by forming our ideas so of persons and things, as we suppose they appear to them, that we have a faint vanishing notion of that affection; or if the thing be a thing that we so hate that this can't be, we have our love to something else faintly, at least, excited, and so in the mind, as it were, referred to that place. We think this is like that.

239. *Spiritual knowledge.* From what has been said under the foregoing head, we know wherein spiritual knowledge consists. For seeing, in order to the knowledge of spiritual things, there must be those things in the mind (at least in order to a knowledge anything clear and adequate), sinners must be destitute even of the ideas of many spiritual and heavenly things and of divine excellencies, because they don't experience them. 'Tis impossible for them so much as to have the idea of faith, trust in God, holy resignation, divine love, Christian charity, because his mind is not possessed of those things, and therefore can't have an idea of the excellencies and beauties of God and Christ, of which those things are the image. He knows not the things of the Spirit of God.   (Undated)

On the Medium of moral Government—particularly Conversation*

1. By *conversation*, I mean intelligent beings expressing their minds one to another, in words, or other signs intentionally directed to us for our notice, whose immediate and main design is to be significations of the mind of him who gives them. Those signs are evidences distinguished from works done by any, from which we may argue their minds. The first and most immediate design of the work is something else than a mere signification to us of the mind of the efficient. Thus, I distinguish God's communicating his mind to us by word or conversation, from his giving us opportunity to learn it by philosophical reasoning; or, by God's works which we observe in the natural world.

2. There is a great difference between God's *moral* government of his creatures, that have understanding and will, and his general government of providential disposal.—The nature, design, and ends of the latter, by no means require that it should be declared and made visible by a revelation of the methods, rules, particular views, designs, and ends of it: these are secret things that belong to God; in which men's understandings and wills are no way concerned. There is no application to these faculties in it; nor are these faculties any otherwise concerned, than the qualities or properties of inanimate and senseless things.

But it is quite otherwise with respect to God's moral government of a kingdom or society of intelligent and willing creatures; to which society he is united as its head, ruling for its good. The nature of that requires, that it should be declared, open and visible. How can any moral government be properly and sufficiently established and maintained in a kingdom of intelligent agents, consisting in exhibiting, prescribing, and enforcing methods, rules, and ends of their own intelligent voluntary actions, without declaring, and particularly promulgating to their understandings, those methods, rules, and enforcements? The moral government of a society, in the very nature of it, implies, and consists in an application to their understandings, in directing the intelligent will, and enforcing the direction by the declaration made.

3. It is needful, in order to a proper moral government, that the ruler should enforce the rules of the society, by threatening just punishments, and promising the most suitable and wise rewards. But without word or voluntary declaration, there is no threatening or promising in the case, in a proper sense. To leave the subject to find out what reward would be wise, if there

---

* *Works of President Edwards*, vol. 7 (New York, 1830).

appear in the state of things room for every subject to guess at it in some degree, would be a different thing from *promising* it. And to leave men to their own reason, to find out what would be a just, deserved, and, all things considered, a wise punishment, though we should suppose some sufficiency in every one's reason for this, would be a different thing from *threatening* of it.

It is needful in a moral kingdom, not in a ruined and deserted state—the union between the head and members remaining—that there should be conversation between the governors and governed. It is requisite that the former should have intercourse with the latter in a way agreeable to their nature; that is by way of *voluntary signification* of their mind to the governed, as the governed signify their minds voluntarily one to another. There should be something equivalent to conversation between the rulers and ruled; and thus the rulers should make themselves visible. The designs and ends of government should be made known; it should be visible what is aimed at, and what grand ends or events are in view, and the mind of the rulers should be declared as to the rules, measures, and methods, to be observed by the society. If the rulers are sovereign, absolute disposers, it is necessary their will should be particularly declared, as to the good and evil consequence of obedience or disobedience, which they intend as moral enforcements of the rules and laws, to persuade the will to a compliance. For they can reach the will, or affect it at all, no further than they are made known.—It is requisite something should be known, particularly, of the nature, weight, and degree of the rewards and punishments, and of their time, place, and duration.

4. Thus, it is requisite that it should be declared what is the end for which God has made us, and made the world; supports it, provides for it, and orders its events. For what end mankind are made in particular; what is intended to be their main employment; what they should chiefly aim at in what they do in the world: how far God, the Creator, is man's end; and what man is to aim at with respect to God, who stands in no need of us, and cannot be in the least dependent on us: how far, and in what respect, we are to make God our highest end; and how we are to make ourselves, or our fellow-creatures, our end: what benefits man will have by complying with his end; what evils he shall be subject to by refusing, or failing so to comply, in a greater or lesser degree. If we have offended, and deserved punishment, it must be known on what terms (if at all) we may be forgiven and restored to favor; and what benefits we shall receive, if we are reconciled.

It is apparent, that there would be no hope that these things would ever be determined among mankind, in their present darkness and disadvantages, without a revelation. Without a revelation—now extant, or once extant, having some remaining influence by tradition—men would undoubtedly for ever be at a loss, what God expects from us, and what we may expect from him; what we are to depend upon as to our concern with God, and what ground we are to go upon in our conduct and proceedings that relate to him; what end we are to aim at; what rule we are to be directed by; and what good, and what harm, is to be expected from a right or wrong conduct. Yea, without a revelation, men would be greatly at a loss concerning God; what he is; what manner of being; whether properly intelligent and willing; a being that has will and design, maintaining a proper, intelligent, voluntary dominion over the world. Notions of the first being, like those of Hobbes and Spinosa, would prevail. Especially would they be at a loss concerning those perfections of God, which he exercises as a moral governor. For we find that some of the deists, though they, from revelation, have been taught these; yet, having cast off revelation, apparently doubt of them all. Lord Bolingbroke, in particular, insists that we have no evidence of them.

5. And though, with regard to many, when they have a revelation fully setting forth the perfections of God—giving a rational account of them, and pointing forth their consistence—their reason may rest satisfied in them; this is no evidence that it is not exceeding needful that God should tell us of them. It is very needful that God should declare to mankind what manner of being he is. For, though reason may be sufficient to confirm such a declaration after it is given, and enable us to see its consistence, harmony, and rationality, in many respects; yet reason may be utterly insufficient first to discover these things.

Yea, notwithstanding the clear and infinitely abundant evidences of his *being*, we need that God should tell us that there is a great Being, who *understands*, who *wills*, and who has made and governs the world. It is of unspeakable advantage, as to the *knowledge* of this, that God has told us of it; and there is much reason to think, that the notion mankind in general have entertained in all ages concerning a Deity, has been very much originally owing to revelation.

On the supposition, that God has a moral kingdom in the world, that he is the head of a moral society, consisting either of some part of mankind, or of the whole; in what darkness must the affairs of this moral kingdom be carried on, without a communication between the head and the body; the ruler never making himself known to the society by any word, or other equivalent expression whatsoever, either by himself, or by any mediators, or messengers?

6. So far as we see, all moral agents are *conversible* agents. It seems to be so agreeable to the nature of moral agents, and their state in the universal system, that we observe none without it; and there are no beings that have even the semblance of intelligence and will, but possess the faculty of con-

versation; as in all kinds of birds, beasts, and even insects. So far as there is any appearance of something like a mind, so far they give *significations* of their minds one to another, in something like conversation among rational creatures. And, as we rise higher in the scale of beings, we do not see that an increase of perfection diminishes the need or propriety of communication and intercourse of this kind, but augments it. And accordingly, we see most of it among the most perfect beings. So we see conversation by voluntary immediate significations of each other's minds, more fully, properly, and variously, between mankind, than any other animals here below. And if there are creatures superior to mankind united in society, doubtless still voluntary converse is more full and perfect.

Especially do we find conversation proper and requisite between intelligent creatures concerning *moral* affairs, which are most important: affairs wherein especially moral agents are concerned, as joined in society, and having union and communion one with another. As to other concerns that are merely personal and natural, wherein we are concerned more separately, and by ourselves, and not as members of society, in them there is not equal need of conversation.

7. Moral agents are *social* agents; affairs of morality are affairs of society. It is concerning moral agents as united in society, in a commonwealth or kingdom, that we have been speaking. Particular moral agents so united, need conversation. The affairs of their social union cannot well be maintained without conversation. And if so, what reason can be given, why there should be no need of conversation with the head of the society? The head of the society, so far as it is united with it on a *moral* ground, is a social head. The head belongs to the society, as the natural head belongs to the body. And the union of the members with the head is greater, stricter, and more important, than one with another. And if their union with other members of the society require conversation, much more their greater union with the head. By all that we see and experience, the *moral* world, and the *conversible* world, are the same thing; and it never was intended, that the affairs of society, in any that are united in society among intelligent creatures, should be upheld and carried on without conversation.

There is no more reason to deny God any conversation with 'his moral kingdom, in giving laws, and enforcing them with promises and threatenings, than to deny him any conversation with them in another world, when judging them. But, can any that believe a future state, rationally imagine, that when men go into another world to be judged by their Supreme Governor, nothing will pass or be effected through the immediate interposition of the judge, but all things be left wholly to go on according to laws of nature established from the beginning of the world: and that souls pass into another state by a law of nature, as a stone, when shaken off from a building, falls down by gravity, without any miraculous signification from God? But there is as much reason to suppose this, as to deny any miraculous interposition in giving and establishing the laws of the moral society. If judgment and execution by law, be by immediate interposition and declaration, why not legislation?

8. The *ground* of moral behavior, and all moral government and regulation, is society, or mutual intercourse and social regards. The special medium of union and communication of the members of the society, and the being of society as such, is conversation; and the well-being and happiness of society is friendship. It is the highest happiness of all moral agents; but friendship, above all other things that belong to society, requires conversation. It is what friendship most naturally and directly desires. By conversation, not only is friendship maintained and nourished, but the felicity of friendship is tasted and enjoyed. The happiness of God's moral kingdom consists, in an inferior degree, in the members' enjoyment of each other's friendship; but infinitely more in the enjoyment of their head. Therefore, here especially, and above all, is conversation requisite.

9. Conversation between God and mankind in this world, is maintained by God's *word* on his part, and by *prayer* on ours. By the former, he speaks and expresses his mind to us; by the latter, we speak and express our minds to him. Sincere friendship towards God, in all who believe him to be properly an intelligent, willing being, does most apparently, directly and strongly, incline to prayer; and it no less disposes the heart strongly to desire to have our infinitely glorious and gracious Friend expressing his mind to us by his word, that we may know it. The same light which has directed the nations of the world in general to prayer, has directed them to suppose, that God, or the gods, have revealed themselves to men. And we see, that the same infidelity that disposes men to deny any divine revelation, disposes them to reject as absurd the duty of prayer.

10. If God's moral kingdom, or the society of his friends and willing subjects, shall be in a most happy state in another world—in the most complete friendship, and in perfect union with God their head, as some of the deists pretend to believe—is it reasonable to suppose any other, than that they will fully enjoy the sweets of their friendship one with another, in the most perfect conversation, either by words, or some more perfect medium of expressing their minds? And shall they have at the same time, no conversation at all with their glorious head, the fountain of all the perfection and felicity of the society, in friendship with whom their happiness chiefly consists? That friendship, and the happiness they have in it, is begun in this world; and this is the state wherein they are trained up for that more perfect

state: and shall they nevertheless live here wholly without any intercourse with God of this sort; though their union with him, as their moral head, and their great friend, begins here; and though their happiness, as consisting in friendship to him, and also the enjoyment of that subordinate happiness of holding a virtuous and holy conversation one with another, be begun here? The need of conversation in order properly to support and carry on the concerns of *society*, may well appear, by considering the need of it for answering all the purposes of *friendship*, which is one of the main concerns of society, in some respects the main social concern, and the end of all the rest.

Let us suppose, that some friend, above all others dear to us, in whose friendship consisted the main comfort of our life, should leave us in possession of something he had contrived and accomplished, some manifold complicated effect that he had produced which we might have always in our view. Suppose also that this work should be a very great and manifold evidence of the excellencies of our friend's mind, of his great, fixed, and firm benevolence to us; and that he should withdraw for ever, and never have any conversation with us; that no word should ever pass, or any thing of that nature; and that no word should be left behind in writing, nor any word ever spoken left in the memory: would this sufficiently and completely answer the purposes of this great friendship, and satisfy its ends and desires, or be a proper support of this great end of society? I cannot but think, every sober, considerate person will at once determine, that it would be very far from it, for such reasons as these,—that it would not give us those views of things, pertaining to the support and enjoyment of friendship, suitable to the nature of intelligent, volitive, and conversible beings; not giving the direct and immediate view, nor at all tending, in so great a degree and so agreeable a manner, to affect and impress the mind. And as, for these reasons, this alone would not answer the ends and purposes of society in this respect; so, for the same reasons, it would not answer the other purposes of society.

11. As we may suppose, that God will govern mankind, in that moral kingdom which he hath mercifully set up among them, in a manner agreeable to their nature; so it is reasonable to suppose, that he would make his moral government, with respect to them, *visible*, not only in declaring the *general* ends, methods, and rules of his government, but also by making known the chief of his more *particular* aims and designs. As in human kingdoms, in order to the wisdom, righteousness, and goodness of the administration being properly visible—so far as is requisite for encouraging and animating of the subject, and in order to the suitable convenience, satisfaction, and benefit of the whole society of intelligent agents—it is needful, not only that the general end, *viz.* the public good, should be known, but also the particular design of many of the principal parts of the administration, among which

we may reckon the main negotiations, treaties, and changes of affairs, the cause and end of wars engaged in, the ground of treaties of peace and commerce, the design of general revolutions in the state of the kingdom, &c. Otherwise the society is not governed in a manner becoming their rational and active nature; but affairs are carried on in the dark, and the members have no opportunity to consent or concur, to approve or disapprove, to rejoice in the goodness, wisdom, and benefit of the administration, and to pay proper regards to those in whose hands the government is, &c. These things are necessary for the establishment and confirmation of the government. God's moral government over his moral kingdom on earth, cannot, in such like respects, be carried on in a visible manner, and in a way suitable to our nature, without divine history and prophecy. Without divine history, we cannot properly see the grounds and foundation of divine administrations, the first formation or erection of God's moral kingdom, the nature and manner of the main revolutions to which it has been subject, which are the ground of future designs, and to which future events and intended revolutions have a relation. It is also necessary that those past events should be known, in order that the reason, wisdom, and benefit of the present state of the kingdom, and of God's present dispensations towards it, may be known. And prophecy is needful to reveal the future designs and aims of government, and what good things are to be expected.

These things are necessary, in order to the proper establishment, health and prosperity, of God's moral, intelligent kingdom. Without them, the government of an infinitely wise and good head, is not sensible. There is no opportunity to see the effects and success of the administration. There is no opportunity to find it by experience. Neither the designs of government, nor the accomplishment of those designs, are sensible; and the government itself, with respect to fact, is not made visible.

12. If it be said, that reason and the light of nature, without revelation, are sufficient to show us, that the end of God's government, in his moral kingdom, must be, to promote these two things among mankind, *viz.* their virtue and their happiness:

In reply, I would ask, What satisfaction can men without revelation have, with respect to the design, wisdom, and success of God's government, as to these ends, when wickedness so generally prevails and reigns, through all ages hitherto, in the far greater part of the world; and the world, at all times, is so full of calamities, miseries, and death, having no prophecies of a better state of things in which all is to issue at last, in the latter ages of the world; or assuring us that all these miserable changes and great confusion are guided by Infinite Wisdom to that great final issue, and without any revelation of a future state of happiness to the city of God in another world?

13. OBJECT: God does maintain a moral government over all mankind: but we see, in fact, that many are not governed by revelation, since the greater part of the world have been destitute of divine revelation: which shows that God does not look upon conversation as necessary in order to his moral government of mankind; as God judges for himself, and acts according to his own judgment.

ANSWER 1: What I have been speaking of, is God's moral government over a society of moral agents, which are his kingdom, or a society that have God for their king, united to them as the head of the society; as it is with earthly kings with respect to their own kingdoms, where the union between king and subjects is not broken and dissolved; and not of a society or country of rebels, who have forsaken their lawful sovereign, withdrawn themselves from subjection to him, and cast off his government: though they may still be under the king's power, and moral dominion, in some sense, as he may have it in his power and design, to conquer, subdue, judge, and punish them for their rebellion. But yet the sense in which such a nation is under the moral government of this king, and may be said to be his kingdom or people, is surely extremely diverse from that of a kingdom remaining in union with their king. In the case of a people broken off from their king, maintaining of intercourse by conversation is in no wise in like manner requisite. The reasons for such intercourse, which take place in the other case, do not take place in this.

In that case, society ceases; *i.e.* that union ceases between God and man, by which they should be of one society. And where society ceases, there the argument for conversation ceases. If a particular member of the society were wholly cut off, and ceases to be of the society—the union being entirely broken—the argument for conversation, the great medium of social concerns, ceases. So if the body be cut off from the head, or be entirely disunited from it, intercourse ceases. Moral government in a society is a *social* affair; wherein consists the intercourse between superior and inferior constituents, between that which is original, and that which is dependent, directing and directed in the society. It is proper, in this case, that the rebel people should have sufficient means of knowing the end of their rebellion, and that it is their duty to be subject to their king, to seek reconciliation with him, and to inquire after his will. But while they remain obstinate in their rebellion, and the king has not received them into favor, the state of things does not require, that he should particularly declare his intentions with respect to them, or should open to them the designs and methods of his administration. It is not necessary that he should publish among *them* the way and terms of reconciliation; make revelations of his goodness and wisdom and the great benefits of his government; converse with them as their friend, and so open the way for their being happy in so great a friend; or that he should so particularly and immediately publish among them, particular statutes and rules for their good, as a society of moral agents, &c. Conversation, in this sense, when there is an utter breach of the union, is not to be expected, nor is it requisite, though judging and condemning may.

ANSWER 2: So far as the union between God and the Heathen world has not been utterly broken; so far they have not been left utterly destitute of all benefit of divine revelation. They are not so entirely and absolutely cast off, but that there is a possibility of their being reconciled; and God has so ordered the case, that there is an equal possibility of their receiving the benefit of divine revelation.

If the Heathen world, or any parts of it, have not only enjoyed a mere possibility of being restored to favor, but have had some advantages for it, so, a great part, yea, mostly the greater part of the Heathen world, have not been left merely to the light of nature. They have had many things, especially in the times of the Old Testament, that were delivered to mankind in the primitive ages of the world by revelation, handed down from their ancestors by tradition; and many things borrowed from the Jews. And, during those ages, by many wonderful dispensations towards the Jews—wherein God did in a most public and striking manner, display himself and show his hand —the world had, from time to time, notices sufficient to convince them, that there was a divine revelation extant, and sufficient to induce them to seek after it. And things sufficient to make revelation public, to spread it abroad —to extend the fame of it and its effects to the utmost end of the earth, and to draw men's attention to it—have been vastly more and greater in later times, than in the primitive ages.

ANSWER 3: The nations that are separated from the true God, and live in an open and obstinate full rejection of him as their supreme moral Governor, reject all friendly intercourse while their state is such. They are open enemies; and, so far as God treats them as such, he does not exercise any friendly moral government over them. And they have light sufficient without revelation, for any other exercise of moral government and intercourse, besides those that are friendly, *viz.* in judging and condemning them. They have light sufficient for that judgment and condemnation, of which they shall be the subjects. For their condemnation shall proceed no further, than proportioned to their light. They shall be condemned for the violation of the law of nature and nations; and the degree of their condemnation shall be only answerable to the degree of the means and advantages they have had for information of the duties of this law, and of their obligations to perform them.

ANSWER 4: What has appeared in those parts of the world which have been destitute of revelation, is so far from being any evidence that revelation

is not necessary, that in those nations and ages which have been most destitute of revelation, the necessity of it has most evidently and remarkably
appeared, by the extreme blindness and delusion which have prevailed and
reigned, without any remedy, or any ability in those nations to extricate
themselves from their darkness.

14. I think, a little sober reflection on those opinions which appear among
the deists, weighing them together with the nature of things, may convince
us, that a general renunciation of divine revelation, after nations have
enjoyed it, would soon bring those nations to be more absurd, brutish, and
monstrous in their notions and practices, than the heathens were before the
gospel came among them. For, (1.) Those nations had many things among
them derived originally from revelation, by tradition from their ancestors,
the ancient founders of nations, or from the Jews, which led them to embrace
many truths contained in the scripture; and they valued such tradition. It
was not in general, their humor to despise such an original of doctrines,
or to contemn them because they had their first foundation in divine revelation, but they valued them the more highly on this account; and had no
notion of setting them aside, in order to the drawing of every thing from the
foundation of their own reason. By this means, they had a great deal more
of truth in matters of religion and morality, than ever human reason would
have discovered without helps. But now, the humor of the deists is, to reject
every thing that they have had from supposed revelation or any tradition
whatsoever, and to receive nothing but what they can clearly see, and demonstrate from the fountain of their own unassisted reason. (2.) The heathens,
by tradition, received and believed many great truths, of vast importance,
that were incomprehensible; and it was no objection with them against
receiving them, that they were above their comprehension. But now, it is a
maxim with the free-thinkers, that nothing is to be believed but what can
be comprehended; and this leads them to reject all the principles of natural
religion (as it is called) as well as revealed. For there is nothing pertaining to
any doctrine of natural religion, not any perfection of God, no, nor his very
existence from eternity, without many things attending it that are incomprehensible. (3.) The heathens of old, in their reasonings, did not proceed
in that exceeding haughtiness and dependence on their own mere singular
understanding, disdaining all dependence on teaching, as our deists do;
which tends to lead one to reject almost all important truths, out of an
affectation of thinking freely, independently, and singularly. Some of the
heathens professed their great need of teaching, and of *divine* teaching.
(4.) The heathens did not proceed with that enmity against moral and divine
truth, not having been so irritated by it. They were willing to pick up some

scraps of this truth which came from revelation, which our deists reject all in the lump.

15. If we suppose that God never speaks to, or converses at all with mankind, and has never, from the beginning of the world, said any thing to them, but has perfectly let them alone, as to any voluntary, immediate, and direct signification of his mind to them, in any respect teaching, commanding, promising, threatening, counselling or answering them; such a notion if established, would tend exceedingly to atheism. It would naturally tend to the supposition, that there is no Being that made and governs the world. And if it should nevertheless be supposed, that there is *some* Being who is, in some respect, the original of all other beings; yet this notion would naturally lead to doubt of his being properly an intelligent, volitive Being; and to doubt of all duties to him implying intercourse, such as prayer, praise, or any address to him, external or internal, or any respect to him at all analogous to that which we exercise towards rulers or friends, or any intelligent beings we here see and know; and so it would tend to overthrow every doctrine and duty of natural religion. Now, in this respect, deism has a tendency to a vastly greater degree of error and brutishness, with regard to matters of religion and morality, than the ancient heathenism. For the heathens in general had no such notion, that the Deity never at all conversed with mankind in the ways above-mentioned; but received many traditions, rules, and laws, as supposing they came from God, or the gods, by revelation.

16. Many of the free-thinkers of late deceive themselves, through the ambiguity or equivocal use of the word *Reason*. They argue that we must make our reason the highest rule by which to judge of all things, even of the doctrines of revelation; because reason is that by which we must judge of revelation itself. It is the rule on which our judgment of the truth of a revelation depends, and therefore undoubtedly must be that, by which particular doctrines of it must be judged: not considering that the word *reason* is here used in two senses. In the former, *viz.* in our judging of the divinity of a supposed revelation, the word means the *faculty* of reason taken in the whole extent of its exercise: in the latter, it is the *opinion* of our reason, or some particular opinions that have appeared rational to us. Now, there is a great difference between these two. It is true, the faculty of reason is that by which we are to judge of every thing, as it is the eye by which we see all truth. And after we have received revelation, still, by the faculty of reason, we receive the particular doctrines of revelation, yea, even those that are most difficult to our comprehension. For, by the faculty of reason we determine this principle, that God knows better than us; and whatever God declares is true. But this is an exceedingly different thing from making an *opinion*, which

we first established without revelation, by reason only, as our rule to judge of particular doctrines which revelation declares. It may be illustrated by this: If there be a man with whom we have the most thorough acquaintance, and have long known to be a person of the soundest judgment and greatest integrity, who goes a journey or voyage to a place where we never were; and, when he returns, gives an account of some strange phœnomena or occurrences that he was an eye-witness of there, which we should not have otherwise believed; but we believe them now to be true, because we rely on his testimony. Here, it would be ridiculous for a man to say, that it is unreasonable to believe him, because what he says is not agreeable to reason, (meaning, by *reason*, that particular *opinion* we should have had, independent of his testimony;) and urging that *reason*, must be our highest rule, and not his testimony, because it is by our *reason* that we judge of the testimony, and credibility of the man that testifies; meaning, in this case, the *faculty* of reason. This would be as unreasonable, as for a man to say, that he never will rely on any representation made by the best microscope or telescope that is different from the representation which he has by the naked eye; because his eye is the rule by which he sees even the optic glass itself, and by which he judges whether it be regularly made, tending to give a true representation of objects; urging that his eye must be the highest rule for him to determine by, because it is by the eye he determines the goodness and sufficiency of the glass itself; and therefore he will credit no representation made by the glass, wherein the glass differs from his eyes; and so will not believe that the blood consists partly of red particles, and partly of a limpid liquor, because it appears all red to the naked eye; not considering the different sense in which he uses the word *eye*. In the former case, *viz.* with respect to judging of the goodness of the optic glass, he means the sense of seeing, or the organ of sight. In the latter, when he says he will not believe the representation of the glass, wherein it differs from his eye, because his *eye* is the highest rule: by the *eye*, he means the particular *representation* he has by his eye, separately, and without the glass.

17. Again: They blunder exceedingly, through not making a distinction between *reason* and a *rule of reason*. They say, that reason is our highest rule by which to judge of all things and therefore they must judge of the doctrines of revelation by it; whereas, they seem not to consider what they mean by reason being the highest rule. It is true, our reason or understanding is the only *judging faculty* by which we determine truth and falsehood. But it is not properly our highest *rule of judging* of truth and falsehood, nor any rule at all. The *judge*, and the *rule* by which he judges, are diverse. A *power* of discerning truth, and a *rule* to regulate and determine the use of that power, are quite different things. The *rule* may be divine revelation, especially in

matters of religion. As it is with the faculty or organ of sight, the organ is not properly the *highest* means, but the only *immediate* means we have of discerning the objects of sight. But if men were talking of *rules* how to *use* their eyes to the best advantage, so as to see most certainly and clearly—to see the most distant or the minutest objects, so as to have the most certain and full information—it would be ridiculous for any one to say that his *eye* was the highest *rule* to regulate his sight.

18. Sometimes, by the word *reason*, is intended the same as *argument* or *evidence*, which the faculty of reason makes use of in judging of truth: as when we say, we should believe nothing without, or contrary to *reason;* that is, we should not give the assent of our judgments without, or against *evidence*, or, something that appears which argues the thing to be true. But if this be meant by them who assert reason to be a rule superior to revelation, it is absurd in them thus to speak of reason as contra-distinguished from revelation. To say, that argument or evidence is a higher rule than revelation, is to make evidence and divine revelation entirely distinct; implying, that divine revelation is not of the nature of evidence or argument. They ought to explain themselves who assert, that *evidence* is superior to the evidence we have by divine revelation. It is true, divine testimony is not the same thing as argument or evidence in general; because it is a particular sort of evidence. There are other particular sorts of evidence; and persons might speak as intelligibly, if they single out any other kind of evidence, and assert, that reason or evidence was superior to that sort of evidence. As for instance, one sort of evidence is human testimony of credible eye-witnesses; another is credible history; another is memory; another is present experience; another is geometrical mensuration; another is arithmetical calculation; another is strict metaphysical distinction and comparison. Now, would it not be an improper and unintelligible way of speaking, to ask, whether *evidence* was not above *experience?* or whether *argument* was not above *mensuration* or *calculation?* If they who plead, that reason is a rule to judge of truth superior to revelation, mean by *reason, that* evidence, which is worthy to influence the faculty of reason; it seems not to be considered by them, that such evidence, when spoken of in general, *comprehends* divine testimony, as well as other sorts of evidence; unless they would entirely set aside divine revelation, as carrying in it no evidence at all. If this be their meaning, they are deceitful; for this is not what they pretend: since it would entirely change the point in dispute, and alter the whole controversy.

Or if, when they say reason is a higher rule than revelation, they mean reason *exclusive* of revelation, or that such arguments of truth as we have without revelation, are better than divine testimony; that is as much as to say, all other arguments are better than divine testimony. For reason or argument, without divine testimony, comprehends all other arguments that are without divine testimony: and then, this is as much as to say, that divine testimony is the very least and lowest of all possible arguments, that ever can occur to the mind of man, in any measure to influence his judgment; which meaning they will hardly own. On the whole, it is manifest, that, let us turn the expressions which way we will, all the boasted proof of their assertion is owing wholly to confusion, and an ambiguous use of terms; it is talking without ideas, and making sounds without fixing any distinct meaning.

19. Here, if any, in disdain of such an imputation, shall say, "I see no necessity of supposing this assertion to be so unreasonable and unintelligible. By reason, we mean *that* evidence which is seen by reason simply considered; reason itself, without dependence on the dictates of another; viewing things as they are in themselves:" such an objector is mistaken, if he thinks he has got clear of the difficulty. All evidence whatsoever, even that by divine revelation, is included in his description of reason. It is by viewing things *as they are* in themselves, and judging by our *own* reason, and not by the reason of another, that we judge there is a divine revelation, and that we judge divine revelation must be agreeable to truth. Reason judges by viewing things as they are in themselves, not the less because it makes use of a *medium* of judgment; and when reason makes use of divine testimony as an evidence or medium of judgment, it judges as much by viewing things as they are in themselves, as when it makes use of any other medium of judgment; as, for instance a measuring rod in judging of distances, a compass in judging of directions and courses, and figures and characters in calculating and determining numbers.

If any should say, that *reason*, in our inquiries after truth, is to be regarded as a rule superior to *experience*, this—according to what would be most naturally suggested to the mind by such a saying, and might generally be supposed to be intended by it according to the more usual acceptation of words—would be a foolish assertion. For by the comparison which takes place in the proposition between *reason* and *experience*, reason would be understood in such a sense as that it might properly be set in opposition to experience, or taken in contradiction to it; and therefore the proposition must be understood thus, *viz.* That our highest rule is what our reason would suggest to us independent of experience, in the same things that are matters of experience. Or, what our reason would lead us to suppose *before* experience, is what we must regard as our highest rule, even in those matters that afterward are tried *by* experience. Certainly, he that should proceed in this manner in his inquiries after truth, would not be thought wise by considerate persons.

20. Yet it is really true, in some sense, that our reason is our highest rule;

and that by which we are to try and judge of all things: even our experience and senses themselves must be tried by it. For we have no other faculty but our reason, by which we can determine of truth or falsehood, by any argument or medium whatsoever. Let the argument be testimony or experience, or what it will, we must judge of the goodness or strength of the argument by reason. And thus it is we actually determine, that *experience* is so good and sure a medium of proof. We consider the nature of it; and our reason soon shows us the necessary connexion of this medium with truth. So we judge of the degree of dependence that is to be had on our senses by reason; by viewing the agreement of one sense with another, and by comparing, in innumerable instances, the agreement of the testimonies of the senses with other criteria of truth, and so rationally estimating the value of these testimonies.

But if this is what is meant by saying, that our reason is a surer rule than experience, it is an improper way of speaking, and an abuse of language. For, take reason thus; and so reason and experience are not properly set in contradiction, or put in comparison one with another; for the former includes the latter, as the genus includes the species, or as a whole includes the several particular sorts comprehended in that whole. For, judging by experience is one way of judging by reason, or rather, experience is one sort of argument which reason makes use of in judging. And to say that reason is a more sure rule than experience, is to say, that arguing is a more sure rule than a particular way of arguing: or to say that argument (in general) is a more sure rule than that particular sort of argument, *viz.* experience. Or if, by reason, is meant the *faculty of reason*, or that power or ability of the mind, whereby it can see the force of arguments; then such an assertion will appear still more nonsensical. For then, it is as much as to say, that the mind's *ability* to see the force of arguments, is a surer rule by which to judge of truth, than that particular argument, *viz.* experience; which is the same as to say, an ability to judge of arguments is a surer argument than that sort of argument, experience; or that a man's understanding is a better rule to understand by, than such a particular means or rule of understanding.

These observations concerning reason and experience, when these two are compared as rules by which to judge of truth, may be applied to reason and revelation, or divine testimony, when in like manner compared as distinct rules of truth. To insist, that men's own reason is a rule superior to divine revelation, under a pretense, that it is by reason that we must judge even of the authority of revelation; that all pretended revelations must be brought to the test of reason; and that reason is the judge whether they are authentic or not, &c., is as foolish as it would be to assert, for the like reasons, that man's own *reason* is a test of truth superior to *experience*. There is just the same fallacy in the arguments that are brought to support one and the other of these foolish assertions; and both are, for reasons equally forcible, very false, or very nonsensical.

21. If the assertion of those who say, that men's own reason is a higher test of truth than divine revelation, has any sense in it, it must imply a comparison of *different sorts* of arguments or evidences of truth; and so the meaning of it must be, that those evidences of truth, which men find before they have the help of divine revelation, are a better criterion of truth, than any discovery they have by revelation. And their great argument to prove it, is this, that the faculty of reason, by which the mind is able to discern the force of truth, is the only faculty by which we are able to judge of the value and force of revelation itself. It is just such a sort of arguing, as if a person should go about to demonstrate, that a man could more certainly discover the form and various parts of the planets with the naked eye, than with a telescope; because the eye is that by which we see all visible things, yea by which we see and discern how to use and to judge of the goodness of telescopes themselves.

In the argument these men use, to prove that reason is a better test of truth than revelation, they wretchedly deceive themselves, by sliding off from the meaning which they give to the word *reason* in the premises, into another meaning of it exceedingly diverse in the conclusion. In the premises, wherein they assert, that reason is that by which we judge of all things, even of revelation itself, they mean either the *power* of discerning evidence; or the *act* of reasoning in general. The consequence they draw is, therefore, reason is a higher test of truth than revelation. Here if they retained the same sense of the word as in the premises, the conclusion would be perfect nonsense. For then, the conclusion would be thus: The *power* or the *act* of discerning evidence, is a better *evidence* of truth, than divine revelation. But this is not what is intended to be understood. What is intended in the conclusion, is, that the evidence we have before we have revelation, or independently of it, is better and more certain than revelation itself.

22. The outward provision which God makes through the ages of the world for the temporal benefit and comfort of mankind, in causing his sun to shine, and his rain to descend upon them, and in numberless other things, is a great argument that God was not determined to be their everlasting, irreconcileable enemy. And if God be reconcileable, it will follow, that he must make a revelation to mankind, to make known to them the terms and methods of reconciliation. For God, who is offended, alone can tell us, on what terms he is willing to be reconciled; and how he will be at peace with us, and receive us to favor. And there surely is nothing which can be pretended to be any revelation of this kind, if the holy scripture is not.

23. OBJECTION. The scriptures are communicated to but few of mankind; so that if a revelation of the method of reconciliation be necessary, a very great part of those who enjoy these external benefits and bounties of divine providence, still have no opportunity to obtain reconciliation with God, not having the benefit of that revelation. So that, notwithstanding these seeming testimonies of favor and placableness, it is all one to them, as if God was irreconcileable. For still, for want of the knowledge of the method of reconciliation, it is all one to them, as though there were no such method, and as though no reconciliation were possible.—To this, I answer,

1st. The case of mankind is not just the same as if there were no such thing as reconciliation for mankind, or as though reconciliation were utterly impossible. For although the circumstances of a great part of the world be such, that their reconciliation be very improbable, yet is not utterly impossible. There is a way of reconciliation, and it is publicly known in the world; and God has ever afforded opportunity to the generality of the habitable world, that if the minds of men had been as much engaged in the search of divine truth as they ought to have been, they might have felt after God, and found him; and might probably have come to an acquaintance with divine revelation.

2d. If there have been some parts of mankind, in some ages, for whom it was next to impossible that they should ever come to know that revelation which God has made, yet that hinders not the force of the argument for God's placableness to sinners and the existence of a revealed method of reconciliation. The common favors of Providence may be a proof, that God intends favor to *some* among mankind, but yet be no proof that he intends that *all* shall actually have the benefits of his favor. None will deny, but that those outward blessings of God's goodness were intended for the temporal benefit of *mankind;* and yet there are numbers who never actually receive any temporal benefit by many of them. None will doubt, but that God aimed at men's outward good, in providing grain, and grapes, and other fruits, which the earth produces for man's subsistence and comfort in the world; as also the most useful animals. But yet a very great part of the world were for a long time wholly destitute of the most useful of these. All the innumerable nations that dwelt on this American side of the globe, were from age to age, till the Europeans came hither, wholly destitute of wheat, rye, barley, pease, wines, horses, neat cattle, sheep, goats, swine, poultry, and many other useful animals and fruits, which abounded in the other continent.

And it is probable, that some of those gifts of nature and providence, which are most useful to mankind, were what all men remained without the benefit of for many ages; as metals, wine, and many things used for food, clothing, and habitations. The loadstone, with regard to its polar direction, was doubtless intended for the use of mankind; but yet it is but lately that any of them have had any benefit of it. Glass is a great gift of providence, and yet but lately bestowed; and also some of the most useful medicines. And with regard to those things which are most universally useful, some have the benefit of them in vastly lesser degrees than others; as the heat of the sun, vegetation, &c.

24. If it should be further objected, That, if God's true aim in these outward benefits of providence, which have the appearances of favor, be real favors to mankind, and so that the true happiness of mankind should be the consequence; one would think it would have the same effect in all places where those blessings are bestowed.

I answer, that it will not follow. God may grant things in all parts of the world, the main design of which may evidently be the benefit of mankind, and yet not have that effect in all places where they are given. As the main design of him who orders the existence of rain in the world, is making the earth fruitful; yet it does not follow, that he designed this should actually be the effect of all parts of the globe where the rain falls. For it falls on the sea as well as the dry land, which is more than one half the globe; but yet *there* it cannot answer this intention.

25. Reason alone cannot certainly determine, that God will not insist on some satisfaction for injuries he receives. If we consider what have in fact been the general notions of mankind, we shall see cause to think, that the dictates of men's minds, who have been without revelation, have been contrariwise, *viz.* that the Deity will insist on some satisfaction. Repentance makes some satisfaction for many injuries that men are guilty of one towards another; because it bears some proportion to the degree of injury. But reason will not certainly determine, that it is proper for God to accept of repentance as some satisfaction for an offense, when that repentance is infinitely disproportionate to the heinousness of the offense, or the degree of injuriousness that is offered. And reason will not certainly determine, that the offense of forsaking and renouncing God in heart, and treating him with such indignity and contempt, as to set him below the meanest and vilest things, is not immensely greater, and more heinous, than any injury offered to men; and that therefore all our repentance and sorrow fall infinitely short of proportion in measure and degree. If it be said, that we may reasonably conclude, and be fully satisfied in it, that a good God will forgive our sin on repentance; I ask, what can be meant by repentance in the case of them that have no love nor true gratitude to God in their hearts, but who discover such an habitual disregard and contempt of God in their conduct, as to treat created things, of the lowest value, with greater respect than him? If it be said, that thereby is meant being sorry for the offense; I ask, whether that sorrow is worthy

to be accepted as true repentance, that does not arise from any change of heart, or from a better mind, a mind more disposed to love God, and honor him, being now so changed as to have less disregard and contempt? whether or not the sorrow which arises only from fear and self-love, with a heart still in rebellion against God, be such as we can be certain will be accepted? If not, how shall a man, who at present has no better heart, but yet is greatly concerned for himself through fear, know how to obtain a better heart? How does it appear, that he, if he tries only from fear and self-love, can make himself better, and make himself love God? what proper tendency can there be in the heart to make itself better, until it sincerely repents of its present badness? and how can the heart have sincerity of repentance of the present badness, until it begins to be better, and so begins to forsake its badness, by truly disapproving it, from a good disposition, or a better tendency arising in it? If the disposition remain just the same, then no sincere disapprobation arises; but the reigning disposition, instead of destroying, on the contrary, approves and confirms itself. The heart can have no tendency to make itself better, until it begins to have a better tendency; for therein consists its badness, *viz.* having no good tendency or inclination. And to begin to have a good tendency, or, which is the same thing, to begin to have a sincere inclination to be better, is the same thing as to begin already to be better. So that it seems, that they that are now under the reigning power of an evil heart, can have no ability to help themselves, how sensible soever they may be of their misery, and concerned through fear and self-love to be delivered; but they need this from God, as part of their salvation, *viz.* that God should give them sincere repentance, as well as pardon and deliverance from the evil consequences of sin. And how shall they know, without revelation, that God will give sinners a better heart, to enable them truly to repent; or in what way they can have any hope to obtain it of him? And if men could obtain some sincere repentance of their being wholly without that love of God that they ought to have; yet how can reason determine, that God will forgive their sin, until they wholly forsake it? or until their repentance is perfect? until they relinquish all their sinful contempt, ingratitude, and regardlessness of God? or, which is the same thing, until they fully return to their duty, *i.e.* to that degree of love, honor, gratitude and devotedness to God, that is their duty? If they have robbed God, who can certainly say that God will forgive them, until they restore all that they have robbed him of, and give him the whole that he claims by the most absolute right? But where is any man that repents with such a perfect repentance? and if there be ever any instances of it in this world, who will say, that it is in every man's power to obtain it? or that there certainly are no lower terms of forgiveness? and if there are, who can tell certainly where to set the bounds, and say precisely to what degree a man must repent? How great must his sorrow be in proportion to his offences, &c.? Or, who can say, how long a man's day of probation shall last? Will reason alone certainly determine, that if a man goes on for a long time presumptuously in his contempt, rebellion, and affronts, presuming on God's goodness, depending, that though he does thus abuse his grace as long as he pleases, yet if he repents at any time, God will forgive him, and receive him to favor, forgiving all his presumptuous aggravated rebellion, ingratitude and provocation and will receive him into the arms of his love? will reason alone fully satisfy the mind, that God stands ready to pardon and receive to favor such a sinner, after long continuance in such horrid presumption and most vile ingratitude? Or, will reason fully determine for a certainty, that God will do it, if men thus presumptuously spend their youth, the best part of their lives, in obstinate and ungrateful wickedness, depending that God will stand ready to pardon afterward: and, in short, how can reason alone be sufficient to set the bounds, and say how long God will bear with and wait upon presumptuous sinners? how many acts of such ingratitude and presumption he will be ready to forgive, and on what terms, &c.? I say, how can reason fix these limits, with any clear evidence that shall give the mind a fixed establishment and satisfaction?

Therefore if there be any such thing as the forgiveness and salvation of sinful men; new relations of God to men, and concerns of God with men, and a new dependence of men on God, will arise, no less, probably much more important, than those which are between God as man's creator, and the author of his natural good. And as God must manifest his perfections in a new work of redemption or salvation, contrived and ordered by his infinite wisdom, and executed by his power—in a perfect consistence with his justice and holiness, and a greater manifestation of his goodness, than is made in his works as the author of nature—so these things must be the foundation of new regards to God, new duties, and a new religion, founded on those displays of his perfections in the work of salvation, and on the new relations God sustains towards men, and the new dependence of men on God, and new obligations laid on men in that work, which may be called *revealed religion*, different from that natural religion which is founded on the works of God, as the creator and the author of nature, and our concerns with God in that work; though not at all contrary to it.

The light of nature teaches that religion which is necessary to continue in the favor of the God that made us: but it cannot teach us that religion which is necessary to our being restored to the favor of God, after we have forfeited it. (Undated)

II

The Colonial South and the Middle Colonies

Unlike the literature of Puritan New England, that of the colonial South and the Middle colonies belongs mostly to the eighteenth century. Little was written in those regions earlier: in the South, some works by George Sandys and John Smith, some elegies and histories arising from Bacon's Rebellion in Virginia, and several promotional tracts; in New Amsterdam, some poems in Latin and Dutch by a group of Dutch Calvinist ministers; in Pennsylvania, an early anti-slavery essay and some miscellaneous works by the learned German Pietist Francis Pastorius, but nothing by the Quakers, who thought belles-lettres frivolous.

The South. Lack of means, not of desire, probably explains the scarcity of literature in the early South. The region had no paper mills or printing presses until the 1720's. Once established, southern presses rolled off several volumes by local poets and the many essays and poems that regularly appeared in such lively periodicals as the Maryland, South Carolina, and Virginia *Gazettes*. Given means for publication, polite literature in the South flourished, since many upper-class southerners considered verse and essay writing necessary accomplishments for a gentleman. Works by many southern writers appeared in the chief periodicals of eighteenth-century England. Some who wrote gathered into convivial literary clubs loosely modelled on those of London. The mid-eighteenth-century poets of Annapolis, for example, kept a lengthy record of the meetings of their Tuesday Club, replete with drawings, poems, and toasts. While poetry and the essay came later to the South than to New England, drama came earlier, because there were few Puritans about to condemn it and none in power to forbid it. In 1736, students at William and Mary College produced plays by Addison and Farquhar. By the 1750's, cities like Charleston and Williamsburg supported travelling companies of English actors. For their productions southern poets often wrote prologues, and two or three southerners wrote plays themselves. In all, literature became a popular diversion in the South between 1700 and the Revolution, and for a few a serious art. Just how popular and how serious remain uncertain. Scholars have just begun to dig out and evaluate the literary record of the early South. The selections that follow include both recently uncovered and classic early southern works.

Heading the list of classics for their wit and precision are the writings of the Virginian WILLIAM BYRD II (1674–1744). He was born at Westover, a 26,000-acre James River estate with a main building of elegant proportions and appointments. Yet he spent all but two years between the ages of ten and thirty-one living abroad. England offered what Virginia could not: a sound classical education, training at the Middle Temple in London, and the friendship of important writers like Wycherly and Congreve. Byrd returned to England periodically, but for the rest he stayed at Westover, writing, making the best of a stormy marriage, and trying to maneuver himself into the Virginia ruling hierarchy. By the time of his death he had amassed 180,000 acres and, like his contemporary Cotton Mather, a personal library of over three thousand volumes, plus a fellowship in the Royal Society.

Much of what we know about the social life of colonial Virginia we know through Byrd's extensive *Diaries*. But far more than they are social records, the *Diaries* are confessions, the secret, wholly private ruminations of a unique man, writing in code to free and to safeguard his candor. Unlike a Puritan, Byrd does not scrutinize his soul for signs of grace. Instead he records his daily routine: what he ate for dinner, what play or coffeehouse he attended, what he read in Italian, Dutch, Hebrew, Greek, or Latin; whether he said or forgot to say his prayers, whether he "danced his dance" (did his exercises), his success or failure as a rake in Williamsburg or London. What he chooses to record—his way of seeing himself—expresses the transformation of the English personality under the influence of the southern frontier. Byrd experienced America, compared to the temptations of London, as a deprivation. Yet he was determined to make the best of it, which meant turning it as nearly as possible into London. Always counting fretfulness a vice, he commanded himself to make do. In his *Journey to the Land of Eden*, for instance, he remarks that "My knees pained me very much, though I broke not the laws of traveling by uttering the least complaint." With the same resigned restraint he tells the Earl of Orrery that life in Virginia "reconciles a man to himself." His hunger for society going unsatisfied, Byrd turns even the labor of managing a plantation, as he tells the Earl, into a sort of "amusement," and he notes appreciatively that at least Virginia has none of London's grime and crime. Thus the rather wearied but contented tone of the *Diary* as Byrd charges himself with acting like a gentleman while living in "this silent country." The effect of repetition in the *Diary* comes from his determination to maintain, though on the frontier, a gentleman's regime. Each day's entry appears in monotone declarative sentences or sentence fragments that preserve the bare fact that he said his prayers, read a bit in some foreign or classical tongue, got around in local society—did, in short, what a gentleman is supposed to do. Each day he scrutinizes his life to see how well he stuck to the mark.

The mark Byrd aimed at included the exercise of his sexual prowess. No reader can miss his coarsely matter-of-fact fascination with love-making. His somberly bemused interest in matrimonial relations, in aphrodisiacs and anaphrodisiacs—indeed the sexual and amorous undercurrent in much southern writing—sharply distinguishes the southern literary tradition from the northern Puritan tradition, to whose taste Byrd would have seemed impiously crude. Byrd's longings for women are at one extreme social and at the other pathological. Desire sometimes arises from his belief that feminine company can polish a man's behavior and sharpen his wit. He carefully divides his public and private lives, and vows to say nothing profane or indecent in good company. Man of honor and friend to temperance though he is, his principles keep clashing with his inclinations. His *Diaries* show him alternately proud of his potency and humiliated by his need to demonstrate it. As he fails to control his inclinations, guilt follows lust, and he often goes to sleep asking God's pardon for polluting himself. The doleful sketch of himself as a dismal, solemn, bashful lover in "Inamorato L'Oiseaux" (a Frenched version of his own name) may explain his need to prove himself as a sexual machine. The conflict in Byrd between the man of honor and the frontier lecher reminds one of the later, more intensely destructive conflicts in such southern heroes as Faulkner's Quentin Compson. Altogether, Byrd emerges through his sketches and *Diaries* as nothing on the heroic scale, but with the winningly fallible humanity of some character in Chaucer.

Byrd's most considered work is his *History of the Dividing Line*, a product of his having helped to settle a boundary dispute between Virginia and North Carolina in 1728. The *History* is a somewhat bowdlerized version of his earlier, lustier *Secret History*, which he disinfected of its *Tom Jones*-like quarreling, vomiting, drunkenness, diarrhea, and raunchiness. But he also elegantly polished the account. The later version turns the exhausting backwoods march into an urbane sort of *Travels* that combines scenic description, natural curiosities, humorous reflections, and woodcraft. Byrd makes a genial and sly guide to the American frontier. Always intent on observing manners, he provides a wealth of precise and solid information on Indian clothing, habits, and sexual practices. Ever a philosopher of love, he tells us that bear meat enhances potency and argues for miscegenation as bound to improve race relations: "a sprightly lover is the most prevailing missionary." Ever paternal, he is outraged that among the Indians women do the heavy work. And especially, Byrd is ever a gentleman. Morally and aesthetically he keeps his distance from the frontier vulgarity he observes. His own love of energy, of "dancing his dance," sets him apart from the lazy North Carolinians, loitering away their lives in Lubberland. He explains the quick collapse of the earlier southern settlements by the settlers' indolent hope that in America to want is to have. Polite but rugged, in love with propriety but aghast at effeminacy, Byrd is a New World version of the ideal of the Christian gentleman, a uniquely native mixture of scout and gent.

The same blend of strength and grace explains Byrd's power as a writer and makes the *History* more than a cultural document. Byrd had a sharp eye and an answerable pen. He did not have to labor under the supernaturalism of New England, which usually turned nature into something abstract. Nor was he burdened with the "poetic." To come from the gentility of Cooper and Irving's descriptions of the frontier to Byrd is to feel that this is the way the frontier must have been. The *History* gives one of the most solidly alive pictures of the frontier in all American literature. A century before Cooper, Byrd gave the dignity of print to native material. If art, as Emerson said, is the statement of an enormous preference, Byrd was an artist. He risked writing about what interested him, even if it were only how to cook a glue broth. His idiomatic style laced with wit, his resilient rhythms—as relaxed but firmly composed as his toughly elegant self—give presence and a shapely delight to his head-on descriptions of opossums and bears. His chillingly perfect rendering of a rattlesnake as it eats a squirrel is worthy of a first-rate novelist.

While this realism in Byrd represents an artistic gain over the supernaturalism or gentility of much other American writing about nature, it also represents a loss. The loss comes in philosophy, indeed thought. And the loss persists to distinguish southern literature from northern.

Significantly few important American philosophers have been raised in the South. Emerson, James, Pierce, Santayana, and Dewey were all born or trained in New England. The gain, however, comes in close notation of the social and natural scene, the kind of realism that characterizes such later southern writers as the Fugitives. To generalize broadly, the metaphysical and inward identifies the Puritan tradition in American writing, the tradition of Melville and Hawthorne; the social and outward identifies the southern tradition.

Such generalizations, of course, must be elaborately qualified, especially after the Civil War. And even colonial southern culture is not summed up in Byrd. In fact, the following selection from *The Religion of the Bible* (probably written by a southern Presbyterian named James Reid) attacks what Byrd stands for. Addressed to the inhabitants of King William County in Tidewater Virginia in 1769, it deplores the failure of the upper classes to live up to the concept of the Christian gentleman. Berating the southern ruling classes for their pride, greed, miscegenation, gluttony, and arrogance, it mocks the very ideal which Byrd strove to perpetuate by his daily ritual. Against this ideal the author opposes the medieval Christian idea of "gentilesse," the civility attaching not to money, birth, property, or horse racing, but only to greatness of soul. He denounces the "young Ass-queers" who, like Byrd, spend their time wenching and attending cockfights and live to "Play without ceasing." Many southern descriptions of southern life treat this seemingly regional prankishness, illustrated by Byrd and a few friends ordering a Quaker to drink the Queen's health on his knees—the same rather sadistic, boyish capering that leads Huck and Tom to lock up Nigger Jim.

Life in Maryland also supplied subjects and a tone for several interesting writers. We know little about the lives of the two early Maryland poets RICHARD LEWIS (fl. 1725–1746) and EBENEZER COOK (fl. 1708–1732). Lewis, a schoolmaster in Annapolis, was perhaps the most skillful neoclassic poet in America. In versifying his journey toward the Patapsco River, near present Baltimore, he craftily uses alliterative and rhythmic techniques to give variety and emphasis to his many detailed, affectionate vignettes of American scenery and wildlife along the way. The journey he describes is metaphorical as well. As the poem moves from day to night, youth to age, nature to God, exploring man's relation to the universe in view of eighteenth-century science and philosophy, the journey becomes an image of life itself. Reprinted several times in America and England, the poem won Lewis much praise. Pope, however, included him in *The Dunciad* for writing about trifles like the mocking-bird—a standard English reaction to colonial attempts at local color.

Ebenezer Cook, apparently a tobacco trader in Maryland, wrote several elegies, a poem on the economics of tobacco, a verse history of Bacon's Rebellion, and two differing versions of *The Sot-weed Factor*. The difference is that the second version finds little to praise in Maryland while the first, reprinted here, finds nothing at all to praise. In rollicking hudibrastic verse whose close rhythms and metronomic beat themselves express his unequivocal, curt contempt, Cook shows his distaste for everything in the place: the inhabitants are thieves, bumpkins, or drunks who sleep with lice, guzzle rum for breakfast, get bilked by local merchants, take their suits to corrupt courts, and live at the mercy of nature at her strangest and most ferocious. Much of what galls Cook reappears for disapproval in later southern writing: the dis-respect for law returns in the Georgia rednecks wrestling before the statehouse in the nineteenth-century sketches of Augustus Baldwin Longstreet; the omnipresent drunken torpor and flashing savagery foreshadow the landscapes of Tennessee Williams; the mean, cheating merchants live again in the awful Snopes family of Faulkner's Yokna-patawpha saga. More important, there also recurs the distance between a gentlemanly narrator and the corrupt, vulgar lower classes he observes.* Cook revealingly signed his poem "Ebenezer Cook, Gent." The frontier world which the tobacco factor finds hot, uncomfortable, and vastly weird is the same world from which Byrd escapes through his daily ritual.

As in Byrd's *History*, the narrator's aloof stance is a loss but also a gain. Lost is the *pietas*, the pride in the community, that marks much New England writing. With some exceptions, the contrasting mark of much early southern writing is its distaste for the place. The gain, how-ever, is in clear-sightedness and vigor. Cook ridicules lower-class vulgarity by transcribing lower-class speech. He thus introduces into the poem a hoard of local words and phrases—Americanisms—and by malice produces a poetic language strikingly different from the language

---

* For a discussion of this theme see Kenneth S. Lynn, *Mark Twain and Southwestern Humor* (Boston, 1959).

of contemporary English poetry. The difference makes *The Sot-weed Factor* one of the first genuinely American poems.

A generation after Cook, a spirited group of Maryland writers grew up around the Annapolis Tuesday Club and *The Maryland Gazette*, founded in 1745. The following selection of their works illustrates the social nature of literature in the mid-eighteenth-century South and the taste for satirical writing in southern gazettes. The essay is probably by the founder of the Tuesday Club, ALEXANDER HAMILTON (1712–1756), a physician and litterateur in Annapolis. In a vision framework, Hamilton evaluates the belletristic writing published in the *Gazette* during its first three years. He flatters local culture little more than does Ebenezer Cook; he regrets the "Vice and Ignorance that prevail in this *Infant Province*" due to lack of education, and he complains that the *Gazette* puts him to sleep. Only pages of footnotes could identify all of the local writers to whom Hamilton alludes. To explain his judgments, at least in part, three of the writers he mentions have been included: "Juba," "Ned Type" (Benjamin Franklin, who had visited the Tuesday Club), and "that wonderful Imitator of Horace," probably the poet JAMES STERLING (1701–1763; Sterling's present imitation of Horace, however, appeared later than the one Hamilton names). Franklin's poem takes off on a speech delivered by Governor Gooch to a special session of the Virginia Assembly following a fire which destroyed the capitol at Williamsburg in 1747. It also takes off on the reply of the Council, which lamented that the religious enthusiasm introduced into Virginia by itinerant preachers might prove even more inflammatory. Actually, the capitol magniloquently praised by Gooch was little more than an old courthouse.

Marylanders enjoyed Franklin's parody of the extravagant tone of the speeches, whose language he followed closely. By satirizing the Council's willingness to see the old courthouse as "the CAPITOL!" and its bloated sense of affront to the Virginia aristocracy, "the CREAM of the British Nation," Franklin turned the gentleman's self-applauding hauteur back on the Gent himself.

Benjamin Franklin and Philadelphia. Franklin was the outstanding personality and writer of what was an ambitious if provincial culture. By the middle of the eighteenth century, Philadelphia had become the third largest city in the English empire, after London and Liverpool. By the end of the century it had become the first American literary center. The many wealthy people who settled in the city and its suburbs built the fine homes and held the literary salons where the city's cultured and active social life was concentrated. Franklin organized a group of self-taught writers and philosophers into a club called The Junto. Later a group of poets and essayists gathered around the influential William Smith, provost of the University of Pennsylvania, including such original and gifted writers as Thomas Godfrey, Nathaniel Evans, and Francis Hopkinson. Some noted scientists also lived in Philadelphia, such as the botanists John and William Bartram and the physician Benjamin Rush. The culture boom, one writer complained, made local housewives more interested in poems than in puddings.

Since the *Autobiography* of BENJAMIN FRANKLIN (1706–1790) is essential reading, what follows ignores the facts of Franklin's life for the sake of the larger view. Like Cotton Mather, whom he knew during his boyhood in Boston, Franklin remains one of the most intriguing and controversial figures in American culture. Judgments of him become judgments of America, in no way more so than by arousing both admiration and abhorrence in both critics and sympathizers. What, then, was Franklin like?

Foremost, he was remarkably independent and self-reliant. Always willing to go it alone, he achieved an exhilarating personal freedom. One rarely finds him halted by a sense of difficulty or mystery, and never incapacitated; he might have adopted the saying which Balzac inscribed on the head of his cane: "I crush every obstacle." Less kindly, one could say that he lacked the tragic sense. Yet he achieved his freedom by a difficult and classic route. The original self-made man, he grew up in Boston but scoffed at hallowed Harvard. In his teens he left his family and went to Philadelphia. He became the first dropout in American culture, the prototype of many later Ishmaels, Huck Finns, and catchers in the rye. Franklin, however, dropped back in, and moving into ever wider circles, became one of the most famous men in an age of famous men, a citizen of the world. Always shedding old skins, making himself new, he was forever growing.

Franklin maintained the process of self-renewal by refusing to force old solutions on new problems. Pragmatic and open-ended, he believed with Emerson that "every wall is a door." "The best public Measures," he said, are "seldom *adopted from previous Wisdom*, but *forc'd by the*

Occasion." A master of getting things done, he thrived on practical challenges: how to keep the city streets clean, improve the postal system, use the energy of a rocking chair to fan oneself and swat flies, reach a book down from a high shelf. In allowing problems to suggest their own solutions he anticipated Emerson, James, and Dewey, the later line of American pragmatists. Fabulously inventive and successful, he avoided any suggestion of superiority and refused to take himself seriously. In his parody of a meditation by an English minister, chosen here, he scorns puritanical breast-beating and proposes that instead of complaining that we are not angels, we should be happy that we are not oysters. The beautiful "Optimistic Meditation" that closes his parody declares that time eases pain, and that man is free to behold nature and to use his reason. Borrowing the form and language of religious discourse, the declamatory confidence of the "Meditation" suggests how Franklin made personal freedom the basis of a new, secular religion.

Merely to relate Franklin's freedom, pragmatism, and optimism to later ideals of American personality is to omit the important question of value: to what end? The use Franklin made of his qualities often turns his readers against him and against America. D. H. Lawrence treated him as a specimen of American aridity, a "Snuff-colored little man" concerned with everything but his own soul. Melville considered him "everything but a poet." William Carlos Williams accused him of a satanic pride in wanting to touch and try everything, get his hands on it, manipulate it. To be sure, Franklin's desire to control nature, to question what men accept ordinarily as their limitations, can produce a space flight or, just as easily, a Captain Ahab. Other critics of American culture denounce Franklin as a high priest of capitalism, worshipping at the shrine of Get Ahead. Are his stoves, bifocals, and rocking chairs anything more than the work-saving comforts of barbecue patio America, the pampering gadgetry of the ultimate bourgeois? Surely again, in becoming the first millionaire Franklin at times adopted an ultimately vicious view of human nature. His famous essay "The Way to Wealth"—an anthology of aphorisms culled from his Poor Richard almanacs—puts industry and frugality in the service of a colorlessly vulgar and ungenerous ideal: "Fools make feasts and wise men eat them." Equating generosity with stupidity and sponging with wisdom, Franklin's watchword seems to be "Look out for number one." In the essay "On the Laboring Poor," reprinted here, he belittles a proposed welfare program as bound to multiply beggars by encouraging indolence, and he adds that the trouble with the poor is that they waste their money at alehouses. He came to believe that the state was supreme, superseding private interests, and to think of the common man as a menace to social order.

On the other hand, Franklin often "got ahead" by acts of principled benevolence that at once eased his own life and benefited the race. Like Cotton Mather, whose influence he acknowledged, he hoped to do good. Franklin the technocrat hoped to do good to mankind by improving its material condition, and he refused to patent his inventions. Equally, Franklin hoped to alleviate such social ills as slavery. He wrote his essay "On the Slave Trade" (dated only twenty-four days before his death) in response to attempts by southern congressmen to justify slavery, following a proposal to Congress by Franklin's own Society for Abolition. The essay applies the pro-slavery arguments of the representative from Georgia to Europeans, a typical Franklin strategy. Typically too, Franklin connects abolition with a large ideal of freedom that shudders at the dehumanizing effects of slavery on the intellect and the "social affections." His penny pinching itself aims at this large freedom. In "The Way to Wealth" he explains that his prescriptions reflect the need to master one's financial affairs in order to be independent: "Be industrious and free; be frugal and free." It could be said that he desired wealth only to secure leisure enough to indulge his interests.

The problem of whether Franklin was benefactor or social climber, saint or salesman, occurs in considering Franklin the writer as well. He felt that his youthful experiments in writing had contributed to his worldly success. Prose, he concluded, should be "smooth, clear, and short," since the contrary qualities "are apt to offend, either the Ear, the Understanding, or the Patience." The strength of this unimprovable formula for a style that intends to communicate and persuade appears in Franklin's letter to Mary Stevenson explaining the relation between heat and color—an essential example of his clear-headed, self-effacing genius for putting complicated matters in simple terms. His formula resembles the Puritan theory of the plain style, with a difference. The plain style intended making God's word available to its audience by speaking to it simply; Franklin's style intends coercing its audience by not offending it. In much of his prose Franklin adopted a manner which he accurately termed "modest diffidence." He noted, for instance, that he published his "Proposal relating to the Education of Youth in Pennsylvania" under the name of some public-minded men, to avoid "according to my usual Rule, the presenting myself to the Public as the Author of any Scheme for their Benefit." He turned this rule into a narrative device.

In order to persuade, Franklin often chooses some downtrodden or passive spokesman, such as the widow Silence Dogood or Poor Richard. He wins converts to his views by winning sympathy for the woebegone, feeble, or oppressed persons, the naifs and witless Yankees who defend them. This doubleness of Franklin's style, this subtly arm-bending diffidence, makes him a sort of pastoralist, regarding the great urban world from the viewpoint of a simpler, truer one, usually to mock its extravagance and self-importance, as he uses the demoralized Widow Dogood to make fun of the self-appointedly great of Boston. An inveterate jokester and punster, he was forbidden to write the Declaration of Independence, Jefferson reportedly said, because he might slip a joke into it, as he does even in his sober letter on the barometer to Mary Stevenson. After discussing the medicinal use of cantharides, an aphrodisiac, he adds that "thousands owe their lives to this knowledge." With some of the cleverness of the dropout forced to shift for himself, the resourcefulness of a Huck Finn, he enjoyed showing up or putting on his rivals and superiors. Indeed the cultivated self-mistrust in Franklin's writing, to be less kind again, amounts to getting ahead without seeming to—the art of the soft sell. More interested in persuasion than in expression, Franklin is perhaps more justly called a great rhetorician than a great writer.

In one minor literary genre Franklin did excel. He was probably the greatest parodist in the history of American literature. Given here, along with his parody of Governor Gooch's speech and the English minister's meditation, are his parodies of a New England elegist, of an edict by the King of Prussia, and of a Yankee sermonizer (Father Abraham's speech). Parody is an exquisite literary act. It succeeds only with a writer quickly sensitive to how style registers conduct. Sensitive in just this way, Franklin's parodies and burlesques not only propose or attack an idea; they equally propose or attack a way of thinking. The target of Franklin's mimicry is the larger vehicle: the pompousness of southern oratory, the cold arrogance of royal proclamations, the solemnity and parochialism of the New England elegy. The occasion of his satire always moves beyond the immediate one of slavery, conscription, or elegiac writing. Eventually what is at stake is a style of thought. His parody of the New England elegy repudiates the whole New England culture, the way of feeling that the style and form epitomize. Able to take off on anybody, Franklin conveys through his parodies and burlesques a great literary freedom and power matching his personal freedom and power. His many identifications with others indicate the many selves one can be. Many of the specific roles Franklin chose to play—a New England widow, a southern congressman, a young pregnant Philadelphia girl—derive from the ever more distinct American scene. His flexibility and sympathy themselves seem products of a mobile, restless democratic society in which people seek out new identities, confident that one can be and do anything.

With his knack for impersonation, his ability to feel himself into someone else's place, his remarkable variety of voices, Franklin unexpectedly reminds one of Whitman. Whitman also loved roles and poses, and postured himself into magic kinship with the expanding variety of American life. Statesman, scientist, writer, printer, librarian, educator, soldier, Franklin lived out Whitman's mimic oneness with America:

> Of every hue and caste am I, of every rank and religion,
> A farmer, mechanic, artist, gentleman, sailor, quaker,
> Prisoner, fancy-man, rowdy, lawyer, physician, priest.
>
> I resist any thing better than my own diversity. . .
>
> (*Song of Myself*)

And like Whitman, Franklin through his many phases remained "one of the roughs." In Franklin as in William Byrd, the American environment had begun to transform English character. Proud of being a Leather Apron Man rather than a son of Harvard, Franklin eloquently had inscribed on his tombstone, "Printer." His accomplished roughness predicts the ideal gardener Thomas Jefferson sought who could also play the French horn, the long list of American writers—Cooper, Melville, Hemingway, Faulkner, Mailer—who combined culture and masculinity, the downright and the transcendent.

Their progenitor was Poor Richard, the rough-hewn provincial naif whose very diffidence evidenced his shrewd intelligence and literary power. Probably the only resolution to the problem of Franklin is to say that he was modest *and* assertive, saint *and* salesman, benefactor *and* social climber. Neither half alone affords as perfect a mirror of America, or describes Franklin so well, as the uneasy union.

On literature in the colonial South see Hennig Cohen, *The South-Carolina Gazette 1732–1755* (Columbia, S.C., 1953); Richard Beale Davis, *George Sandys Poet-Adventurer* (New York, 1955); Jay B. Hubbell, *The South in American Literature 1607–1900* (Durham, N.C., 1954); Howard Mumford Jones, *The Literature of Virginia in the Seventeenth Century*, 2d ed. (Charlottesville, Va., 1968); Edmund S. Morgan, *Virginians at Home* (Charlottesville, Va., 1952); Louis B. Wright, ed., *The Prose Works of William Byrd of Westover* (Cambridge, Mass., 1966) and *The First Gentlemen of Virginia* (San Marino, Cal., 1940).

On Franklin and the literature of the Middle colonies see Alfred Owen Aldridge, *Franklin and his French Contemporaries* (New York, 1957); Carl and Jessica Bridenbaugh, *Rebels and Gentlemen: Philadelphia in the Age of Franklin* (New York, 1942); I. Bernard Cohen, *Franklin and Newton* (Philadelphia, 1956); Verner W. Crane, *Benjamin Franklin and a Rising People* (Boston, 1954); Bruce Ingham Granger, *Benjamin Franklin: An American Man of Letters* (Ithaca, N.Y., 1964); Ellis Raesly, *Portrait of New Netherland* (New York, 1945); Carl Van Doren, *Benjamin Franklin* (New York, 1938).

WILLIAM BYRD II

(1674–1744)

To compare the following selections from Byrd with those on pp. 142–154 is to begin a comparison of New England and the South. Sewall and Byrd were almost contemporaries, and the differences in their recorded lives show some of the contrast between life in the two sections in which they lived. Sewall presumably could not have written *Inamorato L'Oiseaux* because his personality differed from Byrd's and because his view of himself and the world differed from Byrd's. Some of the activities of the two men are so similar as to make the comparisons more striking; the accounts of social visits exemplify the contrast. Byrd is a Christian, but of quite a different sort from Sewall. Byrd is also a new man, an American, and his descriptions in the "Letter to Charles, Earl of Orrery" reveal his nationalistic spirit. *The History of the Dividing Line* shows the same spirit, much tempered by a sense of reality. The early frontier becomes believable in his descriptions.

The Religion of the Bible and Religion of King William County provides a contrast to Byrd's accounts and furnishes a view to be balanced with Byrd's. However different New England and the South may be, they cannot be characterized as holy and barbaric or Christian and heathen. The differences are in kind rather than quality between two vastly disparate cultures.

*Inamorato L'Oiseaux**

NEVER *did the sun shine upon a Swain who had more combustible matter in his constitution than the unfortunate Inamorato. Love broke out upon him before his Beard, and he cou'd distinguish sexes long before he cou'd the difference betwixt Good & Evil. . . . Tis well he had not a Twin-sister as Osyris[1] had, for without doubt like him he wou'd have had an amourette with her in*

---

* Maude H. Woodfin and Marion Tinling, eds., *Another Secret Diary of William Byrd* (Richmond, Va., 1942).

[1] Osiris: Egyptian god of the underworld whose sister, Isis, was also his wife.

his mothers belly. Love was born to him so long before Reason, that it has ever since slighted its rebukes, as much as old Fopps do the good sence of a young man. However this Frailty has never been without some check, For Diana threw such a Weight of Grace into the opposite scale, that the Ballance has commonly been held very even. And if the Love-scale has happen'd to be carry'd down sometimes, the Counterpoise has not fail'd to mount it up again very suddenly. The struggle between the Senate and the Plebeans in the Roman Commonwealth, or betweext the King and the Parliament in England, was never half so violent as the Civil war between this Hero's Principles and his Inclinations. Sometimes Grace wou'd be uppermost and sometimes Love, neither wou'd yeild and neither cou'd conquer. Like Cesar and Pompey one cou'd not bear an Equal nor t'other a superior. It must be confesst indeed, His Principles have been sometimes happily supported by the misadventures of his Love, by wch means its own cannon have been turn'd against it self. *This Foible has been an unhappy Clogg to all his Fortunes, and hinder'd him From reaching that Eminence in the World, which his Freinds and his Abilitys might possibly have advanct him to.* Nature gave him all the Talents in the World for business except Industry, which of all others is the most necessary. This is the spring and life and spirit of all preferment, and makes a man bustle thro all difficulty, and foil all opposition. *Laziness mires a man in the degree in which he was born, and clogs the wheels of the finest qualifications.* Fortune may make a Lazy Fellow great: but he will never make himself so. Diligence gives Wings to ambition by which it soars up to to [sic] the highest pitch of advancement. These Wings Inamorato wanted, as he did constancy, which is another ingredient to raise a great Fortune. To What purpose is it for a man to be always upon the wing, if he only fly backward and forward. He must go right out or else he will never go far. He shou'd fix one certain end in his own thoughts, and towards that all his designs, and all his motions shou'd unalterably tend. *But poor Inamorato had too much mercury to fix to one thing. His Brain was too hot to jogg on eternally in the same dull road. He liv'd more by the lively movement of his Passions, than by the cold and unromantick dictates of Reason. This made him wavering in his Resolutions, and inconstant after he had taken them. He wou'd follow a scent with great eagerness for a little while, but then a fresh scent wou'd cross it and carry him as violently another way.* One while the ease with which the Judges loll in their Coaches and doze upon the Bench, tempted him to study the Law: but he was soon taken off by the rapine and mercenariness of that Profession. Then the Gaity of St James's made him fancy to be a Courteour: but the falsness and treachery, the envy and corruption in fashion there quickly made him abandon that pursuit. When this fit was over he was charm'd with the Glory of serving in the army, and thought it a shame for a proper Fellow to live at home in ease, when the Libertys of Europe were in danger: but before he had provided his Equipage, he was discourag'd by the confinement, dependance, & barbarity of that service. *In some frolicks no state appear'd so happy to him as matrimony, the convenience, the tenderness the society of that condition, made him resolve upon his own ruine, and set up for a Wife. He fancy'd it too sullen too splenatique to continue single, and too liable to the inconveniences that attend accidental and promiscuous gallantry. In this humour he'd work himself violently in love with some nymph of good sence, whose Understanding forsooth might keep under all the impertinent starts of a Womans temper. And when he was in love no man ever made so disingageing a figure. Instead of that life and gaity, that freedome and pushing confidence which hits the Ladys, he wou'd look as dismal as if he appear'd before his Judge, and not his mistress. Venus and all the Graces wou'd leave him in the lurch in the critical time when they shou'd have assisted him most. When he ought to have had the most fire he had the most flegm, and he was all form and constraint when he shou'd have the most freedome and spirit. He wou'd look like a fool, & talk like a Philosopher, when both his Eys and his Tongue shou'd have sparkled with wit and waggery. He wou'd sigh as rufully as if he sat over a dead freind, and not a live mistress. No wonder this awkward conduct was without success for what woman wou'd venture upon a solemn swain that lookt more like her Confessor than her Gallant, and put her more in mind of a sullen Husband than a sprightly lover? The miscarriage of an honourable amour never disturb'd him so much, but that he wou'd sleep and look much better in his dispair, than he did in the hottest of his Expectation. He was not in half the jeopardy of hanging himself when he lost a mistress, that he was while he was in danger of getting her. While there was hopes he wou'd be assiduous to a fault, not considering that a little neglect in love (like saltpetre in Gunpowder) serves to give force to ye Passion. Whenever his bashfulness gave him leave to declare his mind something wou'd rise in his throat and intercept the untimely Question. A Woman is with more ease deliver'd of a huge boy, than he was of the painfull secret. His Ey-balls wou'd roul with as much gastliness as he had been strangled. Twas melancholly to see how his heart panted, his spirits flutter'd, his hands trembled, his knees knockt against one another, and the whole machine was in a deplorable confusion. You may guess how ingageing a Declaration must be that was attended with so many sorrowfull symptomes. It moved the Nymphs pity at least, if it cou'd not move her inclination. If she cou'd not be kind to a man to whome she had created so much disturbance, yet she cou'd not forbear being civil. Thus whenever Inamorato lost a mistress, he got a freind by way of equivalent, and so Providence made a good Bargain for him when he wou'd have made a wofull one for himself.* His Person was agreable enough tho he had a certain cast of pride in his look, which clouded some of the grace of it. Hardly any body likt him that did not know him, and nobody hated him that did. He had almost as many freinds as he had acquaintance and nobody ever fell out with him for any other reason: but because they thought he neglected them.

His conversation was easy, sensible and inoffensive, never bordering either upon profaness, or indecency. He was always tender of the modesty of those that were present, and of the reputation of those that were absent. He was incapable of saying a shocking thing, or of acting an unjust one. He was the never failing freind of ye unfortunate, and good nature was the constantest of all his virtues. He pay'd his Court more to obscure merit, than to corrupt Greatness. *He never cou'd flatter any body, no not himself, which were two invincible bars to all preferment.* He was much readyer to tell people of their faults, than their fine qualitys, because they were already too sensible of these, whereas they were too ignorant of the first. *His soul is so tun'd* to those things that are right, that he is too ready *to be moved at those that are wrong. This makes him passionate, and sorely sensible of Injurys, but he punishes himself more by the resentment than he dos the Party by revenge. If the sun go down upon his wrath twill be sure to rise upon his reconciliation. An Injury never festers or rankles upon his mind: but wasts its self in the First sally of indignation. He is frugal in all Expences upon himself, that he may be generous to the Distresst. He takes more pleasure to supply the wants of others than his own Wantoness.* His religion is more in substance than in form, and he is more forward to practice vertue than profess it. He is sincere to an indiscretion himself, and therefore abhors dissimulation in other people. He can sooner be reconcil'd to a professt Enimy than to a pretended Freind. Of all cheats in the world he has least charity for the Holy Cheat, that makes Religion bawd for his Interest and serves the Devil in the Livery of Godliness. His memory is in nothing so punctual as in performing of Promises. He thinks himself as firmly bound by his Word as by his hand & seal, and wou'd be as much asham'd to be put in mind of one, as to be sue'd for the other. He knows the World perfectly well, and thinks himself a citizen of it without the [. . .] distinctions of kindred sect or Country. He has learning without ostentation. By Reading he's acquainted with ages past, and with the present by voyageing & conversation, *He knew how to keep company with Rakes without being infected with their Vices, and had the secret of giveing Virtue so good a grace that Wit it self cou'd not make it ridiculous. He cou'd return from one of the Convents in Drury Lane with as much innocence, as any of the saints from a meeting. He Lov'd to undress wickedness of all its paint, and disguise, that he might loath its deformity.* His discretion never gave him an opportunity to try his courage, for he wou'd never provoke a [. . .] sober man, nor be provokt by a man in drink.

He never interlop't with anothers wife or mistress, but dealt altogether where the Trade was open & free for all Adventurers. If he reflected upon any one t'was by Irony, which a wise man wou'd take for a banter, and a fool for a complement. His Tongue was so far from embroiling the rest of his Person that upon some occasions it has happily protected it. *He abhors all excesses of strong drink because it wholly removes those Guards that can defend a man from doing & suffering Harm. He's a great freind to temperance, because tis the security of all the other virtues.* It disarms Flesh & bloud of those Tempests wth which it puts out all the lights of Reason. By talking little he is quit of a World of Folly & repentance. His silence proceeds not from want of matter, but from plenty of discretion. He is so great a freind to exactness, that he sometimes allows too little to the frailty of mankind. He wishes every body so perfect, that he overlooks the impossibility of reaching it in this World. He wou'd have men Angells before their time, and wou'd bring down that perfection upon Earth which is the peculiar priviledge of Heaven. This makes him a little too severe upon Faults, which it wou'd not be unjust to forgive. However he wou'd not have Transgressours punisht to procure them pain, but reformation. It proceeds from his hatred of the fault, and not of the offender. *He loves retirement, that while he is acquainted with the world, he may not be a stranger to himself.* Too much company distracts his thoughts, and hinders him from digesting his observations in good sence. It makes a man superficial, penetrateing no deeper than the surface of things. One notice crowds out another, haveing no time to sink into the mind. *A constant hurry of visits & conversation gives a man a habit of inadvertency, which betrays him into faults without measure & without end.* For this reason he commonly reserv'd the morning to himself, and bestow'd the rest upon his business and his freinds. *He often frequented the company of Women, not so much to improve his mind as to polish his behaviour.* There is something in female conversation, that softens the roughness, tames the wildness, & refines the indecency too common amongst the men. *He laid it down as a maxime that without the Ladys, a schollar is a Pedant, a Philosopher a Cynick, all morality is morose, all & behaviour either too Formal or too licentious. He has an excellent talent at keeping a secret, which neither love nor ressentment, Vanity nor lightness can ever draw from him. All the ingenious tortures of the Inquisition cant force him to betray either his Faith, or his Freind.* He always thought Ingratitude the most monstrous of all the vices, because it makes a man unfit for society, which subsists by mutual returns of kindness. *His good-nature is so universal as to extend to all Brute creatures. He can not see them ill us'd without the tenderest sentiments of compassion. They are helpless and must submit to all sorts of tyrany while men have some way or other of righting themselves. They have no refuge, no freind, no laws to protect them from injury, but are liable to suffer by the neglect, the wantoness, and cruelty of men. This hard fate he bemoans with a very sensible concern, and the rather, because they have often more merit than their oppressors.* (1723)

From *The Secret Diary**

1709

APRIL 6. . . . My wife and I disagreed about employing a gardener. I ate milk for breakfast. John made an end of trimming the boat, which he performed very well. I settled my accounts and read Italian. I ate nothing but fish for dinner and a little asparagus. We played at billiards. I read more Italian. In the evening we walked about the plantation after I read in Dr. Lister's book to the ladies. My wife and I continued very cool. . . .

7. . . . The men began to work this day to dig for brick. I settled my accounts and read Italian. I reproached my wife with ordering the old beef to be kept and the fresh beef used first, contrary to good management, on which she was pleased to be very angry and this put me out of humor. I ate nothing but boiled beef for dinner. I went away presently after dinner to look after my people. When I returned I read more Italian and then my wife came and begged my pardon and we were friends again. I read in Dr. Lister again very late. I said my prayers. I had good health, good thoughts, and bad humor, unlike a philosopher.

8. . . . My wife and I had another foolish quarrel about my saying she listened on the top of the stairs, which I suspected, in jest. However, I bore it with patience and she came soon after and begged my pardon. I settled my accounts and read some Dutch. Just before dinner Mr. Custis came and dined with us. He told us that my father Parke instead of being killed was married to his housekeeper which is more improbable. He told us that the distemper continued to rage extremely on the other side the Bay and had destroyed abundance of people. I did not keep to my rule of eating but the one dish. . . . The Indian woman died this evening, according to a dream I had last night about her.

October 6. I rose at 6 o'clock and said my prayers and ate milk for breakfast. Then I proceeded to Williamsburg, where I found all well. I went to the capitol where I sent for the wench to clean my room and when I came I

* Louis B. Wright and Marion Tinling, eds., *The Great American Gentleman* (New York, 1963).

kissed her and felt her, for which God forgive me. Then I went to see the President, whom I found indisposed in his ears. I dined with him on beef. Then we went to his house and played at piquet where Mr. Clayton came to us. We had much to do to get a bottle of French wine. . . .

December 3. . . . Eugene pissed abed again for which I made him drink a pint of piss. I settled some accounts and read some news. About 12 o'clock I went to court where I found little good company. However I persuaded Mr. Anderson and Colonel Eppes to come and dine with me. I ate a venison pasty for dinner. In the evening Mr. Anderson and I walked to Mr. Harrison's where we found Frank W-l-s and James Burwell and Isham Randolph. Here I ate custard and was merry. I stayed till 9 o'clock and when I came home my wife was in bed. . . .

1710

January 22. . . . About 11 o'clock we went to church and before we went in Mr. Harrison's horse ran away with his coach and broke down my mother's tombstone. Mr. Anderson gave us a good sermon and after church he and Colonel Hill and Mrs. Anderson and Mrs. B-k-r came and dined with us and so did Mr. C-s. I ate beef for dinner but ate too much. They went away about 4 o'clock and then Mr. C-s and I took a walk about the plantation. My daughter was indisposed and had a fever, for which I gave her a vomit of the tincture of ipecac. . . .

23. . . . My daughter slept very well this night and was well this morning. thank God. . . .

24. I could not sleep all night for the disturbance my daughter gave me. . . , I had my father's grave opened to see him but he was so wasted there was not anything to be distinguished. . . . In the evening I read nothing by my wife's desire. I had good health, good thoughts, and good humor, thanks be to God Almighty.

February 26. . . . In the afternoon we saw a good battle between a stallion and Robin about the mare, but at last the stallion had the advantage and covered the mare three times. The Captain's bitch killed another lamb for which she was beat very much. We took another walk about the plantation. My maid Anaka was very well again, thank God, and so was Moll at the quarters. My wife was out of humor with us for going to see so filthy a sight as the horse to cover the mare. In the evening we drank a bottle of wine and were very merry till 9 o'clock. . . .

1711

February 6. I rose about 9 o'clock but was so bad I thought I should not have been in condition to go to Williamsburg, and my wife was so kind to [say] she would stay with me, but rather than keep her from going I resolved to go if possible. I was shaved with a very dull razor, and ate some boiled milk for breakfast but neglected to say my prayers. About 10 o'clock I went to Williamsburg without the ladies. As soon as I got there it began to rain, which hindered about [sic] the company from coming. I went to the President's where I drank tea and went with him to the Governor's and found him at home. Several gentlemen were there and about 12 o'clock several ladies came. My wife and her sister came about 2. We had a short Council but more for form than for business. There was no other appointed in the room of Colonel Digges. My cold was a little better so that I ventured among the ladies, and Colonel Carter's wife and daughter were among them. It was night before we went to supper, which was very fine and in good order. It rained so that several did not come that were expected. About 7 o'clock the company went in coaches from the Governor's house to the capitol where the Governor opened the ball with a French dance with my wife. Then I danced with Mrs. Russell and then several others and among the rest Colonel Smith's son, who made a sad freak. Then we danced country dances for an hour and the company was carried into another room where was a very fine collation of sweetmeats. The Governor was very gallant to the ladies and very courteous to the gentlemen. About 2 o'clock the company returned in the coaches and because the drive was dirty the Governor carried the ladies into their coaches. My wife and I lay at my lodgings. Colonel Carter's family and Mr. Blair were stopped by the unruliness of the horses and Daniel Wilkinson was so gallant as to lead the horses himself through all the dirt and rain to Mr. Blair's house. My cold continued bad. I neglected to say my prayers and had good thoughts, good humor, but indifferent health, thank God Almighty. It rained all day and all night. The President had the worst clothes of anybody there.

7. . . . I went to see Mr. Clayton who lay sick of the gout. About 11 o'clock my wife and I went to wait on the Governor in the President's coach. We went there to take our leave but were forced to stay all day. The Governor had made a bargain with his servants that if they would forbear to drink upon the Queen's birthday, they might be drunk this day. They observed their contract and did their business very well and got very drunk today, in such a manner that Mrs. Russell's maid was forced to lay the cloth, but the cook in that condition made a shift to send in a pretty little dinner. I ate some mutton cutlets. In the afternoon I persuaded my wife to stay all night

in town and so it was resolved to spend the evening in cards. My cold was very bad and I lost my money. About 10 o'clock the Governor's coach carried us home to our lodgings where my wife was out of humor and I out of order. . . .

April 29. . . . I settled all my affairs and then went to Mr. Bland's to take my leave, which I did about 9 o'clock. Then I rode to my sister Custis' and found them pretty well, only my sister was melancholy. I comforted her as well as I could and then took a walk with my sister and brother in the orchard. About one o'clock Dr. Cocke came from Williamsburg and soon after we went to dinner and I ate boiled beef. In the afternoon we sat and talked till 3 o'clock and then I took my leave and went to Green Spring, and the Doctor returned home. I found a great deal of company with Colonel Ludwell who went away in the evening and we took a walk and romped with the girls at night. I ate some partridge and about 10 went to bed. I said a short prayer and had good health, good thoughts, and good humor, thank God Almighty. I had wicked inclinations to Mistress Sarah Taylor.

30. . . . I took my leave about 6 o'clock and found it very cold. I met with nothing extraordinary in my journey and got home about 11 o'clock and found all well, only my wife was melancholy. We took a walk in the garden and pasture. We discovered that by the contrivance of Nurse and Anaka Prue got in at the cellar window and stole some strong beer and cider and wine. I turned Nurse away upon it and punished Anaka. I ate some fish for dinner. In the afternoon I caused Jack and John to be whipped for drinking at John [Cross] all last Sunday. In the evening I took a walk about the plantation and found things in good order. . . . The weather was very cold for the season. I gave my wife a powerful flourish and gave her great ecstasy and refreshment.

May 1. I rose about 8 o'clock because the child had disturbed me in the night and read a chapter in Hebrew and some Greek in Lucian. I said my prayers and ate boiled milk for breakfast. I wrote to Mr. Randolph to have some copies of his county records and sent G-r-l with the letter. I caused Bannister to draw off a hogshead of cider which was very good. . . . I forgave Anaka, on my wife's and sister's persuasion, but I caused Prue to be whipped severely and she told many things of John Grills for which he was to blame, particularly that he lost the key of the wine cellar and got in at the window and opened the door and then because he had not the key the door was left open and anybody went in and stole the beer and wine &c. In the evening I took a walk with my wife and sister. . . . I received a letter with some records from Will Randolph. I gave my wife a short flourish.

October 20. I rose about 6 o'clock and drank tea with the Governor, who made use of this opportunity to make the Indians send some of their great men to the College, and the Nansemonds sent two, the Nottoways two, and the Meherrins two. He also demanded one from every town belonging to the Tuscaroras. About 9 the Governor mounted and we waited on him to see him exercise the horse and when all the militia was drawn up he caused the Indians to walk from one end to the other and they seemed very much afraid lest they should be killed. The Governor did nothing but wheel the foot, and Colonel Ludwell and I assisted him as well as we could. About noon the Governor ordered lists to be taken of the troops and companies that the people might make their claim to be paid, because they had been on the service five days. When this was done he gave liberty to the people to go home, except a troop and company for the guard that night. Then we went and saw the Indian boys shoot and the Indian girls run for a prize. We had likewise a war dance by the men and a love dance by the women, which sports lasted till it grew dark. Then we went to supper and I ate chicken with a good stomach. We sat with the Governor till he went to bed about 11 o'clock and then we went to Major Harrison's to supper again but the Governor ordered the sentry to keep us out and in revenge about 2 o'clock in the morning we danced a [g-n-t-r] dance just at his bed's head. However we called for the captain of the guard and gave him a word and then we all got in except Colonel Ludwell and we kept him out about quarter of an hour. Jenny, an Indian girl, had got drunk and made us good sport. . . .

November 13. . . . Mr. Graeme and I went out with bows and arrows and shot at partridge and squirrel which gave us abundance of diversion but we lost some of our arrows. We returned about one o'clock but found that Frank Lightfoot had broken his word by not coming to us. About 2 o'clock we went to dinner and I ate some venison pasty and were very merry. In the afternoon we played at billiards and I by accident had almost lost some of my fore teeth by putting the stick in my mouth. Then we went and took a walk with the women and Mr. Graeme diverted himself with Mrs. Dunn. In the evening came Mr. Mumford who told me all was well again at Appomattox. We played at cards and drank some pressed wine and were merry till 10 o'clock. I neglected to say my prayers but rogered my wife, and had good health, good thoughts, and good humor, thank God Almighty.

1712

January 1. I lay abed till 9 o'clock this morning to bring my wife into temper again and rogered her by way of reconciliation. I read nothing because Mr. Mumford was here, nor did I say my prayers, for the same reason. However I ate boiled milk for breakfast, and after my wife tempted me to eat some pancakes with her. Mr. Mumford and I went to shoot with our bows and arrows but shot nothing, and afterwards we played at billiards till dinner, and when we came found Ben Harrison there, who dined with us. . . . I took a walk about the plantation and at night we drank some mead of my wife's making which was very good. I gave the people some cider and a dram to the negroes. . . .

From *The London Diary**

1718

JANUARY 30. I rose about 9 o'clock, and read a chapter in Hebrew and two chapters in Greek. I said my prayers, and had boiled milk for breakfast. The weather was cold and cloudy, the wind northeast. I wrote a letter to Mrs. O-r-d and then drew a little till 2 o'clock and then ate some battered eggs. After dinner I put several things in order, and then read some English till five, and then went to Will's Coffeehouse, where I drank two dishes of chocolate, and stayed till 8 o'clock; and then went to Lady Guise's, where I stayed all the evening and ate some roasted goose for supper. About 12 o'clock I took leave and went home in the chair and said my prayers, and kissed the maid till I polluted myself, for which God forgive me. The weather was warmer, and it thawed.

31. I rose about 8 o'clock and read a chapter in Hebrew and four in Greek. I said my prayers, and had boiled milk for breakfast. The weather was cold and cloudy. About ten my drawing master came to me and stayed about an hour. I sent for twelve bottles of wine from Mr. U-t-n. I wrote a letter to Virginia till 2 o'clock and then ate some mutton cutlets. After dinner I put several things in order and read some English till 5 o'clock, and then went to visit Mrs. W-n-m but she was from home. Then I went to my Lady Dunkellen's, and sat with her about half an hour, and then went to both playhouses, and from thence to Will's Coffeehouse, where I drank two dishes of chocolate and stayed till 9 o'clock, and then went to the Spanish Ambassador's, where I won three pounds at basset and came home about twelve in a chair and said my prayers. I slept very well, thank God.

April 17. I rose about 8 o'clock and read a chapter in Hebrew and some Greek in Homer. I said my prayers, and had boiled milk for breakfast. The weather was cloudy and warm, the wind west. I finished my letter to my dear Miss Smith and about 12 o'clock came my cousin Daniel Horsmanden and stayed with me about half an hour. At two I ate some mutton cutlets for dinner. In the afternoon I put several things in order and took a nap till five

* Louis B. Wright and Marion Tinling, eds., *The London Diary* (New York, 1958).

and then prepared my things for the masquerade and dressed me in the [sight] of my mistress. About eight I first showed my habit to my landlady, then I went to Mrs. B-r-t, then to Lady Guise's and about 10 o'clock I went to Haymarket, where was abundance of company and I was exceedingly well entertained and particularly I put one woman's hand upon my business and spent. I met with pretty Mrs. H-n-t-n who was a great romp. Here I stayed till 5 o'clock in the morning and then went home in the chair and neglected to say my prayers.

18. I rose about 10 o'clock and read a chapter in Hebrew and some Greek in Homer. I said my prayers, and had boiled milk for breakfast. The weather was warm and cloudy, the wind west. About 10 o'clock I received my letter back again that I wrote to Miss Smith, but I am sure she had read it. I wrote some English till 2 o'clock and then ate some battered eggs. After dinner I put several things in order and then took a nap. Then I read some French till five, when I went to visit Mrs. U-m-s where I drank tea, and then called at the play and afterwards went to Will's Coffeehouse, where I found my Lord Dunkellen, who told me Miss Smith had shown my letter to her father. He told me many other things. Then I ate a jelly and went to visit Mrs. H-n-t-n and would have laid with her but she thought herself too dirty. About ten I went to the Spanish Ambassador's where I saw my cousins Horsmanden and several other ladies of my acquaintance. About twelve I went home and said my prayers.

July 21. I rose about 7 o'clock and read a chapter in Hebrew and some Greek in Homer. I said my prayers, and had milk for breakfast. The weather was warm and cloudy, the wind west. About 11 o'clock I went to visit Mrs. Southwell but everybody was out. Then I went into the City and read the news at Garraway's Coffeehouse and then went to dine with old Mr. Perry, where I found a letter from Virginia. I ate some roast mutton. After dinner I wrote a letter into the country and then went to visit my daughter whom I found in good health, thank God. Then I went to Lady Guise's where I stayed till 7 o'clock and then went to walk in the park, where I met Mr. C-p-r and then picked up two women and carried them to supper and ate some Scotch collops and then went with one of them to the bagnio and lay with her all night and rogered her three times to her great satisfaction.

1719

January 28. I rose about 11 o'clock, having had my asses' milk, and read a chapter in Hebrew and some Greek in Homer. I said my prayers, and had milk porridge for breakfast. I danced my dance. About one o'clock my Lord Percival came and stayed about half an hour. I read some English till

3 o'clock and then ate some brains. After dinner I put several things in order till 5 o'clock and then I went to see Mrs. U-m-s where I drank tea and stayed till six and then went to Will's, where I met Lord Orrery and went with him to Mrs. Smith a [g-t] woman that lives in Queen Street where I met with Mrs. C-r-t-n-y and went to bed with her and rogered her two times. We lay till 10 o'clock and then rose and I went to Will's and ate a jelly and then walked home and said Lord have mercy on me.

29. I rose about 8 o'clock, having had my asses' milk, and read a chapter in Hebrew and some Greek in Lucian. I said my prayers, and had milk porridge for breakfast. The weather was cold and cloudy, the wind east. I danced my dance. About 10 o'clock came Colonel Blakiston and stayed about half an hour. About one o'clock I went to Will's Coffeehouse and read the news and then went to Colonel Blakiston's to dinner and ate some boiled beef. After dinner Colonel [Shutz] and I played at piquet and I won a guinea. Then I went and called in at the play and then went to Will's Coffeehouse and from thence I went to Mrs. C-d-g-n but she was out so I went to Betty S-t-r-d and drank some wine with her and then went to the bagnio and lay all night and rogered her four times.

December 2. I rose about 8 o'clock and read a chapter in Hebrew and some Greek. I said my prayers, and had boiled milk for breakfast. The weather was cold, the wind northeast. I danced my dance and wrote a letter to my cousin Ch-d-k by John Rand who was going there. I read some English till dinner and then ate some hashed beef. After dinner I took a walk of about three miles and almost tired myself. In the evening I read some English till supper and then ate some boiled turkey. After supper one of the maids was frightened into fits by a boy, which put all the family into a bustle. About nine I retired and took the maid by the cunt, which made me commit uncleanness, for which God forgive me.

*Letter to Charles, Earl of Orrery**

Virginia, July 5, 1726.

My Lord,—

Soon after my arrival I had the honour to write to Your Ldsp to acquaint you that we had happaly escaped all the Dangers of the Sea, and were safely landed at my own House. There was nothing frightfull in the whole Voyage but a suddain Puff that carried away our Topmast, which in the falling gave a very bad crack, but we received no other Damage, neither were our Women

* *Virginia Magazine of History and Biography*, XXXII (1924).

terrified at It. The beautifullest Bloom of our Spring when we came Ashore, gave Mrs. Byrd a good impression of the Country. But since that the Weather is grown Warm, and some days have been troublesome eno' to make Her wish herself back in England. She now begins to be seasoned to the Heat, and to think more favourably of our Clymate. She comforts herself with the thought that a warm Sun is necessary to ripen our fine Fruit, and so pays herself with the Pleasure of one Sense, for the Inconvenience that attends the others. I must own to Yr Ldship that we have about three months that impatient People call warm, but the Colonel would think them cool enough for a pair of Blankets, and perhaps a comfortable Counterpain into the Bargain. Yet there are not 10 days in the whole summer that Yr Ldsp would complain of, and they happen when the Breazes fail us and it is a dead Calme. But then the other nine Months are most charmingly delightfull, with a fine Air and a Serene Sky that keeps us in Good Health and Good Humour. Spleen and vapours are as absolute Rarities here as a Winter's Sun, or a Publick Spirit in England. A Man may eat Beef, be as lazy as Captain Hardy, or even marry in this Clymate, without having the least Inclination to hang himself. It would cure all Mr. Hutchinson's distempers if the Ministry would transport him hither unless they sent Lady G—(?) along with him. Your Ldsp will allow it to be a fair Commendation of a Country that it reconciles a Man to himself, and makes him suffer the weight of his misfortunes with the same tranquility that he bears with his own Frailtys. After your September is over, I shall wish your Ldsp a little of our Sunshine to disperse that Fogg and Smoake with which your Atmosphere is loaded. Tis miraculous that any Lungs can breath in an Air compounded of so many different Vapours and Exhalations like that of dirty London. For my part mine were never of a texture to bear it in winter without great convulsions, so that nothing could make me amends for that uneasiness but the pleasure of being near your Lordship. Besides the advantage of a pure Air, we abound in all kinds of Provisions without expence (I mean we who have Plantations). I have a large Family of my own, and my Doors are open to Every Body, yet I have no Bills to pay, and half-a-Crown will rest undisturbed in my Pocket for many Moons together. Like one of the Patriarchs, I have my Flocks and my Herds, my Bond-men and Bond-women, and every Soart of Trade amongst my own Servants, so that I live in a kind of Independence on every one but Providence. However this Soart of Life is without expence, yet it is attended with a great deal of trouble. I must take care to keep all my people to their Duty, to set all the Springs in motion and to make every one draw his equal Share to carry the Machine forward. But then 'tis an amusement in this silent Country and a continual exercise of our Patience and Economy.

Another thing My Lord that recommends this Country very much—we sit securely under our Vines and our Fig Trees without any Danger to our Property. We have neither publick Robbers nor private, which Your Ldsp will think very strange, when we have often needy Governors, and pilfering Convicts sent amongst us. The first of these it is suspected have some-times an inclination to plunder, but want the pow'r, and tho' they may be Tyrants in their Nature, yet they are Tyrants without Guards, which makes them as harmless as a Scold would be without a Tongue. Neither can they do much Injustice by being partial in Judgment, because in the Supreme Court the Council have each an equal Vote with them. Thus both the Teeth and the Claws of the Lion are secured, and He can neither bite nor tear us, except we turn him loose upon Ourselves. I wish this was the Case with all his Majesty's good Subjects, and I dare say Your Ldsp has the goodness to wish so too. Then we have no such Trades carried on amongst us, as that of Horse-breakers, [Housebreakers?] Highway-men, or Beggers. We can rest securely in our Beds with all our Doors and Windows open, and yet find every thing exactly in place the next Morning. We can travel all over the Country by Night and by Day, unguarded and unarmed, and never meet with any Person so rude as to bid us Stand. We have no Vagrant Mendicants to seize and deafen us wherever we go, as in your Island of Beggers. Thus My Lord we are very happy in our Canaans if we could but forget the Onions and Fleshpots of Egypt. There are so many Temptations in England to inflame the Appetite and charm the Senses, that we are content to run all Risques to enjoy them. They always had I must own too strong an Influence upon me, as Your Ldsp will belive when they could keep me so long from the more solid pleasures of Innocence and Retirement. . . .

From *The History of the Dividing Line**

As it happened some ages before to be the fashion to saunter to the Holy Land and go upon other Quixote adventures, so it was now grown the humor to take a trip to America. The Spaniards had lately discovered rich mines in their part of the West Indies, which made their maritime neighbors eager to do so too. This modish frenzy, being still more inflamed by the charming account given of Virginia by the first adventurers, made many fond of removing to such a Paradise.

Happy was he, and still happier she, that could get themselves transported,

* Louis B. Wright, ed., *The Prose Works of William Byrd* (Cambridge, 1966).

fondly expecting their coarsest utensils in that happy place would be of massy silver.

This made it easy for the Company to procure as many volunteers as they wanted for their new colony, but, like most other undertakers who have no assistance from the public, they starved the design by too much frugality; for, unwilling to launch out at first into too much expense, they shipped off but few people at a time, and those but scantily provided. The adventurers were, besides, idle and extravagant and expected they might live without work in so plentiful a country.

These wretches were set ashore not far from Roanoke Inlet, but by some fatal disagreement or laziness were either starved or cut to pieces by the Indians.

Several repeated misadventures of this kind did for some time allay the itch of sailing to this new world, but the distemper broke out again about the year 1606. Then it happened that the Earl of Southampton and several other persons eminent for their quality and estates were invited into the Company, who applied themselves once more to people the then almost abandoned colony. For this purpose they embarked about an hundred men, most of them reprobates of good families and related to some of the Company who were men of quality and fortune.

The ships that carried them made a shift to find a more direct way to Virginia and ventured through the capes into the Bay of Chesapeake. The same night they came to an anchor at the mouth of Powhatan, the same as James River, where they built a small fort at a place called Point Comfort.

This settlement stood its ground from that time forward, in spite of all the blunders and disagreement of the first adventurers and the many calamities that befell the colony afterwards. The six gentlemen who were first named of the Company by the Crown and who were empowered to choose an annual president from among themselves were always engaged in factions and quarrels, while the rest detested work more than famine. At this rate the colony must have come to nothing had it not been for the vigilance and bravery of Captain Smith, who struck a terror into all the Indians round about. This gentleman took some pains to persuade the men to plant Indian corn, but they looked upon all labor as a curse. They chose rather to depend upon the musty provisions that were sent from England; and when they failed they were forced to take more pains to seek for wild fruits in the woods than they would have taken in tilling the ground. Besides, this exposed them to be knocked in the head by the Indians and gave them fluxes into the bargain, which thinned the plantation very much. To supply this mortality, they were reinforced the year following with a greater number of people, amongst which were fewer gentlemen and more laborers, who, however, took care not to kill themselves with work. These found the first adventurers in a very starving condition but relieved their wants with the fresh supply they brought with them. From Kecoughtan[1] they extended themselves as far as Jamestown, where, like true Englishmen, they built a church that cost no more than fifty pounds and a tavern that cost five hundred. . . .

. . . about the year 1620 a large swarm of dissenters fled thither from the severities of their stepmother, the church. These saints, conceiving the same aversion to the copper complexion of the natives with that of the first adventurers to Virginia, would on no terms contract alliances with them, afraid, perhaps, like the Jews of old, lest they might be drawn into idolatry by those strange women.

Whatever disgusted them I can't say, but this false delicacy, creating in the Indians a jealousy that the English were ill affected toward them, was the cause that many of them were cut off and the rest exposed to various distresses.

This reinforcement was landed not far from Cape Cod, where for their greater security they built a fort and near it a small town, which, in honor of the proprietors, was called New Plymouth. But they still had many discouragements to struggle with, though by being well supported from home they by degrees triumphed over them all.

Their brethren, after this, flocked over so fast that in a few years they extended the settlement one hundred miles along the coast, including Rhode Island and Martha's Vineyard.

Thus the colony throve apace and was thronged with large detachments of Independents and Presbyterians who thought themselves persecuted at home.

Though these people may be ridiculed for some pharisaical particularities in their worship and behavior, yet they were very useful subjects, as being frugal and industrious, giving no scandal or bad example, at least by any open and public vices. By which excellent qualities had they much the advantage of the southern colony, who thought their being members of the established church sufficient to sanctify very loose and profligate morals. For this reason New England improved much faster than Virginia, and in seven or eight years New Plymouth, like Switzerland, seemed too narrow a territory for its inhabitants. . . .

Surely there is no place in the world where the inhabitants live with less labor than in North Carolina. It approaches nearer to the description of Lubberland[2] than any other, by the great felicity of the climate, the easiness of raising provisions, and the slothfulness of the people. Indian corn is of

[1] Modern Hampton, Virginia.

[2] Cockaigne, a fabulous land of ease and plenty, subject of a thirteenth-century fabliau. [Wright's note].

so great increase that a little pains will subsist a very large family with bread, and then they may have meat without any pains at all, by the help of the low grounds and the great variety of mast that grows on the high land. The men, for their parts, just like the Indians, impose all the work upon the poor women. They make their wives rise out of their beds early in the morning, at the same time that they lie and snore till the sun has risen one-third of his course and dispersed all the unwholesome damps. Then, after stretching and yawning for half an hour, they light their pipes, and, under the protection of a cloud of smoke, venture out into the open air; though if it happen to be never so little cold they quickly return shivering into the chimney corner. When the weather is mild, they stand leaning with both their arms upon the cornfield fence and gravely consider whether they had best go and take a small heat at the hoe but generally find reasons to put it off till another time. Thus they loiter away their lives, like Solomon's sluggard, with their arms across, and at the winding up of the year scarcely have bread to eat. To speak the truth, 'tis a thorough aversion to labor that makes people file off to North Carolina, where plenty and a warm sun confirm them in their disposition to laziness for their whole lives.

26. Since we were like to be confined to this place till the people returned out of the Dismal, 'twas agreed that our chaplain might safely take a turn to Edenton to preach the Gospel to the infidels there and christen their children. He was accompanied thither by Mr. Little, one of the Carolina commissioners, who, to show his regard for the church, offered to treat him on the road with a fricassee of rum. They fried half a dozen rashers of very fat bacon in a pint of rum, both which being dished up together served the company at once both for meat and drink.

Most of the rum they get in this country comes from New England and is so bad and unwholesome that it is not improperly called "kill-devil." It is distilled there from foreign molasses, which, if skillfully managed, yields near gallon for gallon. Their molasses comes from the same country and has the name of "long sugar" in Carolina, I suppose from the ropiness of it, and serves all the purposes of sugar, both in their eating and drinking. When they entertain their friends bountifully, they fail not to set before them a capacious bowl of bombo, so called from the admiral of that name. This is a compound of rum and water in equal parts, made palatable with the said long sugar. As good humor begins to flow and the bowl to ebb they take care to replenish it with sheer rum, of which there always is a reserve under the table. . . .

This fort [at an Indian village] was a square piece of ground, enclosed with substantial puncheons or strong palisades about ten feet high and leaning a little outwards to make a scalade more difficult. Each side of the square might be about a hundred yards long, with loopholes at proper distances through which they may fire upon the enemy. Within this enclosure we found bark cabins sufficient to lodge all their people in case they should be obliged to retire thither. These cabins are no other but close arbors made of saplings, arched at the top and covered so well with bark as to be proof against all weather. The fire is made in the middle, according to the Hibernian fashion, the smoke whereof finds no other vent but at the door and so keeps the whole family warm, at the expense both of their eyes and complexion. The Indians have no standing furniture in their cabins but hurdles to repose their persons upon which they cover with mats or deerskins. We were conducted to the best apartments in the fort, which just before had been made ready for our reception and adorned with new mats that were very sweet and clean.

The young men had painted themselves in a hideous manner, not so much for ornament as terror. In that frightful equipage they entertained us with sundry war dances, wherein they endeavored to look as formidable as possible. The instrument they danced to was an Indian drum, that is, a large gourd with a skin braced taut over the mouth of it. The dancers all sang to this music, keeping exact time with their feet while their head and arms were screwed into a thousand menacing postures.

Upon this occasion the ladies had arrayed themselves in all their finery. They were wrapped in their red and blue matchcoats, thrown so negligently about them that their mahogany skins appeared in several parts, like the Lacedaemonian damsels of old. Their hair was braided with white and blue peak and hung gracefully in a large roll upon their shoulders.

This peak consists of small cylinders cut out of a conch shell, drilled through and strung like beads. It serves them both for money and jewels, the blue being of much greater value than the white for the same reason that Ethiopian mistresses in France are dearer than French, because they are more scarce. The women wear necklaces and bracelets of these precious materials when they have a mind to appear lovely. Though their complexions be a little sad-colored, yet their shapes are very straight and well proportioned. Their faces are seldom handsome, yet they have an air of innocence and bashfulness that with a little less dirt would not fail to make them desirable. Such charms might have had their full effect upon men who had been so long deprived of female conversation but that the whole winter's soil was so crusted on the skins of those dark angels that it required a very strong appetite to approach them. The bear's oil with which they anoint their persons all over makes their skins soft and at the same time protects them from every species of vermin that use to be troublesome to other uncleanly people.

We were unluckily so many that they could not well make us the compliment of bedfellows according to the Indian rules of hospitality, though a grave matron whispered one of the commissioners very civilly in the ear that if her daughter had been but one year older she should have been at his devotion. It is by no means a loss of reputation among the Indians for damsels that are single to have intrigues with the men; on the contrary, they account it an argument of superior merit to be liked by a great number of gallants. However, like the ladies that game,[3] they are a little mercenary in their amours and seldom bestow their favors out of stark love and kindness. But after these women have once appropriated their charms by marriage, they are from thenceforth faithful to their vows and will hardly ever be tempted by an agreeable gallant or be provoked by a brutal or even by a fumbling husband to go astray.

The little work that is done among the Indians is done by the poor women, while the men are quite idle or at most employed only in the gentlemanly diversions of hunting and fishing. In this, as well as in their wars, they now use nothing but firearms, which they purchase of the English for skins. Bows and arrows are grown into disuse, except only amongst their boys. Nor is it ill policy, but on the contrary very prudent, thus to furnish the Indians with firearms, because it makes them depend entirely upon the English, not only for their trade but even for their subsistence. Besides, they were really able to do more mischief while they made use of arrows, of which they would let silently fly several in a minute with wonderful dexterity, whereas now they hardly ever discharge their firelocks more than once, which they insidiously do from behind a tree and then retire as nimbly as the Dutch horse used to do now and then formerly in Flanders.

We put the Indians to no expense but only of a little corn for our horses, for which in gratitude we cheered their hearts with what rum we had left, which they love better than they do their wives and children. Though these Indians dwell among the English and see in what plenty a little industry enables them to live, yet they choose to continue in their stupid idleness and to suffer all the inconveniences of dirt, cold, and want rather than disturb their heads with care or defile their hands with labor.

The whole number of people belonging to the Nottoway town, if you include women and children, amount to about two hundred. These are the only Indians of any consequence now remaining within the limits of Virginia. The rest are either removed or dwindled to a very inconsiderable number, either by destroying one another or else by the smallpox and other diseases. Though nothing has been so fatal to them as their ungovernable passion for

---

[3] Engage in prostitution. [Wright's note].

rum, with which, I am sorry to say it, they have been but too liberally supplied by the English that live near them. . . .

The care Colonel Spotswood took to tincture the Indian children with Christianity produced the following epigram, which was not published during his administration for fear it might then have looked like flattery.

> Long has the furious priest assayed in vain,
> With sword and faggot, infidels to gain,
> But now the milder soldier wisely tries
> By gentler methods to unveil their eyes.
>
> Wonders apart, he knew 'twere vain t'engage
> The fixed preventions of misguided age.
> With fairer hopes he forms the Indian youth
> To early manners, probity, and truth.
>
> The lion's whelp thus, on the Libyan shore,
> Is tamed and gentled by the artful Moor,
> Not the grim sire, inured to blood before.

I am sorry I can't give a better account of the state of the poor Indians with respect to Christianity, although a great deal of pains has been and still continues to be taken with them. For my part, I must be of opinion, as I hinted before, that there is but one way of converting these poor infidels and reclaiming them from barbarity, and that is charitably to intermarry with them, according to the modern policy of the Most Christian King in Canada and Louisiana. Had the English done this at the first settlement of the colony, the infidelity of the Indians had been worn out at this day with their dark complexions, and the country had swarmed with people more than it does with insects. It was certainly an unreasonable nicety that prevented their entering into so good-natured an alliance. All nations of men have the same natural dignity, and we all know that very bright talents may be lodged under a very dark skin. The principal difference between one people and another proceeds only from the different opportunities of improvement. The Indians by no means want understanding and are in their figure tall and well proportioned. Even their copper-colored complexion would admit of blanching, if not in the first, at the farthest in the second generation. I may safely venture to say, the Indian women would have made altogether as honest wives for the first planters as the damsels they used to purchase from aboard the ships. 'Tis strange, therefore, that any good Christian should have refused a wholesome, straight bedfellow, when he might have had so fair a portion with her as the merit of saving her soul.

We rested on our clean mats very comfortably, though alone, and the next morning went to the toilet of some of the Indian ladies, where, what with the charms of their persons and the smoke of their apartments, we were almost blinded. They offered to give us silk-grass baskets of their own making, which we modestly refused, knowing that an Indian present, like that of a nun, is a liberality put out to interest and a bribe placed to the greatest advantage. Our chaplain observed with concern that the ruffles of some of our fellow travelers were a little discolored with puccoon,[4] wherewith the good man had been told those ladies used to improve their invisible charms. . . .

By the way one of our men killed another rattlesnake with eleven rattles, having a large gray squirrel in his maw, the head of which was already digested while the body remained still entire. The way these snakes catch their prey is thus: they ogle the poor little animal till by force of the charm he falls down stupefied and senseless on the ground. In that condition the snake approaches and moistens first one ear and then the other with his spawl, and after that the other parts of the head to make all slippery. When that is done, he draws this member into his mouth and after it, by slow degrees, all the rest of the body.

. . . Certainly no Tartar ever loved horseflesh or Hottentot guts and garbage better than woodsmen do bear. The truth of it is, it may be proper food perhaps for such as work or ride it off, but, with our chaplain's leave, who loved it much, I think it not a very proper diet for saints, because 'tis apt to make them a little too rampant. And, now, for the good of mankind and for the better peopling an infant colony, which has no want but that of inhabitants, I will venture to publish a secret of importance which our Indian disclosed to me. I asked him the reason why few or none of his countrywomen were barren. To which curious question he answered, with a broad grin upon his face, they had an infallible secret for that. Upon my being importunate to know what the secret might be, he informed me that if any Indian woman did not prove with child at a decent time after marriage, the husband, to save his reputation with the women, forthwith entered into a bear diet for six weeks, which in that time makes him so vigorous that he grows exceedingly impertinent to his poor wife, and 'tis great odds but he makes her a mother in nine months. And thus much I am able to say besides for the reputation of the bear diet, that all the married men of our company were joyful fathers within forty weeks after they got home, and most of the single men had children sworn to them within the same time, our chaplain always excepted,

[4] The colonists seemed to apply the term "puccoon," in any number of spellings, to red dye used by the Indians, whatever the source of the coloring. [Wright's note].

who, with much ado, made a shift to cast out that importunate kind of devil by dint of fasting and prayer.

. . . This is what I thought proper to remark for the service of all those whose business or diversion shall oblige them to live any time in the woods. And because I am persuaded that very useful matters may be found out by searching this great wilderness, especially the upper parts of it about the mountains, I conceive it will help to engage able men in the good work if I recommend a wholesome kind of food of very small weight and very great nourishment, that will secure them from starving in case they should be so unlucky as to meet with no game. The chief discouragement at present from penetrating far into the woods is the trouble of carrying a load of provisions. I must own, famine is a frightful monster and for that reason to be guarded against as well as we can. But the common precautions against it are so burdensome that people cannot tarry long out and go far enough from home to make any effectual discovery. The portable provisions I would furnish our foresters withal are glue broth and rockahominy: one contains the essence of bread, the other of meat. The best way of making the glue broth is after the following method: take a leg of beef, veal, venison, or any other young meat, because old meat will not so easily jelly. Pare off all the fat, in which there is no nutriment, and of the lean make a very strong broth after the usual manner, by boiling the meat to rags till all the goodness be out. After skimming off what fat remains, pour the broth into a wide stewpan, well tinned, and let it simmer over a gentle, even fire till it come to a thick jelly. Then take it off and set it over boiling water, which is an evener heat and not so apt to burn the broth to the vessel. Over that let it evaporate, stirring it very often till it be reduced, when cold, into a solid substance like glue. Then cut it into small pieces, laying them single in the cold, that they may dry the sooner. When the pieces are perfectly dry, put them into a canister, and they will be good, if kept dry, a whole East India voyage. This glue is so strong that two or three drams, dissolved in boiling water with a little salt, will make half a pint of good broth, and if you should be faint with fasting or fatigue, let a small piece of this glue melt in your mouth and you will find yourself surprisingly refreshed.

One pound of this cookery would keep a man in good heart above a month and is not only nourishing but likewise very wholesome. Particularly it is good against fluxes, which woodsmen are very liable to, by lying too near the moist ground and guzzling too much cold water. But as it will be only used now and then, in times of scarcity when game is wanting, two pounds of it will be enough for a journey of six months.

But this broth will be still more heartening if you thicken every mess with half a spoonful of rockahominy, which is nothing but Indian corn parched without burning and reduced to powder. The fire drives out all the watery parts of the corn, leaving the strength of it behind, and this, being very dry, becomes much lighter for carriage and less liable to be spoilt by the moist air. Thus half a dozen pounds of this sprightly bread will sustain a man for as many months, provided he husband it well and always spare it when he meets with venison, which, as I said before, may be very safely eaten without any bread at all.

By what I have said, a man needs not encumber himself with more than eight or ten pounds of provisions, though he continue half a year in the woods. These and his gun will support him very well during that time, without the least danger of keeping one single fast. And though some of his days may be what the French call *jours maigres*, yet there will happen no more of those than will be necessary for his health and to carry off the excesses of the days of plenty, when our travelers will be apt to indulge their lawless appetites too much. (*c.* 1730).

(JAMES REID?)

(fl. 1769)

From *The Religion of the Bible and Religion of King William County Compared**

CHAP. III

OF A KING WILLIAM COUNTY GENTLEMAN

AMONG Philosophers and Divines it is a maxim that Virtue is the sole and only Nobility: Virtus sola atque unica nobilitatis est[1]: but in King William County it is quite the reverse, for there one may be a Gentleman without having any Virtue at all. If a King Williamite has Money, Negroes and Land enough he is a compleat Gentleman. These are screens which supply the place of wit, hide all his deffects, usher him into (what they call) the best of company, and draws upon him the smiles of the fair Sex. His madness then passes for wit, his extravagance for flow of spirit, his insolence for bravery, and his cowardice for wisdom. His money gilds over all his stupidities, and although an Ass covered over with gold is still an Ass, yet in King William County a fool covered over with the same metal, changes his nature, and commences a GENTLEMAN. Learning and good sense; religion and refined Morals; charity and benevolence have nothing to do in the composition. These are qualifications only proper for a dull, plodding, thoughtfull fellow, who can live in a closet by himself, and who cannot appear in polite company for want of Negroes: Nor at horseraces and Cock matches for want of skill in those valuable, delightful, and manly, I had almost said heroic exercises.

Now tell me, for God's sake, O ye Sons of King William County! how money, which in itself is only a piece of mere insignificant dust, can add any real worth to the person who possesses it? How Negroes, in themselves,

* Richard Beale Davis, ed., *The Colonial Virginia Satirist* (Philadelphia 1967).
[1] "Virtue is the one and only true nobility" (Loeb).

253

ignorant, stupid, thoughtless, wicked, profane and of base principles, can add any intrinsic honour to the soul of their Master? Or how a quantity of dirty Acres, the unfeeling, motionless clods of the field, can add any wisdom, any knowledge or any understanding to a Clod Pate?—But I only speak according to my own received Opinions, and perhaps it is my ignorance of Polite life that makes me reason thus. A man who was born in a Country where Learning & Religion are accounted the most valuable qualifications, and who has been most of his life immured in the lonely, forsaken habitation of Books, and only conversant with the dead, ought not to be accounted a proper judge of what constitutes a modern Gentleman among the living. Consequently I perceive that although I may pique myself upon my reasonings, the effects of dull study, yet daily experience convinces me that I reason wrong; for I have seen a man who was looked upon as a fellow unworthy of a Gentleman's notice because he had no Land and Negroes, who having, by some means or other, acquired both, became a Gentleman all of a sudden; but not knowing how to manage with prudence the helm of his affairs, he suffered Shipwreck, fell back into his primitive obscurity, and died unnoticed, unpitied, unlamented.

Now this to such an odd, old fashioned, whimsical fellow as I am, who pretends to walk according to reason, seems very absurd. A man, by my rule, must be measured by the greatness or littleness of his Soul, and not of his estate. The mind is the standard of the man. Virtue and good sense ought to be esteemed though clothed in rags, loaded with misery, and placed on a dunghill: When on the contrary, Vice, ignorance and immorality should be branded with infamy and reproach though decked in scarlet, surrounded with all the glittering show of gaudy Pageantry, and seated on a throne. Theology, Philosophy and Reason tell me so, and the customs of King William County will never be able to erase from my Soul their just Dictates.

CHAP. IV

THE MANNER OF AUGMENTING AN ESTATE

VOLTAIRE was a fellow of very whimsical notions, and I'll prove it before this Chapter be concluded.—The son being made a Gentleman by the Negroes & Land given him by his father, who perhaps sprung from a race of Ignoramuses, and who still continued one himself, thinking money bestowed on the education of his Heir apparent would be only thrown away, only imbibed into him this noble Lesson; "by all fair means endeavour to get money, and if you cannot get it that way, get money by any means." This son, full of his own merit, and elevated with the figure he cuts in the world, and with his own importance, immediately assumes the swaggering air and looks big. He drinks, fights, bullies, curses, swears, whores, games, sings, whistles, dances, jumps, capers, runs, talks baudy, visits Gentlemen he never saw, has the rendez-vous with Ladies he never spoke to, writes Billets-dou[ce?] to filles des joies whom he stiles women of Quality, eats voraciously, sleeps, snores, & takes snuff. This comprehends his whole life, and renders him a Polite Gentleman, or to use the modern elegant phrase—a damn'd honest Fellow.

Nevertheless of all this he must not forget to augment his Estate, for if that go to ruin his Gentlemanship, his Wit, his Politeness, & Wisdom all go to the Pot together. To prevent this therefore he, at his liesure [*sic*] hours, & when the time sits heavy upon his hand for want of Polite company, impregnates his own Negroe wenches, as a very easy way of augmenting his wealth. Solomon tells us that he had seen Servants upon horses and Princes walking upon foot. The meaning of which passage is, that fornication & adultery break down all distinction; for if a King should have a Son by a poor Girl, that son is a Prince although he should all his life reign betwixt the horns of the Plough; and if a Princess should accept the embrace of a Clown, the child is but of the same rank with his father even though he should ascend the throne: So that Solomon might very readily see Servants upon horses and Princes walking beside them on foot, and no doubt he did see it. But were he alive now he would behold Slave SON running before his Gentleman Father; Slave Brother driving the Oxen of Brother Gentleman; Slave Sister wiping the shoes of Lady Sister, and washing the dirty Posteriors of the MASTERS their young Brothers. Thus the Heir enlarges his Estate, whilst his Sisters, through the assistance of their Portions, pass into captivity and are subjected to the caprices of an Animal who has nothing of the man in him but the shape: for, as a favourite Author words it, he is a man in shape only, and not in reality who does things unbecoming a rational Being.

Voltaire I say was a fellow of whimsical notions. He affirms that Negroes are not sprung from the same stock that we are, but he is absolutely mistaken. If they were not descended from the same origin, but were of a different nature, then a child begot by a white man upon a negro wench, would never be able to propagate its species; as we know the production of a Jack Ass and a Mare, cannot produce its own kind. But children propagated betwixt white & black people are as capable of producing their Species as any other Beings, which entirely destroys Monsieur Voltaire's hypothesis, and corroborates this undeniable axiom, viz. That an ignorant, vicious, rich Gentleman differs in nothing from his ignorant, vicious, poor Negro, but in the colour of his skin, and in his being the greater blacguard [*sic*] of the two.

CHAP. XXXIII

EVERY MAN THE CENTER OF A CIRCLE AT ONE TIME, AND A PART OF THE CIRCUMFERENCE AT ANOTHER

SOMETIME ago I was surprised how a man, who was reckoned a wise and learned Being in one County, should be esteemed a fool and an ignoramus in another neighboring County; and as I found that this was generaly the case, I began to look around me for the reasons of this temporary wisdom and folly. I soon found out the cause. A man in his own native County, who is so much indebted to the blind Goddess as to be the son of a rich father, when he grows up becomes the Oracle of all his contemporaries, though inferior to them in point of wit. Men of Genius easily give up the superiority to such fellows as covet it, because they have other matters of greater consequence to employ themselves about; and to the disgrace of human nature a fool of Quantity (I refuse the word quality) is caressed, esteemed, flattered and adored by all who are dependent upon him, by those who do not care to dissoblige him, and by such as want to raise themselves at his expense.

In such cases the honest man keeps at a distance, because he is modest, and modesty never appears till called for; consequently the modest man never appears at the Levee of the great. Surrounded therefore by Scoundrels, Slaves, Ignoramuses and Gamesters, what can a young man of fortune, in this County, expect, but to hear panegyrics which he has not deserved, and to have his mind tinctured with the grossest vanity. These encomia flattering his self-love render him a compleat coxcomb; he looks upon his inferiors as animals of a different species, & upon his slaves as beasts of burden created by God for his service. Thus among his inferiors and slaves he appears as a kind of Demi-God; but when he goes to another County his Divinityship falls prostrate, as Dagon did before the Ark, for strangers will not willingly pay him any implicite homage. One County is jealous of its neighbour County; they vie with one another, and consequently refuse this self-conceited Booby the incense that was offered him in the place of his nativity. This offends the mighty man; through a principle of false courage he resents it, and his posteriors are honoured with the just punishment of a kickage: He returns to his own County; brags of his prowess; tells a thousand lies, and swears ten thousand oaths to corroborate them, is credited by his sycophants, & again shines with his former lustre.

Every man acts in a circle, and is the centre of some particular circle. The Master of a family, who is the centre there, in a greater circle is only one who makes apart of the circumference. A King who is the centre of that circle w^{ch}.

comprehends all his subjects, in a company of Kings, where the mind would be the standard of the man, would, perhaps, be only a part of the Periphery. Thus every individual of the human race has a circle whereof he is the centre, from the king to the beggar; but when out of that place they become of no account, and so it is in this County, for a man is great, learned and wise in the sphere of his friends and relations, but elsewhere he is a mere cypher. A candle gives light in the dark, not in the presence of the Sun; so a talkative, boasting, lying, conceited, idle fop, though ignorant and stupid among men of wisdom, is wise, learned and judicious amidst people of the same stature, providing he is richer than they; but if poor, they will dispute the superiority with him, because in this place poverty & wisdom are reckoned incompatible.

The fool of Quantity however will always have admirers, and will be the centre of a circle where he can appear with stupid majesty; for as a dwarf never appears to greater disadvantage then when walking beside a man of gigantic stature, because his own littleness is thereby the more conspicuous: So in this County (and for ought I know every where else) the young Ass-queers will ever appear disgraceful to humanity in the company of men of true literature, because their ignorance and stupidity is, by such a comparison, made more manifest. Sensible men cannot confine their knowledge to cock-matches and horse races, and that is all the Youth here learn. Had I the naming of this County, I would give it a more suitable name than the one it now bears; one absolutely significant of the qualities of the inhabitants, that learned travelers might anticipate what kind of mental entertainment they would meet with there. I would call it Golgotha, which is, when interpreted, the place of a Scull.

CHAP. XXXIV

THE CONCLUSION

I LAY my account that I shall be much censured and calumniated by every snarling Ass-queer in this County for this performance, which, though undertaken with a design to make them wiser and better, will be construed into a libel, a lampoon, or the breathings of ill-nature revenge levelled at particular persons, although nothing is more untrue. But I am very little concerned about the censure of such sort of worthies. The esteem of men of true learning, virtue and candour, I shall ever value above every thing, but those noble qualifications themselves; for the sneers and reflections of such as may be destitute of them, I despise them, just as much as I value the former. If such stupid Ass-queers, who have not sense enough to conceal their nonsense, would study to gain my approbation, they must always calumniate me, for I should esteem their praises and encomia as absolutely derogatory of my honour. The tongue of Ignorance is not capable of making me uneasy; nor will my spirits ever succumb under the aspersions of a people who do not even know that they know nothing; for by knowing this, they would know something, & consequently be in a fair way of acquiring some wisdom. But wisdom is a thing which, I think I may venture to say, no young Ass-queer in King William County ever put up a petition to God for; and as all true wisdom cometh from him, I know no other way of a King Williamite's arriving at it. Prayer is here an unfashionable, ungenteel, and unpolite, I had almost said a very beggarly exercise. To bow the knee, except to a young Lady, is reckoned below the dignity of a polite Gentleman; and therefore that passage of Scripture wch. desires us to pray without ceasing, a King Williamite reads, Play without ceasing, and he literaly understands the words, & actualy puts them in execution.

It is a common received opinion that things which are rare and uncommon attract our attention, raise our curiosity, and afford us pleasure and delight; but I find that from this general rule there is an exception; for nothing is more rare and uncommon than Virtue, and yet in this County it is taken no notice of: Though I do not wonder at it, for the virtuous man is often poor, despised and solitary, whilst vice rides in a chariot, lives splendidly, and commands respect. I do not envy those grand Personages, who are only constant in Inconstancy; and though I am sometime grieved that my lot is cast among them, yet I usualy comfort myself with this suggestion, viz. that a man's being in a stable does not make him a horse. I therefore live contented, and freely yield up to the young Ass-queers around the smiles and favours of the fair sex, the dazling gifts of blind fortune, the intoxicating pleasures of life, the applause of the stupid rabble, and every other empty joy that wealth or titles can procure them; and to conclude this performance shall present them with an Epigram which I have literaly translated from the Hebrew Manuscript of Rabbi Ben Ezra Hekkalpasi,[2] and which is as follows:

> By Moses' Law we find an ass
> In consecration could not pass;
> They must redeem it, or its neck
> They were, by law, oblig'd to break.

[2] Probably an invented author.

Was such Law now in use, Good Lord!
How many necks would we see gor'd!
Not all the Lambs from pole to pole
Would be sufficient to keep whole
Half of their necks, which, every day,
Throughout the universe do bray.

But now the case is alter'd quite,
We Ass-queers view in different light;
For spite of every Law of Moses,
Those Asses daily show their noses;
And treated are with great respect,
To make amends for that neglect,
Or rather most profound abuse
Their fathers met with from the Jews.   (1769)

RICHARD LEWIS

(fl. 1725–1746)

While Lewis' poem has been cut for inclusion here, even this version may seem quite lengthy. If the poem were included only so that a student could study its prosody, a few lines would suffice; but to see all the elements mentioned in the Introduction (p. 220)—particularly the journey—most of the poem must be read. The journey motif recurs repeatedly in American literature, although some justify it in contemporary literature on the basis that Americans are now a mobile people. Lewis borrowed much from English poetry of the period, but the pride—like Byrd's—is his own.

From *Description of the Spring.*
A Journey from Patapsco in Maryland to Annapolis,
*April 4, 1730**

AT length the *wintry* Horrors disappear,
And *April* views with Smiles the infant Year;
The grateful Earth from frosty Chains unbound,
Pours out its *vernal* Treasures all around,
Her Face bedeckt with Grass, with Buds the Trees are
        crown'd.
In this soft Season, ere the Dawn of Day,
I mount my Horse, and lonely take my Way,
From woody Hills that shade *Patapsco's* Head
(In whose deep Vales he makes his stony Bed,
From whence he rushes with resistless Force,   10
Tho' huge rough Rocks retard his rapid Course,)
Down to *Annapolis*, on that smooth Stream
Which took from fair *Anne-Arundel* its Name.

* *The Gentleman's Magazine*, II (March, 1732).

And now the *Star* that ushers in the Day,
'Begins to pale her ineffectual Ray.
The *Moon* with blunted Horns now shines less bright,
Her fading Face eclips'd with growing Light;
The fleecy Clouds with streaky Lustre glow,
And Day quits Heaven to view the Earth below.
O'er yon tall *Pines* the *Sun* shews half its Face,   20
And fires their floating Foliage with his Rays:
Now sheds aslant on Earth its lightsome Beams,
That trembling shine in many-colour'd Streams.
Slow-rising from the Marsh, the Mist recedes,
The Trees, emerging, rear their dewy Heads;
Their dewy Heads the *Sun* with Pleasure views,
And brightens into Pearls the pendent Dews.
   The *Beasts* uprising, quit their leafy Beds,
And to the cheerful *Sun* erect their Heads;
All joyful rise, except the filthy *Swine*,   30
On obscene Litter stretch'd they snore supine:
In vain the Day awakes, Sleep seals their Eyes,
Till Hunger breaks the Band and bids them rise.
Mean while the *Sun* with more exalted Ray,
From cloudless Skies distributes riper Day;
Thro' sylvan Scenes my Journey I pursue,
Ten thousand Beauties rising to my View;
Which kindle in my Breast poetic Flame,   ⎫
And bid me my *Creator's* praise proclaim;   ⎬
Tho' my low Verse ill-suits the noble Theme. ⎭   40
   Here various Flourets grace the teeming Plains,
Adorn'd by Nature's Hand with beauteous Stains.
First-born of *Spring*, here the *Pacone* appears,
Whose golden Root a silver Blossom rears.
In spreading Tufts, see there the *Crowfoot* blue,
On whose green Leaves still shines a globous Dew;
Behold the *Cinque-foil*, with its dazzling Dye
Of flaming yellow, wounds the tender Eye.
But there enclos'd the grassy *Wheat* is seen,
To heal the aching sight with cheerful Green.   50
   Safe in yon Cottage dwells the *Monarch Swain*, ⎫
His *Subject Flocks*, close grazing, hide the Plain; ⎬
For him they live; and die t'uphold his Reign.   ⎭
Viands unbought his well-till'd Lands afford,

And smiling *Plenty* waits upon his Board;
Health shines with sprightly Beams around his Head.
And *Sleep*, with downy Wings, o'er shades his Bed,
His *Sons* robust his daily Labours share,
Patient of Toil, Companions of his Care.
And all their Toils with sweet Success are crown'd.   60
In graceful Ranks there *Trees* adorn the Ground,
The *Peach*, the *Plum*, the *Apple* here are found.
Delicious Fruits!—Which from their Kernels rise,
So fruitful is the Soil—so mild the Skies.
The lowly *Quince* yon sloping Hill o'er-shades,
Here lofty *Cherry-Trees* erect their Heads:
High in the Air each spiry Summit waves,
Whose Blooms thick-springing yield no space for Leaves;
Evolving Odours fill the ambient Air,
The *Birds* delighted to the Grove repair: 70
On ev'ry Tree behold a tuneful Throng,
The vocal Vallies echo to their Song.
    But what is *He*,[1] who perch'd above the rest,
Pours out such various Musick from his Breast!
His Breast, whose Plumes a cheerful White display,
His quiv'ring Wings are dress'd in sober Grey.
Sure all the *Muses* this their Bird inspire!
And he, alone, is equal to the Choir
Of warbling Songsters who around him play,
While, Echo like, *He* answers ev'ry Lay.   80
The chirping *Lark* now sings with sprightly Note
Responsive to her Strain *He* shapes his Throat.
Now the poor widow'd *Turtle* wails her Mate,
While in soft Sounds *He* cooes to mourn his Fate.
Oh sweet Musician, thou dost far excel
The soothing Song of pleasing *Philomel*!
Sweet is her Song, but in few Notes confin'd;
But thine, thou *Mimic* of the feath'ry Kind,
Runs thro' all Notes!—*Thou* only know'st them *All*,
At once the *Copy*—and th' *Original*.   90
    My *Ear* thus charm'd, my *Eye* with Pleasure sees
Hov'ring about the Flow'rs th' industrious *Bees*.

---

[1] The mockingbird.

Like them in Size, the *Humming Bird* I view, ⎫
Like them, *He* sucks his Food, the Honey Dew, ⎬
With nimble Tongue, and Beak of jetty Hue. ⎭
He takes with rapid Whirl his noisy Flight,
His gemmy Plumage strikes the Gazer's Sight;
And as he moves his ever-flutt'ring Wings,
Ten thousand Colours he around him flings.

   While such Delights my Senses entertain, ⎫
I scarce perceive that I have left the *Plain*; ⎬   100
'Till now the Summit of a *Mount* I gain: ⎭
Low at whose sandy Base the *River* glides,
Slow-rolling near their Height his languid Tides;
Shade above Shade, the Trees in rising Ranks,
Cloath with eternal Green his steepy Banks:
The Flood, well pleas'd, reflects their verdant Gleam
From the smooth Mirror of his limpid Stream.

   But see the *Hawk*, who with acute Survey,
Tow'ring in Air predestinates his Prey   110
Amid the Floods!—Down dropping from on high,
He strikes the *Fish*, and bears him thro' the Sky.
The Stream disturb'd no longer shews the Scene
That lately stain'd its silver Waves with green;
In spreading Circles roll the troubled Floods,
And to the Shores bear off the pictur'd Woods.

   Now looking round I view the out-stretch'd *Land*,
O'er which the Sight exerts a wide Command;
The fertile Vallies, and the naked Hills,
The Cattle feeding near the chrystal Rills;   120
The Lawns wide-op'ning to the sunny Ray,
And mazy Thickets that exclude the Day.
Awhile the Eye is pleas'd these Scenes to trace,
Then hurrying o'er the intermediate Space,
Far-distant Mountains dress'd in Blue appear,
Now I behold the Em'rald's vivid Green,
Now scarlet, now a purple Die is seen;
In brightest Blue his Breast *He* now arrays,
Then strait his Plumes emit a golden Blaze.
Thus whirring round he flies, and varying still   130
He mocks the *Poet's* and the *Painter's* Skill;
Who may for ever strive with fruitless Pains,

To catch and fix those beauteous changeful Stains,
While Scarlet now, and now the Purple shines,
And Gold to Blue its transient Gloss resigns.
Each quits, and quickly each resumes its Place,
And ever-varying Dies each other chase.
Smallest of Birds, what Beauties shine in thee!
A living *Rainbow* on thy Breast I see.

While with delight on this soft Scene I gaze,   140
The *Cattle* upward look, and cease to graze,
But into Covert run thro' various Ways.
And now the Clouds in black Assemblage rise,
And dreary Darkness overspreads the Skies,
Thro' which the Sun strives to transmit his Beams,
"But sheds his sickly Light in straggling Streams.
Hush'd is the Musick of the wood-land Choir,
Fore-knowing of the Storm, the Birds retire
For Shelter, and forsake the shrubby Plains,
And a dumb Horror thro' the Forest reigns;   150
In that lone House which opens wide its Door,
Safe may I tarry till the Storm is o'er.
Hark how the *Thunder* rolls with solemn Sound!
And see the forceful *Lightning* dart a Wound
On yon tall Oak!—Behold its Top laid bare!
Its Body rent, and scatter'd thro' the Air
The Splinters fly!—Now—now the *Winds* arise,
From different Quarters of the low'ring Skies;
Forth issuing fierce, the *West* and *South* engage,
The waving Forest bends beneath their Rage: 160
But where the winding Valley checks their Course,
They roar and ravage with redoubled Force:
With circling sweep in dreadful Whirlwinds move
And from its Root tear up the gloomy Grove,
Down rushing fall the Trees, and beat the Ground
In Fragments flie the shatter'd Limbs around;
Tremble the Under-woods, the Vales resound.
Follows, with patt'ring Noise, the icy *Hail*,
And *Rain*, fast falling, floods the lowly Vale.
Again the *Thunders* roll, the *Lightnings* fly,   170
And as they first disturb'd, now clear the Sky;
For lo! the *Gust* decreases by Degrees,

The dying *Winds* but sob amidst the Trees;
With pleasing Softness falls the silver Rain,
Thro' which at first faint gleaming o'er the Plain,
The Orb of Light scarce darts a wat'ry Ray
To gild the Drops that fall from ev'ry Spray;
But soon the dusky Vapours are dispell'd,
And thro' the Mist that late his Face conceal'd,
Bursts the broad *Sun*, triumphant in a Blaze   180
Too keen for Sight—Yon Cloud refracts his Rays;
The mingling Beams compose th' *ethereal Bow*,
How sweet, how soft, its melting Colours glow!
Gaily they shine, by heav'nly Pencils laid,
Yet vanish swift—How soon does *Beauty* fade!

    Onwards the *Ev'ning* moves in Habit grey,
And for her Sister *Night* prepares the Way.
The plumy People seek their secret Nests,
To Rest repair the ruminating Beasts;
Now deep'ning Shades confess th' Approach of Night,   190
Imperfect Images elude the Sight:
From earthly Objects I remove mine Eye,
And view with Look erect the vaulted Sky,
Where dimly shining now the Stars appear,
At first thin-scatt'ring thro' the misty Air;
Till Night confirm'd, her jetty Throne ascends,
On her the *Moon* in cloudy State attends;
But soon unveil'd her lovely Face is seen,
And *Stars* unnumber'd wait around their Queen.
Rang'd by their *Maker's* Hand in just Array,   200
They march Majestic thro' th' ethereal Way.
   Are these bright Luminaries hung on high
Only to please with twinkling Rays our Eye?
Or may we rather count each *Star* a *Sun*,
Round which *full peopled Worlds* their Courses run?
Orb above Orb harmoniously they steer
Their various Voyages thro' Seas of Air.
    Snatch me some *Angel* to those high Abodes,
The Seats perhaps of *Saints* and *Demigods*!
Where such as bravely scorn'd the galling Yoke   210
Of *vulgar Error*, and her Fetters broke;
Where *Patriots*, who to fix the publick Good,

In Fields of Battle sacrific'd their Blood;
Where *pious Priests*, who Charity proclaim'd,
And *Poets* whom a *virtuous Muse* enflam'd;
Philosophers who strove to mend our Hearts,
And such as polish'd Life with *useful Arts*,
Obtain a Place; when by the Hand of Death
Touch'd, they retire from this poor Speck of Earth;
Their *Spirits* freed from bodily Alloy,   220
Perceive a Fore-tast of that endless Joy,
Which from Eternity hath been prepar'd,
To crown their Labours with a vast Reward.
While to these Orbs my wand'ring Thoughts aspire,
A falling *Meteor* shoots his lambent Fire,
Thrown from the heav'nly Space he seeks the Earth,
From whence he first deriv'd his humble Birth.
    The *Mind* advis'd by this instructive Sight,
Descending sudden from th' aereal Height,
Obliges me to view a different Scene,   230
Of more Importance to myself, tho' mean.
These distant Objects I no more pursue,
But turning inward my reflective View,
My working Fancy helps me to survey
In the just Picture of this *April Day*,
My Life o'er past,—a Course of thirty *Years*,
Blest with few Joys, perplex'd with num'rous Cares.
    In the dim Twilight of our *Infancy*,
Scarce can the Eye surrounding Objects see.
Then thoughtless *Childhood* leads us pleas'd and gay,   240
In Life's fair Morning thro' a flow'ry Way:
The *Youth* in Schools inquisitive of Good,
Science pursues thro' *Learning's* mazy Wood;
Whose lofty Trees, he, to his Grief perceives,
Are often bare of *Fruit*, and only fill'd with *Leaves*:
Thro' lonely wilds his tedious Journey lies,
At last a brighter Prospect cheers his Eyes;
Now the gay Fields of *Poetry* he views,
And joyous listens to the *tuneful Muse;*
Now *History* affords him vast Delight,   250
And opens lovely Landscapes to his Sight:
But ah! too soon this Scene of Pleasure flies;
And o'er his Head tempestuous Troubles rise,

He hears the Thunders roll, he feels the Rains,
Before a friendly Shelter he obtains;
And thence beholds with Grief the furious Storm
The *noon tide* Beauties of his *Life* deform:
He views the *painted Bow* in distant Skies;
Hence, in his heart some Gleams of Comfort rise;
He hopes the *Gust* has almost spent its Force,   260
And that he safely may pursue his Course.
   Thus far *my life* does with the *Day* agree,
Oh! may its coming Stage from Storms be free,
While passing thro' the World's most private Way,
With Pleasure I my *Maker's* Works survey;
Within my Heart let *Peace* a Dwelling find,
Let my *Good-will* extend to *all Mankind*:
Freed from *Necessity*, and blest with *Health*;
Give me *Content*, let others toil for *Wealth*.
In *busy* Scenes of Life let me exert   270
A *careful Hand*, and wear an *honest Heart*;
And suffer me my *leisure* Hours to spend,
With chosen *Books*, or a well-natur'd *Friend*.
Thus journeying on, as I advance in Age,
May I look back with Pleasure on my Stage;
And as the setting *Sun* withdrew his Light
To rise on other Worlds serene and bright,
Cheerful may I resign my vital Breath,
Nor anxious tremble at th' Approach of *Death*;
Which shall, I hope, but strip me of *my Clay*,   280
And to a better World my Soul convey.
   Thus musing, I my silent Moments spend,
Till to the *River's* Margin I descend,
From whence I may discern my *Journey's* End:
Annapolis adorns its further Shore,
To which the *Boat* attends to bear me o'er.
   And now the moving *Boat* the Flood divides,
While the *Stars* 'tremble on the floating Tides.
Pleas'd with the Sight again I raise mine Eye
To the bright Glories of the azure Sky;   290
And while these Works of God's creative Hand,
The *Moon* and *Stars*, that move at his Command
Obedient thro' their circling Course on high,
Employ my Sight,—struck with amaze I cry,

Almighty Lord! Whom Heav'n and Earth proclaim
The *Author* of their universal Frame,
Wilt thou vouchsafe to view the *Son of Man*,
The Creature, who but *Yesterday* began
Thro' animated Clay to draw his Breath,
To morrow doom'd a Prey to ruthless Death!   300
   Tremendous God! May I not justly fear,
That I, unworthy Object of thy Care,
Into this World by thy bright Presence tost,
Am in th' Immensity of *Nature* lost!
And that my Notions of the *World above*,
Are but Creations of my own *Self-Love*!
To feed my coward Heart, afraid to die,
With *fancied* Feasts of *Immortality*!
   These Thoughts, which thy amazing Works suggest,
Oh glorious *Father*, rack my troubled Breast.   310
   Yet, *Gracious God*, reflecting that my Frame
From *Thee* deriv'd in animating Flame,
And that whate'er I am, however mean,
By thy Command I enter'd on this Scene
Of Life—thy wretched *Creature of a Day*,
Condemn'd to travel thro' a tiresome Way;
Upon whose Banks (perhaps to cheer my Toil)
I see thin Verdures rise, and *Daisies* smile:
Poor Comforts these, my Pains t'alleviate!
While on my Head tempestuous Troubles beat.   320
And must I, when I quit this Earthly Scene,
Sink total into *Death*, and never rise again?
   No sure,—These *Thoughts* which in my Bosom roll,
Must issue from a *never-dying Soul*;
These active *Thoughts* that penetrate the Sky,
Excursive into dark Futurity;
Which hope eternal Happiness to gain,
Could never be bestow'd on *Man* in vain.
   To *Thee, O Father*, fill'd with fervent Zeal,
And sunk in humble Silence I appeal;   330
Take me, my great *Creator*, to *Thy Care*,
And gracious listen to my ardent Prayer!
   Supreme of Beings, omnipresent Pow'r,
My great Preserver from my natal Hour,

Fountain of Wisdom, boundless Deity,
Omniscient God, my Wants are known to *Thee*, ⎞
With Mercy look on mine Infirmity! ⎟
Whatever State thou shalt for me ordain, ⎠
Whether my Lot in Life be *Joy* or *Pain*;
Patient let me sustain thy wise Decree,   340
And learn to know *myself*, and *honour Thee*.

(1732)

EBENEZER COOK

(fl. 1708–1732)

The poem contrasts sharply with the easy, pastoral scenes that occur in the preceding selection. The section where the speaker is driven from his bed to the orchard only to find there frogs, a rattlesnake and mosquitoes exemplifies the humor that underlays the poem, but that tone springs from incidents of suffering and bitterness. The portrait of the country can scarcely be called flattering. Instead of recounting the quiet, rural, comfortable life in the colonies, Cook settled on the vulgar, rough, objectionable qualities of people and of nature. Instead of focusing on the psychological and spiritual problems, as some New England writers did, Cook looked at the external facts to be confronted. Such literature confirms our expectations that life in the colonies was lived by human beings, not altogether in the studies of Puritan ministers in New England.

From *The Sot-weed*[1] *Factor**

Condemn'd by Fate to way-ward Curse,
Of Friends unkind, and empty Purse;
Plagues worse then fill'd *Pandora's* Box,
I took my leave of *Albion's* Rocks:
With heavy Heart, concern'd that I
Was forc'd my Native Soil to fly,
And the *Old World* must bid good-buy.
But Heav'n ordain'd it should be so,
And to repine is vain we know:
Freighted with Fools, from *Plymouth* sound,   10
To *Mary-Land* our Ship was bound;

---

[1] Sot-weed: tobacco, the weed that inebriates.
* *The Sot-weed Factor: Or, a Voyage to Maryland. A Satyr* (London, 1708). *N.B.* The lettered footnotes are Cook's own; the numbered notes are the editor's.

Where we arriv'd in dreadful Pain,
Shock'd by the Terrours of the Main;
For full three Months, our wavering Boat,
Did thro' the surley Ocean float,
And furious Storms and threat'ning Blasts,
Both tore our Sails and sprung our Masts:
Wearied, yet pleas'd, we did escape
Such Ills, we anchor'd at the (*a*) *Cape*;
But weighing soon, we plough'd the *Bay*,   20
To (*b*) *Cove* it in (*c*) *Piscato-way*,
Intending there to open Store,
I put myself and Goods a-shore:
Where soon repair'd a numerous Crew,
In Shirts and Drawers of (*d*) *Scotch-cloth* Blue.
With neither Stockings, Hat, nor Shooe.
These *Sot-weed* Planters Crowd the Shoar,
In Hue as tawny as a Moor:
Figures so strange, no God design'd,
To be a part of Humane Kind: 30
But wanton Nature, void of Rest,
Moulded the brittle Clay in Jest.
At last a Fancy very odd
Took me, this was the Land of *Nod*;
Planted at first, when Vagrant *Cain*,
His Brother had unjustly slain:
Then conscious of the Crime he'd done,
From Vengeance dire, he hither run;
And in a Hut supinely dwelt,
The first in *Furs* and *Sot-weed* dealt.   40
And ever since his Time, the Place,
Has harbour'd a detested Race;
Who when they cou'd not live at Home,
For Refuge to these Worlds did roam;
In hopes by Flight they might prevent,
The Devil and his fell intent;

(*a*) By the *Cape*, is meant the *Capes* of *Virginia*, the first Land on the Coast of *Virginia* and *Mary-Land*.
(*b*) To *Cove* is to lie at Anchor safe in Harbour.
(*c*) The Bay of *Piscato-way*, the usual place where our Ships come to an Anchor in *Mary-Land*.
(*d*) The Planters generally wear Blue *Linnen*.

Obtain from Tripple Tree[2] repreive,
And Heav'n and Hell alike deceive:
But e're their Manners I display,
I think it fit I open lay
My Entertainment by the way;
That Strangers well may be aware on,
What homely Diet they must fare on.
To touch that Shoar, where no good Sense is found,
But Conversation's lost, and Manners drown'd.
I crost unto the other side,
A River whose impetuous Tide,
The Savage Borders does divide;
In such a shining odd invention,
I scarce can give its due Dimention.
The *Indians* call this watry Waggon
(*e*) *Canoo*, a Vessel none can brag on;
Cut from a *Popular-Tree*, or *Pine*,
And fashion'd like a Trough for Swine:
In this most noble Fishing-Boat,
I boldly put myself a-float;
Standing Erect, with Legs stretch'd wide,
We paddled to the other side:
Where being Landed safe by hap,
As *Sol* fell into *Thetis* Lap.
A ravenous Gang bent on the stroul,[3]
Of (*f*) Wolves for Prey, began to howl;
This put me in a pannick Fright,
Least I should be devoured quite:
But as I there a musing stood,
And quite benighted in a Wood,
A Female Voice pierc'd thro' my Ears,
Crying, *You Rogue drive home the Steers*,
I listen'd to th'attractive sound,
And straight a Herd of Cattel found
Drove by a Youth, and homewards bound:
Cheer'd with the sight, I straight thought fit,
To ask where I a Bed might get.

50

60

70

80

---

[2] The gallows.
(*e*) A *Canoo* is an *Indian* Boat, cut out of the body of a Popler-Tree.
[3] Stroll.
(*f*) Wolves are very numerous in *Mary-Land*.

The surley Peasant bid me stay,
And ask'd from whom (g) I'de run away.
Surpriz'd at such a saucy Word,
I instantly lugg'd out my Sword;
Swearing I was no Fugitive,
But from *Great-Britain* did arrive,
In hopes I better there might Thrive.   90
To which he mildly made reply,
I beg your Pardon, Sir, *that I*
Should talk to you Unmannerly;
But if you please to go with me
To yonder House, you'll welcome be.
Encountring soon the smoaky Seat,
The Planter old did thus me greet:
"Whether you come from Gaol or Colledge,
"You're welcome to my certain Knowledge;
"And if you please all Night to stay,   100
"My Son shall put you in the way."
Which offer I most kindly took,
And for a Seat did round me look:
When presently amongst the rest,
He plac'd his unknown *English* Guest,
Who found them drinking for a whet,[4]
A Cask of (h) Syder on the Fret,[5]
Till Supper came upon the Table,
On which I fed whilst I was able.
So after hearty Entertainment,   110
Of Drink and Victuals without Payment;
For Planters Tables, you must know,
Are free for all that come and go.
While (i) Pon and Milk, with (j) Mush well stoar'd,
In wooden Dishes grac'd the Board;
With (k) Homine and Syder-pap,
(Which scarce a hungry Dog wou'd lap)

(g) 'Tis supposed by the Planters, that all unknown Persons are run away from some Master.
[4] A dram that whets the appetite.
(h) Syder-pap is a sort of Food made of Syder and small Homine, like our Oat-meal.
[5] Liquor in an effervescent state.
(i) Pon is Bread made of *Indian-Corn*.
(j) Mush is a sort of Hasty-pudding made with Water and *Indian* Flower.
(k) Homine is a Dish that is made of boiled *Indian*-Wheat, eaten with Molossus, or Bacon-Fat.

Well stuff'd with Fat, from Bacon fry'd,
Or with *Molossus* dulcify'd.
Then out our Landlord pulls a Pouch,   120
As greasy as the Leather Couch
On which he sat, and straight begun,
To load with Weed his *Indian* Gun;[6]
In length, scarce longer than ones Finger,
Or that for which the Ladies linger:
His Pipe smoak'd out with aweful Grace,
With aspect grave and solemn pace;
The reverend Sire walks to a Chest,
Of all his Furniture the best,
Closely confin'd within a Room,   130
Which seldom felt the weight of Broom;
From thence he lugs a Cag of Rum,
And nodding to me, thus begun:
I find, says he, you don't much care,
For this our *Indian* Country Fare;
But let me tell you, Friend of mine, ⎫
You may be glad of it in time,   ⎬
Tho' now your Stomach is so fine;   ⎭
And if within this Land you stay,
You'll find it true what I do say.   140
This said, the Rundlet[7] up he threw,
And bending backwards strongly drew:
I pluck'd as stoutly for my part,
Altho' it made me sick at Heart,
And got so soon into my Head
I scarce cou'd find my way to Bed;
Where I was instantly convey'd
By one who pass'd for Chamber-Maid;
Tho' by her loose and sluttish Dress,
She rather seem'd a *Bedlam-Bess*:   150
Curious to know from whence she came,
I prest her to declare her Name.
She Blushing, seem'd to hide her Eyes,
And thus in Civil Terms replies;
In better Times, e'er to this Land,

---

[6] Tobacco pipe.
[7] Small cask.

I was unhappily Trapann'd;[8]
Perchance as well I did appear,
As any Lord or Lady here,
Not then a Slave for twice two (*a*) Year.
My Cloaths were fashionably new,   160
Nor were my Shifts of Linnen Blue;
But things are changed now at the Hoe,
I daily work, and Bare-foot go,
In weeding Corn or feeding Swine,
I spend my melancholy Time.
Kidnap'd and Fool'd, I hither fled,
To shun a hated Nuptial (*b*) Bed,
And to my cost already find,
Worse Plagues than those I left behind.
Whate'er the Wanderer did profess,   170
Good-faith I cou'd not choose but guess
The Cause which brought her to this place,
Was supping e'er the Priest said Grace.
Quick as my Thoughts, the Slave was fled,
(Her Candle left to shew my Bed)
Which made of Feathers soft and good,
Close in the (*c*) Chimney-corner stood;
I threw me down expecting Rest,
To be in golden Slumbers blest:
But soon a noise disturb'd my quiet,   180
And plagu'd me with nocturnal Riot;
A Puss which in the ashes lay,
With grunting Pig began a Fray;
And prudent Dog, that Feuds might cease,
Most strongly bark'd to keep the Peace.
This Quarrel scarcely was decided,
By stick that ready lay provided;
But *Reynard* arch and cunning Loon,
Broke into my Appartment soon;

---

[8] Kidnapped.

(*a*) 'Tis the Custom for Servants to be obliged for four Years to very servile Work; after which time they have their Freedom.

(*b*) These are the general Excuses made by *English* Women, which are sold, or sell themselves to *Mary-Land*.

(*c*) Beds stand in the Chimney-corner in this Country.

In hot pursuit of Ducks and Geese,   190
With fell intent the same to seize:
Their Cackling Plaints with strange surprize,
Chac'd Sleeps thick Vapours from my Eyes:
Raging I jump'd upon the Floar,
And like a Drunken Saylor Swore;
With Sword I fiercly laid about,
And soon dispers'd the Feather'd Rout:
The Poultry out of Window flew,
And *Reynard* cautiously withdrew:
The Dogs who this Encounter heard,   200
Fiercly themselves to aid me rear'd,
And to the Place of Combat run,
Exactly as the Field was won.
Fretting and hot as roasting Capon,
And greasy as a Flitch of Bacon;
I to the Orchard did repair,
To Breathe the cool and open Air;
Expecting there the rising Day,
Extended on a Bank I lay:
But Fortune here, that saucy Whore,   210
Disturb'd me worse and plagu'd me more.
Than she had done the night before.
Hoarse croaking (*d*) Frogs did 'bout me ring,
Such Peals the Dead to Life wou'd bring,
A Noise might move their Wooden King.
I stuff'd my Ears with Cotten white
For fear of being deaf out-right,
And curst the melancholy Night:
But soon my Vows I did recant,
And Hearing as a Blessing grant;   220
When a confounded Rattle-Snake,
With hissing made my Heart to ake:
Not knowing how to fly the Foe,
Or whether in the Dark to go;
By strange good Luck, I took a Tree,
Prepar'd by Fate to set me free;

(*d*) Frogs are called *Virginea* Bells, and make, (both in that Country and *Mary-Land*) during the Night, a very hoarse ungrateful Noise.

Where riding on a Limb a-stride,
Night and the Branches did me hide,
And I the Devil and Snake defy'd.
Not yet from Plagues exempted quite,   230
The curst Muskitoes did me bite;
Till rising Morn' and blushing Day,
Drove both my Fears and Ills away;
And from Night's Errors set me free.
Discharg'd from hospitable Tree;
I did to Planters Booth repair,
And there at Breakfast nobly Fare,
On rashier broil'd of infant Bear:
I thought the Cub delicious Meat,
Which ne'er did ought but Chesnuts eat;   240
Nor was young Orsin's flesh the worse,
Because he suck'd a Pagan Nurse.
Our Breakfast done, my Landlord stout,
Handed a Glass of Rum about;
Pleas'd with the Treatment I did find,
I took my leave of Oast so kind;
Who to oblige me, did provide,
His eldest Son to be my Guide,
And lent me Horses of his own,
A skittish Colt, and aged Rhoan,   250
The four-leg'd prop of his Wife *Joan.*
Steering our Barks in Trot or Pace,
We sail'd directly for a place
In *Mary-Land* of high renown,
Known by the Name of *Battle-Town.*

[The Sot-weed factor's horse is stolen at an inn, where he meets a planter
who invites him to his plantation.]

. . . in an antient *Cedar* House,
Dwelt my new Friend, a (*a*) Cockerouse;
Whose Fabrick, tho' 'twas built of Wood,
Had many Springs and Winters stood;
When sturdy Oaks, and lofty Pines   260
Were level'd with (*b*) Musmelion Vines,

(*a*) Cockerouse, is a Man of Quality.
(*b*) Musmilleon Vines are what we call Muskmilleon Plants.

And Plants eradicated were,
By Hurricanes into the air;
There with good Punch and apple Juice,
We spent our Hours without abuse:
Till Midnight in her sable Vest,
Persuaded Gods and Men to rest;
And with a pleasing kind surprize,
Indulg'd soft Slumbers to my Eyes.
Fierce (c) *Æthon* courser of the Sun,   270
Had half his Race exactly run;
And breath'd on me a fiery Ray,   ⎞
Darting hot Beams the following Day, ⎬
When snug in Blanket white I lay: ⎠
But Heat and (d) *Chinces* rais'd the Sinner,
Most opportunely to his Dinner;
Wild Fowl and Fish delicious Meats,   ⎞
As good as *Neptune's* Doxy[9] eats, ⎬
Began our Hospitable Treat;   ⎠
Fat Venson follow'd in the Rear,   280
And Turkies wild Luxurious Chear:
But what the Feast did most commend,
Was hearty welcom from my Friend.
Thus having made a noble Feast;
And eat as well as pamper'd Priest,
Madera strong in flowing Bowls,
Fill'd with extream, delight our Souls;
Till wearied with a purple Flood,
Of generous Wine (the Giant's blood,
As Poets feign) away I made,   290
For some refreshing verdant Shade;
Where musing on my Rambles strange,
And Fortune which so oft did change;
In midst of various Contemplations
Of Fancies odd, and Meditations,
I slumber'd long - - - - - - - - - - - - - - - -
Till hazy Night with noxious Dews,
Did Sleep's unwholsom Fetters lose:

(c) *Æthon* is one of the Poetical Horses of the Sun.
(d) *Chinces* are a sort of Vermin like our *Bugs* in *England*.
[9] Sweetheart.

With Vapours chil'd, and misty air,
To fire-side I did repair: 300
Near which a jolly Female Crew,
Were deep engag'd at *Lanctre-Looe*;[10]
In Nightrails white, with dirty Mein,
Such Sights are scarce in *England* seen:
I thought them first some Witches bent,
On Black Designs in dire Convent.
Till one who with affected air,
Had nicely learn'd to Curse and Swear:
Cry'd Dealing's lost is but a Flam,[11]
And vow'd by G-d she'd keep her *Pam*.[12]   310
When dealing through the board had run,
They ask'd me kindly to make one;
Not staying often to be bid,
I sat me down as others did:
We scarce had play'd a Round about,
But that these *Indian* Froes[13] fell out.
D - - m you, says one, tho' now so brave,
I knew you late a Four Years Slave;
What if for Planters Wife you go,
Nature design'd you for the Hoe.   320
Rot you replies the other streight,
The Captain kiss'd you for his Freight;
And if the Truth was known aright,
And how you walk'd the Streets by night,
You'd blush (if one cou'd blush) for shame,
Who from *Bridewell* or *Newgate* came.
From Words they fairly fell to Blows,
And being loath to interpose,
Or meddle in the Wars of Punk,[14]
Away to Bed in hast I slunk.   330
Waking next day, with aking Head,
And Thirst, that made me quit my Bed;
I rigg'd myself, and soon got up,

---

[10] A card game, similar to whist.
[11] A delusion.
[12] The jack of trumps (usually clubs in Loo), the highest card in the deck.
[13] *Dutch:* woman.
[14] Prostitute.

To cool my Liver with a Cup
Of (*a*) *Succahana* fresh and clear,
Not half so good as *English* Beer;
Which ready stood in Kitchin Pail,
And was in fact but *Adam's* Ale;
For Planters Cellars you must know,
Seldom with good *October* flow,   340
But Perry Quince and Apple Juice,
Spout from the Tap like any Sluce;
Untill the Cask's grown low and stale,
They're forc'd again to (*b*) Goad and Pail:
The soathing drought scarce down my Throat,
Enough to put a Ship a float,
With Cockerouse as I was sitting,
I felt a Feaver Intermitting;
A fiery Pulse beat in my Veins,
From Cold I felt resembling Pains: 350
This cursed seasoning I remember,
Lasted from *March* to cold *December*;
Nor would it then its *Quarters* shift,
Until by *Cardus*[15] turn'd a drift,
And had my Doctress wanted skill,
Or Kitchin Physick at his will,
My Father's Son had lost his Lands,
And never seen the *Goodwin-Sands*:
But thanks to Fortune and a Nurse
Whose Care depended on my Purse,   360
I saw myself in good Condition,
Without the help of a Physitian:
At length the shivering ill relieved,
Which long my Head and Heart had grieved;
I then began to think with Care,
How I might sell my *British* Ware,
That with my Freight I might comply,
Did on my Charter-party lie:
To this intent, with Guide before,
I tript it to the Eastern Shoar;   370

(*a*) *Succahana* is Water.
(*b*) A *Goad* grows upon an *Indian* Vine, resembling a Bottle, when ripe it is hollow; this the Planters make use of to drink water out of.
[15] A thistle valued for its healing powers.

While riding near a Sandy Bay,
I met a *Quaker, Yea* and *Nay*:
A Pious Conscientious Rogue,
As e'er woar Bonnet or a Brogue,
Who neither Swore nor kept his Word,
But cheated in the Fear of God;
And when his Debts he would not pay,
By Light within he ran away.
With this sly Zealot soon I struck
A Bargain for my *English* Truck,   380
Agreeing for ten thousand weight,
Of *Sot-weed* good and fit for freight,
Broad *Oronooko* bright and sound,
The growth and product of his ground;
In Cask that should contain compleat,
Five hundred of Tobacco neat.
The Contract thus betwixt us made,
Not well acquainted with the Trade,
My Goods I trusted to the Cheat,
Whose crop was then aboard the Fleet;   390
And going to receive my own,
I found the Bird was newly flown:
Cursing this execrable Slave,
This damn'd pretended Godly Knave;
On due Revenge and Justice bent,
I instantly to Counsel went,
Unto an ambodexter (c) *Quack*,
Who learnedly had got the knack
Of giving Glisters, making Pills,
Of filling Bonds, and forging Wills;   400
And with a stock of Impudence,
Supply'd his want of Wit and Sense;
With Looks demure, amazing People,
No wiser than a Daw in Steeple;
My Anger flushing in my Face,
I stated the preceding Case:
And of my Money was so lavish,
That he'd have poyson'd half the Parish,
And hang'd his Father on a Tree,

(c) This Fellow was an Apothecary, and turn'd an Attorney at Law.

For such another tempting Fee;   410
Smiling, said he, the Cause is clear,
I'll manage him you need not fear;
The Case is judg'd, good Sir, but look ⎫
In *Galen*, No—in my Lord *Cook*,   ⎬
I vow to God I was mistook: ⎭
I'll take out a Provincial Writ,
And Trounce him for his Knavish Wit;
Upon my Life we'll win the Cause,
With all the ease I cure the (*d*) *Yaws*:
Resolv'd to plague the holy Brother,   420
I set one Rogue to catch another;
To try the Cause then fully bent,
Up to (*e*) *Annapolis* I went,
A City Situate on a Plain,
Where scarce a House will keep out Rain;
The Buildings fram'd with Cyprus rare,
Resembles much our *Southwark* Fair:
But Stranger here will scarcely meet,
With Market-place, Exchange, or Street;
And if the Truth I may report,   430
'Tis not so large as *Tottenham Court*.
St. *Mary's* once was in repute,   ⎫
Now here the Judges try the Suit,   ⎬
And Lawyers twice a Year dispute: ⎭
As oft the Bench most gravely meet, ⎫
Some to get Drunk, and some to eat ⎬
A swinging share of Country Treat. ⎭
But as for Justice right or wrong,
Not one amongst the numerous throng,
Knows what they mean, or has the Heart,   440
To give his Verdict on a Stranger's part:
Now Court being call'd by beat of Drum,
The Judges left their Punch and Rum,
When Pettifogger Docter draws,
His Paper forth, and opens Cause:
And least I shou'd the better get,
Brib'd *Quack* supprest his Knavish Wit.
So Maid upon the downy Field,

(*d*) The *Yaws* is the *Pox*.
(*e*) The chief of *Maryland* containing about twenty four *Houses*.

Pretends a Force, and Fights to yeild:
The Byast Court without delay,   450
Adjudg'd my Debt in Country Pay;
In (*f*) Pipe staves, Corn, or Flesh of Boar,
Rare Cargo for the *English* Shoar:
Raging with Grief, full speed I ran,
To joyn the Fleet at (*g*) *Kicketan*;
Embarqu'd and waiting for a Wind,
I left this dreadful Curse behind.

   May Canniballs transported o'er the Sea
Prey on these Slaves, as they have done on me;
May never Merchant's, trading Sails explore   460
This Cruel, this Inhospitable Shoar;
But left abandon'd by the World to starve,
May they sustain the Fate they well deserve:
May they turn Savage, or as *Indians* Wild,
From Trade, Converse, and Happiness exil'd;
Recreant to Heaven, may they adore the Sun,
And into Pagan Superstitions run
For Vengence ripe - - - - - - - - - - - - - -
May Wrath Divine then lay those Regions wast
Where no Man's (*) Faithful, nor a Woman Chast.   (1708) 470

(*f*) There is a Law in this Country, the Plantiff may pay his Debt in Country pay, which consists in the produce of his Plantation.
(*g*) The homeward bound Fleet meets here.
* The Author does not intend by this, any of the *English* Gentlemen resident there.

(ALEXANDER HAMILTON?)

(1712–1756)

The four selections in this group illustrate the humorous wit of a group of Maryland writers. While some of the humor can be followed only with difficulty by a modern reader, the spirit of the wit can readily be apprehended. The ludicrous verse is not many steps from the serious poetry of Richard Lewis (pp. 260–269), for example. Even to recognize the presence of such wit helps us once more to see that Jonathan Edwards did not represent the thinking of men in all of the colonies. The view of the world shown in the selections below has too seldom been understood as a part of American literature that continued along with the New England literature until the latter ceased to be dominant in the nineteenth century.

*A Literary History of the Maryland Gazette**

> *All human Race would fain be Wits;*
> *But Millions miss for one that hits.*
> *Say*, Britain, *could you ever boast*
> *Three* Poets *in an Age, at most?*
>
> *Our chilling Climate hardly bears*
> *A Sprig of* Bays *in fifty Years:*
> *While ev'ry Fool his Claim alledges,*
> *As if it grew on common Hedges.*

Dr. Swift's Poetry: *A Rhapsody.*

* J. A. Leo Lemay, "Hamilton's Literary History of the *Maryland Gazette*," *William and Mary Quarterly*, 3rd Ser., XXIII (April 1966). As noted in the Introduction to Part Two, Hamilton's essay is too allusive and localized to be fully annotated here. Interested students should consult Lemay's article.

Mr. Green,

The other Night, looking over a Bundle of your *News-Papers*, to which I often have recourse when satiated with more serious and solid Compositions, after I had perused several *Poems* and *Essays* with which you have obliged the Public, I came at last to *a long-winded Paper*, wrote by a *Native of Maryland;* the tedious Prolixity of which lulled me asleep in my elbow Chair, before I had half run over that important and *ponderous Performance.* So soon as the *drowsy god* had clapt his *leaden Cap* over my Temples, I was carried into the *Region of Visions*, and dreamed such a comical *Dream*, that I cannot help relating it to you; and if you think it worth While, you may communicate it to the Public.

I found myself in a spacious Hall, where were assembled several strange Persons, who, by their Gesture and Discourse, appeared to be *Poets, Politicians*, and *Philosophers:* Some wrote, some disputed, others repeated *Verses* upon various Subjects, and many dispatched certain *Pacquets*, which all seemed directed to you. While I admired this strange *Medley*, and was at a Loss what to make of it, you enter'd the Hall: Immediately I made up to you, bluntly asking, who these odd Fellows were, and what they were about? I am not surprized, you replied, that you do not know them; for I cannot say any of them are the *Minions of Fame*, tho' they aim at being thought so with all their Might: In short, they are *my Authors*, who oblige me with their *Compositions* in *Prose* and *Verse*, to fill up a Gap in my *Gazette*, in a Scarcity of News. There seems to be a Multitude of them, said I; to take Notice of every particular would be tiresome, but pray be so kind as to make me better acquainted with some of the most remarkable of them, whom I shall pitch upon. —With all my Heart, said you. So, having prepared a small *Nipperkin of Punch*, we took our Seat at one End of the Hall, and as we handled the Bowl to and again, I made my Questions, which you civilly answered. . . .

While we thus talked, a tall raw-boned Person hastily passed by us in a furious Manner, expanding his Arms, and stamping with his Foot. —"Ha, ye Gods! ye immortal Essences! What a noble Conception was there! Stop, stop the gaudy fugitive Thought, lest it outfly my *Pegasus*"—Is this Person, said I, *a Pindaric Poet,* or a *religious Zealot?* Methinks his Behaviour somewhat resembles Madness.—That there Gentleman, Sir, is the *first Rate Poet* in our *Province;* a most thundering and verbose *Son of the Nine Muses;* he has a Fancy like lightning; and not only in his *Compositions*, but in his common *Discourse*, he darts out Notions and Conceptions which no Mortal but himself ever thought of. He deals much in *ideal Beings, figurative Personages*, and antient *Pagan Mythology;* and is desirous to be understood by none but *People of Taste.* —But this must be a strange *Taste*, said I, which makes the relishing of what is romantic and obscure to almost all your *Readers*, an essential *Criterion of Taste.* —Why the Gentleman himself is romantic in most Things he does or says; tho' it must be owned, abstracting from this strange volatile Humour, he has a good Measure of Sense and Learning.— I'm sorry to find him then in the Company of these *Fops:* But here's to his good Success, and may he be crowned *Poet Laureat* of *Maryland.* —I'll pledge you there; for he is one of my prime *Authors,* and I wish he would write oftner.

That old Gentleman, with the Spectacles on his Nose, looks like an *Author of Quality and Distinction.* —You have guessed right; he transcends the common Class of *Authors,* not in Wit and Accuracy of Stile (for many of *my own Authors* excell him in both), but in Honour and Titles. —If he be not one of *your Authors,* pray what Business has he here? —He is not here in *Person,* but in *Effigie,* for I borrowed a Performance of him from a *Brother Gazette-Publisher:* 'Tis a *Speech* (for he is a notable *Speech-maker*) upon the dreadful Fire that consumed the *Capitol* of our *neighbouring Province,* which coming into the Hands of a certain *Northern Bard, Ned Type* by Name, he did him the Honour to paraphrase it into *long Iambics,* and so metamorphosed his *lame Prose* into *hobbling Verse.* —The Gentleman seems to have weak Eyes. —Right: His Eyes are so weak that he cannot bear the *New Light,* and was therefore so incensed against *Wh-tf-ld,* and his Brethren *Lanthorn-Carriers,* that he paid them off in a most unparallel'd and inimitable Speech.[1]

Pray who is that young dapper Gentlemen, so particularly precise and affected in his Carriage, so seemingly pointed, exact and prolix in his Discourse; who seems to dictate to all round him, talks much of Mr. *Pope,* and often quotes *Horace?* I am much mistaken if he also is not a *Poet.* —You're right; this Gentlemen has a large Share in my Paper, and sets up for a delicate Taste in *Poetry:* As to his Abilities that Way, I am not learned enough to judge; yet those who set up for *Men of Taste and Literature,* in this our *Woodland Country,* affirm that he is no great Proficient in it: However, about this, *Doctors* differ. His name is *Philo-Musaeus,* sometimes *Philo-musus:* he is Author of several Pieces, some in the *Ode Way,* or as others chuse to call it, in the *Odd Way,* —You'll never forbear punning, Friend *Jonas*—which relish a little of *Sternhold* and *Hopkins;* tho' some Judges say, that there is a little Fire mixt with his Phlegm. . . . —This *Philo-Musaeus,* said I, must be one of your distinguished *Authors,* for he seems to have more Enemies than one; observe that Chap with the broad round Face, bashful and awkward in his Carriage, who grins upon poor *Philo* with a most inveterate Sneer. —O Sir,

---

[1] Ned Type's (Benjamin Franklin's) poem follows, and those by "Juba" and James Sterling.

that's *Philokalus*, the obscurest and most abusive of all my *Authors*. —Thrust him up in that obscure Corner with Mr. *Q*. then, said I, and see which will make the best Figure; what untimely Birth did he bring forth, pray? —Why Sir, he is of that Sect of *polemical Writers*, who mistake Raillery and Billingsgate for Argument and good Sense. —Well, here's to his Reformation, poor Soul. —But pray what does he rail at honest *Philo* for? —Because he imagines he has classed him among his *Dunces*, seeing he has not given him a Place among the *Worthies* in his *Satyrical Epistle*. —But pray what is the Design and Drift of that same *Satyrical Epistle*, Friend *Jonas*? —Why, so far as I can see, it is to ridicule the Vice and Ignorance that prevail in this *Infant Province*, which Vice and Ignorance, he seems to say, arises from the Want of good Education, *Universities*, and *Seminaries of Learning*. —There he is right; but I think he should also have brought in bad and indifferent *Poets*, and all wretched Authors, among his other *Fops*, and then he could very properly have attributed their Folly and Vanity to Want of *Learning* and *Good Manners:* —But we have said enough of him.

Methinks you have got a devilish Clan of *Poets* here. —O yes, Numbers of the *Rhiming Species*. There's *Juba*, the *Monitor of the Ladies*. Here's *Ignotus*, very properly so called, a puny *Translator*. There's that wonderful Imitator of *Horace*, in his *Ode*, beginning *Otium divos*, &c. And here is *Eumolpus*, that solemn Dealer in *blank Verse*, the Body of whose *Muse*, too large for her small Wings, like a *squab Gosling*, comes souse down as often as she attempts to soar. —This Sort of Poetry by some is thought the easiest, but is surely the most difficult; because where the Jingle of Rhime is wanting, there must be a strong Fancy, just Sentiment, and lively Colouring, to make it even tolerable. —This Gentlemen then, said I, has mistaken himself much, if I judge right; for there is little else in that *Poem* of his, but a tolerable Cadence and Measure in the Lines. —He is surely a *dead Poet:* and therefore, here is Peace to his *Manes*. . . .

Hey! Hey! what a Hurly Burly have we here! *Jonas*, this is not fair; —three against two: I have a good Mind to assist the weakest Party. —You had better sit still and drink your Punch. —Here's to you. —Well, well, as to drink is better than to quarrel at any Time, I'll drink, and do you go on with the History of your *Champions*. —These two upon one Side, are the *Freeholder* and *Americano Britannus*, and these three that engage them are the *Native of Maryland*—What! that prolix Drivler, interrupted I, who has given us a Preface long enough, and as fit for the History of *China* or *Japan*, as for the Subject he was to go upon? —Yes Sir, and *Philanthropos*, and his Friend *Anonymous*. Brave Fellows all. —And what do they quarrel about? —Why, the Pretence upon one Side is *the Liberty of the Subject*, and the

Security of every Man's Purse and Property. That on the other is the Cause of *injur'd Magistracy,* and to chastise the daring and *insolent Contempt of Authority;* both specious and plausible Subjects of Debate, to cover over something else that is meant, to wit, whether a *Court-House* shall be built in *this Place* or in *that Place,* agreeable to the Interest, not of the Public, but of either contending Party. —But why should the Public be annoy'd with this tedious Dispute, might it not have been better let alone? —I grant it, Sir, but they pay me for it, and I'll publish any Thing for Money, if it is not impious or treasonable. —You're right, *Jonas,* but go on, —What the *Freeholder* has said is well enough, and the Gentleman may pass, in these Parts, for a tolerable *Patriot-Writer.* But, as for the *Native of Maryland,* he is abundantly too prolix, and becomes tiresome by a Multiplicity of Words and little Substance; and indeed in some Places he is absurd, where he asserts an *unlimited uncontroulable Power* in any *Magistrate* whatsoever, or in any *Constitution,* to levy whatever they please upon the People; for here, he plainly pleads the Cause of Oppression, and advances a gross Absurdity, in supposing the Constitution an Enemy to itself. —He does not advance greater absurdities than *Philanthropos,* who does not deserve the Name he assumes. Look at this Passage in his Letter. —*A Birth-Right,* an inherent *Right*—Ha, ha, ha, ho, ho,—Confound the Nonsense! No, the Right of any Prince, whether *hereditary* or *elective* is not *inherent* but *derived;* it is a *Right in Trust,* committed to him upon certain Conditions by the *People,* which Conditions, if he observes not, he forfeits this Right; and a Man can no more be born a *King,* than he can be born a *Reverend Commissary.* —Here again, *I know of no Essential or Fundamental of the constitution but Parliaments.* Ha, ha, ha. —Don't you know *Wiseacre?* Why the *People,* the *Constituents* of these *Parliaments,* are the *Essential* and *Fundamental* of the *Constitution,* the *Parliaments* being only the *Creatures of the People.* —Hey, hey, hey! *Their Existence was before the Law, their Origin cannot be founded on any Law, we have Laws for the Choice and Regulation of them, but not for their Existence.* Ha, ha, ha, ho, Excellent! so much for *Parliaments; that is, we have Laws for their Existence, but not for their Existence.* Quod erat demonstrandum. —You Mr. *Philanthropos,* shall have a *hereditary Right* to be *King of the Blunderers.* I think Friend *Jonas,* these Disputes are altogether needless, and ought not to be drawn out to such a great Length, because, in the first Place, they do not answer the pretended Purpose for which they were broached, and it is only in the Power of the *Legislature* to determine such Cavils, and secondly, they breed Animosities and Heartburnings, among People that were formerly good Neighbours, and disturb the Quiet of Society. However, here's a Health to the *Freeholder,* and all true *Whigs,* (ay, ay, to all true Whigs, says you) for if any one of these *Partizens* deserves the Name of an honest Fellow, he seems, in my Opinion, to have the best Title to it.

Here there stepp'd into the Hall a stately grave Person, who took a Survey of the whole *Posse of Authors*, and then with a scornful Smile turned towards the Place where we were. —What Stranger is that, said I? —I believe, answer'd you, his Name is *Public Opinion*, he is a Person of nice Taste, and hard to please; I never yet could reconcile him to any of my *Authors*. —Here coming close up to us, he stopp'd our Enquiry; after he had tasted of our Bowl, he asked what we were about. —Taking a View of my *Authors*, said you. —Authors! replied he, sneeringly, I believe such a Rabble of *Authors* never were before heard of, —An't you afraid of bringing your Paper into Contempt, and disobliging your Readers, by being concerned with these *Writers* and their Performances, without scrupulously weighing the Value of their Works, before you trouble the Public with them? —As for their *Works*, said you, I never gave my self the Trouble to weigh the Value of any of them, my *Types* are always in Readiness for them, when they send me a *Piece of Money*, and instead of reading the *Author's Piece*, to find the value of it, I read the *Money Bill* he sends along with it, and according as that is more or less in Value, so I put a greater or less Value upon the *Author* and his Performance. —Strange way of judging! But do you think the Public will judge so? —Undoubtedly Sir, for we daily find that many People are much taken notice of and esteemed, who have nothing but Money to recommend them, any more than these *Performances of my Authors*, paltry and insignificant as you take them to be. —This *Sophistical* Argument, said he, smells rank of the *Native of Maryland*, and his Friend *Philanthropos*. —May be so, said you, but come, here's to our better Acquaintance.—

We were here interrupted by a great Noise at the Door, and looking out, I saw a certain precise *Quaker*, engaged in a Dispute with half a Dozen, whilst one bawl'd out, *I disassent, ho! I disassent, ho!* —Hey, said you, here's more *Authors* from another Quarter, these are not *Gazette Gentlemen*. —Lo, here is Friend *Ezekiel*, engaged with mighty *Joshua* and his Adherents. Here I was bit in the Leg by a curs'd *Musketo*, so the whole Vision vanishing, I left off dreaming and fell to scratching.

Don Francisco de Quevedo Villegas (1748)

BENJAMIN FRANKLIN ("NED TYPE")

(1706–1790)

Verses on the Virginia Capitol Fire*

Mr. Printer,

It may entertain the curious and learned Part of your Subscribers, if you give them the following genuine *Speech* and *Address*, which, for the *Importance* of the *Subject*, *Grandeur* of *Sentiment*, and *Elegance* of *Expression*, perhaps exceed Any they have hitherto seen. For the Benefit of more common Readers, I have turn'd them, with some Paraphrase, into *plain English Verse*. I am told by Friends, that my Performance is excellent: But I claim no other Praise than what regards my *Rhyme*, and my *Perspicuity*. All the other Beauties I acknowledge, are owing to the *Original*, whose true Sense I have every where follow'd with a scrupulous Exactness. If envious Critics should observe, that some of my Lines are *too short* in their Number of Feet, I own it; but then, to make ample Amends, I have given *very good Measure* in most of the others. I am, Sir, your constant Reader,   NED TYPE

[*Here follow The Speech of Sir William Gooch, the Humble Address of the Council, and the Governor's Answer.—Ed.*]

The SPEECH Versyfied.

L - - D have Mercy on us!—the CAPITOL! the CAPITOL! is burnt down!
O astonishing Fate! — which occasions this Meeting in Town.
And this *Fate* proves a *Loss*, to be deplored the more,
The said *Fate* being th' *Effect* of Malice and *Design*, to be sure.
And yet 'tis hard to comprehend how a Crime of so flagitious a Nature
Should be committed, or even *imagined*, by any but an *irrational* Creature.

* Leonard F. Labaree, ed., *The Papers of Benjamin Franklin*, III (New Haven, 1961).

290

But when you consider, that the first *Emission of Smoke* was not from below,
And that Fires kindled by Accident *always burn slow,*
And not with half the Fury as when they *burn on Purpose* you know
You'll be forced to ascribe it (with Hearts full of Sadness)   10
To the horrid Machinations of desperate Villains, instigated by infernal
    Madness.
  God forbid I should accuse or excuse any without just Foundation,
Yet I may venture to assert—for our own Reputation,
That such superlative Wickedness never entred the Hearts of Virginians,
    who are the CREAM of the British Nation.
  The Clerks have been examin'd, and clear'd by the May'r,
Yet are willing to be examin'd again by you, and that's fair.
And will prove in the Face of the Country, if requir'd,
That it was not by their *Conduct* our Capitol was fir'd.
I must add, to do 'em Justice, that the Comfort we have,
In enjoying our authentic Registers, which those Clerks did save,   20
Is owing to their Activity, Resolution and Diligence,
Together with Divine Providence
All which would have been in vain, I protest,
If the Wind, at the bursting out of the Flames, had not changed from *East*
    to *Northwest.*
  Our Treasury being low, and my Infirmities great,
I would have kept you prorogu'd till the Revisal of the Laws was compleat;
But this Misfortune befalling the *Capitol* of the Capital of our Nation
Require your immediate Care and Assistance for its *Instauration.*
  To press you in a Point of such Usefulness manifest,
Would shew a Diffidence of your sincere Zeal for the public Interest   30
For which you and I always make such a laudable Pother,
And for which we've so often *applauded one Another.*
  The same public Spirit which within these Walls us'd to direct you all,
Will determine you (as Fathers of your Country) to apply Means effectual
For restoring the ROYAL FABRIC to its former Beauty
And Magnificence, according to your Duty;
With the like Apartments, elegant and spacious
For all the *weighty* purposes of Government, so capacious.
  Mean time the College and Court of Hustings our *Weight* may sustain,
But pray let us speedily have our CAPITOL, our *important* CAPITOL again.   40

The COUNCIL's Answer.

We the King's *best Subjects*, the Council of this Dominion,
Are deeply affected (as is every true Virginian)
With the unhappy Occasion of our present Meeting:
——In Troth we have but a sorry Greeting.
We are also not a little touch'd (in the Head) with the same *Weakness* as
  your Honour's,
And therefore think this raging Fire which consum'd our *Capitol*, should
  incite us to reform our Manners:
The best *Expedient* at present to avert the Indignation divine,
And *nobly* to express our *Gratitude* for the *Justice*, which (temper'd with
  Mercy) doth shine,
In *preserving* our Records, tho' Red hot,
And like Brands pluck'd out of the Flames, in which they were going to pot, 50
Without this *Expedient* we shall be ruin'd quite.
Besides, This FIRE puts us in Mind of NEW-LIGHT;
And we think it Heav'n's Judgment on us for tolerating the Presbyterians,
Whose Forefathers drubb'd ours, about a hundred Year-hence.
We therefore resolve to abate a little of our Drinking, Gaming, Cursing and
  Swearing,
And make up for the rest, by persecuting some itinerant Presbyterian.
An *active Discharge* of our *important* Trusts, according to your Honour's
  Desire,
Is the wisest *Project of Insurance* that can be, of the Public Safety, from the
  Attempts of such as would *set it on fire.*
'Tis *a Project* also for advancing the Honour and Interest of our King and
  Nation,
And *a Project* for engaging Heaven's Protection from Generation to Genera-
  tion. 60
We take this Opportunity, that we may not be suspected of Malignity,
To congratulate you, Sir, on your Promotion to the Baronet's Dignity;
A fresh Instance of just Regard to your long and faithful Services, we say,
Because from Carthagena your Honour came safe away.[1]
And you lent and sent such *great Assistance*[2] for reducing CANADA.

---

[1] Sir William Gooch, governor of Virginia, 1727–49, had raised and led 400 men to assist British forces in the attack on Cartagena, 1740, where he was seriously wounded and contracted a fever. He was created a baronet Nov. 4, 1746. [Labaree's note].
[2] One WHOLE Company.

The BARONET's Reply.

The just Sense you express for the Loss of our CAPITOL,
    which to be sure was a fatal Mishap,
Your affectionate Concern for the *Infirmities of my Honour*,
And Joy at my new Title, of which our good K—g is the Donor,
Claim sincere Acknowledgments of Thankfulness,
And Gratitude, for this obliging Address.   70
    And, (lest here and hereafter we're left in the Lurch)
To promote *true Religion*, (I mean our own Church)
I'll heartily concur with you, and lend a few Knocks
To suppress these confounding New Light Heterodox.
Then if from our Sins, we also refrain,
Perhaps we may have our CAPITOL! our dear CAPITOL! our glorious ROYAL
    CAPITOL again.   (1747)

"JUBA"

To the Ladies of Maryland*

Would you, my Fair, triumphant lead along
Of sighing, passive Slaves, a shining Throng?
Say, would you learn the happy pleasing Art
To charm, and to secure the captive Heart?
The Muse thro' all her various Maze pursue,
Her Theme is Beauty, and she sings to you.
  Shun Affectation in your Air and Dress;
The clipt, lispt Accent, and the prim set Face:
Easy each Motion, natural and free,
Not pinch'd with cramp, strait-laced Formality: 10
Bid Grace and Dignity from conscious Worth,
From Virtue, and fair Honour's Spring, beam forth.
Let not your Cheek the painted Falshood know,
But flame with the pure native Crimson's Glow,
Whose Tincture does from modest Merit flow:
A native Grace shall more attractive prove
Than all th'Auxiliaries of Art, to move.
Affect to please the Men of Sense alone,
And scorn the *Foppling Flutters* of the Town:
A Freedom disengaged, and careless Ease,   20
Shall the unwary Heart, unaiming, seize:
(Love's richest Gift) an easy, graceful Smile,
Pow'rful to charm, proves an alluring Wile;
On which hid Darts shall certain Conquests wait,
While yielding Slaves to you resign their Fate.

* *The Maryland Gazette*, No. 8 (June 14, 1745).

Fly Books; they'll turn your Head, and spoil your Charms;
Philosophy your ev'ry Grace disarms,
Yet deign to make the lighter Muse your Care,
'Twill form the Wit, and give the Debonnair:
Mix'd with the social Choir, the Dance now grace;   30
And artful moving, swim the mystic Maze:
Or with the full join'd Concert tuneful sing,
Or wake, with skilful Touch, the speaking String.
The Parent of the Graces, Smiles and Loves,
Those gay, those Heart-ensnaring Lures approves.
Those fav'rite Arts her Empire's Power sustain,
Those fav'rite Arts her *Cupids* still maintain.
Be neat, not nice; be rather clean than fine;
And let plain Elegance around you shine.
Of Novel Vanities th' Expences shun,   40
Nor through the Lab'rinths of the Fashion run:
To please the more, be careless still to please;
So shall you charm with more becoming Ease.
With fairer Grace neglected Beauties glow,
And Charms, the less adorn'd, more lovely show.   (1745)

JAMES STERLING

(1701–1763)

The 22d Ode of the first Book of Horace *imitated; and inscribed to the Lady of his late Excellency Samuel Ogle, Esquire**

1.

The christian hero, pure from sin,
Serene, and fortify'd within,
Defies the rage of civil jars,
Assembly-feuds, and foreign wars;
   Nor wants the troops, brave *Amherst*[1] led,
He, safe in sanctity of life,
From the *French* sword and *Indian* knife,
N'er dreads a circumcision of the head.

2.

   Whether he purposes to go;
Thro' *Apalachian* rocks and snow.   10
Cannadean-forests, *Funda's* frost,
Or bleak *Ontario's* barbarous coast;
   Or visits *Niagara's Fall*:
With soul, not liable to fear,
He sees tremendous dangers near;
Smiling, he sees; superior to them all.

* *The American Magazine* (October, 1758).
[1] Jeffrey Amherst (1717–1797), supreme commander of the British forces during the French and Indian War.

3.

'Tis true, *fair Friend*; no evil can
Surprize the heav'n-protected man.
—As thro' thy pleasing lawns I stray'd;
(While *Virtue*, like a blooming maid,
 Employ'd my tho'ts on all her charms)
From neighb'ring groves, with threat'ning eyes,
A *Buffalo* of monstrous size,
Rush'd sudden forth, nor gave my soul alarms!

    20

4.

Such never drank *Ohio's* floods,
Or bellow'd in *Virginian*-woods;
Such and so fierce did ne'er advance
'Gainst *Spanish Don* with daring lance;
 Such ne'er in *Hole of Hockley*[2] bled.
Yet *me* unarm'd the savage saw,
With fear and reverential awe,
Spurning the ground, he came, he gaz'd, he fled.

    30

5.

Place me on *Hudson's* dreary shore,
Where icy mountains, bursting, roar;
Where Hyperborean tempests blow;
Where tree or shrub can never grow.
 (*Virtue*, bright goddess! I'm prepar'd)
Place me, where howling swamps extend;
A gloomy wild, without an end!
Yet *Virtue* there shall be her vot'ry's guard!

    40

6.

Cast me amidst the hissing brood,
When sultry *Sirius* fires their blood;
Where from th' inhospitable brake
Dire basilisks their rattles shake:
 Yet, *Virtue*, thou shalt cheer the place;
And, strongly imag'd in my mind,
Within my raptur'd heart inshrin'd,
Shalt sweetly talk, and smile with *Ogle's* grace! (1758)

---

[2] A bull-baiting pit.

BENJAMIN FRANKLIN

(1706–1790)

One of the most elusive figures in American literature, Franklin is here represented by selections that reveal some parts of the large range of his interests and activities. Many of these are mentioned in the Introduction (pp. 223–228). Known widely as a politician and scientist, Franklin was also an inveterate writer of satire and parody. Using the persona of Silence Dogood or of Poor Richard, Franklin cut through pious homilies with such thrusts as his recipe "to make a New-England Funeral Elegy." In the "Parody of a Meditation" he used the proverb of one having his cake and eating it. Poor Richard battles reality with his pithy sayings, and we begin to see in them a popular type of current humor—the put-on. Such humor rests, in part, on the audience's confusion over when the humorist is using it and when he is not. Reading these humorous pieces places us on guard as we read the other selections, so that we are better prepared to watch for his many rhetorical devices. Capable of writing serious scientific descriptions or discussions, Franklin was also quite able to adopt, or to shift to, an apparently naïve position even in the midst of such works. He could, in other words, mislead the careless reader and cause him to mistake Franklin's position. The selections below on the poor and on the slave trade must be carefully read to determine Franklin's views.

Silence Dogood, No. 7*

Give me the Muse, whose generous Force,
Impatient of the Reins,
Pursues an unattempted Course,
Breaks all the Criticks Iron Chains. Watts.[1]

---

* Leonard W. Labaree, ed., *The Papers of Benjamin Franklin*, I (New Haven, Conn., 1959).
[1] Isaac Watts (1674–1748), English hymn writer.

298

To the Author of the *New-England Courant*.

Sir,

It has been the Complaint of many Ingenious Foreigners, who have travell'd amongst us, *That good Poetry is not to be expected in New-England.* I am apt to Fancy, the Reason is, not because our Countreymen are altogether void of a Poetical Genius, nor yet because we have not those Advantages of Education which other Countries have, but purely because we do not afford that Praise and Encouragement which is merited, when any thing extraordinary of this Kind is produc'd among us: Upon which Consideration I have determined, when I meet with a Good Piece of New-England Poetry, to give it a suitable Encomium, and thereby endeavour to discover to the World some of its Beautys, in order to encourage the Author to go on, and bless the World with more, and more Excellent Productions.

There has lately appear'd among us a most Excellent Piece of Poetry, entituled, *An Elegy upon the much Lamented Death of Mrs. Mehitebell Kitel, Wife of Mr. John Kitel of Salem, &c.* It may justly be said in its Praise, without Flattery to the Author, that it is the most *Extraordinary* Piece that ever was wrote in New-England. The Language is so soft and Easy, the Expression so moving and pathetick, but above all, the Verse and Numbers so Charming and Natural, that it is almost beyond Comparison,

> *The Muse disdains*
> *Those Links and Chains,*
> *Measures and Rules of vulgar Strains,*
> *And o'er the Laws of Harmony a Sovereign Queen she reigns.* Watts.

I find no English Author, Ancient or Modern, whose Elegies may be compar'd with this, in respect to the Elegance of Stile, or Smoothness of Rhime; and for the affecting Part, I will leave your Readers to judge, if ever they read any Lines, that would sooner make them *draw their Breath* and Sigh, if not shed Tears, than these following.

> *Come let us mourn, for we have lost a Wife, a Daughter, and*
> * a Sister,*
> *Who has lately taken Flight, and greatly we have mist her.*

In another Place,

> *Some little Time before she yielded up her Breath,*
> *She said, I ne'er shall hear one Sermon more on Earth.*
> *She kist her Husband some little Time before she expir'd,*
> *Then lean'd her Head the Pillow on, just out of Breath and tir'd.*

But the Threefold Appellation in the first Line

> *a Wife, a Daughter, and a Sister,*

must not pass unobserved. That Line in the celebrated Watts,

> GUNSTON *the Just, the Generous, and the Young,*

is nothing Comparable to it. The latter only mentions three Qualifications of *one* Person who was deceased, which therefore could raise Grief and Compassion but for *One*. Whereas the former, (*our most excellent Poet*) gives his Reader a Sort of an Idea of the Death of *Three Persons*, viz.

> *a Wife, a Daughter, and a Sister,*

which is *Three Times* as great a Loss as the Death of *One*, and consequently must raise *Three Times* as much Grief and Compassion in the Reader.

I should be very much straitned for Room, if I should attempt to discover even half the Excellencies of this Elegy which are obvious to me. Yet I cannot omit one Observation, which is, that the Author has (to his Honour) invented a new Species of Poetry, which wants a Name, and was never before known. His Muse scorns to be confin'd to the old Measures and Limits, or to observe the dull Rules of Cricks;

> *Nor Rapin gives her Rules to fly, nor Purcell Notes to sing.* Watts.

Now 'tis Pity that such an Excellent Piece should not be dignify'd with a particular Name; and seeing it cannot justly be called, either *Epic*, *Sapphic*, *Lyric*, or *Pindaric*, nor any other Name yet invented, I presume it may, (in Honour and Remembrance of the Dead) be called the KITELIC. Thus much in the Praise of *Kitelic Poetry*.

It is certain, that those Elegies which are of our own Growth, (and our Soil seldom produces any other sort of Poetry) are by far the greatest part, wretchedly Dull and Ridiculous. Now since it is imagin'd by many, that our Poets are honest, well-meaning Fellows, who do their best, and that if they had but some Instructions how to govern Fancy with Judgment, they would make indifferent good Elegies; I shall here subjoin a Receipt for that purpose, which was left me as a Legacy, (among other valuable Rarities) by my Reverend Husband. It is as follows,

A RECEIPT TO MAKE A NEW-ENGLAND
FUNERAL ELEGY

For the Title of your Elegy. Of these you may have enough ready made to your Hands; but if you should chuse to make it your self, you must be sure not to omit the Words *Aetatis Suae*, which will Beautify it exceedingly.

For the Subject of your Elegy. Take one of your Neighbours who has lately departed this Life; it is no great matter at what Age the Party dy'd, but it will be best if he went away suddenly, being *Kill'd, Drown'd,* or *Froze to Death.*

Having chose the Person, take all his Virtues, Excellencies, &c. and if he have not enough, you may borrow some to make up a sufficient Quantity: To these add his last Words, dying Expressions, &c. if they are to be had; mix all these together, and be sure you *strain* them well. Then season all with a Handful or two of Melancholly Expressions, such as, *Dreadful, Deadly, cruel cold Death, unhappy Fate, weeping Eyes,* &c. Have mixed all these Ingredients well, put them into the empty Scull of some *young Harvard;* (but in Case you have ne'er a One at Hand, you may use your own,) there let them Ferment for the Space of a Fortnight, and by that Time they will be incorporated into a Body, which take out, and having prepared a sufficient Quantity of double Rhimes, such as, *Power, Flower; Quiver, Shiver; Grieve us, Leave us; tell you, excel you; Expeditions, Physicians; Fatigue him, Intrigue him;* &c. you must spread all upon Paper, and if you can procure a Scrap of Latin to put at the End, it will garnish it mightily; then having affixed your Name at the Bottom, with a *Mœstus Composuit,* you will have an Excellent Elegy.

N.B. This Receipt will serve when a Female is the Subject of your Elegy, provided you borrow a greater Quantity of Virtues, Excellencies, &c. Sir, Your Servant,   Silence Dogood (1722)

*Parody of a Meditation**

I

THE PARODY

YOU gave us in your last a melancholy Account of Human Life, in the Meditation upon that Subject. The gloomy and splenetick Part of your Readers like it much; but as for me, I do not love to see the dark Side of Things; and besides, I do not think such Reflections upon Life altogether Just. The World is a very good World, and if we behave our selves well, we shall doubtless do very well in it. I never thought even *Job* in the right, when he repin'd that the Days of a Man are *few* and *full of Trouble;* for certainly both these Things cannot be together just Causes of Complaint; if our Days are full of Trouble, the fewer of 'em the better. But as for the Author of the Meditation above-mention'd, besides what he says in common with *Job*, he seems to complain in several respects very weakly, and without the least shadow of Reason; in particular, That he cannot be alive now, and ten Years ago, and ten Years hence, at the same time: With very little Variation, as you shall see, his elegant Expressions will serve for a Child who laments that he cannot eat his Cake and have his Cake.

All the few days we live are full of Vanity; and our choicest Pleasures sprinkled with bitterness:

All the few Cakes we have are puffed up with Yeast; and the nicest Gingerbread is spotted with Flyshits!

The time that's past is vanish'd like a dream; and that which is to come is not yet at all.

The Cakes that we have eaten are no more to be seen; and those which are to come are not yet baked.

The present we are in stays but for a moment, and then flies away, and returns no more:

The present Mouthful is chewed but a little while, and then is swallow'd down, and comes up no more.

Already we are dead to the years we have liv'd; and shall never live them over again:

Already we have digested the Cakes we have eaten, and shall never eat them over again.

But the longer we live, the shorter is our life; and in the end we become a little lump of clay.

*Alfred Owen Aldridge, "A Religious Hoax by Benjamin Franklin, "*American Literature*, XXXVI (May 1964).

And the more we eat, the less is the Piece remaining; and in the end the whole will become Sir-reverence![1]

O vain, and miserable world! how sadly true is all this story!

O vain, and miserable Cake-shop! *&c.*

Away with all such insignificant Meditations. I am for taking *Solomon's* Advice, *eating Bread with Joy, and drinking Wine with a merry Heart.* Let us rejoice and bless God, that we are neither Oysters, Hogs, nor Dray-Horses; and not stand repining that He has not made us Angels; lest we be found unworthy of that share of Happiness He has thought fit to allow us.

II

THE OPTIMISTIC MEDITATION

Most happy are we, the sons of men, above all other creatures, who are born to behold the glorious rays of the sun, and to enjoy the pleasant fruits of the earth.

With what pleasure did our parents first receive us, first to hear us cry, then to see us smile, and afterwards to behold us growing up and thriving in the world.

By their good examples and a vertuous education, they put us in the right path to happiness, as all good parents do;

Then we, by making a right use of that share of reason with which God hath endued us, spend our days in gaining and enjoying the blessings of life, which are innumerable.

If we meet with crosses and disappointments, they are but as sowr sauce to the sweet meats we enjoy, and the one hath not a right relish without the other.

As time passes away, it carries our past pains with it, and returns no more; and the longer we live the fewer misfortunes we have to go through.

If death takes us off in the heighth of our prosperity, it takes us from the pains which may ensue.

And a great blessing attends old age, for by that we are naturally wean'd from the pleasures of youth, and a more solid pleasure takes place, The thoughts of our having so far escaped all the hazards that attend mankind, and a contemplation on all our former good actions.

And if we have done all the good we could, we have done all that we might, and death is no terror to a good man.

And after we are far declined, with hearty praises and thanks we recommend our soul to God, the eternal Being from whom we received it.

Then comes the grave, and the sweet sleep of death, pleasant as a bed to a weary traveller after a long journey. (1734)

[1] A turd.

The Way to Wealth*

AS CLEARLY SHOWN IN THE PREFACE OF
AN OLD ALMANAC ENTITLED
"POOR RICHARD IMPROVED"

COURTEOUS READER:

I have heard that nothing gives an author so great pleasure as to find his works respectfully quoted by others. Judge, then, how much I must have been gratified by an incident I am going to relate to you. I stopped my horse lately where a great number of people were collected at an auction of merchants' goods. The hour of the sale not being come, they were conversing on the badness of the times; and one of the company called to a plain, clean, old man, with white locks: "Pray, Father Abraham, what think you of the times? Will not these heavy taxes quite ruin the country? How shall we ever be able to pay them? What would you advise us to do?" Father Abraham stood up and replied: "If you would have my advice, I will give it you in short; for *A word to the wise is enough*, as Poor Richard says." They joined in desiring him to speak his mind, and gathering round him he proceeded as follows:

"Friends," said he, "the taxes are indeed very heavy, and if those laid on by the government were the only ones we had to pay, we might more easily discharge them, but we have many others and much more grievous to some of us. We are taxed twice as much by our idleness, three times as much by our pride, and four times as much by our folly, and from these taxes the commissioners cannot ease or deliver us by allowing an abatement. However, let us hearken to good advice and something may be done for us; *God helps them that help themselves*, as Poor Richard says.

"I. It would be thought a hard government that should tax its people one-tenth part of their time, to be employed in its service, but idleness taxes many of us much more; sloth by bringing on diseases, absolutely shortens life. *Sloth, like rust, consumes faster than labor wears, while the used key is always bright*, as Poor Richard says. *But dost thou love life, then do not squander time, for that is the stuff life is made of*, as Poor Richard says. How much more than is necessary do we spend in sleep, forgetting that *The sleeping fox catches no poultry*, and that *There will be sleeping enough in the grave*, as Poor Richard says.

"*If time be of all things the most precious, wasting time must be*, as Poor Richard says, *the greatest prodigality*, since, as he elsewhere tells us, *Lost time is never found again, and what we call time enough always proves little*

---

* John Bigelow, ed., *Complete Works of Benjamin Franklin*, I (New York, 1887).

enough. Let us then up and be doing, and doing to the purpose; so by diligence shall we do more with less perplexity. *Sloth makes all things difficult, but industry all things easy;* and *He that riseth late must trot all day, and shall scarce overtake his business at night;* while *Laziness travels so slowly that Poverty soon overtakes him. Drive thy business, let not that drive thee;* and *Early to bed and early to rise, makes a man healthy, wealthy, and wise,* as Poor Richard says.

"So what signifies wishing and hoping for better times? We may make these times better if we bestir ourselves. *Industry need not wish, and he that lives upon hopes will die fasting. There are no gains without pains; then help, hands, for I have no lands;* or if I have they are smartly taxed. *He that hath a trade hath an estate, and he that hath a calling hath an office of profit and honor,* as Poor Richard says; but then the trade must be worked at and the calling followed, or neither the estate nor the office will enable us to pay our taxes. If we are industrious we shall never starve, for *At the working man's house hunger looks in but dares not enter.* Nor will the bailiff nor the constable enter, for *Industry pays debts, while despair increaseth them.* What though you have found no treasure, nor has any rich relation left you a legacy, *Diligence is the mother of good luck, and God gives all things to industry. Then plough deep while sluggards sleep, and you shall have corn to sell and to keep.* Work while it is called to-day, for you know not how much you may be hindered to-morrow. *One to-day is worth two to-morrows,* as Poor Richard says; and further, *Never leave that till to-morrow which you can do to-day.* If you were a servant would you not be ashamed that a good master should catch you idle? Are you then your own master? Be ashamed to catch yourself idle when there is so much to be done for yourself, your family, your country, and your king. Handle your tools without mittens; remember that *The cat in gloves catches no mice,* as Poor Richard says. It is true there is much to be done, and perhaps you are weak-handed, but stick to it steadily and you will see great effects; for *Constant dropping wears away stones;* and *By diligence and patience the mouse ate in two the cable;* and *Little strokes fell great oaks.*

"Methinks I hear some of you say, 'Must a man afford himself no leisure?' I will tell thee, my friend, what Poor Richard says: *Employ thy time well, if thou meanest to gain leisure; and, since thou art not sure of a minute, throw not away an hour.* Leisure is time for doing something useful; this leisure the diligent man will obtain, but the lazy man never; for *A life of leisure and a life of laziness are two things. Many, without labor, would live by their wits only, but they break for want of stock;* whereas industry gives comfort and plenty and respect. *Fly pleasures, and they will follow you. The diligent spinner has a large shift; and now I have a sheep and a cow, everybody bids me good morrow.*

"II. But with our industry we must likewise be steady, settled, and careful, and oversee our own affairs with our own eyes, and not trust too much to others; for, as Poor Richard says:

> *I never saw an oft-removed tree,*
> *Nor yet an oft-removed family,*
> *That throve so well as those that settled be.*

And again, *Three removes are as bad as a fire;* and again, *Keep thy shop, and thy shop will keep thee;* and again: *If you would have your business done, go; if not, send.* And again:

> *He that by the plough would thrive,*
> *Himself must either hold or drive.*

And again, *The eye of a master will do more work than both his hands;* and again, *Want of care does us more damage than want of knowledge;* and again, *Not to oversee workmen is to leave them your purse open.* Trusting too much to others' care is the ruin of many; for, *In the affairs of this world men are saved, not by faith, but by the want of it;* but a man's own care is profitable; for, *If you would have a faithful servant, and one that you like, serve yourself. A little neglect may breed great mischief; for want of a nail the shoe was lost; for want of a shoe the horse was lost; and for want of a horse the rider was lost, being overtaken and slain by the enemy; all for want of a little care about a horse-shoe nail.*

"III. So much for industry, my friends, and attention to one's own business; but to these we must add frugality, if we would make our industry more certainly successful. A man may, if he knows not how to save as he gets, keep his nose all his life to the grindstone and die not worth a groat at last. *A fat kitchen makes a lean will;* and

> *Many estates are spent in the getting,*
> *Since women for tea forsook spinning and knitting,*
> *And men for punch forsook hewing and splitting.*

If you would be wealthy, think of saving as well as of getting. The Indies have not made Spain rich, because her outgoes are greater than her incomes.

"Away then with your expensive follies, and you will not then have so much cause to complain of hard times, heavy taxes, and chargeable families; for

> *Women and wine, game and deceit,*
> *Make the wealth small and the want great.*

And further, *What maintains one vice would bring up two children.* You may think, perhaps, that a little tea, or a little punch now and then, diet a little more costly, clothes a little finer, and a little entertainment now and then, can be no great matter; but remember, *Many a little makes a mickle*. Beware of little expenses: *A small leak will sink a great ship*, as Poor Richard says; and again, *Who dainties love, shall beggars prove;* and moreover, *Fools make feasts, and wise men eat them.*

"Here you are all got together at this sale of fineries and knick-knacks. You call them *goods;* but if you do not take care they will prove *evils* to some of you. You expect they will be sold cheap, and perhaps they may for less than they cost; but if you have no occasion for them they must be dear to you. Remember what Poor Richard says: *Buy what thou hast no need of, and ere long thou shalt sell thy necessaries.* And again, *At a great pennyworth pause a while.* He means, that perhaps the cheapness is apparent only, and not real; or the bargain, by straitening thee in thy business, may do thee more harm than good. For in another place he says, *Many have been ruined by buying good pennyworths.* Again, *It is foolish to lay out money in a purchase of repentance;* and yet this folly is practised every day at auctions for want of minding the Almanac. Many a one, for the sake of finery on the back, have gone with a hungry belly and half-starved their families. *Silks and satins, scarlet and velvets, put out the kitchen fire*, as Poor Richard says.

"These are not the necessaries of life; they can scarcely be called the conveniences; and yet, only because they look pretty, how many want to have them! By these and other extravagances the genteel are reduced to poverty and forced to borrow of those whom they formerly despised, but who, through industry and frugality, have maintained their standing; in which case it appears plainly that *A ploughman on his legs is higher than a gentleman on his knees*, as Poor Richard says. Perhaps they have had a small estate left them, which they knew not the getting of: they think, *It is day, and will never be night;* that a little to be spent out of so much is not worth minding; but *Always taking out of the meal-tub, and never putting in, soon comes to the bottom*, as Poor Richard says; and then, *When the well is dry, they know the worth of water.* But this they might have known before, if they had taken his advice. *If you would know the value of money, go and try to borrow some; for he that goes a borrowing goes a sorrowing*, as Poor Richard says; and indeed so does he that lends to such people, when he goes to get it again. Poor Dick further advises and says,

> *Fond pride of dress is sure a very curse;*
> *Ere fancy you consult, consult your purse.*

And again, *Pride is as loud a beggar as Want, and a great deal more saucy.* When you have bought one fine thing you must buy ten more, that your appearance may be all of a piece; but Poor Dick says, *It is easier to suppress the first desire than to satisfy all that follow it.* And it is as truly folly for the poor to ape the rich, as for the frog to swell in order to equal the ox.

> *Vessels large may venture more,*
> *But little boats should keep near shore.*

It is, however, a folly soon punished; for, as Poor Richard says, *Pride that dines on vanity sups on contempt. Pride breakfasted with Plenty, dined with Poverty, and supped with Infamy.* And after all, of what use is this pride of appearance, for which so much is risked, so much is suffered? It cannot promote health, nor ease pain; it makes no increase of merit in the person; it creates envy; it hastens misfortune.

"But what madness must it be to *run in debt* for these superfluities? We are offered by the terms of this sale six months' credit; and that, perhaps, has induced some of us to attend it, because we cannot spare the ready money, and hope now to be fine without it. But ah! think what you do when you run in debt; you give to another power over your liberty. If you cannot pay at the time, you will be ashamed to see your creditor; you will be in fear when you speak to him; you will make poor, pitiful, sneaking excuses, and by degrees come to lose your veracity, and sink into base, downright lying; for, *The second vice is lying, the first is running in debt*, as Poor Richard says; and again, to the same purpose, *Lying rides upon Debt's back;* whereas a freeborn Englishman ought not to be ashamed nor afraid to see or speak to any man living. But poverty often deprives a man of all spirit and virtue. *It is hard for an empty bag to stand upright.*

"What would you think of that prince or of that government who should issue an edict forbidding you to dress like a gentleman or gentlewoman, on pain of imprisonment or servitude? Would you not say that you were free, have a right to dress as you please, and that such an edict would be a breach of your privileges, and such a government tyrannical? And yet you are about to put yourself under such tyranny when you run in debt for such dress! Your creditor has authority, at his pleasure, to deprive you of your liberty by confining you in gaol till you shall be able to pay him. When you have got your bargain you may perhaps think little of payment, but, as Poor Richard says, *Creditors have better memories than debtors; creditors are a superstitious sect, great observers of set days and times.* The day comes round before you are aware, and the demand is made before you are prepared to satisfy it; or, if you bear your debt in mind, the term, which at first seemed so long, will, as it lessens, appear extremely short. Time will seem to have added wings to his heels as well as his shoulders. *Those have a short Lent who owe money to be paid at Easter*. At present, perhaps, you may think yourselves in thriving circumstances, and that you can bear a little extravagance without injury, but—

> *For age and want save while you may;*
> *No morning sun lasts a whole day.*

Gain may be temporary and uncertain, but ever, while you live, expense is constant and certain; and *It is easier to build two chimneys than to keep one in fuel*, as Poor Richard says; so, *Rather go to bed supperless than rise in debt*.

> *Get what you can, and what you get hold;*
> *'Tis the stone that will turn all your lead into gold.*

And, when you have got the Philosopher's stone, sure you will no longer complain of bad times or the difficulty of paying taxes.

"IV. This doctrine, my friends, is reason and wisdom; but, after all, do not depend too much upon your own industry and frugality and prudence, though excellent things, for they may all be blasted, without the blessing of Heaven; and therefore ask that blessing humbly, and be not uncharitable to those that at present seem to want it, but comfort and help them. Remember Job suffered and was afterwards prosperous.

"And now, to conclude, *Experience keeps a dear school, but fools will learn in no other*, as Poor Richard says, and scarce in that, for it is true *We may give advice, but we cannot give conduct*. However, remember this, *They that will not be counselled cannot be helped;* and further, that *If you will not hear Reason, she will surely rap your knuckles*, as Poor Richard says."

Thus the old gentleman ended his harangue. The people heard it and approved the doctrine, and immediately practised the contrary, just as if it had been a common sermon; for the auction opened, and they began to buy extravagantly. I found the good man had thoroughly studied my Almanacs, and digested all I had dropped on these topics during the course of twenty-five years. The frequent mention he made of me must have tired any one else, but my vanity was wonderfully delighted with it, though I was conscious that not a tenth part of the wisdom was my own which he ascribed to me, but rather the gleanings that I had made of the sense of all ages and nations. However, I resolved to be the better for the echo of it, and though I had at first determined to buy stuff for a new coat, I went away resolved to wear my old one a little longer. Reader, if thou wilt do the same thy profit will be as great as mine. I am, as ever, thine to serve thee,

RICHARD SAUNDERS. (1736)

Letter to Mary Stevenson*

CRAVEN STREET, 11 June, 1760.

It is a very sensible question you ask, how the air can affect the barometer, when its opening appears covered with wood? If indeed it was so closely covered as to admit of no communication of the outward air to the surface of the mercury, the change of weight in the air could not possibly affect it. But the least crevice is sufficient for the purpose; a pinhole will do the business. And if you could look behind the frame to which your barometer is fixed, you would certainly find some small opening.

There are indeed some barometers in which the body of mercury at the lower end is contained in a close leather bag, and so the air cannot come into immediate contact with the mercury; yet the same effect is produced. For, the leather being flexible, when the bag is pressed by any additional weight of air, it contracts, and the mercury is forced up into the tube; when the air becomes lighter, and its pressure less, the weight of the mercury prevails, and it descends again into the bag.

Your observation on what you have lately read concerning insects is very just and solid. Superficial minds are apt to despise those who make that part of the creation their study, as mere triflers; but certainly the world has been much obliged to them. Under the care and management of man, the labors of the little silkworm afford employment and subsistence to thousands of families, and become an immense article of commerce. The bee, too, yields us its delicious honey, and its wax useful to a multitude of purposes. Another insect, it is said, produces the cochineal, from which we have our rich scarlet dye. The usefulness of the cantharides, or Spanish flies, in medicine, is known to all, and thousands owe their lives to that knowledge. By human industry and observation, other properties of other insects may possibly be hereafter discovered, and of equal utility. A thorough acquaintance with the nature of these little creatures may also enable mankind to prevent the increase of such as are noxious, or secure us against the mischiefs they occasion. These things doubtless your books make mention of; I can only add a particular late instance which I had from a Swedish gentleman of good credit. In the green timber, intended for ship-building at the King's yards in that country, a kind of worms were found, which every year became more numerous and more pernicious, so that the ships were greatly damaged before they came into use. The King sent Linnæus, the great naturalist, from Stockholm, to inquire into the affair, and see if the mischief was capable of any remedy. He

* Bigelow, III.

found, on examination, that the worm was produced from a small egg, deposited in the little roughnesses on the surface of the wood, by a particular kind of fly or beetle; from which the worm, as soon as it was hatched, began to eat into the substance of the wood, and after some time came out again a fly of the parent kind, and so the species increased. The season in which the fly laid its eggs, Linnæus knew to be about a fortnight (I think) in the month of May, and at no other time in the year. He therefore advised, that, some days before that season, all the green timber should be thrown into the water, and kept under water till the season was over. Which being done by the King's order, the flies, missing their usual nests, could not increase; and the species was either destroyed or went elsewhere; and the wood was effectually preserved; for, after the first year, it became too dry and hard for their purpose.

There is, however, a prudent moderation to be used in studies of this kind. The knowledge of nature may be ornamental, and it may be useful; but if, to attain an eminence in that, we neglect the knowledge and practice of essential duties, we deserve reprehension. For there is no rank in natural knowledge of equal dignity and importance with that of being a good parent, a good child, a good husband or wife, a good neighbour or friend, a good subject or citizen—that is, in short, a good Christian. Nicholas Gimcrack, therefore, who neglected the care of his family, to pursue butterflies, was a just object of ridicule, and we must give him up as fair game to the satirist.

Adieu, my dear friend, and believe me ever

Yours affectionately,

B. FRANKLIN.

From *Letter to Mary Stevenson**

Sept. 20, 1761

. . . As to our other subject, the different degrees of heat imbibed from the sun's rays by cloths of different colors, since I cannot find the notes of my experiment to send you, I must give it as well as I can from memory.

But first let me mention an experiment you may easily make yourself. Walk but a quarter of an hour in your garden when the sun shines, with a part of your dress white, and a part black; then apply your hand to them alternately, and you will find a very great difference in their warmth. The black will be quite hot to the touch, the white still cool.

Another. Try to fire paper with a burning glass. If it is white, you will not easily burn it;—but if you bring the focus to a black spot, or upon letters, written or printed, the paper will immediately be on fire under the letters.

* I. Bernard Cohen, ed., *Benjamin Franklin's Experiments* (Cambridge, Mass., 1941).

Thus fullers and dyers find black cloths, of equal thickness with white ones, and hung out equally wet, dry in the sun much sooner than the white, being more readily heated by the sun's rays. It is the same before a fire; the heat of which sooner penetrates black stockings than white ones, and so is apt sooner to burn a man's shins. Also beer much sooner warms in a black mug set before the fire, than in a white one, or in a bright silver tankard.

My experiment was this. I took a number of little square pieces of broad cloth from a taylor's pattern card, of various colors. There were black, deep blue, lighter blue, green, purple, red, yellow, white, and other colors, or shades of colors. I laid them all out upon the snow in a bright sun-shiny morning. In a few hours (I cannot now be exact as to the time) the black being warmed most by the sun, was sunk so low as to be below the stroke of the sun's rays; the dark blue almost as low, the lighter blue not quite so much as the dark, the other colors less as they were lighter; and the quite white remained on the surface of the snow, not having entered it at all.

What signifies philosophy that does not apply to some use?—May we not learn from hence, that black cloaths are not so fit to wear in a hot sunny climate or season, as white ones; because in such cloaths the body is more heated by the sun when we walk abroad, and we are at the same time heated by the exercise, which double heat is apt to bring on putrid dangerous fevers? That soldiers and seamen who must march and labor in the sun, should in the *East* or *West-Indies* have an uniform of white? That summer hats for men or women, should be white, as repelling that heat which gives head-achs to many, and to some the fatal stroke that the French call the *Coup de Soleil*? That the ladies summer hats, however, should be lined with black, as not reverberating on their faces those rays which are reflected upwards from the earth or water? That the putting a white cap of paper or linen *within* the crown of a black hat, as some do, will not keep out the heat, though it would if placed *without*. That fruit walls being blacked may receive so much heat from the sun in the day-time, as to continue warm in some degree through the night, and thereby preserve the fruit from frosts, or forward its growth?—with sundry other particulars of less or greater importance, that will occur from time to time to attentive minds?—

On the Laboring Poor*

SIR:—I have met with much invective in the papers, for these two years past, against the hardheartedness of the rich, and much complaint of the great oppressions suffered in this country by the laboring poor. Will you

* Bigelow, IV.

admit a word or two on the other side of the question? I do not propose to be an advocate for oppression or oppressors. But when I see that the poor are, by such writings, exasperated against the rich, and excited to insurrections, by which much mischief is done, and some forfeit their lives, I could wish the true state of things were better understood, the poor not made by these busy writers more uneasy and unhappy than their situation subjects them to be, and the nation not brought into disrepute among foreigners by public groundless accusations of ourselves, as if the rich in England had no compassion for the poor, and Englishmen wanted common humanity.

In justice, then, to this country, give me leave to remark that the condition of the poor here is, by far, the best in Europe; for that, except in England and her American colonies, there is not in any country of the known world, not even in Scotland or Ireland, a provision by law to enforce a support of the poor. Everywhere else necessity reduces to beggary. This law was not made by the poor. The legislators were men of fortune. By that act they voluntarily subjected their own estates, and the estates of all others, to the payment of a tax for the maintenance of the poor, encumbering those estates with a kind of rentcharge for that purpose, whereby the poor are vested with an inheritance, as it were, in all the estates of the rich. I wish they were benefited by this generous provision in any degree equal to the good intention with which it was made, and is continued. But I fear the giving mankind a dependence on any thing for support, in age or sickness, besides industry and frugality during youth and health, tends to flatter our natural indolence, to encourage idleness and prodigality, and thereby to promote and increase poverty, the very evil it was intended to cure; thus multiplying beggars instead of diminishing them.

Besides this tax, which the rich in England have subjected themselves to in behalf of the poor, amounting in some places to five or six shillings in the pound, of the annual income, they have, by donations and subscriptions, erected numerous schools in various parts of the kingdom, for educating, gratis, the children of the poor in reading and writing; and in many of those schools the children are also fed and clothed. They have erected hospitals at an immense expense for the reception and cure of the sick, the lame, the wounded, and the insane poor, for lying-in women, and deserted children. They are also continually contributing towards making up losses occasioned by fire, by storms, or by floods, and to relieve the poor in severe seasons of frost, in times of scarcity, &c., in which benevolent and charitable contributions no nation exceeds us. Surely, there is some gratitude due for so many instances of goodness.

Add to this all the laws made to discourage foreign manufactures, by laying heavy duties on them, whereby the rich are obliged to pay much higher prices for what they wear and consume, than if the trade was open. These are so many laws for the support of our laboring poor, made by the rich, and continued at their expense; all the difference of price between our own and foreign commodities, being so much given by our rich to our poor, who would indeed be enabled by it to get by degrees above poverty, if they did not, as too generally they do, consider every increase of wages only as something that enables them to drink more and work less; so that their distress in sickness, age, or times of scarcity, continues to be the same as if such laws had never been made in their favor.

Much malignant censure have some writers bestowed upon the rich for their luxury and expensive living, while the poor are starving, &c.; not considering that what the rich expend, the laboring poor receive in payment for their labor. It may seem a paradox if I should assert that our laboring poor do in every year receive *the whole revenue of the nation;* I mean not only the public revenue, but also the revenue or clear income of all private estates, or a sum equivalent to the whole.

In support of this position I reason thus. The rich do not work for one another. Their habitations, furniture, clothing, carriages, food, ornaments, and every thing in short, that they or their families use and consume, is the work or produce of the laboring poor, who are, and must be continually, paid for their labor in producing the same. In these payments the revenues of private estates are expended, for most people live up to their incomes. In clothing or provisions for troops, in arms, ammunition, ships, tents, carriages, &c., &c., (every particular the produce of labor,) much of the public revenue is expended. The pay of officers, civil and military, and of the private soldiers and sailors, requires the rest; and they spend that also in paying for what is produced by the laboring poor.

I allow that some estates may increase by the owners spending less than their income; but then I conceive that other estates do at the same time diminish by the owners spending more than their income, so that when the enriched want to buy more land, they easily find lands in the hands of the impoverished, whose necessities oblige them to sell; and thus this difference is equalled. I allow also, that part of the expense of the rich is in foreign produce or manufactures, for producing which the laboring poor of other nations must be paid; but then I say, we must first pay our own laboring poor for an equal quantity of our manufactures or produce, to exchange for those foreign productions, or we must pay for them in money, which money, not being the natural produce of our country, must first be purchased from abroad, by sending out its value in the produce or manufactures of this country, for which manufactures our laboring poor are to be paid. And indeed, if we did not export more than we import, we could have no money at all. I allow farther, that there are middle men, who make a profit, and even get estates, by purchasing the labor of the poor, and selling it at advanced prices to the rich; but then they cannot enjoy that profit, or the incomes of estates, but by spending them in employing and paying our laboring poor, in some shape or ·other, for the products of industry. Even beggars, pensioners, hospitals, and all that are supported by charity, spend their incomes in the same manner. So that finally, as I said at first, *our laboring poor receive annually the whole of the clear revenues of the nation*, and from us they can have no more.

If it be said that their wages are too low, and that they ought to be better paid for their labor, I heartily wish that any means could be fallen upon to do it, consistent with their interest and happiness; but, as the cheapness of other things is owing to the plenty of those things, so the cheapness of labor is in most cases owing to the multitude of laborers, and to their under-working one another in order to obtain employment. How is this to be remedied? A law might be made to raise their wages; but if our manufactures are too dear they will not vend abroad, and all that part of employment will fail, unless by fighting and conquering we compel other nations to buy our goods, whether they will or no, which some have been mad enough at times to propose.

Among ourselves, unless we give our working people less employment, how can we, for what they do, pay them higher than we do? Out of what fund is the additional price of labor to be paid, when all our present incomes are, as it were, mortgaged to them? Should they get higher wages, would that make them less poor, if, in consequence, they worked fewer days of the week proportionably? I have said, a law might be made to raise their wages; but I doubt much whether it could be executed to any purpose, unless another law, now indeed almost obsolete, could at the same time be revived and enforced; a law, I mean, that many have often heard and repeated, but few have ever duly considered. Six *days shalt thou labor.* This is as positive a part of the commandment, as that which says, *The* seventh *day thou shalt rest.* But we remember well to observe the indulgent part, and never think of the other. *Saint Monday* is generally as duly kept by our working people as *Sunday;* the only difference is, that, instead of employing their time cheaply at church, they are wasting it expensively at the alehouse.

I am, Sir, yours, &c.,

Medius.   (1768)

An Edict by the King of Prussia*

DANTZIG, 5 September, 1773.

We have long wondered here at the supineness of the English nation, under the Prussian impositions upon its trade entering our port. We did not, till lately, know the claims, ancient and modern, that hang over that nation; and therefore could not suspect that it might submit to those impositions from a sense of duty or from principles of equity. The following Edict, just made public, may, if serious, throw some light upon this matter.

"FREDERIC, by the grace of God, King of Prussia, etc., etc., etc., to all present and to come (*à tous présens et à venir*), health. The peace now enjoyed throughout our dominions, having afforded us leisure to apply ourselves to the regulation of commerce, the improvement of our finances, and at the same time the easing our *domestic* subjects in their taxes; for these causes, and other good considerations us thereunto moving, we hereby make known that, after having deliberated these affairs in our council, present our dear brothers, and other great officers of the state, members of the same; we, of our certain knowledge, full power, and authority royal, have made and issued this present Edict, viz.:

"Whereas it is well known to all the world, that the first German settlements made in the island of Britain were by colonies of people subject to our renowned ducal ancestors, and drawn from their dominions, under the conduct of Hengist, Horsa, Hella, Uffa, Cerdicus, Ida, and others; and that the said colonies have flourished under the protection of our august house for ages past; have never been emancipated therefrom; and yet have hitherto yielded little profit to the same; and whereas we ourself have in the last war fought for and defended the said colonies against the power of France, and thereby enabled them to make conquests for the said power in America, for which we have not yet received adequate compensation; and whereas it is just and expedient that a revenue should be raised from the said colonies in Britain, towards our indemnification; and that those who are descendants of our ancient subjects, and thence still owe us due obedience, should contribute to the replenishing of our royal coffers (as they must have done, had their ancestors remained in the territories now to us appertaining); we do therefore hereby ordain and command that, from and after the date of these presents, there shall be levied and paid to our officers of the *customs*, on all goods, wares, and merchandises, and on all grain and other produce of the earth, exported from the said island of Britain, and on all goods of whatever

* Bigelow V.

kind imported into the same, a duty of four and a half per cent. *ad valorem,*[1] for the use of us and our successors. And, that the said duty may more effectually be collected, we do hereby ordain that all ships or vessels bound from Great Britain to any other part of the world, or from any other part of the world to Great Britain, shall in their respective voyages touch at our port of Koningsberg, there to be unladen, searched, and charged with the said duties.

"And whereas there hath been from time to time discovered in the said island of Great Britain, by our colonists there, many mines or beds of iron-stone; and sundry subjects of our ancient dominion, skilful in converting the said stone into metal, have in time past transported themselves thither, carrying with them and communicating that art; and the inhabitants of the said island, presuming that they had a natural right to make the best use they could of the natural productions of their country for their own benefit, have not only built furnaces for smelting the said stone into iron, but have erected plating-forges, slitting mills, and steel-furnaces, for the more convenient manufacturing of the same; thereby endangering a diminution of the said manufacture in our ancient dominion; we do therefore hereby further ordain that, from and after the date hereof, no mill or other engine for slitting or rolling of iron, or any plating-forge to work with a tilt-hammer, or any furnace for making steel, shall be erected or continued in the said island of Great Britain. And the lord-lieutenant of every county in the said island is hereby commanded, on information of any such erection within his county, to order, and by force to cause, the same to be abated and destroyed; as he shall answer the neglect thereof to us at his peril. But we are nevertheless graciously pleased to permit the inhabitants of the said island to transport their iron into Prussia, there to be manufactured, and to them returned; they paying our Prussian subjects for the workmanship, with all the costs of commission, freight, and risk, coming and returning; any thing herein contained to the contrary notwithstanding.

"We do not, however, think fit to extend this our indulgence to the article of *wool;* but, meaning to encourage, not only the manufacturing of woollen cloth, but also the raising of wool, in our ancient dominions, and to prevent both, as much as may be, in our said island, we do hereby absolutely forbid the transportation of wool from thence, even to the mother country, Prussia; and, that those islanders may be further and more effectually restrained in making any advantage of their own wool in the way of manufacture, we command that none shall be carried out of one country into another; nor shall any worsted, bay, or woollen yarn, cloth, says, bays, kerseys, serges,

[1] In proportion to the value.

frizes, druggets, cloth-serges, shalloons, or any other drapery stuffs, or woollen manufactures whatsoever, made up or mixed with wool in any of the said counties, be carried into any other county, or be water-borne even across the smallest river or creek, on penalty of forfeiture of the same, together with the boats, carriages, horses, etc., that shall be employed in removing them. Nevertheless, our loving subjects there are hereby permitted (if they think proper) to use all their wool as manure for the improvement of their lands.

"And whereas the art and mystery of making *hats* hath arrived at great perfection in Prussia, and the making of hats by our remoter subjects ought to be as much as possible restrained; and forasmuch as the islanders before mentioned, being in possession of wool, beaver, and other furs, have presumptuously conceived they had a right to make some advantage thereof, by manufacturing the same into hats, to the prejudice of our domestic manufacture; we do therefore hereby strictly command and ordain, that no hats or felts whatsoever, dyed or undyed, finished or unfinished, shall be loaded or put into or upon any vessel, cart, carriage, or horse, to be transported or conveyed out of one county in the said island into another county, or to any other place whatsoever, by any person or persons whatsoever; on pain of forfeiting the same, with a penalty of five hundred pounds sterling for every offense. Nor shall any hat-maker, in any of the said counties, employ more than two apprentices, on penalty of five pounds sterling per month; we intending hereby that such hat-makers, being so restrained, both in the production and sale of their commodity, may find no advantage in continuing their business. But, lest the said islanders should suffer inconveniency by the want of hats, we are further graciously pleased to permit them to send their beaver furs to Prussia; and we also permit hats made thereof to be exported from Prussia to Britain; the people thus favored to pay all costs and charges of manufacturing, interest, commission to our merchants, insurance and freight going and returning, as in the case of iron.

"And, lastly, being willing further to favor our said colonies in Britain, we do hereby also ordain and command, that all the *thieves*, highway and street robbers, housebreakers, forgerers, murderers, s-d-tes, and villains of every denomination, who have forfeited their lives to the law of Prussia, but whom we, in our great clemency, do not think fit here to hang, shall be emptied out of our gaols into the said island of Great Britain, for the better peopling of that country.

"We flatter ourselves that these our royal regulations and commands will be thought *just and reasonable* by our much favored colonists in England; the said regulations being copied from their statutes of 10th and 11th William III. c. 10, 5th George II. c. 22, 23d George II. c. 26, 4th George I. c. 11, and from other equitable laws made by their Parliaments; or from instructions given by their princes; or from resolutions of both Houses, entered into for the good government of their *own colonies in Ireland and America.*

"And all persons in the said island are hereby cautioned not to oppose in any wise the execution of this our Edict, or any part thereof, such opposition being high treason; of which all who are suspected shall be transported in fetters from Britain to Prussia, there to be tried and executed according to the Prussian law.

"Such is our pleasure.

"Given at Potsdam, this twenty-fifth day of the month of August, one thousand seven hundred and seventy-three, and in the thirty-third year of our reign.

"By the King in his Council.

"RECHTMAESSIG, *Sec.*"

Some take this edict to be merely one of the king's *jeux d'esprit;* others suppose it serious, and that he means a quarrel with England; but all here think the assertion it concludes with, "that these regulations are copied from acts of the English Parliament respecting their colonies," a very injurious one; it being impossible to believe that a people distinguished for their love of liberty, a nation so wise, so liberal in its sentiments, so just and equitable towards its neighbors, should, from mean and injudicious views of petty immediate profit, treat its own children in a manner so arbitrary and tyrannical! (1773)

On the Slave Trade*

March 23, 1790.

To the Editor of the Federal Gazette:

SIR:—Reading last night in your excellent paper the speech of Mr. Jackson in Congress against their meddling with the affairs of slavery, or attempting to mend the condition of the slaves, it put me in mind of a similar one made about one hundred years since by Sidi Mehemet Ibrahim, a member of the Divan of Algiers, which may be seen in Martin's account of his consulship, anno 1687. It was against granting the petition of the sect called *Erika*, or Purists, who prayed for the abolition of piracy and slavery as being unjust. Mr. Jackson does not quote it; perhaps he has not seen it. If, therefore, some of its reasonings are to be found in his eloquent speech, it may only show

* Bigelow, X.

that men's interests and intellects operate and are operated on with surprising similarity in all countries and climates, whenever they are under similar circumstances. The African's speech, as translated, is as follows:

ALLAH BISMILLAH, ETC. GOD IS GREAT, AND MAHOMET IS HIS PROPHET.

Have these *Erika* considered the consequences of granting their petition? If we cease our cruises against the Christians, how shall we be furnished with the commodities their countries produce, and which are so necessary for us? If we forbear to make slaves of their people, who in this hot climate are to cultivate our lands? Who are to perform the common labors of our city, and in our families? Must we not then be our own slaves? And is there not more compassion and more favor due to us as Mussulmen than to these Christian dogs? We have now above fifty thousand slaves in and near Algiers. This number, if not kept up by fresh supplies, will soon diminish, and be gradually annihilated. If we then cease taking and plundering the infidel ships, and making slaves of the seamen and passengers, our lands will become of no value for want of cultivation; the rents of houses in the city will sink one half; and the revenue of government arising from its share of prizes be totally destroyed! And for what? To gratify the whims of a whimsical sect, who would have us not only forbear making more slaves, but even manumit those we have.

But who is to indemnify their masters for the loss? Will the state do it? Is our treasury sufficient? Will the *Erika* do it? Can they do it? Or would they, to do what they think justice to the slaves, do a greater injustice to the owners? And if we set our slaves free, what is to be done with them? Few of them will return to their countries; they know too well the greater hardships they must there be subject to; they will not embrace our holy religion; they will not adopt our manners; our people will not pollute themselves by intermarrying with them. Must we maintain them as beggars in our streets, or suffer our properties to be the prey of their pillage? For men accustomed to slavery will not work for a livelihood when not compelled. And what is there so pitiable in their present condition? Were they not slaves in their own countries?

Are not Spain, Portugal, France, and the Italian states governed by despots, who hold all their subjects in slavery, without exception? Even England treats its sailors as slaves; for they are, whenever the government pleases, seized, and confined in ships of war, condemned not only to work, but to fight, for small wages, or a mere subsistence, not better than our slaves are allowed by us. Is their condition then made worse by their falling into our hands? No; they have only exchanged one slavery for another, and I may say a better; for here they are brought into a land where the sun of Islamism gives forth its light, and shines in full splendor, and they have an opportunity of making themselves acquainted with the true doctrine, and thereby saving their immortal souls. Those who remain at home have not that happiness. Sending the slaves home then would be sending them out of light into darkness.

I repeat the question, What is to be done with them? I have heard it suggested that they may be planted in the wilderness, where there is plenty of land for them to subsist on, and where they may flourish as a free state; but they are, I doubt, too little disposed to labor without compulsion, as well as too ignorant to establish a good government, and the wild Arabs would soon molest and destroy or again enslave them. While serving us, we take care to provide them with every thing, and they are treated with humanity. The laborers in their own county are, as I am well informed, worse fed, lodged, and clothed. The condition of most of them is therefore already mended, and requires no further improvement. Here their lives are in safety. They are not liable to be impressed for soldiers, and forced to cut one another's Christian throats, as in the wars of their own countries. If some of the religious mad bigots, who now tease us with their silly petitions, have in a fit of blind zeal freed their slaves, it was not generosity, it was not humanity, that moved them to the action; it was the conscious burthen of a load of sins, and a hope, from the supposed merits of so good a work, to be excused from damnation.

How grossly are they mistaken to suppose slavery to be disallowed by the Alcoran! Are not the two precepts, to quote no more, "*Master, treat your slaves with kindness; Slaves, serve your masters with cheerfulness and fidelity,*" clear proofs to the contrary? Nor can the plundering of infidels be in that sacred book forbidden, since it is well known from it, that God has given the world, and all that it contains, to his faithful Mussulmen, who are to enjoy it of right as fast as they conquer it. Let us then hear no more of this detestable proposition, the manumission of Christian slaves, the adoption of which would, by depreciating our lands and houses, and thereby depriving so many good citizens of their properties, create universal discontent, and provoke insurrections, to the endangering of government and producing general confusion. I have therefore no doubt but this wise council will prefer the comfort and happiness of a whole nation of true believers to the whim of a few *Erika*, and dismiss their petition.

The result was, as Martin tells us, that the Divan came to this resolution: "The doctrine that plundering and enslaving the Christians is unjust, is at best *problematical;* but that it is the interest of this state to continue the practice, is clear; therefore let the petition be rejected."

And it was rejected accordingly.

And since like motives are apt to produce in the minds of men like opinions and resolutions, may we not, Mr. Brown, venture to predict, from this account, that the petitions to the Parliament of England for abolishing the slave trade, to say nothing of other legislatures, and the debates upon them will have a similar conclusion? I am, sir, your constant reader and humble servant,   HISTORICUS.

III

The Revolution and After

FOR many writers of the time, the independence America had wrested from the Old World would be fulfilled only with a cultural independence matching the political. America's cultural independence did not arrive until the time of Emerson, Melville, and Whitman. Yet in the excitement of the Revolution and the post-Revolutionary periods, as never before, the arts in America flourished with an exuberantly ambitious sense of new possibilities, an eagerness to show the Old World what America could do. The increase in the sheer numbers of productive and serious writers during the period makes it impossible to represent or discuss them all here. Writers like Thomas Paine, Thomas Jefferson, Philip Freneau, Royall Tyler, Timothy Dwight, and Charles Brockden Brown are intrinsically important and entertaining. Next to studying them whole, the best course perhaps is to describe the collective interests they shared with their contemporaries, as expressed in the various genres. For a collective interest does underlie very much American writing between the Revolution and 1800. It is—either explicitly, or implicitly through its self-proclaiming zest and bombast—the attempt to define the character, purpose, and destiny of America. The last part of this anthology does not treat individual writers, then, but examples of early national verse, fiction, drama, and literary criticism.

Genres and Writers. For all their pretensions to nationhood, American poets of the period wrote with little awareness of each other or of colonial literary traditions, followed the European direction toward romanticism, and continued to use English verse forms. Many poets were uncomfortably aware, however, of working within the literary conventions of a culture they abominated, conventions unsuited to the American scene yet seemingly inevitable. Independence was more a political than a psychological fact. But poets found some English forms more useful than others, such as the song. Large numbers of songs appeared among the twenty thousand political pamphlets that flooded the country between the Stamp Act of 1765 and 1783. Usually anonymous and written to popular English tunes, the songs provided a defiantly lively and expressive way, John Adams said, of "cultivating the sensations of freedom." Their popularity signifies a vastly wider and more unified audience for literature than had been possible in the colonial period, in part created by a feeling of mutual grievance and a need for common defense. Another specially popular form was the commencement poem, usually a long ode or dialogue recited in colleges, extolling in elevated language the often vague virtues and prospects of young America. Less popular only because of its inherent difficulty was the long epic poem. Imposing in its magnitude and concerned by definition with national origins, the epic obviously appealed to a young nation anxious to declare its identity, acclaim its way of life, and establish itself impressively on the world literary scene.

Two early American epics—*The Columbiad* and *The Conquest of Canaan*—came from members of the politically important group of poets known as the Connecticut Wits. All born in Connecticut, all students at Yale, all in their late teens or early twenties at the start of the Revolution, the Wits also shared and helped to formulate the doctrines of New England Federalism, a blend of Lockean ideas on property, Calvinistic religion, and regional jingoism. The Wit JOHN TRUMBULL (1750–1831) entered Yale at thirteen, later studied law under John Adams, and represented Connecticut in the Continental Congress. He wrote two very popular and artistically successful long satiric poems, *M'Fingal* and *The Progress of Dulness*. His friend TIMOTHY DWIGHT (1752–1817) was the grandson of Jonathan Edwards, and one of the most influential Federalists in America. His enemies called him "Old Pope Dwight," "The Pope of Federalism." Through his voluminous writing and preaching, his anonymous articles for Federalist newspapers, and his presidency of Yale, he mobilized opposition to Jefferson and to lower-class democracy. Among the most ambitious writers of the time, he wrote *The Conquest of Canaan*, an epic of the American Revolution; the long pastoral poem *Greenfield Hill*, excerpted here, which offers Connecticut as a model for American society at large; and the four-volume *Travels*, recording the transformation of New England society after the Revolution. Closely associated with the Connecticut Wits in their conservative programs, FISHER AMES (1758–1808) spoke for New England Federalism through his oratory, pamphleteering, and journalism.

In the Wits' conspiratorial view of history, Jefferson, Paine, and Voltaire were allied in trying to bring down the new Republic, and their henchman was PHILIP FRENEAU (1752–1832). Freneau was a passionate and often vitriolic democrat and, along with Edward Taylor, the most naturally and amply talented early American poet. Born in New York of French Huguenot parents, he moved to Matawan, New Jersey, and attended Princeton with James Madison and the novelist Hugh Henry Brackenridge. Sailing later to the West Indies, he was captured and confined aboard a British prison ship. Its daily horrors made his hatred of England burningly permanent. After the war he edited the most important newspaper in America, the anti-Federalist *National Gazette*, before retiring to his New Jersey farm, there to print his collected poems himself and, impoverished and alcoholic, to grow bitterly disaffected from the republic he helped create. His tortuous career makes many long-standing problems in American culture visible in the eighteenth century.

Much poetry, of course, had been written during the colonial period also, but the writing of fiction after the Revolution introduced a new literary form to the American scene. Its introduction suggests an end to the conditions that inhibited its practice earlier: distaste for the sometimes bawdy flavor of English fiction; the expense of printing and the difficulty of distributing native fiction, which made it simpler and cheaper for colonials to read and import English novels; and a puritanical sense that the imagination was corrupting. The change of taste after the Revolution, as Royall Tyler remarks in *The Algerine Captive*, demanded lighter works than "some dreary somebody's Day of Doom." Tyler's novel met this demand, as did the fiction of Freneau's classmate HUGH HENRY BRACKENRIDGE (1748–1816), author of the long comic novel *Modern Chivalry*. As his present account of a frontier trial might suggest, Brackenridge was by profession a judge and lawyer in western Pennsylvania. Among the first professional writers in America—and by virtue of his productivity and inventiveness, an important one—was the Philadelphian CHARLES BROCKDEN BROWN (1771–1810). Born a Quaker, he took up radical causes but ended his life as a conservative Federalist. He wrote most of his fiction between 1797 and 1799; in one eleven-month spell he produced five novels, including his best-known works, *Wieland* and *Arthur Mervyn*. His feverish Gothic fiction won equally fervent praise abroad; Shelley ranked him with Goethe and Schiller.

Brown's novels initiate a tendency of much pre-Civil War American fiction—indifference to the enveloping social scene. The title of Anthony Trollope's novel sums up the classic concerns of the English novel: *The Way We Live Now*. The way people eat, shake hands, tip their hats, count their money, that is, expresses their inner selves; manners are morals. But the South excepted, most of America until the mid-nineteenth century lacked a vividly defined social scene where manners distinguished social classes. As one character in an early American novel called *The Boarding School* says, "We, in this country, are too much in a state of nature to write good novels yet." Having only a "state of nature" to draw on, early American fiction tends toward reportage—the mere recording of events—or toward fantasy, sheer invention. Fact and fiction merge in the reportage of Brackenridge's "The Trial of Mamachtaga." The literalness and prosiness of much early American fiction may also imply a lingering puritanical uneasiness over the imagination, reinforced by the popularity of Scottish commonsense philosophy in America during the later eighteenth century. When the thinness of the social fabric does not lead to mere narration, it often results in fantasy or melodrama, with a substitution of character for personality, metaphysics for reality, the subjective for the objective, the self for society, as happens in Charles Brockden Brown's "Walstein's School of History," presented here. The need to bypass the contemporary social scene also helps explain the later fantasies of Poe, the subjectivism of *Moby Dick*, and the historicism of *The Scarlet Letter*.*

Finally, the post-Revolutionary period also fermented a sudden abundance and sophistication of drama and literary criticism. Drama outside the South had been sparse before the Revolution, like fiction, and for similar reasons—Puritan hostility to the stage, where presumably debauched actors and actresses glorified vice, and the cost of sustaining a theater. But after the Revolution theaters opened in all of the major American cities, and they often put on native plays. The critical and imaginative writing cannot always be separated. Some of the best criticism appeared in prologues to plays or prefaces to novels, like the ones extracted here from *The Contrast*, *Tears and Smiles*, and *The Algerine Captive*. Much of the criticism confronts what has probably been the central problem of American literature as a whole: how to create a national literature. It raises questions that the triumphs of many later American writers consist of solving. What should an American literature be like? What is the writer's task in a democracy? Many of the answers, we will see, grew from political positions. The literary ideals

* An important discussion of melodrama in American fiction may be found in Richard Chase, *The American Novel and its Tradition* (New York, 1957).

cannot be understood apart from the political and social ideals. Attempts to define the American novel, poem, or play are implicitly statements of what America is and should be.

Of the early dramatists the most prolific was WILLIAM DUNLAP (1766–1839) and the best was ROYALL TYLER (1757–1826). Dunlap, one of the first professional literary men in America, was a brother-in law and companion of the Connecticut Wit Timothy Dwight and a friend of the novelist Charles Brockden Brown. While managing the John Street Theater in New York, he wrote and translated a few dozen plays; he also wrote a novel, a history of the American stage, and a history of American painting. Tyler attended Harvard in the class of 1776, courted the daughter of John Adams (who disliked him), became a lawyer in Maine and Massachusetts, then Chief Justice of Vermont, and ran for the U.S. Senate in 1812 as a mild Federalist. His career confirms what many commentators of the time feared: that in a republic, literary men would be drawn off into public life. Tyler's case meant a real loss to American literature. Able to give form and inner richness to long works, he was one of the most mature American writers before 1800. He wrote one of the two or three best early American novels, *The Algerine Captive* (excerpted here), and many lean, biting satiric poems. His fine comedy *The Contrast*, modelled on *The School for Scandal*, was first produced in New York in 1787, then in Baltimore, Philadelphia, Charleston, and Richmond; it still entertains, and has been produced several times in the twentieth century.

Topics. Post-Revolutionary verse, fiction, drama, and criticism alike afford something absent in America since the early Puritans: the sense of a single culture. The national self-examination of the period created a set of commonplaces and a common imaginative vocabulary, rooted in defining the purposes of the Revolution and the fate of the new republic. Five especially popular topics became the substance of countless works in the period: slavery, utopianism, history, the contrast between America and Europe, and nativism. The discussion of these topics continued late into the century. As it progressed, an initial optimism often turned into a disenchantment that was disenchantment with America itself.

The claims for liberty that accompanied many arguments for independence made the continued existence of slavery in America glaring. The emancipatory fervor of the Revolution lent its own urgency to the attacks on slavery and gave them a new foundation. Freneau's "To Sir Toby" and *The Algerine Captive* link slavery with the greed and economic exploitation of British imperialism. Negroes became important characters in many works. The integration of black people into white society figures in Charles Brockden Brown's "Portrait of an Emigrant," where a Jamaican mulatto actress and her white French husband settle in Philadelphia and, although poor, lead a happily carefree, bohemian life—an early treatment of the black person as an uncomplicated noble savage. Such condescension is common, despite elevated appeals for personal liberty. Even well-intentioned treatments of Negro characters belie a certain derogation of them. Tyler's Fourth of July ode notes the emancipation of Vermont Negroes by rejoicing that, now, "Sambo—is a Citizen." The first stage Negro, Racoon, appears on the haunted night of *The Disappointment* cravenly quaking in his boots. Less crude in its condescension, Dwight's *Greenfield Hill* declares slavery to be an unmitigated evil in every way—except that the slave reaps the benefits of cultivating the New World and of the civilizing process he is forced to serve.

Similar apologies for slavery appear in works by slaves themselves. The few slaves after the Revolution who sued in the courts for their own freedom were not typical. The Long Island slave poet JUPITER HAMMON (1720?–1800?) affirms that God will reward him for obeying his "Kind Master" in his rightful role as the "Dutiful Servant." In fact, Hammon welcomes slavery because it has resulted in his conversion to Christianity. The Boston slave poetess PHILLIS WHEATLEY (*c*. 1753–1784) also regards her enslavement in Christian America as an emancipation from heathen Africa. Having led her out of "Egyptian gloom" to Christ, slavery is only a "seeming cruel fate." She takes a so-thoroughly white view of her situation that her verse sounds identical with that of contemporary white poets as they strove to imitate the elegances of Pope and Dryden; like them, ironically, she exults in America's attainment of "Freedom."

Less condescension betrays itself into the many tales of red-white relationships. Here a feeling that white American culture has turned harsh and destructive offsets the sentimentalizing influence of the "noble savage" ideal. The white writer seems able to identify more closely with his red characters, and he rarely treats them as comic butts.

In "The Trial of Mamachtaga"—with many overtones of a contemporary civil rights case—Brackenridge shows how his red hero, a murderer, is less a criminal than a victim of white insensitivity. J. HECTOR ST. JOHN DE CRÈVECOEUR (1731–1813), known internationally in his time for his *Letters from an American Farmer*—decries the effect of white civilization on the red man in terms of the romantic conflict between nature and civilization. In his Indian tale "Hoppajewot," the Indians welcome the white pioneers to their utopia only to have their forests chopped down, their plant life wasted, their religion and folkways defiled, and their indignation numbed by whiskey. In the wish-fulfilling climax, the Indians dishonor the whites by exposing their pretensions to civilization, and drive them out.

Crèvecoeur's Indian utopia is only one of many utopias projected in the literature of the period. Most of them, like Dwight's *Greenfield Hill*, are meant to suggest the ideal shape of future American society. A widely used vehicle for these imaginings of a perfect America is history. In "Walstein," Charles Brockden Brown describes a narrative method that many American writers found valuable: the use of the past as a metaphor for present problems and future possibilities. Brown's own historical fictions make the Roman republic a model for future America and turn out to be thinly-veiled Federalist tracts against the mob, "the negligent and heedless crowd." Many other writers cast into the form of ancient history their ideals for young America. Timothy Dwight transformed Washington and the Revolution into Joshua's battle against the Canaanites. The American past itself became a vehicle for present ideology. In John Dickinson's "Liberty Song," the often loosely associated groups who migrated to America in the seventeenth century for different reasons, from different classes, to different places, become a single, hardy, pious, like-minded band—the mythical forefathers. The forefathers myth grew up at the time of the Revolution, providing the colonies—north, middle, and south—with a supposed mutual heritage, thus mutual and longstanding interests, creating a sense of national identity by fabricating a common past.

The popularity of history as an imaginative vehicle had many sources. Americans of the time believed that one could learn from history. They considered it a world of timeless moral instruction which could suggest proper behavior for themselves. As Charles Brockden Brown says, the historian can exhibit, far more compellingly and realistically than the political theorist, "in an eloquent narration, a model of right conduct." The actualities of history also furnished ready-made the rich details and events which many writers felt that America lacked. Furthermore, the eighteenth-century cyclical view of history particularly lent itself to American aspirations through its corollary theory of cultural translation. Stated simply, this theory held that the course of history is plotted by the coming-into-dominance of various empires which inevitably decay, civilization moving in its progress westward: the arts and sciences first rose in Greece, were "translated" to Rome as Greece fell, and as Rome fell were translated to England, where they now stood. Stood, Americans gloated, on the point of collapse. The hope that the arts and sciences were preparing to be translated from moribund England to the rising empire of America is one of the favorite commonplaces of post-Revolutionary literature. Two of the many examples are Joseph Warren's "Liberty Song" and John Trumbull's essay on the fine arts. Trumbull sees the arts declining in England as "luxurious effeminacy" begets false taste, and passing to an America which disdains fancy manners and encourages liberty. Growing out of the political situation and the cyclical view of history, the hope for the rising glory of America took extra encouragement from the new romantic currents of the late eighteenth century. The attack on neoclassicism, the new emphasis on originality, the anti-traditionalism—each fed and justified the desire for cultural independence. (Other signs of romanticism are the fascination with Germany, observable in Brown's "Walstein," and the recognition of sublimity in nature. Dramatizing nature's treachery and destructiveness, Freneau's "The Hurricane" and John Singleton Copley's painting "Watson and the Shark" mark the birth of romanticism in America.)

Another vehicle for nationalistic sentiment, even more popular than history, is what Timothy Dwight called "the glorious contrast"—the use of England and Europe as images of what America should not be. Colonial writers like Edwards and Mather had, of course, compared European and American society. But the Revolution magnified the differences, and the "glorious" contrast was a searchingly deliberate means of defining American national qualities. The glorious contrast is perhaps the most deeply embedded and far-reaching topic of post-Revolutionary literature. Interest in it is so intense that the glorious contrast could be called a myth, that is, a narrative pattern designed to give a people hope for the future. Saturating the literature of the period, it appears in works by writers of every political complexion. In "Thoughts on the European War System," Freneau contrasts the warfare rending Europe, arising from monarchy, with the peacefulness of America, owing to democracy. In exhaustive detail the glorious contrast informs Dwight's *Greenfield Hill*, which custom by custom and institution by institution sets the orderly progress of stable, classless America against the alternating butchery and stagnation of monarchical Europe.

But the fullest example is the play which takes its title from the myth, Royall Tyler's *The Contrast*. Tyler's characters extend the contrast between Europe and America to further contrasts between plain and formal speech, country and city manners, homespun and fashionable dress, and so on. These sharpen the dramatic conflict, pitting plainspoken-rural-homespun America against formal-urban-fashionable Europe. More important, the clusters of qualities serve as paradigms of the perfect society and its opposite. A contrast within *The Contrast* occurs in the two Americans of the play: Jonathan—the simple, natural man—and Manley, the refined and cultivated man. Tyler seems unable to imagine a single character in whom nature and culture, refinement and naturalness, can exist together. His distribution of these qualities of the ideal American between Jonathan and Manley points to serious cultural problems, to conflicting ideals which cannot be contained within a single representative man. Perhaps the nearest resolution of the conflict was Franklin's Poor Richard. But in the heady optimism following the Revolution, the Poor Richard type must have seemed a not-exalted-enough example of what America could produce.

A third vehicle for nationalism is the commonplace of the European-ized American, an offshoot of the glorious contrast. Worried about the corrupting influence of European education and manners on American youth, Thomas Jefferson wrote to his friend Walker Maury that "Of all the errors which can possibly be committed in the education of youth, that of sending them to Europe is the most fatal." Such youths, he said, "will lose in science, in virtue, in health and in happiness, for which manners are a poor compensation, were we even to admit the hollow unmeaning manners of Europe to be preferable to the simplicity and sincerity of our own country." The damage done a young man who exchanges his native simplicity for foreign luxury became the concern of dozens of imaginative works in the period. Some poems, like Dwight's "Epistle to Col. Humphreys," address a young man about to debark for the Old World. Two amusing dramatic treatments of the Europeanized American are *The Bucktails* by the New York writer JAMES KIRKE PAULDING (1778–1860) and *Tears and Smiles* by the Philadelphia politico JAMES NELSON BARKER (1784–1858). In *Tears and Smiles* the American, Fluttermore, returns from abroad a Frenchified, effeminate butterfly, proclaiming his social and amorous triumphs in a Paris which the native Frenchman in the play calls an old whore. In *The Bucktails*, two meaningly-named Englishmen, Obsolete and Rust, await the arrival from the New World of Henry and Frank Tudor, whom they expect to be "fresh as an unlick'd cub," "wild men," "aboriginals," in short, "bucktails." Although unsophisticated and untitled, the Tudors, of course, turn out to be gracious and intelligent, admirable examples of how democracy and naturalness coexist with good manners and taste.

These commonplaces of late-eighteenth-century American writing appear fleshed out in a common stock of locales, characters, and language as well. Local country life provides a setting for them in Tyler's "Ode Composed for the Fourth of July" and, more ambitiously, in Dwight's *Greenfield Hill*. American heroes like Washington, Paine, and Franklin often perform as imaginative characters; the very recognition of the persons in America who deserve acclaim helps establish a sense of cultural identity. These historical personages also perform as symbols of the ideal characteristics of the republican. The Revolutionary song "The Dance" stresses Washington's untaught natural grace as gloriously opposed to British foppery. The operetta *Darby's Return* speaks of Washington as an authentic folk hero, a common man not unlike Darby himself, who "left his *farm* a *soldiering* to go."* Washington is only one of many ex-soldiers included amid the wealth of distinctive and near-legendary American types in the literature of the period—the stage Irishman and Scotsman, Racoon the Negro, the Quaker, the Indians of Crèvecoeur and Brackenridge. Of these rather ribald and cocky native types, drawn mostly from the lower classes and the frontier, the most entertaining and significant is the Jonathan figure of *The Contrast*, the

---

* Washington himself attended a performance of the operetta. The author, William Dunlap, noted that when Kathleen asks Darby whether Washington was short or tall, Washington looked embarrassed, expecting the usual eulogy. Darby, however, replies that he has never seen Washington, but once mistook him for someone all "botherum and shine." At this, Dunlap wrote, Washington gave what was "with him extremely rare, a hearty laugh." Indeed, many works make Washington's legendary soberness itself an essential quality of republican virtue.

stage Yankee—a "true born Yankee American son of liberty." He represents a new historical type, a whole new personality on the world scene.

These characters, moreover, speak a self-consciously American language. Jonathan's unaffected native speech, like Huck Finn's, is an instrument of truth, of telling-it-like-it-is. In the Irish brogue and Negro dialect of *The Disappointment*, too, we hear a new literary language hovering between American speech and standard English. The use of such a literary language was risky. Writers feared that they would not be understood, or that they would be censured by the prevailing canons of literary taste. Timothy Dwight forestalled misunderstanding by adding pages of footnotes to *Greenfield Hill* (some included here) to explain his localisms to English readers, and probably also to American readers outside of Connecticut. In the preface to *Tears and Smiles*, James Nelson Barker forestalled censure by admitting that a sour reception awaited an American play whose characters spoke "Columbianisms." In fact, English reviewers did regard American speech as barbaric, and trounced American writers who used it. Not all Americans favored "Columbianisms" either. Some liberals, like Jefferson, allowed for a linguistic gulf between America and England congruent with the geographical and political gulf. But some conservatives, like John Adams, called for an elevated literary language based on British English, of the kind written by Charles Brockden Brown. Both views and both kinds of language are present in the literature of the time, and even today; the issue still exists.

Divisions, Discontents, Prospects.   Indeed the widespread use of the same materials, the unity of imagination in late-eighteenth-century America, must not be mistaken for political unity. The long and often bitter debate on what the new republic should be like created implacable disagreements over many weighty issues. Lower-class democracy, deism, the French Revolution, relations with Europe, the settlement of the frontier, the banking system, property laws—these all posed problems that angrily divided rationalistic liberals like Jefferson and Calvinistic conservatives like Dwight, and went into forming the first American political parties. Regional antagonisms also re-emerged after the relative solidarity of the Revolution. *The Algerine Captive* depicts a New Englander's discomfort in a South that recalls "The Sot-weed Factor," where disrespect for learning makes it "almost synonymous" to "purchase a school-master and a Negro," and where a doctor, to succeed, must, like the rest of the population, "sport, bet, drink, swear."

As these divisions widened, they checked the optimism that immediately followed the Revolution. Liberals and conservatives alike became disillusioned. The choice of foreign heroes by Charles Brockden Brown, a Federalist, suggests that America has no monopoly on goodness. Brown's subjects—infanticide, suicide, murder, rape, arson, madness (the typical American novel)—leave behind a single jaundiced impression of human evil that makes questionable the belief in human goodness and sociability which underlay many arguments for revolution. Brackenridge, another Federalist, shatters the Franklin myth by questioning the social value of lower-class advancement. His present story discloses the dangers of lower-class mob justice, and his important novel *Modern Chivalry* shows how democracy fosters the unjust rise of the mediocre. The arch New England Federalist Timothy Dwight bases his hopes for America's future on a healthy respect for human limitation and on the love of learning, religion, and private ownership that characterizes Connecticut. His fulsome address to the concept of "Competence" in *Greenfield Hill* makes national happiness dependent on modesty in governmental programs and styles of life, as opposed to Jeffersonian hankerings for new thought, France, western expansion, and lower-class enfranchisement.

Not only conservative Federalists became discontented with the emerging shape of the republic, but even ardent democrats like Philip Freneau. While his early poems amount to radical manifestos and revolutionary tracts, his later poems are the seethingly disillusioned testament of some American François Villon. Although ideologically opposed to the Wits, he too saw the Revolution issuing in greed, fashion, despoliation of nature, inhumanity, and poverty. "Verses . . . on Leaving a Great House" loathingly mocks the post-Revolution nouveau-riche; "To a New-England Poet" scorns America's continued fawning on England; in "The American Soldier," a brooding amputee veteran of Saratoga curses an America that rewards its heroes with "famine and a name!" The soldier is but one of many alienated strangers whose hurt and angry voices sound through Freneau's later verse. The most recurrent voice belongs to Freneau himself, the poet brutalized by the public's indifference and forgetfulness. Like some Puritan Jeremiah, he sees the poet's job as reminding the public of a zealously dedicated and high-minded past they had rather forget. Ingratitude, alienation, anti-materialism—the themes of Freneau's poetry—transcend politics in the wider despair of "The Vanity of Existence," which damns ordinary living itself as a "bank of mud" where man's ideals drown under gritty realities. Indeed, Freneau's disenchantment grew as much from his own personality and poetic ambitions as from his politics. His romantic leanings conflicted with his republican and deistic principles. Despite his effectiveness as a propagandist, he preferred writing romantic and lyric verse, and felt misborn in an America busy "edging steel." Nor could he adjust his rationalistic hope to found society upon benign and orderly nature, to his darker romantic impulse that saw nature most profoundly revealed in storms and hurricanes. Man in his poetry thus seems a paradox,

> A Being, sent hither all good to bestow
> Yet filling the world with oppression and woe!

Humanity in Freneau's poetry, as from a great distance, looks foolish, pettily wicked, and exploitative, however grand the scheme of creation or the designs of the republic.

The same ideological divisions and the same discontent direct the late-eighteenth-century dispute over the achievements and prospects of American literature. Unwilling to ask too much from a fragilely young culture, its atmosphere is often tactful and repressed. In America, Tyler cautions in *The Contrast*, "The bold *attempt alone* demands applause." Not everyone called for a distinctive American literature. In his essay presented here, John Trumbull looks to the study of English and classical literature to refine American taste and polish the "rugged ferocity of manners." More often, however, critics decided that on moral and political grounds the need for an American literature was imperative: English writers like Pope and Addison they considered profane and obscene; the value English writers attached to fashion descended from monarchism and disappointed by making homely American ways seem unglamorous.

Still other critics, in the disenchantment at the end of the century, foresaw prospects as dim for American literature as for American society. Freneau blamed "these bleak climes" for starving the imagination. Many Federalists predicted that a nation headed toward democracy had already doomed its culture to mediocrity. For them, poetry and government were joined. They saw the difference between the lettered and unlettered man as a class distinction, hence argued that democracy threatens literature: by creating factions, it turns men from literature to public life; by creating equality, it encourages mediocrity; by emphasizing public opinion, it undermines standards. Fisher Ames feared that literature could not develop in America's "complete unmixed democracy" since its writers would be forced to please a public whose taste was molded by the passion to acquire property. The Federalist design for American literature follows the Federalist design for American society, a literature stressing virtue, modesty, religion, vigor, simplicity—the signs of small-town respectability. Timothy Dwight's defensive remarks on Jonathan Edwards demonstrate the promise of American culture by citing such respectable figures as Edwards, Trumbull, Franklin, Eli Whitney, and Benjamin West; ignoring the unrespectable, Dwight explains that the country's infancy and busyness have prevented it from producing great men.

The Federalists did mount a sensible and reasoned attack on many of the hollowly boastful paeons to young America, and on the bloated, merely wishful claims for its artistic potential. At bottom, they simply stated a fact—that for all the over-optimism of the Revolutionary period, the prefacing everything American with "glory," for all the "rising glory" poems and glorious contrasts, America had yet to produce an imaginative writer of genius. Yet their indictment reveals their own limitations as well. Their Federalist politics kept them from acknowledging the existence, much less the talents, of such unrespectable democrats, deists, and Francophiles as Freneau, Paine, Joel Barlow, and Jefferson; their puritanical scorn for novels and plays made them oblivious to the solid accomplishments of Charles Brockden Brown and Royall Tyler. They found little to admire in American culture because ideologically they despised and feared much of what it had achieved.

And in thinking that democracy doomed culture, and in deciding that American writers of large imagination and singular talent were far off, they were wrong. By the time Dwight's remarks on Edwards appeared in 1821, Irving and Cooper had been published, Emerson and Hawthorne had entered college; and Poe, Thoreau, Melville, and Whitman were already alive.

Further interpretation and description of American literature during this period can be found in the following: On the Revolution and the Federal period see Bernard Bailyn, *The Ideological Origins of the American Revolution* (Cambridge, Mass., 1967); Richard Beale Davis, *Intellectual Life in Jefferson's Virginia* (Chapel Hill, N.C., 1964); Bruce Granger, *Political Satire in the American Revolution* (Ithaca, N.Y., 1960); Russel Nye, *The Cultural Life of the New Nation* (New York, 1960); Moses Coit Tyler, *The Literary History of the American Revolution 1763–1783*, 2 vols. (repr. New York, 1957).

On poetry and poets see Nelson Adkins, *Philip Freneau and the Cosmic Enigma* (New York, 1947); Leon Howard, *The Connecticut Wits* (Chicago, 1943); Lewis Leary, *That Rascal Freneau* (New Brunswick, N.J., 1941); Kenneth Silverman, *Timothy Dwight* (New York, 1969).

On the drama see Julian Mates, *The American Musical Stage before 1800* (New Brunswick, N.J., 1962); Brooks McNamara, *The American Playhouse in the Eighteenth Century* (Cambridge, Mass., 1969); A. H. Quinn, *A History of American Drama*, vol. 1 (New York, 1923); Hugh Rankin, *The Theater in Colonial America* (Chapel Hill, N.C., 1965); G. Thomas Tanselle, *Royall Tyler* (Cambridge, Mass., 1967).

On fiction see Richard Chase, noted in the Introduction, and Terence Martin, *The Instructed Vision* (Indianapolis, 1961).

A spirited recording of Revolutionary songs is *Ballads of the Revolution* sung by Wallace House (Folkways Records #FP 5001).

POETRY

Revolutionary Songs

These few songs, representative of a popular genre, give some sense of the patriotic feeling in the late eighteenth century. Dickinson, writer of the first, was a member of the Continental Congress. Warren's song suggests that the nationalistic sentiments in the poem by Lewis (pp. 260–269) were being changed to more patriotic feelings, while Billings' hymn reflects the continuing belief that Americans were God's chosen people. The last has the spirit found in war songs of many different times and places.

JOHN DICKINSON

(1732–1808)

Liberty Song*

Come join hand in hand, brave Americans all,
And rouse your bold hearts at fair Liberty's call;
No tyrannous acts, shall suppress your just claim,
Or stain with dishonor America's name.
    In freedom we're born, and in freedom we'll live;
        Our purses are ready,
        Steady, Friends, steady,
    Not as *slaves*, but as *freemen* our money we'll give.

* Frank Moore, ed., *Songs and Ballads of the American Revolution*, (New York 1855).

339

Our worthy forefathers—let's give them a cheer—
To climates unknown did courageously steer;   10
Thro' oceans to deserts, for freedom they came,
And, dying, bequeath'd us their freedom and fame.

Their generous bosoms all dangers despis'd,
So highly, so wisely, their birthrights they priz'd;
We'll keep what they gave, we will piously keep,
Nor frustrate their toils on the land or the deep.

The Tree, their own hands had to Liberty rear'd,
They lived to behold growing strong and rever'd;
With transport then cried,—"Now our wishes we gain,
For our children shall gather the fruits of our pain."   20

How sweet are the labors that freemen endure,
That they shall enjoy all the profit, secure,—
No more such sweet labors Americans know,
If Britons shall reap what Americans sow.

Swarms of placemen and pensioners soon will appear,
Like locusts deforming the charms of the year:
Suns vainly will rise, showers vainly descend,
If we are to drudge for what others shall spend.

Then join hand in hand brave Americans all,
By uniting we stand, by dividing we fall;   30
In so righteous a cause let us hope to succeed,
For Heaven approves of each generous deed.

All ages shall speak with amaze and applause,
Of the courage we'll show in support of our laws;
To die we can bear,—but to serve we disdain,
For shame is to freemen more dreadful than pain.

This bumper I crown for our sovereign's health,
And this for Britannia's glory and wealth;
That wealth, and that glory immortal may be,
If she is but just, and we are but free.   40
    In freedom we're born, &c.   (1768)

JOSEPH WARREN

(1741–1775)

A Song on Liberty*

That Seat of Science, Athens, and Earth's proud Mistress, Rome,
Where now are all their Glories? We scarce can find their Tomb.
Then guard your Rights, Americans, nor stoop to lawless Sway,
Oppose, oppose, oppose, oppose for North America.

Proud Albion bow'd to Cæsar, and numerous Lords before,
To Picts, to Danes, to Normans, and many Masters more;
But we can boast Americans have never fallen a Prey,
Huzza! huzza! huzza! huzza for free America.

We led fair Freedom hither, and lo the Desert smil'd,
A Paradise of Pleasure now open'd in the Wild;   10
Your Harvest, bold Americans, no Power shall snatch away,
Preserve, preserve, preserve your Rights in free America.

Torn from a World of Tyrants, beneath this western Sky
We form'd a new Dominion, a Land of Liberty;
The World shall own we're Masters here, then hasten on the Day,
Huzza, huzza, huzza, huzza for Love and Liberty.

God bless this Maiden Climate, and through her vast Domain
May Hosts of Heroes cluster that scorn to wear a Chain,
And blast the venal Sycophant who dare our Rights betray,
Assert yourselves, yourselves, yourselves, for brave America.   20

* *Virginia Gazette*, January 6, 1774.

Lift up your Hearts, my Heroes, and swear, with proud Disdain,
The Wretch that would ensnare you shall spread his Net in vain;
Should Europe empty all her Force we'd meet them in Array,
And shout huzza! huzza! huzza! for brave America.

Some fitter Day shall crown us the Masters of the Main,
In giving Laws and Freedom to subject France and Spain;
And all the Isles o'er Ocean spread shall tremble and obey,
The Lords, the Lords, the Lords, the Lords of North America.

WILLIAM BILLINGS

(1746–1800)

Chester*

A Hymn

Let tyrants shake their iron rod,
  And slavery clank her galling chains;
We fear them not; we trust in God—
  New England's God for ever reigns.

Howe and Burgoyne, and Clinton, too,
  With Prescott and Cornwallis join'd;
Together plot our overthrow,
  In one infernal league combin'd.

When God inspir'd us for the fight,
  Their ranks were broke, their lines were forc'd;   10
Their ships were shatter'd in our sight,
  Or swiftly driven from our coast.

The foe comes on with haughty stride;
  Our troops advance with martial noise;
Their veterans flee before our youth,
  And generals yield to beardless boys.

What grateful offering shall we bring?
  What shall we render to the Lord?
Loud hallelujahs let us sing,
  And praise his name on every chord.   (1778)   20

* Moore.

343

ANONYMOUS

*The Dance**

Cornwallis led a country dance,
   The like was never seen, sir,
Much retrograde and much advance,
   And all with General Greene, sir.

They rambled up and rambled down,
   Join'd hands, then off they run, sir,
Our General Greene to Charlestown,
   The earl to Wilmington, sir.

Greene, in the South, then danc'd a set,
   And got a mighty name, sir,   10
Cornwallis jigg'd with young Fayette,
   But suffer'd in his fame, sir.

Then down he figur'd to the shore,
   Most like a lordly dancer,
And on his courtly honor swore,
   He would no more advance, sir.

Quoth he, my guards are weary grown
   With footing country dances,
They never at St. James's shone,
   At capers, kicks or prances.   20

* Moore. This song appeared soon after the surrender of Cornwallis. It is sung to the tune of "Yankee Doodle."

344

Though men so gallant ne'er were seen,
   While sauntering on parade, sir,
Or wriggling o'er the park's smooth green,
   Or at a masquerade, sir.

Yet are red heels and long-lac'd skirts,
   For stumps and briars meet, sir?
Or stand they chance with hunting-shirts,
   Or hardy veteran feet, sir?

Now hous'd in York he challeng'd all,
   At minuet or all 'amande,   30
And lessons for a courtly ball,
   His guards by day and night conn'd.

This challenge known, full soon there came,
   A set who had the bon ton,
De Grasse and Rochambeau, whose fame
   Fut brillant pour un long tems.

And Washington, Columbia's son,
   Whom easy nature taught, sir,
That grace which can't by pains be won,
   Or Plutus' gold be bought, sir.   40

Now hand in hand they circle round,
   This ever-dancing peer, sir;
Their gentle movements, soon confound
   The earl, as they draw near, sir.

His music soon forgets to play—
   His feet can no more move, sir,
And all his bands now curse the day,
   They jiggèd to our shore, sir.

Now Tories all, what can ye say?
   Come—is not this a griper,   50
That while your hopes are danc'd away,
   'Tis you must pay the piper.   (1781)

Two Slave Poets

The poems by Wheatley and Hammon partially reflect the view expressed by Cotton Mather in *The Negro Christianized* (pp. 164–167). To give thanks for being taken from Africa and christianized seems ironic; it is the white view that is offered in these poems. The reader can speculate for himself about the reasons these poets seem to hold that view. The numerous selections in this text that deal with slavery and with the Negro in America do make it possible to reach some conclusions about the white view of the Negro in early America.

Introduction to *Poems on Various Subjects**

THE following is a copy of a letter sent by the author's master to the publisher.

Phillis was brought from Africa to America in the year 1761, between seven and eight years of age. Without any assistance from school education, and by only what she was taught in the family, she, in sixteen months' time from her arrival, attained the English language, to which she was an utter stranger before, to such a degree, as to read any the most difficult parts of the Sacred Writings, to the great astonishment of all who heard her.

As to her writing, her own curiosity led her to it; and this she learnt in so short a time that in the year 1765 she wrote a letter to the Rev. Mr. Occom, the Indian minister, while in England.

She has a great inclination to learn the Latin tongue, and has made some progress in it. This relation is given by her master who bought her, and with whom she now lives.

John Wheatley. Boston, Nov. 14, 1772.

*Poems on Various Subjects, Religious and Moral (Boston, 1773; following poems from this edition).

TO THE PUBLIC

As it has been repeatedly suggested to the publisher, by persons who have seen the manuscript, that numbers would be ready to suspect that they were not really the writings of Phillis, he has procured the following attestation from the most respectable characters in Boston, that none might have the least ground for disputing their original.

We whose names are underwritten do assure the world, that the poems specified in the following page were (as we verily believe) written by Phillis, a young Negro girl, who was but a few years since brought an uncultivated barbarian from Africa, and has ever since been, and now is, under the disadvantage of serving as a slave in a family in this town. She has been examined by some of the best judges, and is thought qualified to write them.

[Undersigned by Thomas Hutchinson (the Governor of Massachusetts) and by seventeen others.]

PHILLIS WHEATLEY

(c. 1753–1784)

To the University of Cambridge, in New-England

While an intrinsic ardor prompts to write,
The muses promise to assist my pen;
'Twas not long since I left my native shore
The land of errors, and *Egyptian* gloom:
Father of mercy, 'twas thy gracious hand
Brought me in safety from those dark abodes.

Students, to you 'tis giv'n to scan the heights
Above, to traverse the ethereal space,
And mark the systems of revolving worlds.
Still more, ye sons of science ye receive   10
The blissful news by messengers from heav'n,
How *Jesus*' blood for your redemption flows.
See him with hands out-stretcht upon the cross;
Immense compassion in his bosom glows;
He hears revilers, nor resents their scorn:
What matchless mercy in the Son of God!
When the whole human race by sin had fall'n,
He deign'd to die that they might rise again,
And share with him in the sublimest skies,
Life without death, and glory without end.   20

Improve your privileges while they stay,
Ye pupils, and each hour redeem, that bears
Or good or bad report of you to heav'n.
Let sin, that baneful evil to the soul,
By you be shunn'd, nor once remit your guard;
Suppress the deadly serpent in its egg.
Ye blooming plants of human race devine,
An *Ethiop* tells you 'tis your greatest foe;
Its transient sweetness turns to endless pain,
And in immense perdition sinks the soul.   (1773)   30

On Being Brought from Africa to America

'Twas mercy brought me from my *Pagan* land,
Taught my benighted soul to understand
That there's a God, that there's a *Saviour* too:
Once I redemption neither sought nor knew.
Some view our sable race with scornful eye,
"Their colour is a diabolic die."
Remember, *Christians*, *Negroes*, black as *Cain*,
May be refin'd, and join th' angelic train.   (1773)

To the Right Honourable William, Earl of Dartmouth, His Majesty's Principal Secretary of State for North America, &c.[1]

Hail, happy day, when, smiling like the morn,
Fair *Freedom* rose *New-England* to adorn:
The northern clime beneath her genial ray,
Dartmouth, congratulates thy blissful sway:
Elate with hope her race no longer mourns,
Each soul expands, each grateful bosom burns,
While in thine hand with pleasure we behold
The silken reins, and *Freedom's* charms unfold.
Long lost to realms beneath the northern skies

---

[1] In 1772, the Earl of Dartmouth (1731–1801) was appointed Secretary of State for the colonies, to which he proved unsympathetic.

She shines supreme, while hated *faction* dies:　　　　10
Soon as appear'd the *Goddess* long desir'd,
Sick at the view, she lanquish'd and expir'd;
Thus from the splendors of the morning light
The owl in sadness seeks the caves of night.

No more, *America*, in mournful strain ⎞
Of wrongs, and grievance unredress'd complain, ⎬
No longer shalt thou dread the iron chain, ⎠
Which wanton *Tyranny* with lawless hand
Had made, and with it meant t' enslave the land.

Should you, my lord, while you peruse my song,　　　20
Wonder from whence my love of *Freedom* sprung,
Whence flow these wishes for the common good,
By feeling hearts alone best understood,
I, young in life, by seeming cruel fate
Was snatch'd from *Afric's* fancy'd happy seat:
What pangs excruciating must molest,
What sorrows labour in my parent's breast?
Steel'd was that soul and by no misery mov'd
That from a father seiz'd his babe belov'd:
Such, such my case. And can I then but pray　　　30
Others may never feel tyrannic sway?

For favours past, great Sir, our thanks are due,
And thee we ask thy favours to renew,
Since in thy pow'r, as in thy will before,
To sooth the griefs, which thou did'st once deplore.
May heav'nly grace the sacred sanction give
To all thy works, and thou for ever live
Not only on the wings of fleeting *Fame*,
Though praise immortal crowns the patriot's name,
But to conduct to heav'ns refulgent fane,　　　40
May fiery coursers sweep th' ethereal plain,
And bear thee upwards to that blest abode,
Where, like the prophet, thou shalt find thy God.　(1773)

JUPITER HAMMON

(1720?–1800?)

From *The Kind Master and the Dutiful Servant**

MASTER

1. Come my servant, follow me,
   According to thy place;
And surely God will be with thee,
   And send the heav'nly grace.

SERVANT

2. Dear Master, I will follow thee,
   According to thy word,
And pray that God may be with me,
   And save thee in the Lord.

MASTER

3. My Servant, lovely is the Lord,
   And blest those servants be,
That truly love his holy word,
   And thus will follow me.

10

SERVANT

4. Dear Master, that's my whole delight,
   Thy pleasure for to do;
As far as grace and truth's in sight,
   Thus far I'll surely go.

* *An Evening's Improvement* (New York, n.d.).

MASTER

5. My Servant, grace proceeds from God,
  And truth should be with thee;
Whence e'er you find it in his word,
  Thus far come follow me.   20

SERVANT

6. Dear Master, now without controul,
  I quickly follow thee;
And pray that God would bless thy soul,
  His heav'nly place to see.

MASTER

7. My Servant, Heaven is high above,
  Yea, higher than the sky:
I pray that God would grant his love,
  Come follow me thereby.

SERVANT

8. Dear Master, now I'll follow thee,
  And trust upon the Lord;
The only safety that I see,   30
  Is Jesus's holy word.

MASTER

9. My Servant, follow Jesus now,
  Our great victorious King;
Who governs all both high and low,
  And searches things within.

SERVANT

10. Dear Master I will follow thee,
  When praying to our King;
It is the Lamb I plainly see,
  Invites the sinner in.   40

MASTER

11. My Servant, we are sinners all,
    But follow after grace;
I pray that God would bless thy soul,
    And fill thy heart with grace.

SERVANT

12. Dear Master I shall follow then,
    The voice of my great King;
As standing on some distant land,
    Inviting sinners in.

MASTER

13. My Servant we must all appear,
    And follow then our King;
For sure he'll stand where sinners are,
    To take true converts in.

50

SERVANT

14. Dear Master, now if Jesus calls,
    And sends his summons in;
We'll follow saints and angels all,
    And come unto our King.

MASTER

15. My Servant now come pray to God,
    Consider well his call;
Strive to obey his holy word,
    That Christ may love us all. . . .

60

(Undated)

PHILIP FRENEAU

(1752–1832)

The poet's dislike of England, described in the Introduction (pp. 325–326), is amply shown in the first selection, but such feelings could easily be shared by a new nation breaking from her mother country. A late-eighteenth-century poet, Freneau also demonstrates both romantic and neo-classic characteristics. His involvement in the Revolutionary War and his sometime occupation as sea captain can also be seen. His nationalism, his defense and praise of the rustic life, his inclinations toward reform, his respect for and practice of poetic tradition—all these can be seen in the poems that follow. The range of his poetry is greater than Edward Taylor's, and his poetic skill is second only to the Puritan's in the history of American literature until the nineteenth century. With Freneau, a less parochial sophistication became apparent in American poetry. Able to shape his prosody to fit his political and philosophical arguments, Freneau is, in many respects, the poet of his age as Taylor is of the Puritan period.

From *The Political Balance**

OR, THE FATES OF BRITAIN AND AMERICA COMPARED

A TALE

Deciding Fates, in Homer's stile, we shew,
And bring contending gods once more to view.

As Jove the Olympian (who both I and you know,
Was brother to Neptune, and husband to Juno)
Was lately reviewing his papers of state,
He happened to light on the records of Fate:

* Fred Lewis Pattee, ed., *The Poems of Philip Freneau*, II (Princeton, 1902–1907).

In Alphabet order this volume was written—
So he opened at B, for the article Britain—
She struggles so well, said the god, I will see
What the sisters in Pluto's dominions decree.

And first, on the top of a column he read
"Of a king with a mighty soft place in his head,   10
"Who should join in his temper the ass and the' mule,
"The third of his name, and by far the worst fool:

"His reign shall be famous for multiplication,
"The sire and the king of a whelp generation:
"But such is the will and the purpose of fate,
"For each child he begets he shall forfeit a State:

"In the course of events, he shall find to his cost
"That he cannot regain what he foolishly lost;
"Of the nations around he shall be the derision,
"And know by experience the rule of Division."   20

So Jupiter read—a god of first rank—
And still had read on—but he came to a blank:
For the Fates had neglected the rest to reveal—
They either forgot it, or chose to conceal:

When a leaf is torn out, or a blot on a page
That pleases our fancy, we fly in a rage—
So, curious to know what the Fates would say next,
No wonder if Jove, disappointed, was vext.

But still as true genius not frequently fails,
He glanced at the Virgin, and thought of the Scales;   30
And said, "To determine the will of the Fates,
"One scale shall weigh Britain, the other the States."

Then turning to Vulcan, his maker of thunder,
Said he, "My dear Vulcan, I pray you look yonder,
"Those creatures are tearing each other to pieces,
"And, instead of abating, the carnage increases.

"Now, as you are a blacksmith, and lusty stout ham-eater,
"You must make me a globe of a shorter diameter;
"The world in abridgment, and just as it stands
"With all its proportions of waters and lands;   40

"But its various divisions must so be designed,
"That I can unhinge it whene'er I've a mind—
"How else should I know what the portions will weigh,
"Or which of the combatants carry the day?"

Old Vulcan complied, (we've no reason to doubt it)
So he put on his apron and strait went about it—
Made center, and circles as round as a pancake,
And here the Pacific, and there the Atlantic.

        *   *   *

Adjacent to Europe he struck up an island,
(One part of it low, but the other was high land)   50
With many a comical creature upon it,
And one wore a hat, and another a bonnet.

Like emmits or ants in a fine summer's day,
They ever were marching in battle array,
Or skipping about on the face of the brine,
Like witches in egg-shells (their ships of the line).

These poor little creatures were all in a flame,
To the lands of America urging their claim,
Still biting, or stinging, or spreading their sails;
(For Vulcan had formed them with stings in their tails).   60

So poor and so lean, you might count all their ribs,[1]
Yet were so enraptured with crackers and squibs,
That Vulcan with laughter almost split asunder,
"Because they imagined their crackers were thunder."

        *   *   *

At length, to discourage all stupid pretensions,
Jove looked at the globe, and approved its dimensions,
And cried in a transport—"Why what have we here!
"Friend Vulcan, it is a most beautiful sphere!

---

[1] Their national debt being now above *l.* 200,000,000 sterling. [Freneau's note].

"Now while I am busy in taking apart
"This globe that is formed with such exquisite art,   70
"Go, Hermes, to Libra, (you're one of her gallants)
"And ask, in my name, for the loan of her balance."

Away posted Hermes, as swift as the gales,
And as swiftly returned with the ponderous scales,
And hung them aloft to a beam in the air,
So equally poised, they had turned with a hair.

Now Jove to Columbia his shoulders applied,
But aiming to lift her, his strength she defied—
Then, turning about to their godships, he says—
"A body so vast is not easy to raise;   80

"But if you assist me, I still have a notion
"Our forces, united, can put her in motion,
"And swing her aloft, (though alone I might fail)
"And place her, in spite of her bulk, in our scale;

"If six years together the Congress have strove,
"And more than divided the empire with Jove;
"With a Jove like myself, who am nine times as great,
"You can join, like their soldiers, to heave up this weight."

So to it they went, with handspikes and levers,
And upward she sprung, with her mountains and rivers!   90
Rocks, cities, and islands, deep waters and shallows,
Ships, armies, and forests, high heads and fine fellows:

"Stick to it!" cries Jove, "now heave one and all!
"At least we are lifting 'one-eighth of the ball!'
"If backward she tumbles—then trouble begins,
"And then have a care, my dear boys, of your shins!"

When gods are determined what project can fail?
So they gave a hard shove, and she mounted the scale;
Suspended aloft, Jove viewed her with awe—
And the gods,[2] for their pay, had a hearty—huzza!   100

---

[2] American soldiers. [Freneau's note].

But Neptune bawled out—"Why Jove you're a noddy,
"Is Britain sufficient to poise that vast body?
"'Tis nonsense such castles to build in the air—
"As well might an oyster with Britain compare."

*   *   *

"But now, my dear Juno, pray give me my mittens,
"(These insects I am going to handle are Britons)
"I'll draw up their isle with a finger and thumb,
"As the doctor extracts an old tooth from the gum."

Then he raised her aloft—but to shorten our tale,
She looked like a clod in the opposite scale—   110
Britannia so small, and Columbia so large—
A ship of first rate, and a ferryman's barge!

Cried Pallas to Vulcan, "Why, Jove's in a dream—
"Observe how he watches the turn of the beam!
"Was ever a mountain outweighed by a grain?
"Or what is a drop when compared to the main?"

But Momus alledged—"In my humble opinion,
"You should add to Great-Britain her foreign dominion,
"When this is appended, perhaps she will rise,
"And equal her rival in weight and in size."   120

"Alas! (said the monarch), your project is vain,
"But little is left of her foreign domain;
"And, scattered about in the liquid expanse,
"That little is left to the mercy of France;

"However, we'll lift them, and give her fair play"—
And soon in the scale with their mistress they lay;
But the gods were confounded and struck with surprise,
And Vulcan could hardly believe his own eyes!

For (such was the purpose and guidance of fate)
Her foreign dominions diminished her weight—   130
By which it appeared, to Britain's disaster,
Her foreign possessions were changing their master.

Then, as he replaced them, said Jove with a smile—
"Columbia shall never be ruled by an isle—
"But vapours and darkness around her may rise,
"And tempests conceal her awhile from our eyes;

"So locusts in Egypt their squadrons display,
"And rising, disfigure the face of the day;
"So the moon, at her full, has a frequent eclipse,
"And the sun in the ocean diurnally dips.   140

"Then cease your endeavours, ye vermin of Britain—
(And here, in derision, their island he spit on)
"'Tis madness to seek what you never can find,
"Or to think of uniting what nature disjoined;

"But still you may flutter awhile with your wings,
"And spit out your venom and brandish your stings:
"Your hearts are as black, and as bitter as gall,
"A curse to mankind—and a blot on the Ball."[3]   (1782)

The Vanity of Existence*

In youth, gay scenes attract our eyes,
    And not suspecting their decay
Life's flowery fields before us rise,
    Regardless of its winter day.

But vain pursuits and joys as vain,
    Convince us life is but a dream.
Death is to wake, to rise again
    To that true life you best esteem.

---

[3] It is hoped that such a sentiment may not be deemed wholly illiberal. Every candid person will certainly *draw a line between a brave and magnanimous people, and a most vicious and vitiating government.* [Freneau's note].
    * Pattee, II.

So nightly on some shallow tide,
　　Oft have I seen a splendid show;　　　　　　　10
Reflected stars on either side,
　　And glittering moons were seen below.

But when the tide had ebbed away,
　　The scene fantastic with it fled,
A bank of mud around me lay,
　　And sea-weed on the river's bed.　(1781)

From *Sketches of American History**

. . . In the reign of a virgin (as authors discover)
Drake, Hawkins, and Raleigh in squadrons came over
While Barlow and Grenville succeeded to these,
Who all brought their colonies over the seas.

These, left in a wilderness teeming with woes,
The natives, suspicious, concluded them foes,
And murdered them all without notice or warning,
Ralph Lane, with his vagabonds, scarcely returning.

In the reign of king James (and the first of the name,)
George Summers, with Hacluit, to Chesapeake came,　　　10
Where far in the forests, not doomed to renown,
On the river Powhatan they built the first town.

Twelve years after this, some scores of dissenters
To the northernmost district came seeking adventures;
Outdone by the bishops, those great faggot fighters;
They left them to rule with their cassocks and mitres.

Thus banished forever, and leaving the sod,
The first land they saw was the pitch of Cape Cod,
Where famished with hunger and quaking with cold
The planned their New-Plymouth—so called from the old.　　　20

* Pattee, II.

They were, without doubt, a delightful collection;—
Some came to be rid of a Stuart's direction,
Some sailed with a view to dominion and riches,
Some to pray without book, and a few to hang witches.

Some, came on the Indians to shed a new light,
Convinced long before that their own must be right,
And that all who had died in the centuries past
On the devil's lee shore were eternally cast.

These exiles were formed in a whimsical mold,
And were awed by their priests, like the Hebrews of old; 30
Disclaimed all pretenses to jesting and laughter,
And sighed their lives through, to be happy hereafter.

On a crown immaterial their hearts were intent,
They looked towards Zion, wherever they went,
Did all things in hopes of a future reward,
And worried mankind—for the sake of the Lord.

With rigor excessive they strengthened their reign,
Their laws were conceived in the ill-natured strain,
With mystical meanings the saint was perplext,
And the flesh and the devil were slain by a text. 40

The body was scourged, for the good of the soul,
All folly discouraged by peevish control,
A knot on the head was the sign of no grace,
And the Pope and his comrade were pictured in lace.

A stove in their churches, or pews lined with green,
Were horrid to think of, much more to be seen,
Their bodies were warmed with the linings of love,
And the fire was sufficient that flashed from above.

'Twas a crime to assert that the moon was opaque,
To say the earth moved, was to merit the stake; 50
And he that could tell an eclipse was to be,
In the college of Satan had took his degree.

On Sundays their faces were dark as a cloud—
The road to the meeting was only allowed,
And those they caught rambling, on business or pleasure,
Were sent to the stocks, to repent at their leisure.

This day was the mournfullest day in the week—
Except on religion, none ventured to speak—
This day was the day to examine their lives,
To clear off old scores, and to preach to their wives.   60

Their houses were forts, that seemed proof against light;
Their parlors, all day, were the blackness of night:
And, as if at their thresholds a cannon did roar,
The animals hardly dared open their door
'Till the sun disappeared—then, like a mole's snout
In the dusk of the evening, their noses popped out.

In the school of oppression though woefully taught,
'Twas only to be the oppressors they sought;
All, all but themselves were be-deviled and blind,
And their narrow-souled creed was to serve all man-kind.   70

This beautiful system of nature below
They neither considered, nor wanted to know,
And called it a dog-house wherein they were pent,
Unworthy themselves, and their mighty descent.

They never perceived that in Nature's wide plan
There must be that whimsical creature called Man,
Far short of the rank he affects to attain,
Yet a link in its place, in creation's vast chain....   (1784)

The Hurricane*

Happy the man who, safe on shore,
　Now trims, at home, his evening fire;
Unmov'd, he hears the tempests roar,
　That on the tufted groves expire:
Alas! on us they doubly fall,
Our feeble barque must bear them all.

Now to their haunts the birds retreat,
　The squirrel seeks his hollow tree,
Wolves in their shaded caverns meet,
　All, all are blest but wretched we——　　　　10
Foredoomed a stranger to repose,
No rest the unsettled ocean knows.

While o'er the dark abyss we roam,
　Perhaps, with last departing gleam,
We saw the sun descend in gloom,
　No more to see his morning beam;
But buried low, by far too deep,
On coral beds, unpitied, sleep!

But what a strange, uncoasted strand
　Is that, where fate permits no day——　　　　20
No charts have we to mark that land,
　No compass to direct that way——
What Pilot shall explore that realm,
What new Columbus take the helm!

While death and darkness both surround,
　And tempests rage with lawless power,
Of friendship's voice I hear no sound,
　No comfort in this dreadful hour——
What friendship can in tempests be,
What comfort on this raging sea?　　　　30

* Pattee, II.

The barque, accustomed to obey,
   No more the trembling pilots guide:
Alone she gropes her trackless way,
   While mountains burst on either side—
Thus, skill and science both must fall;
And ruin is the lot of all.   (1785)

To an Author*

Your leaves bound up compact and fair,
In neat array at length prepare,
To pass their hour on learning's stage,
To meet the surly critic's rage;
The statesman's slight, the smatterer's sneer—
Were these, indeed, your only fear,
You might be tranquil and resigned:
What most should touch your fluttering mind;
Is that, few critics will be found
To sift your works, and deal the wound.   10

Thus, when one fleeting year is past
On some bye-shelf your book is cast—
Another comes, with something new,
And drives you fairly out of view:
With some to praise, but more to blame,
The mind returns to—whence it came;
And some alive, who scarce could read
Will publish satires on the dead.

Thrice happy Dryden, who could meet
Some rival bard in every street!   20
When all were bent on writing well
It was some credit to excel:—

Thrice happy Dryden, who could find
A Milbourne for his sport designed—
And Pope, who saw the harmless rage
Of Dennis bursting o'er his page
Might justly spurn the critic's aim,
Who only helped to swell his fame.

* Pattee, II.

On these bleak climes by Fortune thrown,
Where rigid Reason reigns alone,   30
Where lovely Fancy has no sway,
Nor magic forms about us play—
Nor nature takes her summer hue
Tell me, what has the muse to do?—

An age employed in edging steel
Can no poetic raptures feel;
No solitude's attracting power,
No leisure of the noon day hour,
No shaded stream, no quiet grove
Can this fantastic century move;   40

The muse of love in no request—
Go—try your fortune with the rest,
One of the nine you should engage,
To meet the follies of the age:—

On one, we fear, your choice must fall—
The least engaging of them all—
Her visage stern—an angry style—
A clouded brow—malicious smile—
A mind on murdered victims placed—
She, only she, can please the taste!   (1788)   50

The American Soldier*

(A PICTURE FROM THE LIFE)

> "*To serve with love,*
> *And shed your blood,*
> *Approved may be above,*
> *And here below*
> (*Examples shew*)
> *'Tis dangerous to be good.*"
> —LORD OXFORD.

Deep in a vale, a stranger now to arms,
Too poor to shine in courts, too proud to beg,
He, who once warred on Saratoga's plains,
Sits musing o'er his scars, and wooden leg.

Remembering still the toil of former days,
To other hands he sees his earnings paid;—
They share the due reward—he feeds on praise,
Lost in the abyss of want, misfortune's shade.

Far, far from domes where splendid tapers glare,
'Tis his from dear bought peace no wealth to win,   10
Removed alike from courtly cringing 'squires,
The great-man's Levee, and the proud man's grin.

Sold are those arms which once on Britons blazed,
When, flushed with conquest, to the charge they came;
That power repelled, and Freedom's fabrick raised,
She leaves her soldier—famine and a name!   (1790)

* Pattee, III.

To Sir Toby*

A SUGAR PLANTER IN THE INTERIOR PARTS OF
JAMAICA, NEAR THE CITY OF SAN JAGO DE LA
VEGA, (SPANISH TOWN) 1784

The motions of his spirit are black as night,
And his affections dark as Erebus.

—SHAKESPEARE.

If there exists a hell—the case is clear—
Sir Toby's slaves enjoy that portion here:
Here are no blazing brimstone lakes—'tis true;
But kindled Rum too often burns as blue;
In which some fiend, whom nature must detest,
Steeps Toby's brand, and marks poor Cudjoe's breast.[1]
Here whips on whips excite perpetual fears,
And mingled howlings vibrate on my ears:
Here nature's plagues abound, to fret and teaze,
Snakes, scorpions, despots, lizards, centipees—   10
No art, no care escapes the busy lash;
All have their dues—and all are paid in cash—
The eternal driver keeps a steady eye
On a black herd, who would his vengeance fly,
But chained, imprisoned, on a burning soil,
For the mean avarice of a tyrant, toil!
The lengthy cart-whip guards this monster's reign—
And cracks, like pistols, from the fields of cane.
  Ye powers! who formed these wretched tribes, relate,
What had they done, to merit such a fate!   20
Why were they brought from Eboe's[2] sultry waste,
To see that plenty which they must not taste—
Food, which they cannot buy, and dare not steal;
Yams and potatoes—many a scanty meal!—
  One, with a gibbet wakes his negro's fears,
One to the windmill nails him by the ears;

---

* Pattee, II.
[1] This passage has a reference to the West India custom (sanctioned by law) of branding a newly imported slave on the breast, with a red hot iron, as an evidence of the purchaser's property. [Freneau's note].
[2] A small negro kingdom near the river Senegal. [Freneau's note].

One keeps his slave in darkened dens, unfed,
One puts the wretch in pickle ere he's dead:
This, from a tree suspends him by the thumbs,
That, from his table grudges even the crumbs!   30

    O'er yond' rough hills a tribe of females go,
Each with her gourd, her infant, and her hoe;
Scorched by a sun that has no mercy here,
Driven by a devil, whom men call overseer—
In chains, twelve wretches to their labors haste;
Twice twelve I saw, with iron collars graced!—

    Are such the fruits that spring from vast domains?
Is wealth, thus got, Sir Toby, worth your pains!—
Who would your wealth on terms, like these, possess,
Where all we see is pregnant with distress—   40
Angola's natives scourged by ruffian hands,
And toil's hard product shipp'd to foreign lands.

    Talk not of blossoms, and your endless spring;
What joy, what smile, can scenes of misery bring?—
Though Nature, here, has every blessing spread,
Poor is the laborer—and how meanly fed!—

    Here Stygian paintings light and shade renew,
Pictures of hell, that Virgil's pencil drew:
Here, surly Charons make their annual trip,
And ghosts arrive in every Guinea ship,   50
To find what beasts these western isles afford,
Plutonian scourges, and despotic lords:—

    Here, they, of stuff determined to be free,
Must climb the rude cliffs of the Liguanee;[3]
Beyond the clouds, in sculking haste repair,
And hardly safe from brother traitors there.—[4]

                         (Published 1792, written earlier)

---

[3] The mountains northward of Kingston. [Freneau's note].

[4] Alluding to the *Independent* negroes in the blue mountains, who for a stipulated reward, deliver up every fugitive that falls into their hands, to the English Government. [Freneau's note].

The Forest Beau*

(A PICTURE FROM REALITY)

When first to feel Love's fire Jack Straw begins,
He combs his hair, and cocks his hat with pins,
Views in some stream, his face, with fond regard,
Plucks from his upper lip the bristly beard,
With soap and sand his homely visage scours
(Rough from the joint attacks of sun and showers)
The sheepskin breeches decorate his thighs—
Next on his back the homespun coat he tries;
Round his broad breast he wraps the jerkin blue,
And sews a spacious soal on either shoe.   10
Thus, all prepared, the fond adoring swain
Cuts from his groves of pine a ponderous cane;
In thought a beau, a savage to the eye,
Forth, from his mighty bosom, heaves the sigh;
Tobacco is the present for his fair,
This he admires, and this best pleases her—
The bargain struck,—few cares his bosom move
How to maintain, or how to lodge his love;
Close at his hand the piny forest grows,
Thence for his hut a slender frame he hews,   20
With art, (not copied from Palladio's rules,)
A hammer and an axe, his only tools,
By Nature taught, a hasty hut he forms
Safe in the woods, to shelter from the storms;—
There sees the summer pass and winter come,
Nor envies Britain's king his loftier home.   (1795)

* Pattee, III.

Thoughts on the European War System*
(BY H. SALEM)[1]

The People in Europe are much to be praised,
That in fighting they choose to be passing their days;
If their wars were abolished, there's room to suppose
Our Printers would growl, for the want of New-News.

May our tidings of warfare be ever from thence,
Nor that page be supplied at Columbia's expense!
No kings shall rise here, at the nod of a court,
Ambition, or Pride, with men's lives for to sport.

In such a display of the taste of the times—
The murder of millions—their quarrels and crimes,   10
A horrible system of ruin we scan,
A history, truly descriptive of man:

A Being, that Nature designed to be blest—
With abundance around him—yet rarely at rest,
A Being, that lives but a moment in years,
Yet wasting his life in contention and wars;
A Being, sent hither all good to bestow,
Yet filling the world with oppression and woe!

But, consider, ye sages, (and pray be resigned)
What ills would attend a reform of mankind—   20
Were wars at an end, and no nation made thinner,
My neighbor, the gun-smith, would go without dinner;
The Printers, themselves, for employment would fail,
And soldiers, by thousands, be starving in jail.   (1795)

---

* Pattee, III.
[1] Freneau sometime used the *persona* Hezekiah Salem.

On the Uniformity and Perfection of Nature*

On one fix'd point all nature moves,
Nor deviates from the track she loves;
Her system, drawn from reason's source,
She scorns to change her wonted course.

Could she descend from that great plan
To work unusual things for man,
To suit the insect of an hour—
This would betray a want of power,

Unsettled in its first design
And erring, when it did combine   10
The parts that form the vast machine,
The figures sketch'd on nature's scene.

Perfections of the great first cause
Submit to no contracted laws,
But all-sufficient, all-supreme,
Include no trivial views in them.

Who looks through nature with an eye
That would the scheme of heaven descry,
Observes her constant, still the same,
In all her laws, through all her frame.   20

No imperfection can be found
In all that is, above, around,—
All, nature made, in reason's sight
Is order all, and *all is right.*   (1815)

* Harry Hayden Clark, ed., *Poems of Freneau* (New York, 1929).

To a New-England Poet*

Though skilled in latin and in greek,
And earning fifty cents a week,
Such knowledge, and the income, too,
Should teach you better what to do:
    The meanest drudges, kept in pay,
    Can pocket fifty cents a day.

Why stay in such a *tasteless land*,
Where ALL must on a *level* stand,
(Excepting people, *at their ease*,
Who choose the *level* where they please:)   10
    See IRVING gone to Britain's court
    To people of *another sort*,
    He will return, with wealth and fame,
    While *Yankees* hardly know *your* name.

Lo! he has kissed a Monarch's—hand!
Before a PRINCE I see him stand,
And with the glittering nobles mix,
Forgetting *times* of seventy-six,
While *you* with terror meet the frown
Of *Bank Directors* of the town,   20
    The home-made *nobles* of our times,
    Who hate the bard, and spurn his rhymes.

Why pause?—like IRVING, haste away,
To England your addresses pay;
And England will reward you well,
When you some pompous story tell
    Of British feats, and British arms,
    The *maids* of honor, and their *charms*.

Dear Bard, I pray you, take the hint,
In England what you write and print,   30
Republished here in shop, or stall,

* Lewis Leary, ed., *The Last Poems of Philip Freneau* (New Brunswick, N.J., 1945).

Will perfectly enchant us all:
  It will assume a different face,
  And post your name at every place,
  From splendid domes of first degree
  Where *ladies* meet, to sip their tea;
  From marble halls, where lawyers plead,
  Or Congress-men talk loud, indeed,
  To huts, where evening clubs appear,
  And 'squires resort—to guzzle Beer.   (1823)   40

Verses Written on Leaving a Great House Of Much Ceremony, but Little Sincerity, Or Hospitality*

> "*This is not mine ain house,*
>   *Ken by the rigging o't,*"
>
>   ALLAN RAMSAY.

CAUTION

Thou, who shalt halt at Beaurepaire,[1]
  On business, or for pleasures sake,
Please to observe some folks are there
  Who notice every step you take,
    Survey your *hat*, inspect your *shoes*,
    But not *omission* will excuse.

You comb your hair, you brush your coat
Almost to thread-bare to the neat,
Yet, in its *knap* a single spot
Will be observed by all you meet: 10
    And you will be no more caress'd,
    But censured as a *clown* at best.

---

* Leary.
[1] An estate in upper New York, some one hundred miles from Lake Cayuga.

If hungry as a famished hawk,
You dare not fill your craving maw,
Or sure to be the country talk,
The laughing stock of high and low:
    Be on your guard at every meal,
    And starve to death to be *genteel*.

Good heaven! what a *Lord* I dreamt—!
The *Lordling* of this House, who sees,   20
Must see, with feelings of contempt,
An insect shivering in the breeze,
    Such creatures, in a wintry day,
    A north-west wind would blow away.

The *Angels*, who in habit *here*,
Were Angels not ten years ago:
I knew them in a humble sphere,—
But see, what *sudden wealth* can do!
    It looks at things with other eyes,
    And *new ideas* strangely rise.   30

I knew them ere their pride begun,
I knew them when of *manners plain;*
When *Julia* wash'd, and *Susan* spun,
And *pewter plates* were scoured by *Jane;*
    When giant *Jacob* drove the *plough*
    He would not wish to hear of—*now*.

Ah, well-a-day! how many dreams
A lofty house makes *mighty men*—
How gay these fluttering females seem
That wore a course *home-spun*—I knew when: 40
    But *now!*—to please both *White & Black*,
    A man must be—*a man of wax*.

Lo! *linsey woolsey* changed to *silk*—
They almost *speak*, and *look* divine;
Madeira laughs at *Butter milk*,
For *twelve* at noon at *six* they dine;
    They cheat in periods of a mile,
    And folly marks their swelling style.

A curse on such preposterous whims!
And why a moment tarry there,   50
Where glittering *Bucks* and madam *Prims*
Disgusted me with *Beaurepaire;*
   A mansion that may suit the vain,
   At which I shall not halt again?

Oh for the hut of Indian *Sam!*
He dwells in yonder woods, they say:
His buckwheat meal and venison ham
Once more would cheer me on my way.
   I'll seek him, be it far or near,
   To find a welcome more sincere. (1822)   60

TIMOTHY DWIGHT

(1752–1817)

Unlike Freneau, Dwight was a staunch Federalist. In the following selection from his best work, *Greenfield Hill*, it is his democratic and pastoral attitudes that are most apparent. The defense of America that appears in so many selections in this text may seem more subtle here, but it is an important ingredient. His view of slavery can be compared to that in earlier selections to determine how the American attitude was changing. The regular quality of the verse is one of the major strengths of his poetry, although when carried through hundreds of lines it can also be one of its weaknesses.

Tyler has a freer more colloquial style than Dwight. Both of the poems that follow have an informality and a relaxed quality that Dwight seldom achieved.

From *Epistle from Dr. Dwight to Col. Humphreys**

. . . Oft has thine eye, with glance indignant seen
Columbia's youths, unfolding into men,
Their minds to' improve, their manners to adorn,
To Europe's climes by fond indulgence borne,
Oft hast thou seen those youths, at custom's shrine,
Victims to pride, to folly, and to sin,
Of worth bereft, of real sense forlorn,
Their land forget, their friends, their freedom spurn;
Each noble cause, each solid good desert,
For splendour happiness, and truth for art;   10
The plain, frank manners of their race despise,
Fair without fraud, and great beyond disguise;
Where, thro' the life the heart uncover'd ran,
And spoke the native dignity of man.

* *The Miscellaneous Works of Colonel Humphreys* (New York, 1790).

FOR these, the gain let Virtue blush to hear,
And each sad parent drop the plaintive tear!
Train'd in foul stews, impoison'd by the stage,
Hoyl'd into gaming, Keyser'd into age,
To smooth hypocrisy by Stanhope led,
To truth an alien, and to virtue dead,   20
Swoln with an English butcher's sour disdain,
Or to a Fribble dwindled from a man,
Homeward again behold the jackdaw run,
And yield his sire the ruins of a son!

WHAT tho' his mind no thought has e'er perplex'd,
Converse illum'd, nor observations vex'd;
Yet here, in each debate, a judge he shines,
Of all, that man enlarges, or refines;
Religion, science, politics, and song;
A prodigy his parts; an oracle his tongue,   30
Hist! hist! ye mere Americans, attend;
Ope wide your mouths; your knees in homage bend,
While Curl discloses to the raptur'd view
What Peter, Paul, and Moses, never knew;
The light of new-born wisdom sheds abroad,
And adds a leanto to the word of God.
What Creole wretch shall dare, with home-made foils,
Attack opinions, brought three thousand miles;
Sense, in no common way to mortals given,
But on Atlantic travellers breath'd by Heaven;   40
A head, en queue, by Monsieur Frizzle dress'd;
Manners, a Paris Taylor's arts invest;
Pure criticism, form'd from *acted* plays;
And graces, that would even Stanhope grace?
Commercial wisdom, merchants here inhale
From him, whose eye hath seen th' unfinish'd bale;
Whose feet have pass'd the shop, where pins were sold,
The wire was silver'd, and the heads were roll'd!
Conven'd, ye lawyers, make your humblest leg!
Here stands the man, has seen Lord Mansfield's wig!   50
Physicians hush'd, hear Galen's lips distil,
From Buchan's contents, all the Art to heal!
Divines, with reverence cease your scripture whims,
And learn this male Minerva's moral schemes;

Schemes theologic found in Drury-lane,
That prove the bible false, and virtue vain!
Heavens! shall a child in learning, and in wit,
O'er Europe's climes, a bird of passage flit;
There, as at home, his stripling self unknown,
By novel wonders stupified to stone,   60
Shut from the wise, and by no converse taught,
No well-read day, nor hour of serious thought,
His head by pleasure, vice, and hurry, turn'd,
All prudence trampled, all improvements spurn'd;
Shall he, with less of Europe in his cap,
Than satchell'd school-boy guesses from the map,
On every subject strutingly decree,
Ken the far shore and search th' unfathom'd sea,
Where learning has her lamp for ages oil'd,
Where Newton ponders, and where Berkeley toil'd?   70
Of all the plagues, that rise in human shape,
Good Heaven, preserve us from the travell'd Ape!

"Peace to all such:" but were there one, whose mind
Bold genius wing'd, and converse pure, refin'd,
By nature prompted science realms to roam,
And both her Indies bring with rapture home;
Who men, and manners, search'd with eagle eye,
Exact to weigh, and curious to descry;
Himself who burnish'd with the hand of care,
'Till kings might boast so bright a gem to wear;   80
Should he, deep plung'd in Circe's sensual bowl,
Imbrue his native manliness of soul,
With eye estrang'd, from fair Columbia turn,
Her youth, her innocence, and beauty scorn;
To that foul harlot, Europe, yield his mind,
Witch'd by her smiles, and to her snares resign'd;
To nature's bloom prefer the rouge of art,
A tinsell'd out-side to a golden heart,
Show, to the bliss by simple freedom given,
To virtue, Stanhope, and Voltaire to Heaven;   90
Who but must wish, the apostate youth to see?
Who but must agonize, were Humpreys he?
But all, thy soul shall 'scape, th' escape to aid,
Fair to thy view be every motive spread.

Of each gay cause the dire effects survey,
And bring the painted tomb disclos'd to day.
Tho' there proud pomp uprears his throne on high;
Tho' there the golden palace lights the sky;
Tho' wealth unfolds her gay, Edenian seats,
Her walk of grandeur, and her wild of sweets;   100
The stage, the park, the ring, the dance, the feast
Charm the pall'd eye, and lure the loathing taste;
Yet there fierce war unceasing sounds alarms;
Pride blows the trump, and millions rush to arms;
See steel and fire extinguish human good!
See realms manur'd with corses, and with blood!
At slaughter's shrine expires the new-born joy,
And all Jehovah's bounty fiends destroy.
See the huge jail in gloomy grandeur rise,
Low'r o'er mankind, and mock the tempted skies!   110
Hear the chain clank! the bursting groan attend!
And mark the neighbouring gibbet's pride ascend,
See earth's fair face insatiate luxury spoils!
For one poor tyrant, lo, a province toils!
To brothels, half the female world is driven,
Lost to themselves, and reprobates of heaven,
There too refinement glances o'er the mind;
And nought but vice, and outside, is refin'd;
To vice auspicious, brilliant manners blend,
The waxen saint, and sinner, foe and friend,   120
Melt from the soul each virtue, as they shine,
And warm th' impoison'd blossom into sin. . . .   (1785)

From *Greenfield Hill**

PART II. THE FLOURISHING VILLAGE

FAIR Verna! loveliest village of the west;
Of every joy, and every charm, possess'd;
How pleas'd amid thy varied walks I rove,
Sweet, cheerful walks of innocence, and love,
And o'er thy smiling prospects cast my eyes,
And see the seats of peace, and pleasure rise,
And hear the voice of Industry resound,

* *Greenfield Hill: a Poem, in Seven Parts* (New York, 1794).

And mark the smile of Competence, around!
Hail, happy village! O'er thy cheerful lawns,
With earliest beauty, spring delighted dawns;   10
The northward sun begins his vernal smile;
The spring-bird carols o'er the cressy rill:
The shower, that patters in the ruffled stream,
The ploughboy's voice, that chides the lingering team,
The bee, industrious, with his busy song,
The woodman's axe, the distant groves among,
The waggon, rattling down the rugged steep,
The light wind, lulling every care to sleep,
All these, with mingled music, from below,
Deceive intruding sorrow, as I go.   20

How pleas'd, fond Recollection, with a smile,
Surveys the varied round of wintery toil!
How pleas'd, amid the flowers, that scent the plain,
Recalls the vanish'd frost, and sleeted rain;
The chilling damp, the ice-endangering street,
And treacherous earth that slump'd beneath the feet.

Yet even stern winter's glooms could joy inspire:
Then social circles grac'd the nutwood fire;
The axe resounded, at the sunny door;
The swain, industrious, trimm'd his flaxen store;   30
Or thresh'd, with vigorous flail, the bounding wheat,
His poultry round him pilfering for their meat;
Or slid his firewood on the creaking snow;
Or bore his produce to the main below;
Or o'er his rich returns exulting laugh'd;
Or pledg'd the healthful orchard's sparkling draught:
While, on his board, for friends and neighbours spread,
The turkey smoak'd, his busy housewife fed;
And Hospitality look'd smiling round,
And Leisure told his tale, with gleeful sound.   40

Then too, the rough road hid beneath the sleigh,
The distant friend despis'd a length of way,
And join'd the warm embrace, and mingling smile,
And told of all his bliss, and all his toil;

And, many a month elaps'd, was pleas'd to view
How well the houshold far'd, the children grew;
While tales of sympathy deceiv'd the hour,
And Sleep, amus'd, resign'd his wonted power.

Yes! let the proud despise, the rich deride,
These humble joys, to Competence allied: 50
To me, they bloom, all fragrant to my heart,
Nor ask the pomp of wealth, nor gloss of art.
And as a bird, in prison long confin'd,
Springs from his open'd cage, and mounts the wind,
Thro' fields of flowers, and fragrance, gaily flies,
Or re-assumes his birth-right, in the skies:
Unprison'd thus from artificial joys,
Where pomp fatigues, and fussful fashion cloys,
The soul, reviving, loves to wander free
Thro' native scenes of sweet simplicity;   60
Thro' Peace' low vale, where Pleasure lingers long,
And every songster tunes his sweetest song,
And Zephyr hastes, to breathe his first perfume,
And Autumn stays, to drop his latest bloom:
'Till grown mature, and gathering strength to roam,
She lifts her lengthen'd wings, and seeks her home.

But now the wintery glooms are vanish'd all;
The lingering drift behind the shady wall;
The dark-brown spots, that patch'd the snowy field;
The surly frost, that every bud conceal'd;   70
The russet veil, the way with slime o'erspread,
And all the saddening scenes of March are fled.

Sweet-smiling village! loveliest of the hills!
How green thy groves! How pure thy glassy rills!
With what new joy, I walk thy verdant streets!
How often pause, to breathe thy gale of sweets;
To mark thy well-built walls! thy budding fields!
And every charm, that rural nature yields;
And every joy, to Competence allied,
And every good, that Virtue gains from Pride!   80

No griping landlord here alarms the door,
To halve, for rent, the poor man's little store.
No haughty owner drives the humble swain
To some far refuge from his dread domain;
Nor wastes, upon his robe of useless pride,
The wealth, which shivering thousands want beside;
Nor in one palace sinks a hundred cots;
Nor in one manor drowns a thousand lots;
Nor, on one table, spread for death and pain,
Devours what would a village well sustain.   90

O Competence, thou bless'd by Heaven's decree,
How well exchang'd is empty pride for thee!
Oft to thy cot my feet delighted turn,
To meet thy chearful smile, at peep of morn;
To join thy toils, that bid the earth look gay;
To mark thy sports, that hail the eve of May;
To see thy ruddy children, at thy board,
And share thy temperate meal, and frugal hoard;
And every joy, by winning prattlers giv'n,
And every earnest of a future Heaven.   100

There the poor wanderer finds a table spread,
The fireside welcome, and the peaceful bed.
The needy neighbour, oft by wealth denied,
There finds the little aids of life supplied;
The horse, that bears to mill the hard-earn'd grain;
The day's work given, to reap the ripen'd plain;
The useful team, to house the precious food,
And all the offices of real good.

There too, divine Religion is a guest,
And all the Virtues join the daily feast.   110
Kind Hospitality attends the door,
To welcome in the stranger and the poor;
Sweet Chastity, still blushing as she goes;
And Patience smiling at her train of woes;
And meek-eyed Innocence, and Truth refin'd,
And Fortitude, of bold, but gentle mind.

Thou pay'st the tax, the rich man will not pay;

Thou feed'st the poor, the rich man drives away.
Thy sons, for freedom, hazard limbs, and life,
While pride applauds, but shuns the manly strife: 120
Thou prop'st religion's cause, the world around,
And shew'st thy faith in works, and not in sound.

    Say, child of passion! while, with idiot stare,
Thou seest proud grandeur wheel her sunny car;
While kings, and nobles, roll bespangled by,
And the tall palace lessens in the sky;
Say, while with pomp thy giddy brain runs round,
What joys, like these, in splendour can be found?
Ah, yonder turn thy wealth-inchanted eyes,
Where that poor, friendless wretch expiring lies!   130
Hear his sad partner shriek, beside his bed,
And call down curses on her landlord's head,
Who drove, from yon small cot, her houshold sweet,
To pine with want, and perish in the street.
See the pale tradesman toil, the livelong day,
To deck imperious lords, who never pay!
Who waste, at dice, their boundless breadth of soil,
But grudge the scanty meed of honest toil.
See hounds and horses riot on the store,
By HEAVEN created for the hapless poor!   140
See half a realm one tyrant scarce sustain,
While meagre thousands round him glean the plain!
See, for his mistress' robe, a village sold,
Whose matrons shrink from nakedness and cold!
See too the Farmer prowl around the shed,
To rob the starving houshold of their bread;
And seize, with cruel fangs, the helpless swain,
While wives, and daughters, plead, and weep, in vain;
Or yield to infamy themselves, to save
Their fire from prison, famine, and the grave.   150

    There too foul luxury taints the putrid mind,
And slavery there imbrutes the reasoning kind:
There humble worth, in damps of deep despair,
Is bound by poverty's eternal bar:
No motives bright the etherial aim impart,
Nor one fair ray of hope allures the heart.

But, O sweet Competence! how chang'd the scene,
Where thy soft footsteps lightly print the green!
Where Freedom walks erect, with manly port,
And all the blessings to his side resort,   160
In every hamlet, Learning builds her schools,
And beggars, children gain her arts, and rules;
And mild Simplicity o'er manners reigns,
And blameless morals Purity sustains.

From thee the rich enjoyments round me spring,
Where every farmer reigns a little king;
Where all to comfort, none to danger rise;
Where pride finds few, but nature all supplies;
Where peace and sweet civility are seen,
And meek good-neighbourhood endears the green.   170
Here every class (if classes those we call.
Where one extended class embraces all,
All mingling, as the rainbow's beauty blends,
Unknown where every hue begins or ends)
Each following each, with uninvidious strife,
Wears every feature of improving life.
Each gains from other comeliness of dress,
And learns, with gentle mien to win and bless,
With welcome mild the stranger to receive,
And with plain, pleasing decency to live.   180
Refinement hence even humblest life improves;
Not the loose fair, that form and frippery loves;
But she, whose mansion is the gentle mind,
In thought, and action, virtuously refin'd.
Hence, wives and husbands act a lovelier part,
More just the conduct, and more kind the heart;
Hence brother, sister, parent, child, and friend,
The harmony of life more sweetly blend;
Hence labour brightens every rural scene;
Hence cheerful plenty lives along the green;   190
Still Prudence eyes her hoard, with watchful care,
And robes of thrift and neatness, all things wear.

But hark! what voice so gaily fills the wind?
Of care oblivious, whose that laughing mind?
'Tis yon poor black, who ceases now his song,

And whistling, drives the cumbrous wain along.
He never dragg'd, with groans, the galling chain;
Nor hung, suspended, on th' infernal crane;
No dim, white spots deform his face, or hand,
Memorials hellish of the marking brand!   200
No seams of pincers, fears of scalding oil;
No waste of famine, and no wear of toil.
But kindly fed, and clad, and treated, he
Slides on, thro' life, with more than common glee.
For here mild manners good to all impart,
And stamp with infamy th' unfeeling heart;
Here law, from vengeful rage, the slave defends,
And here the gospel peace on earth extends.

   He toils, 'tis true; but shares his master's toil;
With him, he feels the herd, and trims the soil;   210
Helps to sustain the house, with clothes, and food,
And takes his portion of the common good:
Lost liberty his sole, peculiar ill,
And fix'd submission to another's will.
Ill, ah, how great! without that cheering sun,
The world is chang'd to one wide, frigid zone;
The mind, a chill'd exotic, cannot grow,
Nor leaf with vigour, nor with promise blow;
Pale, sickly, shrunk, it strives in vain to rise,
Scarce lives, while living, and untimely dies.   220

   See fresh to life the Afric infant spring,
And plume its powers, and spread its little wing!
Firm is its frame, and vigorous is its mind,
Too young to think, and yet to misery blind.
But soon he sees himself to slavery born;
Soon meets the voice of power, the eye of scorn;
Sighs for the blessings of his peers, in vain;
Condition'd as a brute, tho' form'd a man.
Around he casts his fond, instinctive eyes,
And sees no good, to fill his wishes, rise: 230
(No motive warms, with animating beam,
Nor praise, nor property, nor kind esteem,
Bless'd independence, on his native ground,
Nor sweet equality with those around;)

Himself, and his, another's shrinks to find,
Levell'd below the lot of human kind.
Thus, shut from honour's paths, he turns to shame,
And filches the small good, he cannot claim.
To sour, and stupid, sinks his active mind;
Finds joys in drink, he cannot elsewhere find;   240
Rule disobeys; of half his labour cheats;
In some safe cot, the pilfer'd turkey eats;
Rides hard, by night, the steed, his art purloins;
Serene from conscience' bar himself essoins;
Sees from himself his sole redress must flow,
And makes revenge the balsam of his woe.

                    *   *   *

See too, in every hamlet, round me rise
A central school-house, dress'd in modest guise!
Where every child for useful life prepares,
To business moulded, ere he knows its cares;   250
In worth matures, to independence grows,
And twines the civic garland o'er his brows.

Mark, how invited by the vernal sky,
Yon cheerful group of females passes by!
Whose hearts, attun'd to social joy, prepare
A friendly visit to some neighbouring fair.
How neatness glistens from the lovely train!
Bright charm! which pomp to rival tries in vain.

Ye Muses! dames of dignified renown,
Rever'd alike in country, and in town,   260
Your bard the mysteries of a visit show;
For sure your Ladyships those mysteries know:
What is it then, obliging Sisters! say,
The debt of social visiting to pay?

'Tis not to toil before the idol pier;
To shine the first in fashion's lunar sphere;
By sad engagements forc'd, abroad to roam,
And dread to find the expecting fair, at home!
To stop at thirty doors, in half a day,
Drop the gilt card, and proudly roll away;   270
To alight, and yield the hand, with nice parade;

Up stairs to rustle in the stiff brocade;
Swim thro' the drawing room, with studied air;
Catch the pink'd beau, and shade the rival fair;
To sit, to curb, to toss, with bridled mien,
Mince the scant speech, and lose a glance between;
Unfurl the fan, display the snowy arm,
And ope, with each new motion, some new charm:
Or sit, in silent solitude, to spy
Each little failing, with malignant eye;   280
Or chatter, with incessancy of tongue,
Careless, if kind, or cruel, right, or wrong;
To trill of us, and ours, of mine, and me,
Our house, our coach, our friends, our family,
While all th' excluded circle sit in pain,
And glance their cool contempt, or keen disdain:
T' inhale, from proud Nanking, a sip of tea,
And wave a curtsey trim, and flirt away:
Or waste, at cards, peace, temper, health and life,
Begin with sullenness, and end in strife,   290
Lose the rich feast, by friendly converse given,
And backward turn from happiness, and heaven.

   It is, in decent habit, plain and neat,
To spend a few choice hours, in converse sweet;
Careless of forms, to act th' unstudied part,
To mix in friendship, and to blend the heart;
To choose those happy themes, which all must feel,
The moral duties, and the houshold weal,
The tale of sympathy, the kind design,
Where rich affections soften, and refine;   300
T' amuse, to be amus'd, to bless, be bless'd,
And tune to harmony the common breast;
To cheer, with mild good-humour's sprightly ray,
And smooth life's passage, o'er its thorny way;
To circle round the hospitable board,
And taste each good, our generous climes afford;
To court a quick return, with accents kind,
And leave, at parting, some regret behind.

   Such, here, the social intercourse is found;
So slides the year, in smooth enjoyment, round.   310

And when new regions prompt their feet to roam,
And fix, in untrod fields, another home,
No dreary realms our happy race explore,
Nor mourn their exile from their native shore.
For there no endless frosts the glebe deform,
Nor blows, with icy breath, perpetual storm:
No wrathful suns, with sickly splendour glare,
Nor moors, impoison'd, taint the balmy air,
But medial climates change the healthful year;
Pure streamlets wind, and gales of Eden cheer;   320
In misty pomp the sky-topp'd mountains stand,
And with green bosom humbler hills expand:
With flowery brilliance smiles the woodland glade;
Full teems the soil, and fragrant twines the shade.
There cheaper fields the numerous houshold charm,
And the glad sire gives every son a farm;
In falling forests, Labour's axe resounds;
Opes the new field; and wind the fence's bounds;
The green wheat sparkles; nods the towering corn;
And meads, and pastures, lessening wastes adorn.   330
Where howl'd the forest, herds unnumber'd low;
The fleecy wanderers fear no prowling foe;
The village springs; the humble school aspires;
And the church brightens in the morning fires!
Young Freedom wantons; Art exalts her head;
And infant Science prattles through the shade.
There changing neighbours learn their manners mild;
And toil and prudence dress th' improving wild:
The savage shrinks, nor dares the bliss annoy;
And the glad traveller wonders at the joy.   340

All hail, thou western world! by heaven design'd
Th' example bright, to renovate mankind.
Soon shall thy sons across the mainland roam;
And claim, on far Pacific shores, their home;
Their rule, religion, manners, arts, convey,
And spread their freedom to the Asian sea.
Where erst six thousand suns have roll'd the year
O'er plains of slaughter, and o'er wilds of fear,
Towns, cities, fanes, shall lift their towery pride;
The village bloom, on every streamlet's side;   350

Proud Commerce' mole the western surges lave;
The long, white spire lie imag'd on the wave;
O'er morn's pellucid main expand their sails,
And the starr'd ensign court Korean gales.
Then nobler thoughts shall savage trains inform;
Then barbarous passions cease the heart to storm:
No more the captive circling flames devour;
Through the war path the Indian creep no more;
No midnight scout the slumbering village fire;
Nor the scalp'd infant stain his gasping fire: 360
But peace, and truth, illume the twilight mind,
The gospel's sunshine, and the purpose kind.
Where marshes teem'd with death, shall meads unfold;
Untrodden cliffs resign their stores of gold;
The dance refin'd on Albion's margin move,
And her lone bowers rehearse the tale of love.
Where slept perennial night, shall science rise,
And new-born Oxfords cheer the evening skies;
Miltonic strains the Mexic hills prolong,
And Louis murmurs to Sicilian song.   370

Then to new climes the bliss shall trace its way,
And Tartar desarts hail the rising day;
From the long torpor startled China wake;
Her chains of misery rous'd Peruvia break;
Man link to man; with bosom bosom twine;
And one great bond the house of Adam join:
The sacred promise full completion know,
And peace, and piety, the world o'erflow.

DWIGHT'S NOTES (SELECTIONS)

Line 1. This part of the poem, though appropriated to the parish of Green-field, may be considered as a general description of the towns and villages of New England; those only excepted, which are either commercial, new, or situated on a barren soil. Morose and gloomy persons, and perhaps some others, may think the description too highly colored. Persons of moderation and candor may possibly think otherwise. In its full extent, the writer sup-poses it applicable to the best inhabitants only; but he believes the number of these to be great; to others he thinks it partially applicable. Poetical representations are usually esteemed flattering; perhaps this is as little so, as most of them. The inhabitants of New England, notwithstanding some modern instances of declension, are, at least in the writer's opinion, a singular example of virtue and happiness.

It will easily be discovered by the reader, that this part of the poem is designed to illustrate the effects of the state of property, which is the counterpart to that, so beautifully exhibited by Dr. Goldsmith, in the "Deserted Village." That excellent writer, in a most interesting manner, displays the wretched condition of the many, where enormous wealth, splendour, and luxury constitute the state of the few. In this imperfect attempt, the writer wished to exhibit the blessings which flow from an equal division of property, and a general competence.

Wherever an *equal division of property* is mentioned in this work, the reader is requested to remember that that state of things only is intended, in which every citizen is secured in the avails of his industry and prudence, and in which property descends, by law, in equal shares, to the proprietor's children.

L. 26 slump'd: This word, said, in New England, to be of North Country original, is customarily used in New England to denote the sudden sinking of the foot in the earth, when partially thawn, as in the month of March. It is also used to denote the sudden sinking of the earth under the foot.

L. 91 Men in middling circumstances appear greatly to excel the rich in piety, charity, and public spirit; nor will a critical observer of human life hesitate to believe that they enjoy more happiness.

L. 145 Farmer: Farmer of revenue: a superior kind of tax-gatherer, in some countries of Europe.

L. 196 wain: wagon or cart.

L. 208. Some interesting and respectable efforts have been made in Connecticut, and others are now making, for the purpose of freeing the Negroes.

L. 221. The black children are generally sprightly and ingenious, until they become conscious of their slavery. This usually happens when they are four, five, or six years of age. From that time, they usually sink into stupidity, or give themselves up to vice.

L. 237. If we consider how few inducements the blacks have to ingenious or worthy efforts, we shall more wonder that there are, among them, so many, than that there are so few, examples of ingenuity or amiableness.

L. 265 Pier: a looking-glass; from its place, and afterwards from its structure, called a pier-glass.

L. 265. All persons declare formal visiting to be unpleasing and burdensome, and familiar visiting to be pleasing; yet multitudes spend no small part of their lives in formal visiting, and consider themselves as being under a species of obligation to it. In formal visiting, persons go to be seen; in social visiting, to give and to receive pleasure. If common sense were allowed to dictate, or genuine good breeding to influence, we should immediately exchange form and parade for sociability and happiness.

L. 295. I do not remember ever to have seen a lady in full dress who appeared to be so happy, or to behave so easily and gracefully as when she was moderately dressed. An unusual degree of dress seems uniformly to inspire formality, distance, and difficulty of behavior. Toil, taste, and fancy are put to exertion to contrive, and to adjust, the dress, which is expected highly to ornament the person; and the same exertion appears to be used in contriving and fashioning manners which may become the dress.

L. 365 Albion: New Albion; a very desirable country on the western shore of America, discovered by Sir Francis Drake.

L. 369 Mexic hills: a range of mountains running from north to south, at the distance of several hundred miles westward of the Mississippi.

L. 370 Louis: the Mississippi; Sicilian song: pastoral poetry.   (1794)

ROYALL TYLER

(1757–1826)

Prologue to *The Contrast**

Exult each patriot heart!—this night is shewn
A piece, which we may fairly call our own;
Where the proud titles of "My Lord! Your Grace!"
To humble *Mr.* and plain *Sir* give place.
Our Author pictures not from foreign climes
The fashions, or the follies of the times;
But has confin'd the subject of his work
To the gay scenes—the circles of New-York.
On native themes his Muse displays her pow'rs;
If ours the faults, the virtues too are ours.   10
Why should our thoughts to distant countries roam,
When each refinement may be found at home?
Who travels now to ape the rich or great,
To deck an equipage and roll in state;
To court the graces, or to dance with ease,
Or by hypocrisy to strive to please?
Our free-born ancestors such arts despis'd;
Genuine sincerity alone they priz'd;
Their minds, with honest emulation fir'd,
To solid good—not ornament—aspir'd;   20
Or, if ambition rous'd a bolder flame,
Stern virtue throve, where indolence was shame.

* Marius B. Pèladeau, ed., *The Verse of Royall Tyler* (Charlottesville, Va., 1968).

But modern youths, with imitative sense,
Deem taste in dress the proof of excellence;
And spurn the meanness of your homespun arts,
Since homespun habits would obscure their parts;
Whilst all, which aims at splendour and parade,
Must come from Europe, *and be ready made.*
Strange! we should thus our native worth disclaim,
And check the progress of our rising fame.   30
Yet *one*, whilst imitation bears the sway,
Aspires to nobler heights, and points the way.
Be rous'd, my friends! his bold example view;
Let your own Bards be proud to copy *you!*
Should rigid critics reprobate our play,
At least the patriotic heart will say,
"Glorious our fall, since in a noble cause.
The bold *attempt alone* demands applause."
Still may the wisdom of the Comic Muse
Exalt your merits, or your faults accuse.   40
But think not, 'tis her aim to be severe;—
We all are mortals, and as mortals err.
If candour pleases, we are truly blest;
Vice trembles, when compell'd to stand confess'd.
Let not the light Censure on your faults, offend,
Which aims not to expose them, but amend.
Thus does our Author to your candour trust;
Conscious, the *free* are generous, as just.   (1787)

Ode Composed for the Fourth of July*

CALCULATED FOR THE MERIDIAN OF SOME COUNTRY TOWNS IN MASSACHUSETTS, AND RYE IN NEWHAMPSHIRE

Squeak the fife, and beat the drum,
INDEPENDENCE DAY has come!!
Let the roasting pig be bled.
Quick twist off the cockerel's head,
Quickly rub the pewter platter,
Heap the nutcakes fried in butter.
Set the cups and beaker glass,
The pumpkin and the apple sauce,
Send the keg to shop for brandy;
Maple sugar we have handy,   10
Independent, staggering Dick,
A noggin mix of *swinging thick*,
Sal, put on your ruffel skirt,
Jotham, get your *boughten* shirt,
To day we dance to tiddle diddle.
—Here comes Sambo with his fiddle;
Sambo, take a dram of whiskey,
And play up Yankee Doodle frisky.
Moll, come leave your witched tricks,
And let us have a reel of six.   20
Father and Mother shall make two,
Sal, Moll and I stand all a row,
Sambo, play and dance with quality;
This is the day of blest Equality.
Father and *Mother* are but men,
And Sambo—is a Citizen,
Come foot it, Sal—Moll, figure in,
And, mother, you dance up to him;
Now saw as fast as e'er you can do,
And Father, you cross o'er to Sambo.   30
—Thus we dance, and thus we play,
On glorious *Independent Day*—
Rub more rosin on your bow,
And let us have another go.

* Pèladeau.

Zounds, as sure as eggs and bacon,
Here's ensign Sneak and uncle Deacon,
Aunt Thiah, and their Bets behind her
On blundering mare, than beetle blinder.
And there's the 'Squire too with his lady—
Sal, hold the beast, I'll take the baby.   40
Moll, bring the 'Squire our great arm chair,
Good folks, we're glad to see you here.
Jotham, get the great case bottle,
Your teeth can pull its corn cob stopple.
Ensign,—Deacon never mind;
'Squire, drink until your blind;
Come, here's the French—and Guillotine, ⎫
And here is good 'Squire Gallatin,[1]   ⎬
And here's each noisy Jacobin.   ⎭
Here's friend Madison so hearty,   50
And here's confusion to the treaty.[2]
Come, one more swig to southern Demos
Who represent our brother negroes.
Thus we drink and dance away,
This glorious INDEPENDENT DAY!   (1796)

[1] Albert Gallatin (1761–1849), an American statesman and Secretary of the Treasury under Jefferson. The Federalists, of whom Tyler was one, attacked Gallatin, not only politically, but personally, because they were opposed to the French Revolution, and so resented Gallatin's ancestry. [Pèladeau's note].

[2] A reference to the debate in 1796 over the Jay Treaty, in which Gallatin defended the constitutional right of the House of Representatives to consider treaties and said the House could refuse to appropriate finances to implement them. The treaty was one of the major issues in dispute between the Republicans and Federalists in the mid-1790's. [Pèladeau's note].

FICTION

J. HECTOR ST. JOHN DE CRÈVECOEUR

(1731–1813)

Letters from an American Farmer won Crèvecoeur fame that has continued since his own time. The narrative skill and the sensitive interpretation of life in the new nation that he showed in the longer work is quite apparent here. The ability of an early American to empathize with the Indians has continued to be uncommon, yet Crèvecoeur clearly had it. White Americans have often been blind to the minorities in their midst, as many selections in this text show, and they have seldom been able to comprehend the views that those groups have of them. Indeed, these views have seldom become a part of American literature.

*Hoppajewot, the Land of Dreams**

. . . As soon as the narrator had finished his tale, a new speaker arose and announced: "Having only recently returned from Hoppajewot, the Land of Dreams, I am going to tell you how life is carried on there, and what I saw take place. If anyone says to me afterward, 'You dream like a sick man,' or 'You rave like a drunkard,' I shall only say, 'Go and see for yourself.' "

In this land there is neither day nor night; the sun neither rises nor sets; and there is neither hot nor cold, spring nor winter. The people have never seen bows and arrows and tomahawks; and their language has no words that mean *hunter* and *warrior*. Devouring hunger and burning thirst came there once upon a time, according to an ancient tradition, but the chiefs of the land threw them to the bottom of the river, where they remain to this day.

Oh! this wonderful land! If one desires to smoke, he can find a pipe any-

* Percy G. Adams, ed. and trans., *Crèvecoeur's Eighteenth-Century Travels in Pennsylvania and New York* (Lexington, Ky., 1961).

396

where; he has only to lift it to his lips. Anywhere that one wishes he can rest at the foot of a tree. He has only to stretch out his arm and he will encounter the hand of a friend. The earth being always green and the trees covered with leaves, one has need neither of bear skins nor wigwams. If one likes to travel, the current of the rivers takes him wherever he wants to go; he has no need of oars and paddles. Oh! this wonderful land!

"Do you want something to eat?" asks the deer of those who are hungry. "Take my right shoulder, and let me go off into the forest of Ninner Wind[1] where it will soon grow back, and next year I shall return and offer you the left one. But take care not to destroy too much, because if you do, in the end you will not have anything."

"Here," says the beaver, "cut off my beautiful tail; I can do without it until it grows back, since I have just finished building my home. But take care not to be greedy, for it is said: 'Four beavers you will take, but the fifth you will let go in peace.'" Oh! that wonderful land! There one only eats, drinks, smokes, and sleeps.

"Do you want to have a feast?" asks the great fish in the lake. "My job is done; I have just laid ten thousand eggs; cook me in any way you wish. But take care not to be too greedy, for it is said: 'Eighteen fish will you take, but the nineteenth you will let go in peace.'" Oh! that wonderful land! Though the women there never have to anoint themselves with bear grease, they are always beautiful and fresh; they have only to keep the pots boiling and teach the children how to swim.

One day as I was helping at the council fire, an unusual noise was heard, and the great Okemaw[2] who presided there gave orders to investigate. The messenger returned. "The sound," he said, "comes from some great canoes that draw near our shore. They look like sea birds driven before the winds. Our people are in great wonder and know neither what to think nor to say."

"Are there any men on these boats?"

"Yes," the messenger replied. "They are white people with beards, tired from their long voyage, for they come from the land of Cherryhum.[3] They humbly ask permission to land here in order to rest. What says the great Okemaw?"

"Although they are white and bearded," he answered, "and have come from a land which I did not believe to be inhabited, they are wretched and suffering; let them come ashore and rest here for a few days."

I do not know how long it was after their arrival that these strangers,

---

[1] In the Chippeway language "Ninnerwind" meant "all of us." [This and the following notes by Percy G. Adams].

[2] Chief, both in Chippeway and Algonquin.

[3] Europe or England; an Iroquois word.

while walking on the bank of the river, met the great chief of Hoppajewot, from whom they begged a little land on both sides of the place where they were encamped. Surprised at such an unusual request, he said to them, "What do you want it for?"

"To plant some little grains we have brought with us," they answered. "They reproduce a hundredfold, and when one has neither flesh nor fish, one can eat them."

Hardly had the chief given his consent when they set to work scratching the earth and destroying the plant life, to the great astonishment of the people of Hoppajewot, who had never seen anything like it. Some moons later, after their fields of grain had flourished, they again approached the Okemaw, and this time asked for the point of land that formed the entrance to the bay. Finding nothing inconvenient in the request, he granted it. Almost immediately they were seen cutting down the trees with a piece of very sharp metal, digging a hole in the earth, and raising a little mountain of wood, from which, both morning and evening, there issued forth fire and smoke and noise never before heard in the country of Hoppajewot.

Then appeared before the Okemaw, Awakesh,[4] the great forest deer, saying, "Woe be unto you, O Chief of the nation! Woe unto your people! And woe unto us and to the other beasts, if you permit these bearded ones to level and burn the forest which the Good Spirit has given us! Soon there will be no longer on the earth either plants or shade; then we will be forced to flee your land. Take care," he continued; "these white people, so soft-spoken and humble, who on first landing called you brother, will drive you away from here when they have become more numerous. Do you not observe how they behave themselves behind their mountain of fire, noise, and smoke?"

These words produced a strong effect on the men in the assembly, and each one present was set to thinking. But while they were thinking, one came to inform them that the bearded men had scattered themselves over the villages and were deceiving the women and children by telling them stories which they said were worth more than the legends of Hoppajewot. The messengers, their indignation aroused by this underhanded conduct, spoke to the great chief, saying: "The peace of families, the harmony within villages no longer exist; the white people have turned the heads of our women; our medicine men have lost their influence. What right have these foreigners from the land of Cherryhum to come here and speak to our people about the god of their country? Does not each country have its own god as it has its own lakes and rivers? And after all, the god of a land on which

---

4 "Awakesh," or "Awaskesh," meant "deer" both in Chippeway and Algonquin.

the hot and radiant sun shines without ceasing, is he not worth more than the god of a place where the sun rises pale and without heat? What is to be done, O, wise and powerful Okemaw?"

"Let the medicine men, both bearded and unbearded, gather here today," he answered, "and we shall see." The two groups did indeed assemble; and following the custom of Hoppajewot, the strangers were permitted to speak first. Among them were four orators who spoke at such length that the audience had time to smoke two pipes. The first man told of a land where one could go only after death, which astonished the gathering a great deal. That land, he said, lies beyond the sun and knows neither heat nor cold; there the people are happy and content, for need is unknown, and this happiness never ends once it has begun. The second orator explained all that must be done and not done on earth in order to obtain permission to enter into this world of spirits. The third man spoke of a lake of fire, which, though it burns everything thrown into it, does not consume anything, and into which are plunged all those who may not go to the first place. The fourth speaker entertained them with the tale of a court of justice before which appear the spirits of all those who die, and the judgments of which are irrevocable; he assured his audience that if they followed his counsel they would find favor in the eyes of the great judge.

"Those are four good and very long stories," said the Okemaw. "It is now our turn to speak. Beardless medicine men, arise, and tell some of our legends. Begin with the one about the manifestation of the Great Spirit on the mountain of Aratapeskow, when he took two figures of clay and breathed into them the breath of life, the first of which he named Pegick Sagat, meaning First Man, and the second, Sanna Tella, meaning Companion.[5] Speak also of Nassanicomy, who came down from the clouds onto the island of Allisinape[6] and caused to grow there corn, rice, squash, and tobacco, by spitting to the north, to the south, to the east, and to the west."

"Those are only lies and illusions," said the bearded speakers. "We do not want to hear them."

"Since we have listened to you with patience and courtesy," replied the Okemaw, "you should certainly listen to our people with the same patience and the same courtesy. Why do you scorn our traditions? Like yours they are venerated for their old age." And he continued, "Why have you cut down the beautiful trees with which the Creator covered the ground I lent you? You merit his indignation and ours, because, like us, these trees are the work

---

[5] For the first of these two names, Crèvecoeur apparently borrowed the Algonquin word "pegick," or "Payjik," meaning "one," and the Iroquois word for man, "sagat." "Sannatella" meant "wife" in the Iroquois tongue.

[6] Algonquin for "man."

of his hands. Why do you keep us away from your mountain with the fire, smoke, and noise of death, we who have received you as brothers? If that is the way men conduct themselves in your country of Cherryhum, your Great Spirit is not so good as ours, for here you have found peace and good faith, and you have brought with your tales division and trouble. Go away, return to your mountain, and let us think and live as our ancestors have lived and thought."

In place of replying civilly, the white men arose, made a great deal of noise, and left the assembly saying things that could not be understood; and from that moment, the two parties swore an implacable hate.

Some time after, having discovered that these same white medicine men, by making use of a water that was fire to the taste, were attempting to insinuate themselves into the village and make the women believe their stories, the great Okemaw had them come a second time before him, and said to them in a loud voice:

"Obstinate bearded ones! You deceive yourselves if you think you can do here what you have done in the land of the Nishynorbays.[7] You will not seduce us with your firewater and your folly, in order to invade our land, as your countrymen have seduced those other unfortunate ones. We are not so blind nor so easily deceived. Drink the waters yourselves; may they succeed in consuming you and destroying you as they have destroyed so many brave nations! Smash those bottles of poison!"

As the Okemaw's order was being carried out, one of the bearded medicine men, with black eyebrows, a ferocious look, and a proud bearing, more hot-headed than the others, dared to lay hold of the great chief, who, while saying coldly to him, "You have been very badly educated in your country," knocked him down with his powerful arm, and pulled off his hair. But what was his astonishment to see that it was not attached to the skull but was only a wig of borrowed hair!

The Okemaw, as well as all his people, having never seen such a thing before, burst involuntarily into loud laughter. This laughter caused a distraction by which the white medicine man and his companions profited quickly in making their escape, leaving the false hair in the hands of the astonished chief. It was soon apparent that when they reached their companions they spread the alarm among all their habitations and that there was a great movement taking place among them.

Then the Okemaw called for a herd of deer, led by Awakesh, each of whom he ordered to take a flaming torch and set fire to the fields around the white man's mountain. And this they did so speedily that, in spite of the noise, the

---

[7] Indians or Red Men, a Chippeway word.

fire, and the smoke that came from the mountain, everything was burned by daybreak. When the sun rose, the white men were seen going aboard their canoes, carrying everything they had brought with them, and then sailing out of the river with a favorable wind. Since that time one has never heard the bearded white ones spoken of in the land of Hoppajewot. That is my story.

The orator, who had been loudly applauded, was going to start another, when several of the officers, remembering that we had yet some distance to go before reaching Niagara, informed us that it was time to leave.

HUGH HENRY BRACKENRIDGE

(1748–1816)

The cry from critics for a native American literature extended well into the nineteenth century, despite the efforts—conscious or unconscious—of some authors to draw upon native materials. Brackenridge was one of the eighteenth-century prose writers who found sufficient material in America for his characters and his settings. *Modern Chivalry*, his long satiric work, contains a multitude of exaggerated incidents of the Pennsylvania frontier. The story that follows has a strong narrative line and realistic detail that give the reader at least the illusion of picturing the frontier.

*The Trial of Mamachtaga, an Indian, at a Court of Oyer and Terminer for the County of Westmoreland, in the Year 1784–5**

I KNOW the particulars of the following story well, because one of the men (Smith) was shingling a house for me in the town of Pittsburgh, the evening before he was murdered by Mamachtaga, and for which murder, and some others, this Indian was tried. Smith had borrowed a blanket of me, saying that he was about to cross the river (Allegheny) to the Indian camp on the west side. Here a party of Indians, mostly Delawares, had come in, it being just after the war, and the greater part of these Indians having professed themselves friendly during the war, and their chief, Killbuck, with his family and that of several others, having remained at the garrison, or on an island in the Ohio river, called Killbuck's Island, and under the reach of the guns of the fort. Mamachtaga had been at war against the settlements with others of the Delawares who were now at this encampment.

* Archibald Loudon, ed., *Selection of Some of the Most Interesting Narratives of Outrages Committed by the Indians* (Carlisle, Pa., 1808).

I went myself over to the encampment, the next morning, and found the Indians there. Two men had been murdered, Smith and another of the name of Evans, and two wounded, one of them a dwarf of the name of Freeman. According to the relation which I got from the wounded, there were four white men together in a cabin when Mamachtaga, without the least notice, rushed in and stabbed Smith mortally, and had stabbed Evans, who had seized the Indian who was entangled with the dwarf among his feet attempting to escape, and who had received wounds also in the scuffle; the other white man had also received a stab. It would appear that the Indian had been in liquor, according to the account of the other Indians and of the white men who escaped. Killbuck appeared greatly cast down, and sat upon a log, silent. Mamachtaga made no attempt to escape. He was now sober, and gave himself up to the guard that came over, affecting not to know what had happened. The seat of justice of Westmoreland county being 30 miles distant, and the jail there not being secure, he was taken to the guard-house of the garrison, to be confined until a court of Oyer and Terminer should be holden in the county. Living in the place and being of the profession of the law, said I to the interpreter, Joseph Nicholas, one day, has that Indian any fur or peltry, or has he any interest with his nation that he could collect some and pay a lawyer to take up his defence for this homicide? The interpreter said that he had some in the hands of a trader in town, and that he could raise from his nation any quantity of racoon or beaver, provided it would answer any purpose. I was struck with the pleasantry of having an Indian for a client, and getting a fee in this way, and told the interpreter to go to the Indian, and explain the matter to him, who did so, and brought me an account that Mamachtaga had forty weight of Beaver, which he was ready to make over, being with a trader in town, William Amberson, with whom he had left it, and that he had a brother who would set off immediately to the Indian towns, and procure an hundred weight or more if that would do any good, but the interpreter stipulated that he should have half of all that should be got, for his trouble in bringing about the contract. Accordingly he was dispatched to the Indian, from whom he brought, in a short time, an order for the beaver in the hand of the trader, with Mamachtaga (his mark). The mark was something like a turkey's foot, as these people have no idea of an hieroglyphic merely abstract, as a straight line or a curve, but it must bear some resemblance to a thing in nature. After this, as it behoved, I went to consult with my client and arrange his defense, if it were possible to make one on which a probable face could be put. Accompanied by the interpreter, I was admitted to the Indian, so that I could converse with him; he was in what is called the black hole, something resembling that kind of hole which is depressed in the floor, and which the southern people have in their cabins, in which to keep their esculent roots from the frost during the winter season. Not going down into the hole as may be supposed, though it was large enough to contain two or three, and was depressed about eight feet, being the place in which delinquent or refractory soldiery had been confined occasionally for punishment, but standing on the floor above, I desired the interpreter to put his questions. This was done, explaining to him the object of the enquiry, that it was to serve him, and by knowing the truth, be prepared for his defense; he affected to know nothing about it, nor was he disposed to rely upon any defense that could be made. His idea was that he was giving the beaver as a commutation for his life. Under this impression it did not appear to me proper that I should take the beaver, knowing that I could do nothing for him; besides, seeing the manner in which the dark and squalid creature was accommodated with but a shirt and breech-clout on, humanity dictated that the beaver should be applied to procure him a blanket and food additional to the bread and water which he was allowed. Accordingly I returned the order to the interpreter, and desired him to procure and furnish these things. He seemed reluctant, and thought we ought to keep the perquisite we had got. On this, I thought it most advisable to retain the order and give it to a trader in town with directions to furnish these articles occasionally to the officer of the guard, which I did, taking the responsibility upon myself to the interpreter for his part of the beaver.

An Indian woman, known by the name of the Grenadier Squaw, was sitting doing some work by the trap-door of the cell, or hole in which he was confined, for the trap-door was kept open and a sentry at the outer door of the guard-house. The Indian woman was led by sympathy to sit by him. I had a curiosity to know the force of abstract sentiment, in preferring greater evils to what with us would seem to be less; or rather the force of opinion over pain. For knowing the idea of the Indians with regard to the disgrace of hanging, I proposed to the Indian woman, who spoke English as well as Indian, and was a Delaware herself, (Mamachtaga was of that nation,) to ask him which he would choose, to be hanged or burnt? Whether it was that the woman was struck with the inhumanity of introducing the idea of death, she not only declined to put the question, but her countenance expressed resentment. I then recollected, and have since attended to the circumstance, that amongst themselves, when they mean to put any one to death, they conceal the determination, and the time, until it is about to be put in execution, unless the blacking the prisoner, which is a mark upon such as are about to be burnt, may be called an intimation; but it is only by those who are accustomed to their manners that it can be understood. However, I got the question put by the interpreter, at which he seemed to hesitate for some time, but said he would rather be shot or be tomahawked. In a few days it made a great noise through the country that I was to appear for the Indian, and having acquired some reputation in the defense of criminals, it was thought possible by some that he might be acquitted by *the crooks of the law,* as the people expressed it; and it was talked of publickly to raise a party and come to town and take the interpreter and me both, and hang the interpreter, and exact an oath from me not to appear in behalf of the Indian. It was, however, finally concluded to come in to the garrison and demand the Indian, and hang him themselves. Accordingly, a party came, in a few days, and about break of day summoned the garrison, and demanded the surrender of the Indian; the commanding officer remonstrated, and prevailed with them to leave the Indian to the civil authority. Upon which they retired, firing their guns as they came through the town. The interpreter, hearing the alarm, sprang up in his shirt, and made for a hill above the town, called Grant's-hill. On seeing him run, he was taken for the Indian, who they supposed had been suffered to escape, and was pursued, until the people were assured that it was not the Indian. In the mean time he had run some miles, and swimming the river, lay in the Indian country until he thought it might be safe to return.

It was not without good reason that the interpreter was alarmed, for having been some years amongst the Indians, in early life a prisoner, and since a good deal employed in the Indian trade, and on all occasions of treaty, employed as an interpreter, he was associated in the public mind with an Indian, and on this occasion, considered as the abetter of the Indian, from the circumstance of employing council to defend him. And before this time a party had come from the Chartiers, a settlement south of the Monongahela, in the neighborhood of this town, and had attacked some friendly Indians on the Island in the Ohio, (Killbuck's Island) under the protection of the garrison, had killed several, and amongst them some that had been of essential service to the whites, in the expeditions against the Indian towns, and on scouting parties, in case of attacks upon the settlements. One to whom the whites had given the name of Wilson, (Captain Wilson) was much regretted by the garrison. A certain Cisna had commanded the party that committed this outrage.

A day or two after his return, the interpreter came to me, and relinquished all interest in the beaver that was lodged with the trader, or expectant from the towns, that he might, to use his own language, wipe his hands of the affair, and be clear of the charge of supporting the Indian. The fact was, that as to beaver from the towns I expected none, having been informed in the mean time by the friendly Indians, that Mamachtaga was a bad man, and was thought so by his nation; that he had been a great warrior; but was mischievous in liquor, having killed two of his own people; that it would not be much regretted in the nation to hear of his death; and that, except his brother, no one would give any thing to get him off.

He had the appearance of great ferocity; was of tall stature, and fierce aspect. He was called Mamachtaga, which signifies trees blown across, as is usual in a hurricane or tempest by the wind, and this name had been given him from the ungovernable nature of his passion. Having, therefore, no expectation of peltry or fur in the case, it was no great generosity in me to press upon the interpreter the taking half the beaver, as his right in procuring the contract; but finding me obstinate in insisting upon it, he got a friend to speak to me, and at length I suffered myself to be prevailed upon to let him off and take all the beaver that could be got to myself.

It did not appear to me advisable to relinquish the defense of the Indian, fee or no fee, lest it should be supposed that I yielded to the popular impression, the fury of which, when it had a little spent itself, began to subside, and there were some who thought the Indian might be cleared, if it could be proved that the white men killed had made the Indian drunk, which was alleged to be the case; but which the wounded and surviving persons denied, particularly the dwarf, (William Freeman,) but his testimony, it was thought, would not be much regarded, as he could not be said to be *man grown*, and had been convicted at the quarter sessions of stealing a keg of whiskey some time before.

At a court of Oyer and Terminer holden for the county of Westmoreland, before Chief Justice M'Kean, and Bryan, Mamachtaga was brought to trial. The usual forms were pursued. An interpreter, not Nicholas, but a certain Handlyn, stood by him and interpreted, in the Delaware language, the indictment and the meaning of it, and the privilege he had to deny the charge, that is, the plea of "*not guilty*." But he could not easily comprehend that it was matter of form, and that he must say "*not guilty*"; for he was unwilling to deny, as unbecoming a warrior to deny the truth. For though he did not confess, yet he did not like to say that he had not killed the men; only that he was drunk, and did not know what he had done; but "supposed he should know which he was under the ground." The court directed the plea to be entered for him, and he was put upon his trial.

He was called upon to make his challenges, which the interpreter explained to him, which he was left to make himself, and which he did as he liked the countenance of the jury, and challenged according to the sourness, or cheerfulness of the countenance, and what he thought indications of a mild temper. The jurors, as they were called to the book, being told in the usual form, "Prisoner, look upon the juror—juror, look upon the prisoner at the bar—are you related to the prisoner?" One of them, a German of a swarthy complexion, and being the first called, took the question amiss, thinking it a reflection, and said with some anger, that "he thought that an uncivil way to treat Dutch people, as if he could be the brother, or cousin, of an Indian"; but the matter being explained to him by another German on the jury, he was satisfied, and was sworn.

The meaning of the jury being on oath, was explained to the Indian, to give him some idea of the solemnity and fairness of the trial. The testimony was positive and put the homicide beyond a doubt; so that nothing remained for me, in opening his defence, but the offering to prove that he was in liquor, and that this had been given him by the white people, the traders in town. This testimony was overruled, and it was explained to the Indian that the being drunk could not by our law excuse the murder. The Indian said "he hoped the good man above would excuse it."

The jury gave their verdict, guilty, without leaving the bar. And the prisoner was remanded to jail. In the mean time there was tried at the same court another person, (John Bradly,) on a charge of homicide, but who was found guilty of *manslaughter* only. Towards the ending of the court, these were both brought up to receive sentence. The Indian was asked what he had to say, why sentence of death should not be pronounced upon him. This was interpreted to him, and he said that he would rather *run awhile*. This was under the idea of the custom among the Indians of giving time to the murderer, according to the circumstances of the case, to run, during which time if he can satisfy the relations of the deceased, by a commutation for his life, a gun, a horse, fur and the like, it is in their power to dispense with the punishment, but if this cannot be done, having not enough to give, or the relations not consenting to take a commutation, he must come at the end of the time appointed, to the spot assigned, and there, by a warrior of the nation, or some relative, son, brother, &c. of the deceased, be put to death, in which case the tomahawk is the usual instrument. No instance will occur in which the condemned will not be punctual to his engagement. And I think it very probable, or rather can have no doubt, but that if this Indian had been suffered to run at this time, that is, go to his nation, on the condition to return at a certain period, to receive the sentence of what he would call the council, he would have come, with as much fidelity, as a man challenged, would on a point of honour come to the place assigned, and at the time when, to risk himself to his adversary. Such is the force of opinion, from education, on the human mind.

Sentence having been pronounced upon the convicted of manslaughter. [*sic*] (In this case, the first part of the sentence, as the law directs, was that of hanging, which is done until the *benefit of clergy is prayed by the prisoner*; but not understanding this, he was not prepared for the shock;—nothing could exceed the contortion of his muscles when a sentence, contrary to what he had expected, was pronounced. Being a simple man, he made a hideous outcry, gave a most woful look to the court, and country and begged for mercy; and it was not for some time after that, having the matter explained to him, and the benefit of clergy being allowed, he could be composed,) sentence of *burning in the hand* being now pronounced; at this moment the sheriff came in with a rope to bind up his hand to a beam of the low and wooden court-house in which we were, in order that the hot iron might be put upon it.

Sentence of hanging had been previously pronounced upon the Indian, on which he had said that he would prefer to be shot; but it being explained to him that this could not be done, he had the idea of hanging in his mind. Accordingly, by a side glance, seeing the sheriff coming in with a rope, which was a bed cord he had procured, having nothing else, in our then low state of trade and manufactures, Mamachtaga conceived that the sentence was about to be executed presently upon him, and that the rope was for this purpose, which coming unaware upon him, he lost the command of himself for a moment; his visage grew black, his features were screwed up, and he writhed with horror and aversion; the surprise not having given time to the mind to collect itself, and on the acquired principle of honour, to conceal its dismay, or on those of reason to bear with and compose itself to its fate. Even when undeceived and made acquainted that he was not to die then, he remained under a visible horror, the idea of immediate death, and especially of hanging, giving a tremor, like the refrigeration of cold upon the human frame.

Before he was taken from the bar, he wished to say something, which was to acknowledge, that his trial had been fair, and to express a wish, that his nation would not revenge his death, or come to war on his account. Being asked as he was taken off, by some of those accompanying the sheriff, in conducting him to jail, whom he thought the judges to be, before whom he had been tried, and who were on the bench in scarlet robes, which was the official custom of that time, and being of the Delaware nation, amongst whom Moravian missionaries had been a good deal, and as it would seem, mixing some recollections which he had derived from this source, he answered that the one, meaning the chief justice, was God, and the other Jesus Christ.

At the same court of Oyer and Terminer was convicted a man for the crime against nature, and at a court of Quarter Sessions a short time after, another, a young man of the name of Jack, had been convicted of larceny, and was now confined in the same jail, and in fact in the same room, for there was but one, with the Indian and the white man before-mentioned; and though, upon account of his youth and family connections, the jury in finding a verdict had recommended him to pardon, for which the supreme executive council of the State had been petitioned some time before; nevertheless he could not restrain the wickedness of his mind and had prevailed upon the white man, guilty of the crime against nature, as he had to die at any rate, to save the disgrace of being hanged, to consent to be murdered by the Indian. The creature was extremely simple, and had actually consented, and Jack had prepared a knife for the purpose, but the Indian refused, though solicited, and offered liquor, saying that he had killed white men enough already.

A child of the jailor had been taken sick, and had a fever. The Indian said he could cure it, if he had roots from the woods, which he knew. The jailor taking off his irons which he had on his feet, took his word that he would not make his escape, while he let him go to the woods to collect roots, telling him that if he did make his escape, the great council, the judges, would hang him, (the jailor,) in his place. But for greater security the jailor thought proper to accompany him to the woods, where roots were collected, which on their return were made use of in the cure of the child.

The warrant for the execution of the Indian and of the white man, came to hand, and the morning of the execution the Indian expressed a wish to be painted, that he might die like a warrior. The jailor, as before, unironed him, and took him to the woods to collect his usual paints, which having done, he returned, and prepared himself for the occasion, painting highly with the rouge which they use on great occasions.

A great body of people assembling at the place of execution, the white man was hung first, and afterwards the Indian ascended a ladder placed to the cross timber of the gibbet; the rope being fastened, when he was swung off it broke, and the Indian fell, and having swooned a little, he rose with a smile, and went up again, a stronger rope in the mean time having been provided, or rather two put about his neck together, so that his weight was supported, and he underwent the sentence of the law, and was hanged till he was dead.

This was during the Indian war, and the place on the verge of the settlement, so that if the Indian had taken a false step, and gone off from the jailor while he was looking for roots for the cure, or for painting, it would have been easy for him to have made his escape; but such is the force of opinion, as we have before said, resulting from the way of thinking amongst the Indians, that he did not seem to think that he had the physical power to go. It was nevertheless considered an imprudent thing in the jailor to run this risk. For if the Indian had made his escape, it is morally certain that in the then state of public mind, the jailor himself would have fallen a sacrifice to the resentment of the people.

ROYALL TYLER

(1757–1826)

Much of the fiction in the early period is episodic. Brackenridge, Brown and others wrote long works of fiction in which they presented episodes in a chapter or a series of chapters and then went on to another episode. Often, little attempt was made to give even the impression that the time between episodes was accounted for in any way. In *The Algerine Captive* Underhill recounts his life as a series of trials rather than in a running account. The effect of this is that some readers are led to feel that they are reading a series of stories rather than a structured long work of fiction. The form of this selection may be usefully compared to Byrd's *History of the Dividing Line*. Few comparable works of long fiction had been written by Americans before *The Algerine Captive*.

From *The Algerine Captive**

CHAP. II.

ARGUMENT:

The Author rescueth from Oblivion a valuable Manuscript Epistle, reflecting great Light on the Judicial Proceedings in the first Settlement of Massachusetts: Apologiseth for the Persecutors of his Ancestor.

I HAVE fortunately discovered, pasted on the back of an old Indian deed, a manuscript which reflects great light upon my ancestor's conduct, and on the transactions of those times; which, according to the beneficial mode of modern historians, I shall transcribe literally.

It should be premised, that in the year 1636, the governor, deputy governor, three assistants, and three ministers (among whom was Hugh Peters, afterwards hung and quartered in England for his adherence to Oliver Cromwell), were entreated by the Massachusetts' court to make a draught of laws, agreeable to the word of God, to report to the next general court; and, in

---

* *The Algerine Captive* (London, 1802). I have omitted the brief verses preceding each chapter. [Ed.].

410

the interim, the magistrates were directed to determine causes according to the laws then established; and, where no laws existed, then as near to the word of God as they could.

Brother UNDERHILL's EPISTLE.

To Master HANSERD KNOLLYS—
these greeting.

Worthee and Beloved,

Remembrin my kind love to Mr. Hilton, I now send you some note of my tryalls at Boston.—Oh that I may come out of this, and al the lyke tryalls, as goold sevene times puryfyed in the furnice.

After the rulers at Boston had fayled to fastenne what Roger Harlakenden was pleased to call the damning errours of Anne Hutchinson upon me, I looked to be sent away in peace; but governour Winthrop sayd I must abide the examining of ye church; accordingly, on the thyrd day of ye weeke, I was convened before them.—Sir Harry Vane, the governour, Dudley, Haines, with masters Cotton, Shepherd, and Hugh Peters, present, with others.— They propounded that I was to be examined, touching a certain act of adultery I had committed with one mistress Miriam Wilbore, wife of Samuel Wilbore, for carnally looking to luste after her, at the lecture in Boston, when master Shepherd expounded.—This mistress Miriam hath since been dealte with for coming to that lecture with a pair of wanton open workt gloves, slit at the thumbs and fingers, for the purpose of taking snuff; for, as master Cotton observed, for what end should those vaine opennings be, but for the intent of taken filthy snuff? and he quoted Gregory Nazianzen upon good works.—Master Peters said, that these opennings were Satan's port-holes of firy temptatione. Mistress Miriam offerd in excuse of her vain attire, that she was newle married, and appeard in her bridall arraye. Master Peters said, that marriage was the ocasion that the devil tooke to caste his firy darts, and lay his pit-falls of temptation, to catche frale flesh and bloode. She is to be further dealt with for taken snuff. How the use of the good creature tobaccoe can be an offence I cannot see.—Oh, my beloved, how these prowde pharisees labour aboute the minte and cummine! Governour Winthrop inquired of mee if I confessed the matter. I said I wished a coppy of there charge.—Sir Harry Vane said, "there was no neede of any coppie, seeing I knew I was guiltie. Charges being made out where there was an uncertaintie whether the accused was guiltie or not, and to lighten the accused into the nature of his cryme, here was no need." Master Cotton said, "Did you not look upon mistress Wilbore?" I confessed that I did. He said, "Then you are verelie guiltie, brother Underhill." I said, "Nay, I did not look at the woman lustfully."—Master Peters said, "Why did you not look at sister Newell or sister Upham?" I said, "Verelie they are not desyrable women, as to temporale graces." Then Hugh Peters and al cryed, "It is enough, he hath confessed, and passed to excommunication." I sayd, "Where is the law by which you condemne me?" Winthrop said, "There is a committee to draught laws. Brother Peters, are you not on that committee? I am sure you have maide a law againste this crynge sin." Hugh Peters replyed, "that he had such a law in his minde, but had not written it downe." Sir Harry Vane said, "It is sufficient." Haynes said, "Ay, law enough for antinomians." Master Cotton tooke a Bible from his coate, and read, *Whoso looketh a woman,* &c.

William Blaxton hath been with me privelie; he weeps over the crynge sins of the times, and expecteth soone to goe out of the jurisdiction. "I came from England," sais he, "because I did not like the lords bishops; but I have yet to praye to be delivered from the lords bretherenne."

Salute brother Fish and others, who, havinge been disappointed of libertie in this wilderness, are ernestlie lookinge for a better countre.

Youre felloe traveller
in this vale of tears,
JOHN UNDERHILL.

Boston, 23th Fourth Month, 1638.

It is with great reluctance I am induced to publish this letter, which appears to reflect upon the justice of the proceedings of our forefathers. I would rather, like the sons of Noah, go backwards, and cast a garment over our fathers' nakedness; but the impartiality of an historian, and the natural solicitude to wipe the stains from the memory of my honoured ancestor, will excuse me to the candid reader. Whoever reflects upon the piety of our forefathers, the noble unrestrained ardour with which they resisted oppression in England, relinquished the delights of their native country, crossed a boisterous ocean, penetrated a savage wilderness, encountered famine, pestilence, and war, and transmitted to us their sentiments of independence,—that love of liberty, which under God has enabled us to obtain our own glorious freedom,—will readily pass over those few dark spots of zeal which clouded their rising sun.

[Underhill is banished to New Hampshire and chosen governor, but is forced again to flee, this time to Albany, where he dies. One of his sons returns to New Hampshire and begets the hero of the novel, Updike Underhill. Too poor to attend college, he teaches himself and opens his own country school; but the students prove incorrigible and burn down the schoolhouse. Updike turns to the study of medicine.]

CHAP. XXI

ARGUMENT:

A Medical Consultation.

A MERRY incident gave me a perfect insight into the practice of the several physicians I have just eulogised. A drunken jockey, having fallen from his horse at a public review, was taken up senseless, and extended upon the long table of the tavern. He soon recovered his breath, and groaned most piteously. As his head struck the ground first, it was apprehended by some, unacquainted with its solidity, that he had fractured his skull. The faculty hastened from all quarters to his assistance. The learned scrupulous physician, after requesting that the doors and windows might be shut, approached the patient; and, with a stately air, declined giving his opinion, as he had unfortunately left at home his 'Pringle on Contusions.'

The cheap doctor immediately pronounced the wound a compound fracture, prescribed half a dose of crude opium, and called for the trepanning instruments. The safe doctor proposed brown paper, dipped in rum and cobwebs, to staunch the blood. The popular physician, the musical doctor, told us a jovial story; and then suddenly relaxing his features, observed, that he viewed the groaning wretch as a monument of justice: that he who spent his days in tormenting horses should now, by the agency of the same animal, be brought to death's door, an event which, he thought, ought to be set home upon our minds by prayer. While my new pupil, pressing through the crowd, begged that he might state the case to the company; and, with an audible voice, winking upon me, began:—The learned doctor Nominativo Hoc Caput, in his treatise on brains, observes, that the seat of the soul may be known from the affections of the man. The residence of a wise man's soul is in his ears; a glutton's in his palate; a gallant's in his lips; an old maid's in her tongue; a dancer's in his toes; a drunkard's in his throat:—By the way, landlord, give us a button of sling. When we learned wish to know if a wound endangers life, we consequently inquire into the affections of the patient, and see if the wound injures the seat of his soul: if that escapes, however deep and ghastly the wound, we pronounce life in no danger. A horse-jockey's soul—gentlemen, I wish your healths—is in his heel, under the left spur. When I was pursuing my studies in the hospitals in England, I once saw seventeen horse-jockeys, some of whom were noblemen, killed by the fall of a scaffold in Newmarket, and all wounded in the heel. Twenty others, with their arms, backs, and necks broken, survived. I saw one noble jockey, with his *nominativo caret*, which is Greek for a nobleman's head, split entirely open. His brains ran down his face like the white of a broken egg; but, as his heel was unhurt, he survived, and his judgment in horses is said not to be the least impaired. Come, pull off the patient's boot, while I drink his better health. Charmed with the harangue, some of the spectators were about following his directions, when the other doctors interfered. They had heard him with disdainful impatience, and now each raised his voice to support his particular opinion, backed by his adherents. Bring the brown paper—compound fracture—cobwebs I say—hand the trepanning instruments—give us some tod, and pull off the boot, echoed from all quarters. The landlord forbad quarrelling in his house. The whole company rushed out to form a ring on the green for the medical professors; and they to a consultation of fisty-cuffs. The practitioner in sheep, horses, and cattle, poured a dose of urine and molasses down the patient's throat; who soon so happily recovered as to pursue his vocation, swop horses three times, play twenty rubbers of all-fours, and get dead drunk again before sunset.

CHAP. XXII

ARGUMENT:

Disappointed in the North, the Author seeketh Treasure in the South.

As my practice increased, my drugs decreased. At the expiration of eighteen months, I found my phials, gallipots, and purse, empty; and my day-book full of items. To present a doctor's bill under seven years, or until my patients died (in which I was not nigh so fortunate as my brother functionaries), was complete ruin to my future practice. To draw upon my father, who had already done for me beyond his ability, was still worse. I had often heard the southern states spoken of as the high road to fortune. I was told that the inhabitants were immensely opulent, paid high fees with profusion, and were extremely partial to the characteristic industry of their New England brethren. By the advice of our attorney, I lodged my accompt-books in his office, with a general power to collect. He advanced me a sum sufficient to pay my travelling expenses; and, with my books and surgeon's instruments, I sat out in the stage for the southward, condemning the illiberality and ignorance of our own people, which prevented the due encouragement of genius, and made them the prey of quacks; intending, after a few years of successful practice, to return in my own carriage, and close a life of reputation and independence in my native state.

CHAP. XXIII

ARGUMENT:

Anecdotes of Dr. Benjamin Franklin, whom the Author visits in Philadelphia.

I CARRIED a request to the late Dr. Benjamin Franklin, then president of the state of Pennsylvania, for certain papers I was to deliver further southward. I anticipated much pleasure from the interview with this truly great man. To see one, who, from small beginnings, by the sole exertion of native genius and indefatigable industry, had raised himself to the pinnacle of politics and letters; a man who, from an humble printer's boy, had elevated himself to be the desirable companion of the great ones of the earth; who, from trundling a wheelbarrow in bye lanes, had been advanced to pass in splendor through the courts of kings; and, from hawking vile ballads, to the contracting and signing treaties, which gave peace and independence to three millions of his fellow citizens, was a sight interesting in the extreme.

I found the doctor surrounded by company, most of whom were young people. He received me with the attention due to a young stranger. He dispatched a person for the papers I wanted; asked me politely to be seated; inquired after the family I sprang from; and told me a pleasing anecdote of my brave ancestor, captain Underhill. I found in the doctor all that simplicity of language which is remarkable in the fragment of his life, published since his decease, and which was conspicuous in my Medical Preceptor. I have since been in a room a few hours with governor Jay, of New York; have heard of the late governor Livingston, of New Jersey; and am now confirmed in the opinion I have suggested, that men of genuine merit, as they possess the essence, need not the parade of great knowledge. A rich man is often plain in his attire; and the man who has abundant treasures of learning, simple in his manners and style.

The doctor, in early life, was economical from principle; in his latter days, perhaps from habit. Poor Richard held the purse-strings of the president of Pennsylvania. Permit me to illustrate this observation by an anecdote. Soon after I was introduced, an airy thoughtless relation, from a New England state, entered the room. It seems he was on a party of pleasure; and had been so much involved in it, for three weeks, as not to have paid his respects to his venerable relative. The purpose of his present visit was to solicit the loan of a small sum of money, to enable him to pay his bills, and transport himself home. He preluded his request with a detail of embarrassments which might have befallen the most circumspect. He said that he had loaded a vessel for B—; and, as he did not deal on credit, had purchased beyond his current cash, and could not readily procure a draft upon home. The doctor inquiring how much he wanted, he replied, with some hesitation, fifty dollars. The benevolent old gentleman went to his escritoir, and counted him out a hundred. He received them with many promises of punctual payment, and hastily took up the writing implements, to draught a note of hand for the cash. The doctor, who saw into the nature of the borrower's embarrassments better than he was aware, and was possessed with the improbability of ever recovering his cash again, stepped across the room, and laying his hand gently upon his cousin's arm, said, "Stop, cousin, we will save the paper; a quarter of a sheet is not of great value, but it is worth saving:"—conveying, at once, a liberal gift and gentle reprimand for the borrower's prevarication and extravagance. Since I am talking of Franklin, the reader may be as unwilling to leave him as I was. Allow me to relate another anecdote. I do not recollect how the conversation was introduced, but a young person in company mentioned his surprise that the possession of great riches should ever be attended with such anxiety and solicitude; and instanced Mr. R—M—, who, he said, though in possession of unbounded wealth, yet was as busy and more anxious than the most assiduous clerk in his counting-house. The doctor took an apple from a fruit-basket, and presented it to a little child, who could just totter about the room. The child could scarce grasp it in his hand. He then gave it another, which occupied the other hand. Then choosing a third, remarkable for its size and beauty, he presented that also. The child, after many ineffectual attempts to hold the three, dropped the last on the carpet, and burst into tears. See there, said the philosopher; there is a little man with more riches than he can enjoy.

CHAP. XXIV

ARGUMENT:

Religious Exercises in a Southern State.

IN one of the states southward of Philadelphia, I was invited, on a Sunday, to go to church. I will not say which, as I am loth to offend; and our fashionable fellow citizens, of the south arm of the union, may not think divine service any credit to them. My friend apologised for inviting me to so humdrum an amusement, by assuring me that, immediately after service, there was to be a famous match run for a purse of a thousand dollars, besides private bets, between 'squire L's imported horse Slammerkin, and colonel F's bay mare Jenny Driver. When we arrived at the church, we found a brilliant collection of well dressed people, anxiously waiting the arrival of the parson—who, it seems, had a small branch of the river M——to pass; and, we afterwards learned, was detained by the absence of his negro boy, who was to ferry him over. Soon after, our impatience was relieved by the arrival of the parson in his canonicals—a young man, not of the most mortified countenance, who, with a switch called a supple jack in his hand, belaboured the back and head of the faulty slave all the way from the water to the church door, accompanying every stroke with suitable language. He entered the church, and we followed. He ascended the reading-desk, and, with his face glowing with the exercise of his supple jack, began the service with, "I said I will take heed unto my ways, that I sin not with my tongue.—I will keep my tongue as it were with a bridle, when I am before the wicked.—When I mused the fire burned within me, and I spake with my tongue," &c. &c. He preached an animated discourse, of eleven minutes, upon the practical duties of religion, from these words, "Remember the sabbath day, to keep it holy;" and read the fourth commandment in the communion. The whole congregation prayed fervently that their hearts might be inclined to keep this holy law. The blessing was pronounced; and parson and people hastened to the horse race. I found the parson as much respected on the turf as upon the hassock. He was one of the judges of the race; descanted, in the language of the turf, upon the points of the two rival horses; and the sleeve of his cassock was heavily laden with the principal bets. The confidence of his parishioners was not ill founded; for they assured me, upon oath and honour, that he was a gentleman of as much uprightness as his grace the archbishop of Canterbury. Ay, they would sport him for a sermon or a song against any parson in the union.

The whole of this extraordinary scene was novel to me. A certain staple of New England which I had with me, called conscience, made my situation, in even the passive part I bore in it, so aukward and uneasy, that I could not refrain from observing to my friend my surprise at the parson's conduct, in chastising his servant immediately before divine service. My friend was so happily influenced by the habits of these liberal enlightened people, that he could not even comprehend the tendency of my remark. He supposed it levelled at the impropriety, not of the minister, but the man; not at the act, but the severity of the chastisement; and observed, with warmth, that the parson served the villain right; and that, if he had been his slave, he would have killed the black rascal, if he was sure he should have to pay a hundred guineas to the public treasury for him.—I will note here, that the reader is requested, whenever he meets with quotations of speeches in the above scenes, excepting those during divine service, that he will please, that is, if his habits of life will permit it, to interlard those quotations with about as many oaths as they contain monosyllables. He may rest assured that it will render the scene abundantly more natural. It is true, I might have inserted them myself, and supported it by illustrations and parodies from grave authors; but I never swear profanely myself, and I think it almost as bad to oblige my readers to purchase the imprecations of others. I give this hint of the introduction of oaths, for the benefit of my readers to the southward of Philadelphia; who, however they may enjoy a scene which reflects such honour upon their country, when seasoned with these palatable expletives, without them, perhaps, would esteem it as tasteless and vapid as a game of cards or billiards without bets, or boiled veal or turkey without ham.

CHAP. XXV

ARGUMENT:

Success of the Doctor's Southern Expedition—He is in Distress—Contemplates a School—Prefers a Surgeon's Berth on board a Ship bound to Africa, via *London.*

I FOUND the southern states not more engaging to a young practitioner than the northern. In the sea-ports of both, the business was engrossed by men of established practice and eminence. In the interior country, the people could not distinguish or encourage merit. The gains were small, and tardily collected; and in both wings of the union, and I believe every where else, fortune and fame are generally to be acquired, in the learned professions, solely by a patient undeviating application to local business.

If dissipation could have afforded pleasure to a mind yearning after professional fame and independence, I might, so long as my money lasted, have been happy at the southward. I was often invited to the turf; and might have had the honour of being intoxicated frequently with the most respectable characters. An association with the well educated of the other sex was not so readily attained. There was a haughty reserve in the manners of the young ladies. Every attempt at familiarity in a young stranger, habituated to the social but respectable intercourse customary in the northern states, excited alarm. With my New England ideas, I could not help viewing, in the anxious efforts of their parents and relatives to repel every approach to innocent and even chastened intercourse, a strong suspicion of that virtue they were so solicitous to protect.

Depressed by the gloomy view of my prospects, and determined never to face my parents again under circumstances which would be burthensome to them, I attempted to obtain practice in the town of F——, in Virginia; but in vain. The very decorum, prudence, and economy, which would have enhanced my character at home, were here construed into poverty of spirit. To obtain medical practice, it was expedient to sport, bet, drink, swear, &c. with my patients. My purse forbad the former; my habits of life the latter. My cash wasted, and I was near suffering. I was obliged to dispose of my books for present subsistence; and, in that country, books were not the prime articles of commerce. To avoid starving, I again contemplated keeping a school. In that country, knowledge was viewed as a handicraft trade. The school-masters, before the war, had been usually collected from unfortunate European youth, of some school learning, sold for their passage into America: so that to purchase a school-master and a negro was almost synonymous. Mr. J——n, and some other citizens of the world who had been cast among them, had, by their writings, influence, and example, brought the knowledge of letters into some repute since the revolution; but I believe those excellent men have yet to lament the general inefficacy of their liberal efforts. This statement, and my own prior experience in school-keeping, would have determined me rather to have preferred labouring with the slaves on their plantations than sustaining the slavery and contempt of a school.

When reduced to my last dollar, and beginning to suffer from the embarrassments of debt, I was invited by a sea captain, who knew my friends, to accept the berth of surgeon in his ship. . . .

[Updike sails for London, where he meets Tom Paine, now a tattered manic-depressive. Then he sails for Africa.]

CHAP. XXX

. . . THE day after our arrival at Cacongo, several Portuguese and negro merchants, hardly distinguishable however by their manners, employments, or complexions, came to confer with the captain about the purchase of our cargo of slaves. They contracted to deliver him two hundred and fifty head of slaves in fifteen days' time. To hear these men converse upon the purchase of human beings, with the same indifference, and nearly in the same language, as if they were contracting for so many head of cattle or swine, shocked me exceedingly. But when I suffered my imagination to rove to the habitation of these victims to this infamous cruel commerce, and fancied that I saw the peaceful husbandman dragged from his native farm, the fond husband torn from the embraces of his beloved wife, the mother from her babes, the tender child from the arms of its parent, and all the tender endearing ties of natural and social affection rended by the hand of avaricious violence, my heart sunk within me. I execrated myself for even the involuntary part I bore in this execrable traffic: I thought of my native land, and blushed. When the captain kindly inquired of me how many slaves I thought my privilege in the ship entitled me to transport for my adventure, I rejected my privilege with horror, and declared I would sooner suffer servitude than purchase a slave. This observation was received in the great cabin with repeated bursts of laughter, and excited many a stroke of coarse ridicule. Captain Russell observed, that he would not insist upon my using my privilege if I had so much of the yankee about me. Here is my clerk, Ned Randolph, will jump at the chance, though the rogue has been rather unlucky in the trade. Out of five-and-twenty negroes he purchased, he never carried but one alive to port, and that poor devil was broken-winded; and he was obliged to sell him for half price in Antigua.

Punctual to the day of the delivery, the contractors appeared, and brought with them about one hundred and fifty negroes—men, women, and children. The men were fastened together in pairs by a bar of iron, with a collar to receive the neck at each extremity; a long pole was passed over their shoulder, and between each two was bound by a staple and ring, through which the pole was thrust, and thus twenty, and sometimes thirty, were connected together; while their conductors incessantly applied the scourge to those who loitered, or sought to strangle themselves by lifting their feet from the ground in despair; which sometimes had been successfully attempted. The women and children were bound with cords, and driven forward by the whip. When they arrived at the factory the men were unloosed from the poles, but still chained in pairs, and turned into strong cells built for the purpose. The dumb sorrow of some, the phrensy of others, the sobbings and tears of the children, and shrieks of the women, when they were presented to our captain, so affected me, that I was hastening from this scene of barbarity on board the ship, when I was called by the mate, and discovered, to my surprise and horror, that, by my station in the ship, I had a principal and active part of this inhuman transaction imposed upon me. As surgeon, it was my duty to inspect the bodies of the slaves, to see, as the captain expressed himself, that our owners were not shammed off with unsound flesh. In this inspection I was assisted by Randolph the clerk, and two stout sailors. It was transacted with all that unfeeling insolence which wanton barbarity can inflict upon defenceless wretchedness. The man, the affrighted child, the modest matron, and the timid virgin, were alike exposed to this severe scrutiny, equally insulting to humanity and common decency.

I cannot even now reflect on this transaction without shuddering. I have deplored my conduct with tears of anguish; and I pray a merciful God, the common parent of the great family of the universe, who hath made of one flesh and one blood all nations of the earth, that the miseries, the insults, and cruel woundings, I afterwards received when a slave myself, may expiate for the inhumanity I was necessitated to exercise towards these MY BRETHREN OF THE HUMAN RACE.

CHAP. XXXI

ARGUMENT:

Treatment of the Slaves on board the Ship.

OF one hundred and fifty Africans, we rejected seventeen as not merchant-able. While I was doubting which to lament most—those who were about being precipitated into all the miseries of an American slavery, or those whom we had rejected as too wretched for slaves—captain Russell was congratulating the slave-contractors upon the immense good luck they had in not suffering more by this lot of human creatures. I understood that, what from wounds received by some of these miserable creatures at their capture, or in their vio-lent struggles for liberty, or attempts at suicide, and what with the fatigue of a long journey, partly over the burning sands of a sultry climate, it was usual to estimate the loss in the passage to the sea-shore at twenty-five in a hundred.

No sooner was the purchase completed, than these wretched Africans were transported in herds aboard the ship, and immediately precipitated between decks, where a strong chain, attached to a staple in the lower deck, was rivetted to the bar before described; and then the men were chained in pairs and hand-cuffed, and two sailors with cutlasses guarded every twenty; while the women and children were tied together in pairs with ropes, and obliged to supply the men with provisions and the slush-bucket; or, if the young women were released, it was only to gratify the brutal lust of the sailors: for though I cannot say I ever was witness to an actual rape, yet the frequent shrieks of these forlorn females in the berths of the seamen left me little charity to doubt of the repeated commission of that degrading crime. The eve after we had received the slaves on board, all hands were piped on deck, and ordered to assist in manufacturing and knotting cat-o'nine-tails, the applica-tion of which, I was informed, was always necessary to bring the slaves to their appetite. The night after they came on board was spent by these wretched people in sobbings, groans, tears, and the most heart-rending bursts of sorrow and despair. The next morning all was still. Surprised by this unexpected silence, I almost hoped that Providence, in pity to these her miser-able children, had permitted some kindly suffocation to put a period to their anguish. It was neither novel nor unexpected to the ship's crew. It is only the dumb fit come on, cried every one: we will cure them. After breakfast, the whole ship's crew went between decks, and carried with them the provisions for the slaves, which they one and all refused to eat. A more affecting group of misery was never seen. These injured Africans, preferring death to slavery, or perhaps buoyed above the fear of dissolution by their religion, which taught them to look with an eye of faith to a country beyond the grave, where they should again meet those friends and relatives from whose endearments they had been torn, and where no fiend should torment or Christian thirst for gold, had resolved to starve themselves, and every eye lowered the fixed resolve of this deadly intent. In vain were the men beaten. They refused to taste one mouthful; and, I believe, would have died under the operation, if the ingenious cruelty of the clerk, Randolph, had not suggested the plan of whipping the women and children in sight of the men; assuring the men they should be tormented until all had eaten. What the torments exercised on the bodies of these brave Africans failed to produce, the feelings of nature effected. The negro, who could undauntedly expire under the anguish of the lash, could not view the agonies of his wife, child, or mother; and though repeatedly encouraged by these female sufferers to persevere unto death, unmoved by their torments, yet, though the *man* dared to die, the *father* relented, and in a few hours they had all eaten their provisions, *mingled with their tears*.

Our slave-dealers being unable to fulfil their contract, unless we tarried three weeks longer, our captain concluded to remove to some other market. We accordingly weighed anchor, steered for Benin, and anchored in the river Formosa, where we took in one hundred and fifteen more slaves. The same process in the purchase was pursued here; and though I frequently assured the captain, as a physician, that it was impracticable to stow fifty more persons between decks without endangering health and life, yet the whole hundred and fifteen were thrust, with the rest, between decks. The stagnant confined air of this infernal hole, rendered more deleterious by the stench of the fæces and violent perspiration of such a crowd, occasioned putrid diseases; and, even while in the mouth of the Formosa, it was usual to throw one or two negro corpses over every day. It was in vain that I remonstrated to the captain. In vain I enforced the necessity of more commodious births, and a more free influx of air for the slaves. In vain I represented that these miserable people had been used to the vegetable diet and pure air of a country life; that at home they were remarkable for cleanliness of person, the very rites of their religion consisting, almost entirely, in frequent ablutions. The captain was by this time prejudiced against me. He observed that he did not doubt my skill, and would be bound by my advice, as to the health of those on board his ship, when he found I was actuated by the interest of the owners; but he feared that I was now moved by some *yankee nonsense about humanity*.

Randolph the clerk blamed me in plain terms. He said he had made seven African voyages with as good surgeons as I was; and that it was their common practice, when an infectious disorder prevailed among the slaves, to make critical search for all those who had the slightest symptoms of it, or whose habits of body inclined them to it; to tie them up and cast them over the ship's side together, and thus at one dash to purify the ship. *What signifies*, added he,

*the lives of the black devils? They love to die. You cannot please them better
than by chucking them into the water.*

When we stood out to sea, the rolling of the vessel brought on the sea sickness, which increased the filth: the weather being rough, we were obliged to
close some of the ports which ventilated the space between decks, and death
raged dreadfully among the slaves. Above two thirds were diseased. It was
affecting to observe the ghastly smile on the countenance of the dying African,
as if rejoicing to escape the cruelty of his oppressors. I noticed one man, who
gathered all his strength, and in one last effort spoke with great emphasis, and
expired. I understood by the linguist, that with his dying breath he invited his
wife and a boy and girl to follow him quickly, and slake their thirst with him
at the cool streams of the fountain of their Great Father, beyond the reach of
the wild white beasts. The captain was now alarmed for the success of his voyage; and, upon my urging the necessity of landing the slaves, he ordered the
ship about, and we anchored near an uninhabited part of the Gold Coast—
I conjecture, not far from Cape St. Paul.

Tents were erected on the shore, and the sick landed. Under my direction
they recovered surprisingly. It was affecting to see the effect gentle usage had
upon these hitherto sullen obstinate people. As I had the sole direction of the
hospital, they looked on me as the source of this sudden transition from the
filth and rigour of the ship to the cleanliness and kindness of the shore. Their
gratitude was excessive. When they recovered so far as to walk out, happy was
he who could, by picking a few berries, gathering the wild fruits of the country,
or doing any menial services, manifest his affection for me. Our linguist has
told me, he has often heard them behind the bushes praying to their God for
my prosperity, and asking him with earnestness, why he put my good *black*
soul into a *white* body. In twelve days all the convalescents were returned to
the ship, except five, who staid with me on shore, and were to be taken on
board the next day.

[Updike himself is captured by an Algerine pirate ship, and thrown into
the hold.]

CHAP. XXXII

. . . THE treatment we gave the unhappy Africans on board the Sympathy
now came full into my mind; and, what was more mortifying, I discovered
that the negro who was captured with me was at liberty, and fared as well as
the sailors on board the vessel. I had not however been confined more than
one half-hour, when the interpreter came to examine me privately respecting
the destination of the ship, to which he suspected I belonged; was anxious to
know if she had her full cargo of slaves; what was her force; whether she had
English papers on board; and if she did not intend to stop at some other

African port. From him I learned that I was captured by an Algerine rover, Hamed Hali Saad captain; and should be carried into slavery at Algiers. After I had lain twenty-four hours in this loathsome place, covered with vermin, parched with thirst, and fainting with hunger, I was startled at a light through the hatchway, which opening softly, a hand presented me a cloth, dripping with cold water, in which a small quantity of boiled rice was wrapped. The door closed again softly, and I was left to enjoy my good fortune in the dark. If Abraham had indeed sent Lazarus to the rich man in torment, it appears to me he could not have received a greater pleasure from the cool water on his tongue than I experienced in sucking the moisture from this cloth. The next day, the same kindly hand appeared again with the same refreshment. I begged to see my benefactor. The door opened further, and I saw a countenance in tears. It was the face of the grateful African who was taken with me. I was oppressed with gratitude. Is this, exclaimed I, one of those men, whom we are taught to vilify as beneath the human species, who brings me sustenance, perhaps at the risk of his life, who shares his morsel with one of those barbarous men who had recently torn him from all he held dear, and whose base companions are now transporting his darling son to a grievous slavery? Grant me, I ejaculated, once more to taste the freedom of my native country, and every moment of my life shall be dedicated to preaching against this detestable commerce. I will fly to our fellow citizens in the southern states; I will on my knees conjure them, in the name of humanity, to abolish a traffic which causes it to bleed in every pore. If they are deaf to the pleadings of nature, I will conjure them for the sake of consistency to cease to deprive their fellow creatures of freedom, which their writers, their orators, representatives, senators, and even their constitutions of government, have declared to be the unalienable birth-right of men.—My sable friend had no occasion to visit me a third time; for I was taken from my confinement, and, after being stripped of the few clothes and the little property I chanced to have about me, a log was fastened to my leg by a chain, and I was permitted to walk the forecastle of the vessel, with the African and several Spanish and Portuguese prisoners. The treatment of the slaves who plied the oars, the management of the vessel, the order which was observed among this ferocious race, and some notices of our voyage, might afford observations which would be highly gratifying to my readers, if the limits of this work would permit. I will just observe, however, that the regularity and frequency of their devotion was astonishing to me, who had been taught to consider this people as the most blasphemous infidels. In ten days after I was captured, the rover passed up the Straits of Gibraltar, and I heard the garrison evening gun fired from that formidable rock; and the next morning we hove in sight of the city of Algiers. . . . (1797)

CHARLES BROCKDEN BROWN

(1771–1810)

In "Portrait of an Emigrant" yet another view of the Negro can be seen. The large number of selections in this text which include comments on or discussions of the Negro—as freeman or as slave, as African or as American—reveal how conscious the white American has been of the black man (although not of how the black man has felt). Yet the textbooks of even ten years ago omitted most selections that showed this consciousness, perhaps thereby participating in the cultural effort to overlook non-white Americans. Brown's picture of the woman is partially realistic—in literary terms—and by no means altogether flattering.

Portrait of an Emigrant*

Extracted from a Letter

I CALLED, as you desired, on Mrs. K——. We had considerable conversation. Knowing, as you do, my character and her's, you may be somewhat inquisitive as to the subject of our conversation. You may readily suppose that my inquiries were limited to domestic and every-day incidents. The state of her own family, and her servants and children being discussed, I proceeded to inquire into the condition of her neighbours. It is not in large cities as it is in villages. Those whose education does not enable and accustom them to look abroad, to investigate the character and actions of beings of a distant age and country, are generally attentive to what is passing under their own eye. Mrs. K—— never reads, not even a newspaper. She is unacquainted with what happened before she was born. She is equally a stranger to the events that are passing in distant nations, and to those which ingross the attention and shake the passions of the statesmen and politicians of her own country; but her mind, nevertheless, is far from being torpid or inactive. She speculates

* The Monthly Magazine and American Review (June 1799).

curiously and even justly on the objects that occur within her narrow sphere.

Were she the inhabitant of a village, she would be mistress of the history and character of every family within its precincts; but being in a large city,[1] her knowledge is confined chiefly to her immediate neighbours; to those who occupy the house on each side and opposite. I will not stop to inquire into the reason of this difference in the manners of villagers and citizens. The fact has often been remarked, though seldom satisfactorily explained. I shall merely repeat the dialogue which took place on my inquiry into the state of the family inhabiting the house on the right hand and next to her's.

"M'Culey," said she, "who used to live there, is gone."

"Indeed! and who has taken his place?"

"A Frenchman and his wife. His wife, I suppose her to be, though he is a man of fair complexion, well formed, and of genteel appearance; and the woman is half negro. I suppose they would call her a mestee. They came last winter from the West-Indies, and miserably poor I believe; for when they came into this house they had scarcely any furniture besides a bed, and a chair or two, and a pine table. They shut up the lower rooms, and lived altogether in the two rooms in the second story."

"Of whom does the family consist?"

"The man and woman, and a young girl, whom I first took for their daughter, but I afterwards found she was an orphan child, whom, shortly after their coming here, they found wandering in the streets; and, though poor enough themselves, took her under their care."

"How do they support themselves?"

"The man is employed in the compting-house of a French merchant of this city. What is the exact sort of employment, I do not know, but it allows him to spend a great deal of his time at home. The woman is an actress in Lailson's pantomimes. In the winter she scarcely ever went out in the day-time, but now that the weather is mild and good she walks out a great deal."

"Can you describe their mode of life, what they eat and drink, and how they spend their time?"

"I believe I can. Most that they do can be seen from our windows and yard, and all that they say can be heard. In the morning every thing is still till about ten o'clock. Till that hour they lie a-bed. The first sign that they exist, is given by the man, who comes half dressed, to the back window; and lolling out of it, smokes two or three segars, and sometimes talks to a dog that lies on the out-side of the kitchen door. After sometime passed in this manner he goes into the room over the kitchen, takes a loaf of bread from the closet, and pours out a tumbler of wine; with these he returns to the front room, but

---

[1] Philadelphia. [Brown's note].

begins as soon as he has hold of them, to gnaw at one and sip from the other. This constitutes their breakfast. In half an hour they both re-appear at the window. They throw out crums of bread to the dog, who stands below with open mouth to receive it; and talk sometimes to him and sometimes to each other. Their tongues run incessantly; frequently they talk together in the loudest and shrillest tone imaginable. I thought, at first, they were quarrelsome; but every now and then they burst into laughter, and it was plain that they were in perfect good humour with each other.

"About twelve o'clock the man is dressed, and goes out upon his business. He returns at three. In the mean time the lady employs herself in washing every part of her body, and putting on a muslin dress, perfectly brilliant and clean. Then she either lolls at the window, and sings without intermission, or plays on a guitar. She is certainly a capital performer and singer. No attention is paid to house or furniture. As to rubbing tables, and sweeping and washing floors, these are never thought of. Their house is in a sad condition, but she spares no pains to make her person and dress clean.

"The man has scarcely entered the house, when he is followed by a black fellow, with bare head and shirt tucked up at his elbows, carrying on his head a tray covered with a white napkin. This is their dinner, and is brought from *Simonet's*. After dinner the man takes his flute, on which he is very skilful; and the woman either sings or plays in concert till evening approaches: some visitants then arrive, and they all go out together to walk. We hear no more of them till next morning."

"What becomes of the girl all this time?"

"She eats, sings, dresses, and walks with them. She often comes into our house, generally at meal times; if she spies any thing she likes, she never conceals her approbation. 'O my, how good *dat* must be! Me wish me had some: will you *gif* me some?' She is a pretty harmless little thing, and one cannot refuse what she asks.

"Next day after they came into this house, the girl, in the morning, while our servant was preparing breakfast, entered the kitchen—'O my!' said she to me, 'what you call dem tings?'

'Buckwheat cakes.'

'Ahah! buckawit cake! O my! how good dey must be! Me likes—will you give me one?'

"Next morning she came again, and we happened to be making *muffins*. 'O my!' cried she, 'you be always baking and baking! What you call dem dere?'

'Muffins.'

'Mofeen? O my! me wish for some, me do.'

"Afterwards she was pretty regular in her visits. She was modest, notwithstanding; and, seeming to be half-starved, we gave her entertainment as often as she claimed it."

"Are not these people very happy?"

"Very happy. When together they are for ever chattering and laughing, or playing and singing in concert. How the man is employed when separate we do not certainly know; but the woman, it seems, is continually singing, and her hands, if not employed in adorning her own person, are plying the guitar. I am apt to think the French are the only people that know how to live. These people, though exiles and strangers, and subsisting on scanty and precarious funds, move on smoothly and at ease. Household cares they know not. They breakfast upon bread and wine, without the ceremony of laying table, and arranging platters and cups. From the trouble of watching and directing servants they are equally exempt. Their cookery is performed abroad. Their clothes are washed in the same way. The lady knows no manual employment but the grateful one of purifying and embellishing her own person. The intervals are consumed in the highest as well as purest sensual enjoyments, in music, in which she appears to be an adept, and of which she is passionately enamoured. When the air is serene and bland, she repairs to the public walks, with muslin handkerchief in one hand, and parti-coloured *parasol* in the other. She is always accompanied by men anxious to please her, busy in supplying her with amusing topics, and listening with complacency and applause to her gay effusions and her ceaseless volubility.

"I have since taken some pains to discover the real situation of this family. I find that the lady was the heiress of a large estate in St. Domingo, that she spent her youth in France, where she received a polished education, and where she married her present companion, who was then in possession of rank and fortune, but whom the revolution has reduced to indigence. The insurrection in St. Domingo destroyed their property in that island. They escaped with difficulty to these shores in 1793, and have since subsisted in various modes and places, frequently pinched by extreme poverty, and sometimes obliged to solicit public charity; but retaining, in every fortune, and undiminished, their propensity to talk, laugh and sing—their flute and their guitar."

Nothing is more ambiguous than the motives that stimulate men to action. These people's enjoyments are unquestionably great. They are innocent: they are compatible, at least, with probity and wisdom, if they are not the immediate fruits of it. Constitutional gaiety may account for these appearances; but as they may flow, in one case, from the absence of reflection and foresight, they may likewise, in another instance, be the product of justice and benevolence.

It is our duty to make the best of our condition; to snatch the good that is within our reach, and to nourish no repinings on account of what is unattainable. The gratifications of sense, of conjugal union, and of social intercourse, are among the highest in the scale; and these are as much in the possession of *de Lisle* and his wife, as of the most opulent and luxuriant members of the community.

As to mean habitation and scanty furniture, their temper or their reason enables them to look upon these things as trifles. They are not among those who witnessed their former prosperity, and their friends and associates are unfortunate like themselves. Instead of humiliation and contempt, adversity has probably given birth to sympathy and mutual respect.

His profession is not laborious; and her's, though not respectable according to our notions, is easy and amusing. Her life scarcely produces any intermission of recreation and enjoyment. Few instances of more unmingled and uninterrupted felicity can be found; and yet these people have endured, and continue to endure, most of the evils which the imagination is accustomed to regard with most horror; and which would create ceaseless anguish in beings fashioned on the model of my character, or of yours. Let you and I grow wise by the contemplation of their example. (1799)

Walstein's School of History*

From the German of Krants of Gotha.

Walstein was professor of history at Jena, and, of course, had several pupils. Nine of them were more assiduous in their attention to their tutor than the others. This circumstance came at length to be noticed by each other, as well as by Walstein, and naturally produced good-will and fellowship among them. They gradually separated themselves from the negligent and heedless crowd, cleaved to each other, and frequently met to exchange and compare ideas. Walstein was prepossessed in their favour by their studious habits, and their veneration for him. He frequently admitted them to exclusive interviews, and, laying aside his professional dignity, conversed with them on the footing of a friend and equal.

Walstein's two books were read by them with great attention. These were justly to be considered as exemplifications of his rules, as specimens of the manner in which history was to be studied and written.

* Harry Warfel, ed., *The Rhapsodist and other Uncollected Writings of Charles Brockden Brown* (New York, 1943).

No wonder that they found few defects in the model; that they gradually adopted the style and spirit of his composition, and, from admiring and contemplating, should, at length, aspire to imitate. It could not but happen, however, that the criterion of excellence would be somewhat modified in passing through the mind of each; that each should have his peculiar modes of writing and thinking.

All observers, indeed, are, at the first and transient view, more affected by resemblances than differences. The works of Walstein and his disciples were hastily ascribed to the same hand. The same minute explication of motives, the same indissoluble and well-woven tissue of causes and effects, the same unity and coherence of design, the same power of engrossing the attention, and the same felicity, purity, and compactness of style, are conspicuous in all.

There is likewise evidence, that each had embraced the same scheme of accounting for events, and the same notions of moral and political duty. Still, however, there were marks of difference in the different nature of the themes that were adopted, and of the purpose which the productions of each writer seemed most directly to promote.

We may aim to exhibit the influence of some moral or physical cause, to enforce some useful maxim, or illustrate some momentous truth. This purpose may be more or less simple, capable of being diffused over the surface of an empire or a century, or of shrinking into the compass of a day, and the bounds of a single thought.

The elementary truths of morals and politics may merit the preference: our theory may adapt itself to, and derive confirmation from whatever is human. Newton and Xavier, Zengis and William Tell, may bear close and manifest relation to the system we adopt, and their fates be linked, indissolubly, in a common chain.

The physician may be attentive to the constitution and diseases of man in all ages and nations. Some opinions, on the influence of a certain diet, may make him eager to investigate the physical history of every human being. No fact, falling within his observation, is useless or anomalous. All sensibly contribute to the symmetry and firmness of some structure which he is anxious to erect. Distances of place and time, and diversities of moral conduct, may, by no means, obstruct their union into one homogeneous mass.

I am apt to think, that the moral reasoner may discover principles equally universal in their application, and giving birth to similar coincidence and harmony among characters and events. Has not this been effected by WALSTEIN?

Walstein composed two works. One exhibited, with great minuteness, the life of Cicero; the other, that of the Marquis of Pombal.[1] What link did his

[1] (1699–1782). Portuguese statesman, exponent of absolutism.

reason discover, or his fancy create between times, places, situations, events, and characters so different? He reasoned thus:—

Human society is powerfully modified by individual members. The authority of individuals sometimes flows from physical incidents; birth, or marriage, for example. Sometimes it springs, independently of physical relation, and, in defiance of them, from intellectual vigour. The authority of kings and nobles exemplifies the first species of influence. Birth and marriage, physical, and not moral incidents, entitle them to rule.

The second kind of influence, that flowing from intellectual vigour, is remarkably exemplified in Cicero and Pombal. In this respect they are alike.

The mode in which they reached eminence, and in which they exercised power, was different, in consequence of different circumstances. One lived in a free, the other in a despotic state. One gained it from the prince, the other from the people. The end of both, for their degree of virtue was the same, was the general happiness. They promoted this end by the best means which human wisdom could suggest. One cherished, the other depressed the aristocracy. Both were right in their means as in their end; and each, had he exchanged conditions with the other, would have acted like that other.

Walstein was conscious of the uncertainty of history. Actions and motives cannot be truly described. We can only make approaches to the truth. The more attentively we observe mankind, and study ourselves, the greater will this uncertainty appear, and the farther shall we find ourselves from truth.

This uncertainty, however, has some bounds. Some circumstances of events, and some events, are more capable of evidence than others. The same may be said of motives. Our guesses as to the motives of some actions are more probable than the guesses than relate to other actions. Though no one can state the motives from which any action has flowed, he may enumerate motives from which it is quite certain, that the action did *not* flow.

The lives of Cicero and Pombal are imperfectly related by historians. An impartial view of that which history has preserved makes the belief of their wisdom and virtue more probable than the contrary belief.

Walstein desired the happiness of mankind. He imagined that the exhibition of virtue and talents, forcing its way to sovereign power, and employing that power for the national good, was highly conducive to their happiness.

By exhibiting a virtuous being in opposite conditions, and pursuing his end by means suited to his own condition, he believes himself displaying a model of right conduct, and furnishing incitements to imitate that conduct, supplying men not only with knowledge of just ends and just means, but with the love and the zeal of virtue.

How men might best promote the happiness of mankind in given situations, was the problem that he desired to solve. The more portraits of human excellence he was able to exhibit the better; but his power in this respect was limited. The longer his life and his powers endured the more numerous would his portraits become. Futurity, however, was precarious, and, therefore, it behoved him to select, in the first place, the most useful theme.

His purpose was not to be accomplished by a brief or meagre story. To illuminate the understanding, to charm curiosity, and sway the passions, required that events should be copiously displayed and artfully linked, that motives should be vividly depicted, and scenes made to pass before the eye. This has been performed. Cicero is made to compose the story of his political and private life from his early youth to his flight from Astura, at the coalition of Antony and Octavius. It is addressed to Atticus, and meant to be the attestor of his virtue, and his vindicator with posterity.

The style is energetic, and flows with that glowing impetuosity which was supposed to actuate the writer. Ardent passions, lofty indignation, sportive elegance, pathetic and beautiful simplicity, take their turns to controul his pen, according to the nature of the theme. New and striking portraits are introduced of the great actors on the stage. New lights are cast upon the principal occurrences. Every where are marks of profound learning, accurate judgment, and inexhaustible invention. Cicero here exhibits himself in all the forms of master, husband, father, friend, advocate, pro-consul, consul, and senator.

To assume the person of Cicero, as the narrator of his own transactions, was certainly an hazardous undertaking. Frequent errors and lapses, violations of probability, and incongruities in the style and conduct of this imaginary history with the genuine productions of Cicero, might be reasonably expected, but these are not found. The more conversant we are with the authentic monuments, the more is our admiration at the felicity of this imposture enhanced.

The conspiracy of Cataline is here related with abundance of circumstances not to be found in Sallust. The difference, however, is of that kind which result from a deeper insight into human nature, a more accurate acquaintance with the facts, more correctness of arrangement, and a deeper concern in the progress and issue of the story. What is false, is so admirable in itself, so conformable to Roman modes and sentiments, so self-consistent, that one is almost prompted to accept it as the gift of inspiration.

The whole system of Roman domestic manners, of civil and military government, is contained in this work. The facts are either collected from the best antiquarians, or artfully deduced from what is known, or invented with a boldness more easy to admire than to imitate. Pure fiction is never employed but when truth was unattainable.

The end designed by Walstein, is no less happily accomplished in the second, than in the first performance. The style and spirit of the narrative is similar; the same skill in the exhibition of characters and deduction of events, is apparent; but events and characters are wholly new. Portugal, its timorous populace, its besotted monks, its jealous and effeminate nobles, and its cowardly prince, are vividly depicted. The narrator of this tale is, as in the former instance, the subject of it. After his retreat from court, Pombal consecrates his leisure to the composition of his own memoirs.

Among the most curious portions of this work, are those relating to the constitution of the inquisition, the expulsion of the Jesuits, the earthquake, and the conspiracy of Daveiro.

The Romish religion, and the feudal institutions, are the causes that chiefly influence the modern state of Europe. Each of its kingdoms and provinces exhibits the operations of these causes, accompanied and modified by circumstances peculiar to each. Their genuine influence is thwarted, in different degrees, by learning and commerce. In Portugal, they have been suffered to produce the most extensive and unmingled mischiefs. Portugal, therefore, was properly selected as an example of moral and political degeneracy, and as a theatre in which virtue might be shewn with most advantage, contending with the evils of misgovernment and superstition.

In works of this kind, though the writer is actuated by a single purpose, many momentous and indirect inferences will flow from his story. Perhaps the highest and lowest degrees in the scale of political improvement have been respectively exemplified by the Romans and the Portuguese. The pictures that are here drawn, may be considered as portraits of the human species, in two of the most remarkable forms.

There are two ways in which genius and virtue may labour for the public good: first, by assailing popular errors and vices, argumentatively and through the medium of books; secondly, by employing legal or ministerial authority to this end.

The last was the province which Cicero and Pombal assumed. Their fate may evince the insufficiency of the instrument chosen by them, and teach us, that a change of national opinion is the necessary prerequisite of revolutions.

Engel, the eldest of Walstein's pupils, thought, like his master, that the narration of public events, with a certain licence of invention, was the most efficacious of moral instruments. Abstract systems, and theoretical reasonings, were not without their use, but they claimed more attention than many were willing to bestow. Their influence, therefore, was limited to a narrow sphere. A mode by which truth could be conveyed to a great number, was much to be preferred.

Systems, by being imperfectly attended to, are liable to beget error and depravity. Truth flows from the union and relation of many parts. These parts, fallaciously connected and viewed separately, constitute error. Prejudice, stupidity, and indolence, will seldom afford us a candid audience, are prone to stop short in their researches, to remit, or transfer to other objects their attention, and hence to derive new motives to injustice, and new confirmations in folly from that which, if impartially and accurately examined, would convey nothing but benefit.

Mere reasoning is cold and unattractive. Injury rather than benefit proceeds from convictions that are transient and faint; their tendency is not to reform and enlighten, but merely to produce disquiet and remorse. They are not strong enough to resist temptation and to change the conduct, but merely to pester the offender with dissatisfaction and regret.

The detail of actions is productive of different effects. The affections are engaged, the reason is won by incessant attacks; the benefits which our system has evinced to be possible, are invested with a seeming existence; and the evils which error was proved to generate, exchange the fleeting, misty, and dubious form of inference, for a sensible and present existence.

To exhibit, in an eloquent narration, a model of right conduct, is the highest province of benevolence. Our patterns, however, may be useful in different degrees. Duties are the growth of situations. The general and the statesman have arduous duties to perform; and, to teach them their duty, is of use: but the forms of human society allow few individuals to gain the station of generals and statesmen. The lesson, therefore, is reducible to practice by a small number; and, of these, the temptations to abuse their power are so numerous and powerful, that a very small part, and these, in a very small degree, can be expected to comprehend, admire, and copy the pattern that is set before them.

But though few may be expected to be monarchs and ministers, every man occupies a station in society in which he is necessarily active to evil or to good. There is a sphere of some dimensions, in which the influence of his actions and opinions is felt. The causes that fashion men into instruments of happiness or misery, are numerous, complex, and operate upon a wide surface. Virtuous activity may, in a thousand ways, be thwarted and diverted by foreign and superior influence. It may seem best to purify the fountain, rather than to filter the stream; but the latter is, to a certain degree, within our power, whereas, the former is impracticable. Governments and general education, cannot be rectified, but individuals may be somewhat fortified against their influence. Right intentions may be instilled into them, and some good may be done by each within his social and domestic province.

The relations in which men, unendowed with political authority, stand to each other, are numerous. An extensive source of these relations, is property.

No topic can engage the attention of man more momentous than this. Opinions, relative to property, are the immediate source of nearly all the happiness and misery that exist among mankind. If men were guided by justice in the acquisition and disbursement, the brood of private and public evils would be extinguished.

To ascertain the precepts of justice, and exhibit these precepts reduced to practice, was, therefore, the favourite task of Engel. This, however, did not constitute his whole scheme. Every man is encompassed by numerous claims, and is the subject of intricate relations. Many of these may be comprised in a copious narrative, without infraction of simplicity or detriment to unity.

Next to property, the most extensive source of our relations is sex. On the circumstances which produce, and the principles which regulate the union between the sexes, happiness greatly depends. The conduct to be pursued by a virtuous man in those situations which arise from sex, it was thought useful to display.

Fictitious history has, hitherto, chiefly related to the topics of love and marriage. A monotony and sentimental softness have hence arisen that have frequently excited contempt and ridicule. The ridicule, in general, is merited; not because these topics are intrinsically worthless or vulgar, but because the historian was deficient in knowledge and skill.

Marriage is incident to all; its influence on our happiness and dignity, is more entire and lasting than any other incident can possess. None, therefore, is more entitled to discussion. To enable men to evade the evils and secure the benefits of this state, is to consult, in an eminent degree, their happiness.

A man, whose activity is neither aided by political authority nor by the *press*, may yet exercise considerable influence on the condition of his neighbours, by the exercise of intellectual powers. His courage may be useful to the timid or the feeble, and his knowledge to the ignorant, as well as his property to those who want. His benevolence and justice may not only protect his kindred and his wife, but rescue the victims of prejudice and passion from the yoke of those domestic tyrants, and shield the powerless from the oppression of power, the poor from the injustice of the rich, and the simple from the stratagems of the cunning.

Almost all men are busy in acquiring subsistence or wealth by a fixed application of their time and attention. Manual or mental skill is obtained and exerted for this end. This application, within certain limits, is our duty. We are bound to chuse that species of industry which combines most profit to ourselves with the least injury to others; to select that instrument which, by most speedily supplying our necessities, leaves us at most leisure to act from the impulse of benevolence.

A profession, successfully pursued, confers power not merely by conferring property and leisure. The skill which is gained, and which, partly or for a time, may be exerted to procure subsistence, may, when this end is accomplished, continue to be exerted for the common good. The pursuits of law and medicine, enhance our power over the liberty, property, and health of mankind. They not only qualify us for imparting benefit, by supplying us with property and leisure, but by enabling us to obviate, by intellectual exertions, many of the evils that infest the world.

Engel endeavoured to apply these principles to the choice of a profession, and to point out the mode in which professional skill, after it has supplied us with the means of subsistence, may be best exerted in the cause of general happiness.

Human affairs are infinitely complicated. The condition of no two beings is alike. No model can be conceived, to which our situation enables us exactly to conform. No situation can be imagined perfectly similar to that of an actual being. This exact similitude is not required to render an imaginary portrait useful to those who survey it. The usefulness, undoubtedly, consists in suggesting a mode of reasoning and acting somewhat similar to that which is ascribed to a feigned person; and, for this end, some similitude is requisite between the real and imaginary situation; but that similitude is not hard to produce. Among the incidents which invention will set before us, those are to be culled out which afford most scope to wisdom and virtue, which are most analogous to facts, which most forcibly suggest to the reader the parallel between his state and that described, and most strongly excite his desire to act as the feigned personages act. These incidents must be so arranged as to inspire, at once, curiosity and belief, to fasten the attention, and thrill the heart. This scheme was executed in the life of "Olivo Ronsica."

Engel's principles inevitably led him to select, as the scene and period of his narrative, that in which those who should read it, should exist. Every day removed the reader farther from the period, but its immediate readers would perpetually recognize the objects, and persons, and events, with which they were familiar.

Olivo is a rustic youth, whom domestic equality, personal independence, agricultural occupations, and studious habits, had endowed with a strong mind, pure taste, and unaffected integrity. Domestic revolutions oblige him to leave his father's house in search of subsistence. He is destitute of property, of friends, and of knowledge of the world. These are to be acquired by his own exertions, and virtue and sagacity are to guide him in the choice and the use of suitable means.

Ignorance subjects us to temptation, and poverty shackles our beneficence. Olivo's conduct shews us how temptation may be baffled, in spite of ignorance, and benefits be conferred in spite of poverty.

He bends his way to Weimar. He is involved, by the artifices of others, and, in consequence of his ignorance of mankind, in many perils and perplexities. He forms a connection with a man of a great and mixed, but on the whole, a vicious character. Semlits is introduced to furnish a contrast to the simplicity and rectitude of Olivo, to exemplify the misery of sensuality and fraud, and the influence which, in the present system of society, vice possesses over the reputation and external fortune of the good.

Men hold external goods, the pleasures of the senses, of health, liberty, reputation, competence, friendship, and life, partly by virtue of their own wisdom and activity. This, however, is not the only source of their possession. It is likewise dependant on physical accidents, which human foresight cannot anticipate, or human power prevent. It is also influenced by the conduct and opinions of others.

There is no external good, of which the errors and wickedness of others may not deprive us. So far as happiness depends upon the retention of these goods, it is held at the option of another. The perfection of our character is evinced by the transient or slight influence which privations and evils have upon our happiness, on the skilfulness of those exertions which we make to avoid or repair disasters, on the diligence and success with which we improve those instruments of pleasure to ourselves and to others which fortune has left in our possession.

Richardson has exhibited in Clarissa, a being of uncommon virtue, bereaved of many external benefits by the vices of others. Her parents and lover conspire to destroy her fortune, liberty, reputation, and personal sanctity.

More talents and address cannot be easily conceived, than those which are displayed by her to preserve and to regain these goods. Her efforts are vain. The cunning and malignity with which she had to contend, triumphed in the contest.

Those evils and privations she was unable to endure. The loss of fame took away all activity and happiness, and she died a victim to errors, scarcely less opprobrious and pernicious, than those of her tyrants and oppressors. She misapprehended the value of parental approbation and a fair fame. She depreciated the means of usefulness and pleasure of which fortune was unable to deprive her.

Olivo is a different personage. His talents are exerted to reform the vices of others, to defeat their malice when exerted to his injury, to endure, without diminution of his usefulness or happiness, the injuries which he cannot shun.

Semlits is led, by successive accidents, to unfold his story to Ronsica, after which, they separate. Semlits is supposed to destroy himself, and Ronsica returns into the country.

A pestilential disease, prevalent throughout the north of Europe, at that time (1630), appears in the city. To ascertain the fate of one connected, by the ties of kindred and love, with the family in which Olivo resides, and whose life is endangered by residence in the city, he repairs thither, encounters the utmost perils, is seized with the reigning malady, meets, in extraordinary circumstances, with Semlits, and is finally received into the house of a physician, by whose skill he is restored to health, and to whom he relates his previous adventures.

He resolves to become a physician, but is prompted by benevolence to return, for a time, to the farm which he had lately left. The series of ensuing events, are long, intricate, and congruous, and exhibit the hero of the tale in circumstances that task his fortitude, his courage, and his disinterestedness.

Engel has certainly succeeded in producing a tale, in which are powerful displays of fortitude and magnanimity; a work whose influence must be endlessly varied by varieties of character and situation of the reader, but, from which, it is not possible for any one to rise without some degree of moral benefit, and much of that pleasure which always attends the emotions of curiosity and sympathy. (1799)

DRAMA

ANDREW BARTON

(fl. 1760–1780)

Many of the important elements in the scenes that follow are discussed in the Introduction (pp. 328–334). The contrasts between Europeans and Americans, among various types of Americans, among various types of speech and dialects, and between city and country abound in these selections. They reveal the manners of a people far from us in time. While we would be mistaken to understand these portraits as life, they can help us to form a more realistic view of the early republic. For example, the characters who are derided and made fun of have some basis in fact; if they did not, no audience ever could have laughed at them. The tradesmen, the Negroes, the Europeans—all the characters—exemplify types that were found in early America. And the concerns of these characters were the concerns of at least some Americans. The scenes, then, can be read as indicative of that period in which people had become so different in their interests from those who first landed in New England. The concerns in the dramas are social, psychological and sometimes political, not theological.

From *The Disappointment**

Characters

PARCHMENT: a scrivener
TRUSHOOP: a cooper
HUM: a tavern keeper
TROWELL: a plasterer
RACCOON: an old debauchee
MOLL PLACKET: a woman of the town,
 Raccoon's mistress

WASHBALL: an avaricious old barber
RATTLETRAP: a supposed conjuror
BUCKRAM: a tailor
QUADRANT: a mathematical instru-
 ment maker

* *The Disappointment; or, the Force of Credulity* (Philadelphia, c. 1780).

439

ACT 1, SCENE 1: *A Tavern.*

PARCH. (To Trushoop) I say Mr. Trushoop, what are the contents of those
  papers?

TRUSH. The devil a hare do I know about it, at all, at all.

HUM. Well gentlemen, I look upon you all to be men of honor. I suppose
  most of you are not altogether strangers to the business in agitation,
  you've all in miniature been informed of it, except Mr. Parchment
  and Mr. Trowell, who are present and shall soon be informed.

PARCH. (Starting up suddenly) Gentlemen, I expected when I was invited
  here, it was to take a cheerful glass with my friends. I had no idea of a
  secret to be divulged, not I—and I earnestly request that, if it is any
  scheme, plot, association, combination, machination, contrivance,
  secret conclave, cabal, privy conspiracy, rout, riot, rebellious-meeting or
  unlawful assembly—infine, if it is anything against the illustrious President
  of the United States, or of the Society of Cincinnati, whom God
  preserve!—the honorable the Vice President of the honorable Senate—
  the honorable the Senate collectively, or individually—The honorable
  the House of Representatives of the United States, that standing Bulwark
  of American freedom, in Congress assembled, or not assembled, or
  either of them—The honorable the Secretary of State—The honorable
  the Secretary of the Treasury—the honorable the Secretary at War—
  the honorable the chief justice of the United States—the honorable the
  associate judges, in their judicial capacity or otherwise—the honorable
  the Attorney-general of the United States—The Right Reverend the
  bishops and clergy of the United States of all denominations, whether in
  church or out of it—the constitution, laws, and government under
  which we live—to be brief—I say gentlemen, if it is any scheme, plot, association, combination, machination, contrivance, secret conclave, cabal,
  private conspiracy, rout, riot, rebellious meeting, or unlawful assembly
  as aforesaid once more, keep it to yourselves, don't let me know a tittle of
  it—I wash my hands of it—for I know it, I'll be a swift witness against
  you, as I profess myself a worthy Citizen a true republican a man of
  honor and a gentleman by birth and education—I'll immediately to the
  Attorney-general, lodge an information against you and hang you every
  mother's son!

WASH. Dear, dear sir! don't think of such a thing.

PARCH. Don't tell me sir. (Raising his voice.)

WASH. Sir! Sir!—you've known me these many, many long years. I've always
  lived peaceably and never was concerned in any of those disturbances

you have mentioned as all my neighbors can testify—Lord! Lord! Mr. Parchment—

PARCH. Mr. Washball, I've nothing to charge you with—but, Sir, my suspicions are—

WASH. Are what?—Lord! Sir, what?

PARCH. Sir, it carries a mysterious countenance!—a damn'd rebellious look—

WASH. Good God sir!—speak to him somebody—do! do! Oh dear! Oh! I'm out of breath.

RAT. Sir, I believe there's none in this company but what are as true republicans as yourself.

BUCK. By my sawl mon! an I ha as grate a regord for the illustrious President of the United States, as ye ha there's na rabels in America mon.

PARCH. I hope there are not—nevertheless, it has a Guy-Faux appearance a damned romantic look.

TROW. How can you say so?

QUAD. I'm surprised at you Mr. Parchment.

TRUS. The devil burn me, but so am I too!

PARCH. I tell you gentlemen, it smells of gunpowder, treason, blood, assassination, slaughter, massacre, and murder.

WASH. I'll give you my bond for five hundred pounds, it is no such thing, indeed, indeed it an't Mr. Parchment—Oh dear! speak to him somebody.

BUCK. Deel damme mon, say that agen and by St. Andra Ize cut aff your heed.

PARCH. I am not to be frightened by you, Mr. Buckram. Damme, Sir, you're mistaken.

HUM. (Aside) Moderate your passion, Mr. Buckram, don't be too rash, let me speak to him—I hope Mr. Parchment you don't suppose any of us capable of conspiring against the government, no Sir!—I answer for all present (yourself excepted), the United States hath not more faithful republicans—the whole business that you were desired to attend upon this evening, I'll instantly communicate—if you'll hear—but, if not—why Sir—

TROW. Aye, do hear—if you don't like it, you can be off, as well as myself.

TRUSH. Arra my dear! an have a little pashence an we'll tell you all an more too, honey.

BUCK. Deel damme mon, if you won't hear, ye may e'en gang aboot your buzness.

RAT. I think him totally unworthy of any communication whatever.

QUAD. Your behavior is very extraordinary—let me tell you, Mr. Parchment— I little expected the like from you.

PARCH. I can't help that Sir—my duty—

HUM. If you are suspicious of us Sir, you're at liberty to quit the company and make what use of our proceedings you think proper—we can answer for ourselves.

TRUSH. Aye, and hang us too, and then turn States Evidence, you devil you!

PARCH. You being my old friends I still regard you, therefore I drop those thoughts. I would not injure your persons or families—I confess I was over-zealous when I made use of the expression.

BUCK. Domme mon and thot's mon leek.

RAT. Come, come, Mr. Parchment, consider.

TROW. Hear, sir, hear!

HUM. I promise you you'll have no cause to repent of it. 'Tis out of pure regard to you we gave you the invitation. (Aside) I could wish him to be one of us. He'd be of infinite service.

PARCH. On condition it is none of those things I have mentioned I am ready to hear.

HUM. I give you on my honor and the sacred word of a mason it is not, and here's my hand upon it. (Shakes hands)

PARCH. I'm satisfied, Mr. Hum.

TROW. Now this is clever. It's just like brethren dwelling together in unity.

TRUS. Fath an it is—it looks well on our side again—by my soul! an it's for all the world now, like to hoores fighting and quarreling and soon make it up again.

TROW. A bad beginning sometimes makes a good ending.

TRUS. That's true for you my dear. (To Parchment) Mind that honey.

HUM. Well silence, gentlemen!—you must know then, that I have very unexpectedly and to my very great joy received a letter from my loving sister-in-law in England, who is heiress to the famous Captain Blackbeard, of blessed memory, enclosing sundry papers, such as original letters, a will, a power of attorney, plans, charts, drafts and memorandums of a vast quantity of treasure etc. etc. that was buried by the pirates, above a century ago, here in America; and these are the papers gentlemen. Please to look over them. (They look over them)

PARCH. Aha!—I beg you ten thousand pardons gentlemen. Since it's an affair of this nature, I join you with all my heart.

* * *

ACT 1, SCENE 3: *A Room in Moll Placket's house.*

(*Enter Raccoon, with a spit, pick-axe, and spade, shouldered.*)

RAC. What shall I do wid dese tings?—dad I'll put dem under de bed. (He steps into the next room, puts them under the bed, and returns.) But where's Mrs. Placket?—She'll be oberjoyed when I tell her—dad I'll dress her off as fine as de Queen of Shebey, when she come to see brudder Solomon—she shall go to de play every night, wid a coach and two footmen to tend her (He calls) Placket! Pet!

PLACK. (Within) Pet's a coming—Pet's a coming, dear Cooney.

(Enter Placket)

RAC. Buss me my dear, and I'll tell you someting dat will make you happy.

PLACK. What! Is your wife dead? say—tell me—for I know that will make us both happy!

RAC. No, no—but it's bery near so good—but you'll tell—

PLACK. No indeed, indeed and double deed—I won't my dear Cooney.

RAC. Well den—I'll not keep my dear Pet in suspense any longer—but you must buss me when I say any ting dat pleases you.

PLACK. Well! so I will, a hundred and a hundred times.

RAC. Well den—but You'll tell? if you do I'll neber forgib you.

PLACK. Trust me dear Cooney—did I ever betray any of your secrets?

RAC. Why no pet—den I'll tell you. Mr. Hum has receib'd a letter from his sister-in-law in England, wid an account of two or tree hunder'd tousand pound, and some oder tings, dat was buried by old Blackbeard de pirate wid de draft where it is hid, and we know de berry spot—(she kisses him) and I'll gib you five hunder'd a year for pin-money (kisses) and we'll ride in de coach togedder (kisses) and we'll go to de play togedder (kisses) and den we'll come home and go to bed togedder (kisses) and den we'll—a little rogue you (kisses again).

PLACK. And do you really think you'll find it?

RAC. Why yes, to be sure child; we know de berry spot!

PLACK. Why if you knew where all the treasure in the world was buried, you'd never obtain it without a conjuror.

RAC. Yes my dear, but we hab a conjuror. Weeb got Mr. Rattletrap, he understands strology and de magic art better den Doctor Foster or any man in de gubberment, and dis night we intend to make de trial— and I must go dis instant and settle de place of meeting.

PLACK. And can you leave me so soon, my dear Cooney?

(Raccoon sings)

SONG VI.

Oh! how joyful shall I be,
When I get de money,
I will bring it all to dee;
O! my diddling honey. (Exit singing)

PLACK. Bye, bye, Cooney. Good luck attend him, for my sake. Poor old fool! He thinks I have a prodigious fondness for him, and so I have for his better part—that's his money. He has been deficient in payment for some time past, and now tells me a cock and a bull story of hidden treasure to amuse and deceive me—accompanied with a deluge of soft sobbering language, such as his pet, his dove, his poor ting, and a thousand such childish expressions and I think I'm up with him, for I call him Cooney, cock-a-pidgeon, sugar-plum, cock-a-dandy, and all the sweet things I can think of; and was anyone to overhear us, they would think us two little children playing baby; and really we do little more. But thank fortune! I'm not at a loss for a friend to make up his deficiency, tho' he thinks me as innocent as a dove; and indeed I'm like a dove, in one respect: for when I lose one mate, I mourn till I get another. . . . (c. 1783)

ROYALL TYLER

(1757–1826)

From *The Contrast**

Characters

JESSAMY   JENNY   JONATHAN

ACT 3, SCENE 1: *A room in New York City*

JESSAMY. . . . Prythee, Jenny, don't spoil your fine face with laughing.

JENNY. Why, mustn't I laugh, Mr. Jessamy?

JESSAMY. You may smile; but, as my lord[1] says, nothing can authorize a laugh.

JENNY. Well, but I can't help laughing.—Have you seen him, Mr. Jessamy?
Ha, ha, ha!

JESSAMY. Seen whom?

JENNY. Why, Jonathan, the New-England colonel's servant. Do you know
he was at the play last night, and the stupid creature don't know where
he has been. He would not go to a play for the world; he thinks it was a
show, as he calls it.

JESSAMY. As ignorant and unpolished as he is, do you know, Miss Jenny, that
I propose to introduce him to the honor of your acquaintance?

JENNY. Introduce him to me! for what?

JESSAMY. Why, my lovely girl, that you may take him under your protection,
as Madame Ramboulliet did young Stanhope; that you may, by your
plastic hand, mould this uncouth cub into a gentleman. He is to make
love to you.

JENNY. Make love to me!—

---

* *The Contrast* (Philadelphia, 1790), modernized by the editor.
[1] Lord Chesterfield (1694–1773), whose *Letters* give a classic portrait of the eighteenth-
century ideal of the gentleman: a symbol of aristocratic pretensions.

JESSAMY. Yes, Mistress Jenny, make love to you; and, I doubt not, when he shall become *domesticated* in your kitchen, that this boor, under your auspices, will soon become *un amiable petit Jonathan*.

JENNY. I must say, Mr. Jessamy, if he copies after me, he will be vastly monstrously polite.

JESSAMY. Stay here one moment, and I will call him.—Jonathan!—Mr. Jonathan! (*Calls.*)

JONATHAN. (*Within.*) Holla! there.—(*Enters.*) You promise to stand by me—six bows you say. (*Bows.*)

JESSAMY. Mrs. Jenny, I have the honour of presenting Mr. Jonathan, Colonel Manly's waiter, to you. I am extremely happy that I have it in my power to make two worthy people acquainted with each other's merit.

JENNY. So, Mr. Jonathan, I hear you were at the play last night.

JONATHAN. At the play! why, did you think I went to the devil's drawing-room?

JENNY. The devil's drawing-room!

JONATHAN. Yes; why an't cards and dice the devil's device, and the play-house the shop where the devil hangs out the vanities of the world upon the tenter-hooks of temptation. I believe you have not heard how they were acting the old boy one night, and the wicked one came among them sure enough, and went right off in a storm, and carried one quarter of the play-house with him. Oh! no, no, no! you won't catch me at a play-house, I warrant you.

JENNY. Well, Mr. Jonathan, though I don't scruple your veracity, I have some reasons for believing you were there; pray, where were you about six o'clock?

JONATHAN. Why, I went to see one Mr. Morrison, the *hocus-pocus* man; they said as how he could eat a case knife.

JENNY. Well, and how did you find the place?

JONATHAN. As I was going about here and there, to and again, to find it, I saw a great crowd of folks going into a long entry that had lanterns over the door; so I asked a man whether that was not the place where they played *hocus-pocus*? He was a very civil kind man, though he did speak like the Hessians; he lifted up his eyes and said, "They play *hocus-pocus* tricks enough there, Got knows, mine friend."

JENNY. Well—

JONATHAN. So I went right in, and they showed me away, clean up to the garret, just like a meeting-house gallery. And so I saw a power of topping folks, all sitting round in little cabins, just like father's corn-cribs, and then there was such a squeaking with the fiddles, and such a tarnal blaze with the lights, my head was near turned. At last the people that sat near me set up such a hissing—hiss—like so many mad cats; and then they went thump, thump, thump, just like our Peleg threshing wheat, and stampt away, just like the nation; and called out for one Mr. Langolee,— I suppose he helps act the tricks.

JENNY. Well, and what did you do all this time?

JONATHAN. Gor, I—I liked the fun, and so I thumpt away, and hiss'd as lustily as the best of 'em. One sailor-looking man that sat by me, seeing me stamp, and knowing I was a cute fellow, because I could make a roaring noise, clapt me on the shoulder and said, "You are a d—d hearty cock, smite my timbers!" I told him so I was, but I thought he need not swear so, and make use of such naughty words.

JESSAMY. The savage!—Well, and did you see the man with his tricks?

JONATHAN. Why, I vow, as I was looking out for him, they lifted up a great green cloth and let us look right into the next neighbor's house. Have you a good many houses in New York made so in that 'ere way?

JENNY. Not many; but did you see the family?

JONATHAN. Yes, swamp it; I see'd the family.

JENNY. Well, and how did you like them?

JONATHAN. Why, I vow they were pretty much like other families;—there was a poor, good-natured curse of a husband, and a sad rantipole of a wife.

JENNY. But did you see no other folks?

JONATHAN. Yes. There was one youngster; they called him Mr. Joseph; he talked as sober and as pious as a minister; but, like some ministers that I know, he was a sly tike in his heart for all that: He was going to ask a young woman to spark it with him, and—the Lord have mercy on my soul!—she was another man's wife.

JESSAMY. The Wabash!

JENNY. And did you see any more folks?

JONATHAN. Why, they came on as thick as mustard. For my part, I thought the house was haunted. There was a soldier fellow, who talked about his row de dow dow, and courted a young woman; but, of all the cute folk I saw, I liked one little fellow—

JENNY. Aye! who was he?

JONATHAN. Why, he had red hair, and a little round plump face like mine, only not altogether so handsome. His name was—Darby;—that was his baptizing name; his other name I forgot. Oh! it was Wig—Wag—Wag-all, Darby Wag-all,—pray, do you know him?—I should like to take a sling with him, or a drap of cider with a pepper-pod in it, to make it warm and comfortable.

JENNY. I can't say I have that pleasure.

JONATHAN. I wish you did; he is a cute fellow. But there was one thing I didn't like in that Mr. Darby; and that was, he was afraid of some of them 'ere shooting irons, such as your troopers wear on training days. Now, I'm a true born Yankee American son of liberty, and I never was afraid of a gun yet in all my life.

JENNY. Well, Mr. Jonathan, you were certainly at the play-house.

JONATHAN. I at the play-house!—Why didn't I see the play then?

JENNY. Why, the people you saw were players.

JONATHAN. Mercy on my soul! did I see the wicked players?—Mayhap that 'ere Darby that I liked so was the old serpent himself, and had his cloven foot in his pocket. Why, I vow, now I come to think on't, the candles seemed to burn blue, and I am sure where I sat it smelt tarnally of brimstone.

JESSAMY. Well, Mr. Jonathan, from your account, which I confess is very accurate, you must have been at the play-house.

JONATHAN. Why, I vow, I began to smell a rat. When I came away, I went to the man for my money again; you want your money, says he; yes, says I; for what, says he; why, says I, no man shall jocky me out of my money; I paid my money to see sights, and the dogs a bit of a sight have I seen, unless you call listening to people's private business a sight. Why, says he, it is the School for Scandalization.—The School for Scandalization!—Oh! ho! no wonder you New York folks are so cute at it, when you go to school to learn it; and so I jogged off.

JESSAMY. My dear Jenny, my master's business drags me from you; would to heaven I knew no other servitude than to your charms.

JONATHAN. Well, but don't go; you won't leave me so.—

JESSAMY. Excuse me.—Remember the cash. (*Aside to him, and—Exit.*)

JENNY. Mr. Jonathan, won't you please to sit down. Mr. Jessamy tells me you wanted to have some conversation with me. (*Having brought forward two chairs, they sit.*)

JONATHAN. Ma'am!—

JENNY. Sir!—

JONATHAN. Ma'am!—

JENNY. Pray, how do you like the city, sir?

JONATHAN. Ma'am!—

JENNY. I say, sir, how do you like New York?

JONATHAN. Ma'am!—

JENNY. The stupid creature! but I must pass some little time with him, if it is only to endeavour to learn whether it was his master that made such an abrupt entrance into our house, and my young mistress' heart, this morning. (*Aside.*) As you don't seem to like to talk, Mr. Jonathan—do you sing?

JONATHAN. Gor, I—I am glad she asked that, for I forgot what Mr. Jessamy bid me say, and I dare as well be hanged as act what he bid me do, I'm so ashamed. (*Aside.*) Yes, ma'am, I can sing—I can sing Mear, Old Hundred, and Bangor.

JENNY. Oh! I don't mean psalm tunes. Have you no little song to please the ladies, such as Roslin Castle, or the Maid of the Mill?

JONATHAN. Why, all my tunes go to meeting tunes, save one, and I count you won't altogether like that 'ere.

JENNY. What is it called?

JONATHAN. I am sure you have heard folks talk about it; it is called Yankee Doodle.

JENNY. Oh! it is the tune I am fond of; and, if I know anything of my mistress, she would be glad to dance to it. Pray, sing!

JONATHAN (*sings*)

Father and I went up to camp,
Along with Captain Goodwin;
And there we saw the men and boys,
As thick as hasty-pudding.
Yankee doodle do, etc.

And there we saw a swamping gun,
Big as log of maple,
On a little deuced cart,
A load for father's cattle.
Yankee doodle do, etc.

And every time they fired it off
It took a horn of powder,
It made a noise—like father's gun,
Only a nation louder.
Yankee doodle do, etc.

There was a man in our town,
His name was—

No, no, that won't do. Now, if I was with Tabitha Wymen and Jemima Cawley down at father Chase's, I shouldn't mind singing this all out before them—you would be affronted if I was to sing that, though that's a lucky thought; if you should be affronted, I have something dang'd cute, which Jessamy told me to say to you.

JENNY. Is that all! I assure you I like it of all things.

JONATHAN. No, no; I can sing more; some other time, when you and I are better acquainted, I'll sing the whole of it—no, no—that's a fib—I can't sing but a hundred and ninety verses: our Tabitha at home can sing it all. —(*Sings.*)

> Marblehead's a rocky place,
> And Cape-Cod is sandy;
> Charlestown is burnt down,
> Boston is the dandy.
>
> Yankee doodle do, etc.

I vow, my own town song has put me into such topping spirits that I believe I'll begin to do a little, as Jessamy says we must when we go a-courting.—(*Runs and kisses her.*) Burning rivers! cooling flames! red-hot roses! pig-nuts! hasty-pudding and ambrosia!

JENNY. What means this freedom? you insulting wretch. (*Strikes him.*)

JONATHAN. Are you affronted?

JENNY. Affronted! with what looks shall I express my anger?

JONATHAN. Looks! why as to the matter of looks, you look as cross as a witch.

JENNY. Have you no feeling for the delicacy of my sex?

JONATHAN. Feeling! Gor, I—I feel the delicacy of your sex pretty smartly (*Rubbing his cheek.*), though, I vow, I thought when you city ladies courted and married, and all that, you put feeling out of the question. But I want to know whether you are really affronted, or only pretend to be so? 'Cause, if you are certainly right down affronted, I am at the end of my tether; Jessamy didn't tell me what to say to you.

JENNY. Pretend to be affronted!

JONATHAN. Aye, aye, if you only pretend, you shall hear how I'll go to work to make cherubim consequences. (*Runs up to her.*)

JENNY. Begone, you brute!

JONATHAN. That looks like mad; but I won't lose my speech. My dearest Jenny—your name is Jenny, I think?—My dearest Jenny, though I have the highest esteem for the sweet favours you have just now granted me— Gor, that's a fib, though; but Jessamy says it is not wicked to tell lies to the women. (*Aside.*) I say, though I have the highest esteem for the favors you have just now granted me, yet you will consider that, as soon as the dissolvable knot is tied, they will no longer be favors, but only matters of duty and matters of course.

JENNY. Marry you! you audacious monster! get out of my sight, or, rather, let me fly from you. (*Exit hastily.*)

JONATHAN. Gor! she's gone off in a swinging passion, before I had time to think of consequences. If this is the way with your city ladies, give me the twenty acres of rock, the bible, the cow, and Tabitha, and a little peaceable bundling.   (1787)

WILLIAM DUNLAP

(1766–1839)

From *Darby's Return**

Characters

DARBY: a soldier in the American army   VILLAGERS

SCENE: *A village in Ireland*

CLOWN: Do *Darby* tell me!—Did you see a whale?
DARBY: Whales! Aye, yes—thick as hops—since you must
        know,
        Dancing Scotch reels—two thousand strong or so.
CLOWN: Oh marcy!
OLD WOMAN: Gooddy!
CLOWN: Odds bobs sningers.
OLD WOMAN: Oh!
DARBY: Well neighbours, now by destinies and fates,
        See me safe landed in the United States;
        And now I'm at the best part of my story,
        For there poor Darby was in all his glory;
        From north to south, where ever I appear'd,
        With deeds and words, my spirits oft they cheer'd;
        But more especially I lik'd to work,
        At one nice little place they call'd New-York;
        Oh! there they lov'd me dearly, never fear
        But Darby loves them too, with heart sincere.

* *Darby's Return* (New York, 1789).

There too I saw some mighty pretty shows;
A revolution without blood or blows;
For as I understood the cunning elves,
The people all revolted from themselves;
Then after joining in a kind confession,
They all agreed to walk in a procession;
So turners, taylors, tinkers, tavern-keepers,
With parsons, blacksmiths, lawyers, chimney
      sweepers,
All neatly dress'd, and all in order fair,
Nice painted standards, waving in the air,
March'd thro' the town—eat beef—and drank
      strong beer.
Soon after that I saw another show,
A man who'd fought to free the land from woe,
Like me had left his *farm* a *soldiering* to go;
But having gain'd his point, he had, *like me*,
Return'd his own *potatoe ground* to see;
But there he couldn't rest;—with one accord
He's call'd to be a kind of——, not a Lord——
I don't know what—he's not a great man, sure,
For poor men love him, just as he was poor!
They love him like a father or a brother.

DERMOT: As we poor Irishmen love one another.
DARBY: Just so.
FATHER LUKE: Why that's the strangest sight of all.
KATHLEEN: How look'd he Darby? Was he short or tall?
DARBY: Why sure I didn't see him: to be sure,
As I was looking hard from out the door,
I saw a man in regimentals fine,
All lace and glitter, bother'um and shine;
And so I look'd at him, till all was gone,
And then, I found that he was not the one.
By this time, boys, I wanted to get home;
I thought you would be glad to see me come;
So, as I've often heard the people say,
The farthest round is much the shortest way,
I went to France. I always did love quiet,
And there I got in the middle of a riot.
There they cried "*vive la nation*," "*liberty*,"
And all the *bag and tails* swore they'd be free;

They caught the fire quite across the ocean,
And to be sure, they're in a nice commotion:
(Down with the bastile—tuck up the jailor.
Cut off my lor's head, then pay his taylor.)
Oh bless their hearts, if they can but get free,
They'll soon be as fat and as jolly as we;
Some took the *liberty* to plunder others,
Because equality is more like brothers.
You may be sure I didn't stay there long.
So here I am boys, hearty hale and strong!
But oh, New-York's the place to get a wife,
Aye, that's the place to lead a merry life.

FATHER LUKE: Why Darby, boy, why didn't you stay there?
DARBY: Because I wish'd to pay a visit here;
To see how all the *Carton* lasses thrive,
And ask ye, sure, if ye are all alive.
But I'll go back again, oh never fear!
I'll not be after leaving them, my dear:
You will not catch me staying a great while,
From where I'm never seen without a smile.
Oh may their little country ever prove,
The land of liberty and seat of love.
Oh bless their little hearts, and all they've got,
And may they soon *have* all that they *have not*. . . .   (1789)

JAMES NELSON BARKER

(1784–1858)

From *Tears and Smiles**

Characters

RANGELY: an aristocratic American   YANK: a simple American
FLUTTERMORE: a Frenchified American   GALLIARD: a Frenchman

ACT 1: *A street*

FLUT. Ay, you wonder, Jack. A little *transformé*, you see.

RAN. You are indeed.

FLUT. Yes, burst from darkness into the blaze of fashion; chang'd in an instant—

RAN. From a worm to a butterfly.

FLUT. Butterfly! yes, faith; good metaphor. Once a bookworm, a college chrysalis; now a butterfly, light, airy, *emerilloné*. 'Gad, a *bonne similitude* —Made the grand tour.

RAN. The grand tour?

FLUT. Yes; just returned. Hey, monsieur? 'Gad, I beg pardon. This sudden *rencontre* with my friend—Give me leave—This is *monsieur Galliard*, from Paris. Monsieur, my friend, Jack Rangely, from—no matter. There; don't shake hands: that's antique. Talk English, Jack; Galliard prefers it; speaks it like a native.

GAL. Oh! lit, ver lit; *presque rien;* noting 'tall.

FLUT. No; believe me, he swears English with the best accent.

GAL. Oh! I'll be dam! You flatte me.

* Paul H. Musser, ed., *James Nelson Barker 1784–1858* (Philadelphia, 1929).

FLUT. Judge!

RAN. And what do you think, M. Galliard, of North America and its savages?

GAL. *Comment?* Sauvage! As I hope to be save, I have not seen—

RAN. I mean its inhabitants: for doubtless we must appear uncivilized to you polished Europeans.

GAL. Your good pardon, sare; *c'est un bon pay;* ver good fine contrée; *tous les hommes*, all de peuple happy; all de vomen belle, beautiful! By gar, I am ravish'd!

RAN. You praise lavishly, M. Galliard.

FLUT. He does, indeed. For my part, I can't conceive what you possibly do in this corner of the globe. No opera; no masquerade, nor *fete*, nor *conversazione;* a diabolical theatre; and not even a *promenade*, where one might—(*Examining his figure.*) Then your women; such dowdies! No air; no manner. And your men: *O Ciel!* such beings!—'Gad, Jack, you must go to Europe! You see what it can do.

RAN. Why, if I could hope ever to attain that brilliancy—

FLUT. Pshaw, man! don't despair. There are very pretty degrees, you know, below the *summit* of excellence. I rather fancy, indeed, that the *eclat* which attended *me* is not to be repeated every day. Why, sir, I was absolutely a comet.

RAN. Indeed!

FLUT. Set Paris in a blaze; shook London to its centre; dazzled most of the Italian cities; made Vienna totter; and was the gaze every where. Ha, monsieur?

GAL. *Oh! oui;* wherever you are, *de peuple gape at you.* Yes; dam 'tis not true.

FLUT. Then for the women. I don't know what can be found so delectable about me; but in strict truth, all ranks—Hark ye, Jack: *entre nous*—(*Whispers.*)

RAN. The princess! Impossible!

FLUT. True; poor Eugene! As to the wives and daughters of petty princes or electors; pretty *amusettes*, or so, for an idle hour. Show you my diary.

RAN. What, did you keep a diary?

FLUT. Not a vulgar gazetteer-like thing; distance of post-towns, and all that— *Le voici!* (*Shows a small morocco book.*)

RAN. Heavens! here's a list of names might become the docket of a sheriff of the county!

FLUT. A few. This side, princes, or so, my particular friends, with whom I've passed whole *days. L'autre coté*, princesses, and that kind of thing, with whom I've pass'd whole—(*ahem*)—hey, monsieur?

GAL. Oh, *by de lor*, you have good mode *pour passer le temps*. Yes.

RAN. Excellent pastimes, I dare swear. But have you gained nothing else? No observations, remarks?

FLUT. Oh! customs and manners, and all that; laws, and the like. O yes; profound too. The English can't dress, talk, nor cook so well as the French. The Italian opera is a dev'lish deal finer than any thing in the world. The *elegantes* have introduced hair-powder into Paris; and the emperor, gun-powder into Germany. Then for laws; for laws. They are every where better than *ours*, because every where else the *bourgeois* are kept under. *En fin*, I have found that the new world is too green to please the palate of a man of *gusto;* and that Europe, like a ripe beauty, is the only object worthy a connoisseur's attention.

GAL. *Eh bien!* For me, I tink Europe is like de old libertine, de courtesane; I am disgust vid her. Amerique is de lit demoiselle you point me in de street; vat you call?

FLUT. Ha! ha! A Quaker!

GAL. Ah! de quake; yes. So *ingenue,* so *modest:* as I hope to be save, I vill choose de *contrée* and de quake for life. I vill marry de *one,* and settle in de *oder.* . . .   (1807)

JAMES KIRKE PAULDING

(1778–1860)

From *The Bucktails**

Characters

OBSOLETE: an English antiquary   HENRY AND FRANK TUDOR: Americans
MISS OBSOLETE: his sister   ASSORTED ENGLISH ARISTOCRATS
MARY AND JANE: Miss Obsolete's friends

ACT 2, SCENE 3: *Obsolete's house in England*

JANE. Well, Mary, don't your heart flutter at the thought of seeing these wild
   men of the forests, these Bucktails as Miss Obsolete calls them?
MARY (*smiling.*) Why, I confess to a little trepidation. I hope they'll treat us to
   the war-whoop and buffalo-dance after dinner.
MISS OBSOLETE. I'm sure it's more than I do. I tremble already like a patient
   in a charming fit of the ague. I hope, brother, you'll not give them too
   much liquor, for they say they are apt to scalp one another in drink. But I
   think I hear the bell. Mercy upon us! they're coming! (*Runs behind a
   great chair.*)
   Enter LORD NOLAND, ADMIRAL, MAJOR, SIR KIT *and* THREADNEEDLE.
NOLAND. Benign Miss Warfield, and you the elder and the younger grace,
   I worship you. (*Bowing.*)
ADMIRAL. And I.
SIR KIT. And I.

---

* *The Bucktails* in J. K. Paulding, *American Comedies* (Philadelphia, 1847).

MAJOR. And I.

THREADNEEDLE. I say ditto to my lord.

JANE. In the name of all the graces I thank—my lord, knight, admiral, major, and ditto to Mr. Threadneedle. (*Courtesies to each.*) Who shall say the age is wanting in chivalry or piety, when here are five gallant knights ready to worship even a heathen deity.

NOLAND. Nay, madam, if thus you treat your votaries, your shrine will be deserted, even though you joined the wit of Minerva to the beauty of Venus.

OBSOLETE. My lord grows classical. That speech certainly found a wrong mouth. It belongs to the most erudite Sir Christopher.

NOLAND. What, my adorer of ancient mummyhood, is it war between us? Allons—"lay on, Macduff." Now will I peach most villainously, and repeat word for word, that gallant speech you made at my levee this blessed morning.

OBSOLETE—(*aside to him.*) For Heaven's sake, my lord! I entreat you by the antiquity of thine ancestors to be as silent as the head of your great great grandsire.

JANE. O tell us by all means, my lord. If there was ever a poor damsel died of a curiosity of the heart, it will be me, if I don't instantly hear the story.

Omnes, except MARY. By all means—the story—the story!

NOLAND. Well, though bound by my nobility to despise the will of the majority, I yield this once, that I may be greatly revenged. You will be pleased, or rather you will be displeased, to know Miss Warfield—

Enter RUST, *trembling.*

Madam—b—b—b—the Aboriginals are come—B—b—b—they—they—
(MISS OBSOLETE *again gets behind the great chair,*
and RUST *behind her.*)

OBSOLETE—(*alarmed.*) Why, what is the blockhead frightened at! He shivers like a poplar leaf.

RUST. S—s—sir—I've never been steady since the last earthquake we encountered at the foot of Mount Ætna.

Enter HENRY *and* FRANK TUDOR. MISS OBSOLETE *remains behind the chair—*
OBSOLETE *eyes them with a sort of alarmed curiosity, and forgets to pay*
the ordinary civilities. MISS OBSOLETE *ventures to peep out, and exclaims*
aside— (NOLAND *and the others laugh at* MR. *and* MISS OBSOLETE).

Why, as I live they are dressed, and look like absolute Christians! If they only had wooden legs, like the admiral, they'd be an ornament to the hospital.

MARY—(*apart to* JANE.) For Heaven's sake, Jane, say something— I am so ashamed at this reception, my feet are grown fast to the floor. Speak, dear Jane—or be dumb forever.

JANE—(*laughing.*) Well, rather than incur the penalty: Gentlemen (*to the Tudors*), to convince you that you have not been invited to dine at an asylum of the deaf and dumb, I am urged to present you to this good silent company, who are so delighted to see you that they have forgot to bid you welcome. As a countrywoman, permit me to present you to Miss Obsolete, who will please to come out of her hiding-place. I assure you, madam, there's no danger. (*Laughs.*)

MISS OBSOLETE. I believe I may venture. (*Comes partly forward, then retires again in a fright.*)

HENRY—(*apart to* FRANK.) What can all this mean, Frank? I begin to be angry.—Could I suppose there was any intention—

FRANK. Pooh, pooh, brother—'tis nothing but the old English hospitality we've heard so much about.

JANE. Mr. Obsolete (*apart*)—Mr. Obsolete, if you don't instantly find the use of your tongue, and do the honors of the house, I'll cast you from the list of my beaux into outer darkness.

OBSOLETE. I go, most lovely, and yet to go am loth. But such a threat would make a Cicero of me, though mum as a mummy. I go—and yet I do not go, for at this moment I am dumbfounded. Beseech thee, mistress Jane, to set my sister Miss Obsolete at them; she hath a never-failing stream of speech, whereas just now I labor under a great drought of ideas.

JANE. Well, this is politeness! Miss Obsolete, pray try and supply the deficiences of your brother.

MISS OBSOLETE. Why what can I do? I don't understand Choctaw, nor Chickasaw, nor Potawottomy, nor any of the polite aboriginal tongues— and as for English, there's no use in talking to them, I suppose.

JANE. It's enough to provoke a saint—though I can't help laughing. Go, then, madam, and try what signs will do.

FRANK (*to* HENRY). "Look, my lord, it comes—angels and ministers!"

HENRY. Hush! she's going to enter into a treaty of peace with us. See—she is plucking the olive branch.

MISS OBSOLETE *advances cautiously from behind her chair, followed by* RUST— *She plucks a branch from a flower pot in the room—motions them to sit down, and attempts a conversation by signs.* FRANK, LORD NOLAND *and the guests laugh aside—while* HENRY *exhibits signs of angry impatience.*

HENRY. What mummery is this? (*Advancing.*) Pray, gentlemen, who of all this good company represents our hospitable entertainer?

LORD NOLAND. Faith, these seem a pair of downright gentlemen after all.— For the honor of old England, I'll welcome them myself—(*Advances.*) Permit me, sir, to answer that question, in behalf of a certain gentleman whose wits seem a little out at the elbows just now. This is Mr. Obsolete, who is struck dumb with the pleasure of seeing you. I am called Lord Noland, and if I might be permitted to act as his substitute, I would offer you my hand, and say you're welcome to England.

HENRY. I thank you, my lord; and to say the truth, I felt a little mortified that Mr. Obsolete did not inquire at least about an old friend of his I left at my father's.

FRANK. And I felt, and do still feel very angry with these young ladies, whom I can't forgive under the price of hearing their voices once at least before I die. (*Bows to* MARY *and* JANE.)

MARY—(*apart to* JANE.) Speak, Jane! The woman is dead within me.

JANE. Speak, Jane! why, you little blushing thing. I begin to believe you have already been struck with an arrow from the quiver of one of these aborigines, who, you know, are very expert at the bow. Pray, gentlemen, are the ladies of your country fond of rural life? I know you can talk of that if nothing else. (*To* MARY.)

HENRY. Those who live in the cities, madam—those who reside in the country are not so fond of retirement. It is easy, however, to give them what taste we please, in this respect, since the most inveterate town lady loves the country—when she's in a crowd—and the most ardent votary of rural shades adores a crowd—when she's alone in the country.

JANE. I should hope, Mr. Tudor, it did not require to be placed at one extreme, in order to admire the other.

HENRY. Perhaps not in all cases, madam. Yet I have very often found, that the ladies who talked most about the charms of rural life, were most often to be seen at public places; and that the most sincere votaries of the repose of the country, were apt to say the least on the subject.

JANE. You don't mean to insinuate that we women talk most of what we think the least?

HENRY. Not among yourselves, madam. (*Bowing.*)

MARY—(*speaking eagerly.*) I'm sure—I'm sure—(*Retires confused, and blushing.*)

FRANK—(*aside.*) They say I'm one of the most impudent fellows in the world— and I believe it, for it can be nothing but the force of contrast that draws my heart towards that little flower of blushing modesty. See how her blood goes and comes of errands from her face to her heart!

OBSOLETE—(*after a deep sigh.*) I begin to breathe again. Pray, Mr. Tudor, are you of the family of Owen Tudor, who married our Queen Katherine?

FRANK—(*to* HENRY.) Bravo! an ox spoke once at Rome, and so did an ass in Judea!

HENRY. I fancy not sir. I remember my grandfather—but who his grandfather was, is more than appears in our family tree.

OBSOLETE. Perhaps by going to the Herald's office you may trace out the descent. Should we meet in London during the winter, I shall be happy to aid your inquiries.

HENRY. I thank you, sir. But I believe I shall not trouble you. I mean not to detract from the advantages of birth and title, but in America, we lay little claim to such distinctions. Those who left this country to settle mine, forgot their pedigrees in toils and dangers; and those of their descendants, who rely upon the mere identity of names to prove their claim to noble blood, only make themselves ridiculous.

NOLAND. Then I presume, sir, there's no distinction between the cobler and the king, and the son of a cobler and a king?

HENRY. The law makes none, and that's sufficient. We are taught to consider a king, and the son of a king, as much the subject of our thoughts and judgment, as the beggar that goes in rags. Man can't remove one step from man—his nature fixes him.

NOLAND—(*apart*.) Why, Sir Kit, this smells of the radical!

SIR KIT. The very radical heat and moisture of democracy, my lord. We must have them at the Alien office. They are certainly of the mischievous sect of the Bucktails, we've read about.

Enter RUST. Dinner waits, sir.

OBSOLETE. My lord, be pleased to hand Miss Obsolete.

NOLAND—(*aside*.) The fiend take my nobility this time, however. O, for the glorious system of equality!

OBSOLETE. Sir Christopher—my daughter's hand. I shall escort Miss Warfield.

FRANK—(*aside*.) Shall I venture? I will—I'll cross that Sir Kit were he twenty knights of Bath or Garter. May it please you, madam.

(*Takes* MARY's *hand and leads her out.*)

SIR KIT. A bucktail! a real bucktail! Why he don't comprehend the first rudiments of etiquette, the very corner-stone and cement of society—a bucktail—I say again a bucktail!

(*Exit.*)

RUST (*walking behind* FRANK, *scrutinizing him closely*.) I don't see the bucktail, after all.

(*Exit.*)
(1815?)

CRITICISM

The pride in the new nation began even before the first immigrants left their old country, as the first selection in this text reveals. That pride has never ceased. In the first centuries of the new nation it permeated the sermons, letters, diaries, poetry, fiction and drama. Trumbull, in his essay on the fine arts, argues for the importance of these, reviews their place in history, and then comes, finally, to their potential in America. His attack on the contemporary literature of Great Britain becomes, in effect, another aspect of the familiar argument that America is the hope of the English-speaking people.

Dwight's defense of Edwards and other Americans does not particularly contain that hope, but his comparisons point to a similar conclusion—that the new nation could no longer be considered culturally impoverished. His pride in the achievements of Americans came from the constant attacks by British critics on the failure of America to produce artists who had made significant achievements. Tyler's plea for American books was calculated to give more stature to native writers and to turn attention to native materials. It would not be apparent to critics for some time that significant American authors writing about the time of Tyler were already doing just what he asked.

Ames thought that America had not produced men of genius, and he believed that he knew why. Democracy and the drive to accumulate property were two most important reasons. But Ames, like the other authors in this group, was confident that geniuses would come, that America would take her place culturally, as well as politically, among nations. The final selection, Barker's Preface to *Tears and Smiles*, permits us to see more clearly one of the reasons for the American authors' complaints. While the critics called for better work and more work from these authors, many Americans preferred the works of Europeans.

463

JOHN TRUMBULL

(1750–1831)

*An Essay on the Use and Advantages of the Fine Arts**

NO SUBJECT can be more important in itself, or better suited to the present occasion, and the exercises of this day, than the Use and Advantages of the fine Arts, and especially those of Polite Literature. These studies are perhaps too much undervalued by the public, and neglected by the youth in our seminaries of science. They are considered as meer matters of trifling amusement, and despised in comparison with the more solid branches of Learning.

The knowledge of Languages, Mathematics, Metaphysics and Philosophy, undoubtedly deserves to engage the attention of the greatest Genius. For skill in these sciences, the World (while the world remains) will revere the memory of a Bacon, a Newton, and a Locke. But when they are carried beyond a certain point; when they are of no advantage to the common purposes of life; when they are employed upon questions which human Reason can never with certainty determine, they degenerate into meer speculations of amusement, and become no farther valuable, than as they serve to enlarge the mind, clear the understanding, and entertain us in the hours of leisure from the important avocations of business. The Geometrical labours for the Quadrature of the Circle, the Metaphysical controversies about the Existence of matter, and the Essence of Spirit, though a field for the display of genius, in what are they more interesting to mankind than the contentions of Antiquaries about the genuineness of a medal, or the disputes of Commentators about the various readings of their antient manuscripts?

Let us consider the advantages which arise to the world from the study of the liberal Arts.

Mankind in the present state, are extremely liable to be led away by mean and sordid vices, to be attached to the low enjoyments of sense, and

---

* Clarence Arthur Brown, ed., *Achievement of American Criticism* (New York, 1954).

thus degraded almost to a level with the brutal creation. As that unceasing thirst for happiness, which is the universal spring of action, must have some object for its gratification; the Divine Being, to raise us above these low desires, hath implanted in our minds a taste for more pure and intellectual pleasures. These pleasures have their source in the fine Arts, and are more especially found in the elegant entertainments of polite Literature. They ennoble the soul, purify the passions, and give the thoughts a better turn. They add dignity to our sentiments, delicacy and refinement to our manners. They set us above our meaner pursuits, and make us scorn those low enjoyments, which perhaps we once esteemed as the perfection of human felicity. I appeal to all persons of judgment, whether they can rise from reading a fine Poem, viewing any masterly work of Genius, or hearing an harmonious concert of Music, without feeling an openness of heart, and an elevation of mind, without being more sensible to the dignity of human nature, and despising whatever tends to debase and degrade it?

These are the delights, which humanize the soul, and polish away that rugged ferocity of manners, which is natural to the uncultivated nations of the world.

In every land, in every age, at the time when the unconquered spirit of freedom, joined with that laudable ambition, which fires the soul to heroic deeds; hath raised the nation to the highest pitch of glory, the fine Arts have been studiously cultivated, and have shined forth with peculiar lustre. For Learning and Glory walk hand in hand through the world. A savage People, before the dawn of literature, may indeed be terrible in arms: but being stained with the blood of cruelty, tarnished with that wild barbarity, which degrades courage into brutality, they never attain to the summit of renown; and either sink unnoticed into oblivion, or leave to posterity a name more infamous for barbarism, than famed for heroic atchievements. While every voice celebrates the bravery of an Alexander, a Scipio, a Caesar, and a Marlborough; who remembers the savage fierceness of the lion-hearted Richard; or what mouth is opened in the praise of that scourge of Asia, the Persian Nadir?

The same ardour of ambition, the same greatness of thought, which inspires the Warrior to brave danger in the conquering field, when diffused among a people will call forth Genius in every station of life, fire the imagination of the Artist, and raise to sublimity the aspiring Muse.

Look into the annals of antiquity. View the Grecians at the aera of learning and politeness, when the fine Arts were carried to their highest glory, when the whole nation were encouragers of science, and every person a judge of literature; when by greatness of genius, correctness of taste and refinement of manners, they rendered themselves famous throughout the world and patterns of imitation to all posterity. Then was the time that Greece produced those Heroes that astonished Europe and Asia with the sound of their victories; then was the time that Athens, Sparta and Thebes gave laws to the world. And could a Nation fail of rising to the highest pitch of fame, when animated with the thundering eloquence of Demosthenes and Pericles, fired to warlike deeds by the martial muse of Homer, and warmed with those noble sentiments which inspire the productions of Aeschylus, Euripides and Sophocles?

The glory of Arts and Arms sunk in Greece and rose again with renewed lustre in Hesperia. Rome distinguished herself for literature, even from the first dawn of her greatness. In her early days, while her unpolished manners bore too near a resemblance to the rough virtues of Sparta, she could boast an Ennius, the boldness of whose thoughts even Virgil himself did not disdain to imitate. Then flourished Accius, Naevius, Pacuvius, those famed dramatic poets, with the bold and spirited Lucilius, the father of the Roman satire. But these writers have sunk into the dark grave of oblivion, and left behind only some small traces of their fame. Then appeared the rough genius of Plautus, the milder elegance of Terence, and the soft muse of Catullus: Then the polished Lucretius, so distinguished for all the graces of poetic expression, that Virgil evidently borrowed from his writings, his style, versification and manner of description. In the mean time Eloquence rose to the highest perfection at Rome. Be Cicero a witness, whose praise is unnecessary, whether as an orator, a patriot, or a philosopher.

But see Rome attains to the summit of greatness. The world submits to her sway. Satiated with the spoils of victory, she sits unmolested on the throne, and diffuses the mild blessings of peace. Then flourish the names dearest to fame, the glories of the Augustan age: The majestic Muse of Virgil, the second who dared attempt the dignity of the epic song; the polished elegance of Horace, graced with the sounding lyre, and armed with the keen sword of satire; the strong and sportive imagination of Ovid; the soft elegiac strains of Tibullus and Propertius; and the historic grandeur of Livy. The world is conscious of their fame. Their characters need not be illustrated by the tedious impertinence of praise.

The Glory of Rome faded by a gradual decay. The Muse still shone, though with tarnished lustre, in the tragedies of Seneca, the satires of Juvenal and Persius, and the heroic poems of Lucan, Statius, Claudian, and Silius Italicus. History produced the nervous, the manly Tacitus; and Philosophy could still show her Seneca and Pliny. Till at length Tyranny usurped the dominion, and Barbarism overspread the land of Italy.

For a nearer instance of the trophies of the liberal Arts, let us view the state of Russia in the last century. In a cold unpolished land, deep-sunk in the shades of savage ignorance, a Monarch rises, who moved with compassion for his subjects, fired with love of glory, and endowed with a soul superior to the age, forms a project of civilizing his country. He sails to other lands, imports the rudiments of the arts, and affords both by precept and example the utmost encouragement to genius. The Nation raises herself from the dust, repels her enemies, extends her borders, leads forth her conquering armies, and now threatens the total subversion of the Ottoman empire.

Britain alone can claim the glory of an equality with Greece and Rome. There for two centuries the Arts have flourished with almost unabated lustre: And the slightest reflection will inform us that this period is by far the most celebrated in the British history. In the glorious reign of Elizabeth, there arose a Spenser, unequalled in all the pleasing charms of luxuriant description; whose fancy transports us to fairy land, and brings us acquainted with a shadowy race, the beings of his own creation. Then a Shakespear, the matchless genius of the drama; endowed with the most noble extravagance of imagination, the strongest powers of humour, the sovereign command of the passions, and the keenest inspection into all the mazes of the human soul. To these succeeded the unbridled wit of Cowley, the soft graces of Waller, and the various grandeur of all-accomplished Dryden. Then with the united charms of every Muse, appeared the immortal Milton; who with the greatest force of natural genius, assisted by all the aids of art, and by the noble descriptions of the inspired writers, hath produced a Poem, almost as much superior to Homer's, in sublimity of conception, as it is in the greatness of its subject:

> A Genius universal as his theme,
> Astonishing as Chaos, as the bloom
> Of blowing Eden fair, as Heav'n sublime.
>
> THOMSON

After a short eclipse in the luxurious reign of Charles II, the reviving Arts shone forth with superior brightness in the prosperous days of William and Anne; while the victorious Marlborough bore Britain's thunder on her foes, and made Europe tremble at the sound of his arms. Then flourished the polished muse of Addison, who revived in England the classic elegance of the Augustan age; whose works, adorned with the highest sublimity of sentiment, and the nicest delicacy of thought, filled with easy humour which points the ridicule at vice, (while they afford instruction and entertainment of the noblest kind to every reader,) may boast as their greatest honour and distinguished excellence, that they are peculiarly calculated to please and improve the fairest part of the creation.

Then arose a Swift, the friend of virtue, the scourge of folly, and the terror of vice; unequalled for manly sense, liveliness of fancy, the powers of wit and humour, and the severest poignancy of satire. Happy, had not his mind, soured with disappointment in the earliest views of his ambition, too often endeavoured by the grossest indelicacy of description to debase the dignity of human nature; and indulged a spirit of misanthropy, which clouds his best productions, and while we admire the force of his Genius, bids us detest the sentiments of his heart. What age shall forget the undying fame of Pope! Whether in pleasing strains he paints the beauties of nature; mourns with the softest notes of elegiac verse; or with moral rapture unfolds all the principles and passions of the human soul: Whether in sportive lays he displays the foibles of the gentler Sex; impales vice and dulness on the point of satire; or holding up the glass of translation, reflects with unabated light the glories of the Maeonian song.

For the power of describing the beauties of rural scenes, and copying the different appearances of nature, what writer can vie with the pleasing Thomson! The liveliness of his paintings, his sublime morality, and his delicacy of thought justly raise him to the highest rank of genius.

Nor must we forget the unaffected ease of Gay and Prior, the spirited wit of Congreve, the delicate fancy of Parnelle, the dramatic powers of Otway, Southern and Rowe, the cervantic humour of Arbuthnot, with the pointed satire and strong imagination of Young. These writers will convey the English glory to the most distant ages of posterity.

Polite Letters at present are much on the decline in Britain; not through a scarcity of authors, or want of encouragement from the public; but by reason of that luxurious effeminacy, which hath caused a decay of genius, and introduced a false taste in writing. Their Men of learning are infected with pedantry. They are great admirers of antiquity and followers in the path of servile imitation. They sacrifice ease and elegance to the affectation of classic correctness, fetter the fancy with the rules of method, and damp all the ardour of aspiring invention. While the men of Genius (who are at present a distinct class of writers) in contempt of the critic chains, throw off all appearance of order and connection, sport in the wildest sallies of imagination, and adopt the greatest extravagance of humour, which too often sinks to buffoonery, or is soured with the malevolence of satire.

America hath a fair prospect in a few centuries of ruling both in arts and arms. It is universally allowed that we very much excel in the force of natural genius: And although but few among us are able to devote their whole lives to study, perhaps there is no nation, in which a larger portion of learning is diffused through all ranks of people. For as we generally possess the middle station of life, neither sunk to vassalage, nor raised to independance, we avoid the sordid ignorance of peasants, and the unthinking dissipation of the great. The heroic love of Liberty, the manly fortitude, the generosity of sentiment, for which we have been so justly celebrated, seem to promise the future advancement and established duration of our glory. Many incidents unfortunate in themselves, have tended to call forth and sustain these virtues. Happy, in this respect, have been our late struggles for liberty! They have awakened the spirit of freedom; they have rectified the manners of the times; they have made us acquainted with the rights of mankind; recalled to our minds the glorious independance of former ages, fired us with the views of fame, and by filling our thoughts with contempt of the imported articles of luxury, have raised an opposition, not only to the illegal power, but to the effeminate manners of Britain. And I cannot but hope, notwithstanding some dangerous examples of infamous defection, that there is a spirit remaining in these Colonies, that will invariably oppose itself to the efforts of usurpation and perfidy, and forbid that Avarice should ever betray us to Slavery.

This Land hath already begun to distinguish itself in literature. It is peculiarly famed for the study of Theology; and though too much infested with the short-lived productions of controversy, can boast of some Divines, who however inelegant in style and expression, have perhaps never been excelled in depth of thought and profoundness of reasoning. Our late writers in the cause of liberty have gained the applause of Europe. Many elegant essays have been produced in the style of wit and humour; nor hath Poetry been entirely uncultivated among us. The encouragement, which is given to the Arts and Sciences, affords a prospect of our future glory.   (1770)

TIMOTHY DWIGHT

(1752–1817)

*Letter on Jonathan Edwards and American Culture**

Dear Sir,

FROM the observations in my last letter you may possibly be induced to believe, that whatever may be the deficiency of our genius and learning, it is not attributable to the causes alleged by Buffon, and de Pauw. In this I hope to convince you that amid all these disadvantages our character is not altogether such, as it frequently appears in the observations of your country-men.

In the Edinburgh Review of Ashe's Travels in America is the following passage, "In short, Federal America has done nothing either to extend, diversify, or embellish, the sphere of human knowledge. Though all she has written were obliterated from the records of learning, there would (if we except the works of Franklin,) be no positive diminution, either of the useful, or the agreeable. The destruction of her whole literature, would not occasion so much regret, as we feel for the loss of a few leaves from an ancient classic."

These declarations are certainly uttered in a sprightly manner. But they are untrue. The late President Edwards has more enlarged the science of Theology than any divine, of whom either England or Scotland can boast; and the loss of his works would occasion more regret than these Reviewers, and I may add without any fear of sober contradiction, than the whole literary world, would feel for the loss, not of a few leaves only, but of the whole works, of half the ancient authors now extant. I do not intend that the Reviewers themselves would feel this regret; but that it would be felt by a vast multitude of man-kind, to whom several writers in that review have been both openly and insidiously hostile: I mean christians. There is not a treatise, written by Mr.

* *Travels; In New-England and New York* (New Haven, 1821–22).

Edwards, except those which were merely occasional, which has not enlarged science. I particularly specify his treatises on Religious affections, on the qualifications for communion in the christian church, on Moral Agency, on Original sin, on GOD's last end in the creation of the world, and on the nature of true Virtue. The subjects of these discussions have long been acknowledged by the whole civilized world to be of the highest importance to man. They are, also, of the most abstruse nature; and require the profoundest thought and the most enlarged comprehension. Two of them are professedly replies to the ablest philosophers, who have written on the Arminian side of the question; that on Moral Agency; and that on Original Sin; and both appear to have terminated the dispute. They have now been published more than fifty years. On one side they have been steadily appealed to as immoveable standards of faith, so far as these subjects are concerned. On the other, they have been bitterly complained of; denounced as heretical; pursued with sarcasms, and sneers; and hunted down with contempt: but they have never been answered. Nothing can explain this fact but the acknowledgment, that they have hitherto been believed to be unanswerable.

I am aware, that it may, and will, be replied to a part of these observations, that I have here taken for granted a main point: viz. that the scheme of Mr. Edwards is true. Of its truth I have not a question; but I will not assume it here. I am not ignorant how many persons disbelieve it; nor how respectable the character is of some, who are in this number. Nor am I ignorant on the other hand, that it is the scheme substantially adopted by all those distinguished men, who, under GOD, produced the reformation; nor that it is substantially found in the creeds, confessions, and catechisms of all the protestant churches, particularly in the articles, and homilies, of your own church; and, let me add, in the prayers also. It was the glory of this great man, that he had no love for innovation. He did not believe that theology was, like philosophy, left in such a situation, that ages might pass on, during which the honest inquirers in the church would be necessarily, and invincibly, ignorant of its fundamental truths. Nor did he think it proper to sacrifice common sense to metaphysics. Though probably the ablest metaphysician, who has appeared, he never warped from the path of common sense. To the Scriptures he yielded the most profound reverence, and the most implicit confidence. At the same time he treated his antagonists with a civility, candor, and moderation, which very few of them, or their followers, have exhibited in return.

The first of my positions is not at all affected by the supposition, that Mr. Edwards' opinions are erroneous: viz. that the loss of his writings would awaken more regret than the loss of a few pages of an ancient author, or even of half the works of all the ancient authors now extant. The question here, is merely concerning a matter of fact. You may say, perhaps, that I assert merely my own opinion. I confess it. The reviewer also asserts nothing but his opinion: and I am fairly warranted to believe, that my own regret for the loss of Mr. Edwards' works would be greater than his for the loss of a few pages of an ancient author, or the whole of many ancient authors. Such a loss would be the loss, perhaps, of a few facts; some of them in a degree interesting to mankind: as the case might be, of a few opinions, and doctrines, of considerable value, or possibly of a fine narrative, or interesting description.

His subjects are the most important in the universe; and his discussions are the clearest, the ablest, and the most decisive, elucidations of them, which the world has ever seen. He has elicited from the Scriptures, truths which have escaped other men; has illustrated them by arguments, which were never before discovered; and has shown their dependence, connexion, and importance, with a comprehensiveness of view, which elsewhere will be sought for in vain.

With regard to the principal subject under examination, principal I mean, with respect to the present debate, the admission, that Mr. Edwards' doctrines are erroneous, will only exhibit it with still higher advantage. What must have been the talents, which could have placed errour in such a light, that all the distinguished men, who have appeared on the side of truth during the last fifty years, not only in Great-Britain, but in the whole Christian world, have been unable to detect his errours? Does truth in its own nature labour under such disadvantages? Or did Mr. Edwards possess such singular and transcendant powers?

Indifference to the subject cannot here be pleaded, nor contempt for Mr. Edwards. The numerous complaints, made of his writings in Great Britain, and the numerous specimens of ill-nature, with which he has been assailed, prove beyond debate, that they have been regarded with far other feelings than indifference. That they would have been answered, had those, who disrelished them so strongly, been able to answer them, there can be no doubt. Look into Boswell's Life of Johnson, and mark the gloom, with which the biographer was distressed, from fear that the system of Mr. Edwards should be the truth; and, what I principally intend, observe the dread, with which Johnson himself regarded the subject of his appeal to him, and the caution with which he avoided reading the book, so pathetically complained of, although Boswell ardently wished him to read it, and although he regarded the Americans with even more contempt than he felt towards the Scots. . . .

The talents of my countrymen have been exhibited, as I think, respectably in various other modes. Dr. Franklin is excepted in this very declaration of the Reviewer from the general disgrace; and has been so often pronounced a distinguished natural philosopher, in the most enlightened countries of

Europe, and by persons of high eminence, that it is too late to attempt a reversal of this sentence. . . .

The poetry of the Americans is treated by these Reviewers with not a little contempt. On this subject I shall say little. It may, however, be observed, that several Reviewers have spoken of it in more favourable terms. It may also be observed without any partiality, that McFingal is not inferiour in wit and humour to Hudibras; and in every other respect is superiour. It has a regular plan, in which all the parts are well proportioned, and connected. The subject is fairly proposed; and the story conducted correctly through a series of advancements, and retardations, to a catastrophe, which is natural and complete. The versification is far better; the poetry is in several instances in a good degree elegant, and in some even sublime. It is also free from those endless digressions, which, notwithstanding the wit discovered in them, are so tedious in Hudibras; the protuberances of which are a much larger mass than the body, on which they grow.

The painters of this country have been holden in honourable estimation in Great-Britain. A high reputation has been attained by West and Copley, by Trumbull and Stuart. As a portrait painter, it is believed, Stuart has rarely if ever been excelled. Several others, younger than these, are also advancing rapidly towards distinction.

Sculpture has not, within my knowledge ever been attempted here. But engraving has already proceeded far, and is very fast advancing.

From the whole of this account, I cannot but persuade myself, that you as a man of candour will think, that the inhabitants of this country have a claim to be considered with some other emotions than those of contempt, and to receive other treatment than sneers and sarcasms. Perhaps you will think, that as much has been done, as in the circumstances could be reasonably expected. From what I have said in a former part of these letters, you will not consider it a small thing to convert an American forest, not merely into a habitable country, but into a pleasant residence. In New-England, according to an estimate, heretofore made, there are probably at the present time (1812) more than 220,000 dwelling-houses. A great part of these are convenient; almost all are comfortable; a great multitude are neat; and not a small number handsome. The inhabitants probably enjoy more of the comforts, and suffer fewer of the evils, of life, than the same number of people in any other part of the world. To accomplish this amid all the difficulties, and dangers, which attended the colonization of the country, has involved a mass of labour, resolution, and fortitude, which in any other case would have claimed respect. To these things was added, necessarily, the establishment of a government, a religion, a system of education, and universally a state of society, by means of which the descendants of those, on whom the burden rested, might so far as their circumstances would permit, be free, enlightened, virtuous, and happy. Occupied in this spacious, and various field, the inhabitants have in few instances had either leisure, or inclination, to write books; and most of those, which have been written, were prompted by some particular occasion.

Let me request you to remember how long your own nation existed, before it could boast of a single well-written book. In the eighth century you had only the venerable Bede; in the ninth, only Alfred; in the tenth and eleventh, none; in the twelfth, William of Malmesbury, is entitled to respect. Roger Bacon adorned the thirteenth. From that time till the sixteenth you had no writer of any distinction, except Fortescue, Chaucer, and Gower. In the sixteenth century, you number only five or six writers of respectability. The seventeenth and eighteenth have filled your hemisphere with constellations. Before Hume and Robertson, you had no historian, superiour to several of ours. The reviewer is disposed to speak contemptuously of Marshall's Life of Washington. Yet there is no piece of biography, written in Great-Britain, if we except those of Johnson, which would not suffer by a comparison with it. The last volume is almost singularly excellent. It ought here to be added, that the ministers, sent out to Europe by Washington, have holden at least as high a rank in European estimation, as those who were their companions from any of the European courts. Of Mr. Jay, Lord Grenville has given a character in the British parliament, which should have made the reviewers hesitate before they published the following declaration: "We have dwelt longer upon this article than its merits justify, not so much for the sake of the work, as for stating, and exemplifying, a most curious and unaccountable fact: the scarcity of all but agricultural, and mercantile, talents in the New World." There are the best reasons for believing, that no foreign minister was holden in higher estimation by the British government, than Mr. King.

I will dismiss the subject with one more remark concerning my countrymen. The speeches of Ames, and several other members of the American Congress have been rarely excelled in eloquence by British orators.

I am, Sir, yours, &. (1812)

ROYALL TYLER

(1757–1826)

Preface to *The Algerine Captive**

ONE of the first observations the author of the following sheets made upon his return to his native country, after an absence of seven years, was the extreme avidity with which books of mere amusement were purchased and perused by all ranks of his countrymen. When he left New England, books of biography, travels, novels, and modern romances, were confined to our sea-ports; or, if known in the country, were read only in the families of clergymen, physicians, and lawyers: while certain funeral discourses, the last words and dying speeches of Bryan Shaheen, and Levi Ames, and some dreary some-body's Day of Doom, formed the most diverting part of the farmer's library. On his return from captivity, he found a surprising alteration in the public taste. In our inland towns of consequence, social libraries had been instituted, composed of books designed to amuse rather than to instruct; and country booksellers, fostering the new-born taste of the people, had filled the whole land with modern travels, and novels almost as incredible. The diffusion of a taste for any species of writing through all ranks, in so short a time, would appear impracticable to an European. The peasant of Europe must first be taught to read, before he can acquire a taste in letters. In New England, the work is half completed. In no other country are there so many people, who, in proportion to its numbers, can read and write, and, therefore, no sooner was a taste for amusing literature diffused, than all orders of country life, with one accord, forsook the sober sermons and practical pieties of their fathers, for the gay stories and splendid impieties of the traveller and the novelist. The worthy farmer no longer fatigued himself with Bunyan's Pilgrim up the 'hill of difficulty' or through the 'slough of despond,' but quaffed wine with Brydone in the hermitage of Vesuvius, or sported with

* *The Algerine Captive* (London, 1802).

Bruce on the fairy-land of Abyssinia: while Dolly the dairy maid, and Jonathan the hired man, threw aside the ballad of the cruel step-mother, over which they had so often wept in concert, and now amused themselves into so agreeable a terror with the haunted houses and hobgoblins of Mrs. Ratcliffe, that they were both afraid to sleep alone.

Although a love of literature, however frivolous, may be pleasing to the man of letters, yet there are two things to be deplored in it. The first is, that, while so many books are vended, they are not of our own manufacture. If our wives and daughters will wear gauze and ribbands, it is a pity they are not wrought in our own looms. The second misfortune is, that novels, being the picture of the times, the New England reader is insensibly taught to admire the levity, and often the vices, of the parent country. While the fancy is enchanted, the heart is corrupted. The farmer's daughter, while she pities the misfortune of some modern heroine, is exposed to the attacks of vice, from which her ignorance would have formed her surest shield. If the English novel does not inculcate vice, it at least impresses on the young female mind an erroneous idea of the world in which she is to live. It paints the manners, customs, and habits, of a strange country; excites a fondness for false splendor; and renders the home-spun habits of her own country disgusting.

There are two things wanted, said a friend to the author: that we write our own books of amusement, and that they exhibit our own manners. Why then do you not write the history of your own life? The first part of it, if not highly interesting, would at least display a portrait of New England manners, hitherto unattempted. Your captivity among the Algerines, with some notices of the manners of that ferocious race, so dreaded by commercial powers, and so little known in our country, would at least be interesting; and I see no advantage which the novel writer can have over you, unless your readers should be of the sentiment of the young lady mentioned by Addison in his Spectator, who, as he informs us, borrowed Plutarch's lives, and, after reading the first volume with infinite delight, supposing it to be a novel, threw aside the others with disgust, because a man of letters had inadvertently told her the work was founded on FACT. (1797)

FISHER AMES

(1758–1808)

From *American Literature**

FEW speculative subjects have exercised the passions more or the judgment less, than the inquiry, what rank our country is to maintain in the world for genius and literary attainments. Whether in point of intellect we are equal to Europeans, or only a race of degenerate creoles; whether our artists and authors have already performed much and promise every thing; whether the muses, like the nightingales, are too delicate to cross the salt water, or sicken and mope without song if they do, are themes upon which we Americans are privileged to be eloquent and loud. It might indeed occur to our discretion, that as the only admissible proof of literary excellence is the measure of its effects, our national claims ought to be abandoned as worthless the moment they are found to need asserting.

Nevertheless, by a proper spirit and constancy in praising ourselves, it seems to be supposed, the doubtful title of our vanity may be quieted in the same manner as it was once believed the currency of the continental paper could, by a universal agreement, be established at par with specie. Yet such was the unpatriotic perverseness of our citizens, they preferred the gold and silver, for no better reason than because the paper bills were not so good. And now it may happen, that from spite or envy, from want of attention or the want of our sort of information, foreigners will dispute the claims of our preëminence in genius and literature, notwithstanding the great convenience and satisfaction we should find in their acquiescence.

In this unmanageable temper or indocile ignorance of Europe, we may be under the harsh necessity of submitting our pretensions to a scrutiny; and as the world will judge of the matter with none of our partiality, it may be discreet to anticipate that judgment, and to explore the grounds upon which

* Seth Ames, ed., *Works of Fisher Ames*, II (Boston, 1854).

it is probable the aforesaid world will frame it. And after all, we should suffer more pain than loss, if we should in the event be stripped of all that does not belong to us; and especially if, by a better knowledge of ourselves, we should gain that modesty which is the first evidence, and perhaps the last, of a real improvement. For no man is less likely to increase his knowledge than the coxcomb, who fancies he has already learned out. An excessive national vanity, as it is the sign of mediocrity, if not of barbarism, is one of the greatest impediments to knowledge.

It will be useless and impertinent to say, a greater proportion of our citizens have had instruction in schools than can be found in any European state. It may be true that neither France nor England can boast of so large a portion of their population who can read and write, and who are versed in the profitable mystery of the rule of three. This is not the footing upon which the inquiry is to proceed. The question is not, what proportion are stone blind, or how many can see, when the sun shines, but what geniuses have arisen among us, like the sun and stars to shed life and splendor on our hemisphere.

This state of the case is no sooner made, than all the fire-fly tribe of our authors perceive their little lamps go out of themselves, like the flame of a candle when lowered into the mephitic vapor of a well. Excepting the writers of two able works on our politics, we have no authors. To enter the lists in single combat against Hector, the Greeks did not offer the lots to the nameless rabble of their soldiery; all eyes were turned upon Agamemnon and Ajax, upon Diomed and Ulysses. Shall we match Joel Barlow against Homer or Hesiod? Can Thomas Paine contend against Plato? Or could Findley's history of his own insurrection vie with Sallust's narrative of Catiline's? There is no scarcity of spelling-book makers, and authors of twelve-cent pamphlets; and we have a distinguished few, a sort of literary nobility, whose works have grown to the dignity and size of an octavo volume. We have many writers who have read, and who have the sense to understand, what others have written. But a right perception of the genius of others is not genius; it is a sort of business talent, and will not be wanting where there is much occasion for its exercise. Nobody will pretend that the Americans are a stupid race; nobody will deny that we justly boast of many able men, and exceedingly useful publications. But has our country produced one great original work of genius? If we tread the sides of Parnassus, we do not climb its heights; we even creep in our path, by the light that European genius has thrown upon it. Is there one luminary in our firmament that shines with unborrowed rays? Do we reflect how many constellations blend their beams in the history of Greece, which will appear bright to the end of time, like the path of the zodiac, bespangled with stars?

If, then, we judge of the genius of our nation by the success with which

American authors have displayed it, our country has certainly hitherto no pretensions to literary fame. The world will naturally enough pronounce its opinion, that what we have not performed we are incapable of performing.

It is not intended to proceed in stripping our country's honors off, till every lover of it shall turn with disgust from the contemplation of its nakedness. Our honors have not faded—they have not been won. Genius no doubt exists in our country, but it exists, like the unbodied soul on the stream of Lethe, unconscious of its powers, till the causes to excite and the occasions to display it shall happen to concur.

*   *   *

It may be properly added, and in perfect consistency with the theory before assumed that fear is the strongest of all passions, that in democracies writers will be more afraid *of* the people, than afraid *for* them. The principles indispensable to liberty are not therefore to be discovered, or if discovered, not to be propagated and established in such a state of things. But where the chief magistrate holds the sword, and is the object of reverence, if not of popular fear, the direction of prejudice and feeling will be changed. Supposing the citizens to have privileges, and to be possessed of influence, or in other words, of some power in the state, they will naturally wish so to use the power they have, as to be secure against the abuse of that which their chief possesses; and this universal propensity of the public wishes will excite and reward the genius, that discovers the way in which this may be done. If we know any thing of the true theory of liberty, we owe it to the wisdom, or perhaps more correctly, to the experience of those nations whose public sentiment was employed to check rather than to guide the government.

It is then little to be expected that American writers will add much to the common stock of political information.

It might have been sooner remarked, that the dramatic art has not afforded any opportunities for native writers. It is but lately that we have had theatres in our cities; and till our cities become large, like London and Paris, the progress of taste will be slow, and the rewards of excellence unworthy of the competitions of genius.

Nor will it be charged, as a mark of our stupidity, that we have produced nothing in history. Our own is not yet worthy of a Livy; and to write that of any foreign nation where could an American author collect his materials and authorities? Few persons reflect, that all our universities would not suffice to supply them for such a work as Gibbon's.

The reasons why we yet boast nothing in the abstruse sciences, are of a different and more various nature. Much, perhaps all, that has been discovered in these, is known to some of our literati. It does not appear that Europe is now making any advances. But to make a wider diffusion of these sciences, and to enlarge their circle, would require the learned leisure, which a numerous class enjoy in Europe, but which cannot be enjoyed in America. If wealth is accumulated by commerce, it is again dissipated among heirs. Its transitory nature no doubt favors the progress of luxury, more than the advancement of letters. It has among us no uses to found families, to sustain rank, to purchase power, or to pension genius. The objects on which it must be employed are all temporary, and have more concern with mere appetite or ostentation than with taste or talents. Our citizens have not been accustomed to look on rank or titles, on birth or office, as capable of the least rivalship with wealth; mere wealth, in pretensions to respect. Of course the single passion that engrosses us, the only avenue to consideration and importance in our society, is the accumulation of property; our inclinations cling to gold, and are bedded in it, as deeply as that precious ore in the mine. Covered as our genius is in this mineral crust, is it strange that it does not sparkle? Pressed down to earth, and with the weight of mountains on our heads, is it surprising, that no sons of ether yet have spread their broad wings to the sky, like Jove's own eagle, to gaze undazzled at the sun, or to perch on the top of Olympus, and partake the banquet of the gods?

At present the nature of our government inclines all men to seek popularity, as the object next in point of value to wealth; but the acquisition of learning and the display of genius are not the ways to obtain it. Intellectual superiority is so far from conciliating confidence, that it is the very spirit of a democracy, as in France, to proscribe the aristocracy of talents. To be the favorite of an ignorant multitude, a man must descend to their level; he must desire what they desire, and detest all that they do not approve; he must yield to their prejudices, and substitute them for principles. Instead of enlightening their errors, he must adopt them; he must furnish the sophistry that will propagate and defend them.

Surely we are not to look for genius among demagogues; the man who can descend so low, has seldom very far to descend. As experience evinces that popularity, in other words, consideration and power, is to be procured by the meanest of mankind, the meanest in spirit and understanding, and in the worst of ways, it is obvious, that at present the excitement to genius is next to nothing. If we had a Pindar, he would be ashamed to celebrate our chief, and would be disgraced, if he did. But if he did not, his genius would not obtain his election for a selectman in a democratic town. It is party that bestows emolument, power, and consideration; and it is not excellence in the sciences that obtains the suffrages of party.

But the condition of the United States is changing. Luxury is sure to introduce want; and the great inequalities between the very rich and the very poor will be more conspicuous, and comprehend a more formidable host of the latter. The rabble of great cities is the standing army of ambition. Money will become its instrument, and vice its agent. Every step, (and we have taken many,) towards a more complete, unmixed democracy is an advance towards destruction; it is treading where the ground is treacherous and excavated for an explosion. Liberty has never yet lasted long in a democracy; nor has it ever ended in any thing better than despotism. With the change of our government, our manners and sentiments will change. As soon as our emperor has destroyed his rivals, and established order in his army, he will desire to see splendor in his court, and to occupy his subjects with the cultivation of the sciences.

If this catastrophe of our public liberty should be miraculously delayed or prevented, still we shall change. With the augmentation of wealth, there will be an increase of the numbers who may choose a literary leisure. Literary curiosity will become one of the new appetites of the nation; and as luxury advances, no appetite will be denied. After some ages we shall have many poor and a few rich, many grossly ignorant, a considerable number learned, and a few eminently learned. Nature, never prodigal of her gifts, will produce some men of genius, who will be admired and imitated. (1809)

JAMES NELSON BARKER

(1784–1858)

Preface to *Tears and Smiles**

A good-natured friend of mine, to whom I submitted the manuscript of my play, before it was acted, after running his eyés over the pages, in a kind tone of voice requested me to throw it into the fire. Astonished and dismayed, I inquired the reason. "My dear sir," said my good-natured friend, "you are young; this is your maiden essay; and therefore I can pardon your inexperience. You meant to have written a comedy?" "I did." "And you have produced nothing, absolutely nothing but a collection of *Columbianisms*, in five parts." "And pray," asked I, "what may a Columbianism be?" "The term," replied my good-natured friend, "was invented and applied by certain hypercritics of our own, who, perhaps from being placed too near the scene, cannot discover the beauties of their own country, and whose refined taste is therefore better pleased with the mellow tints which distance gives to every foreign object. This term of derision they apply to every delineation an American may attempt to make of American manners, customs, opinions, characters, or scenery. Thus, while they rapturously applaud the sentiments of a foreign stage patriot, the lover of his country, in an American play, utters only contemptible Columbianisms. An allusion to the revolution which made us a nation, or to the inestimable characters who achieved it, cannot be heard with patience, though they may search history in vain for parallels to either. They can never pardon the endeavour to depict our national peculiarities, and yet they will listen with avidity to Yorkshire rusticity, or Newmarket slang. They can feel a poetic rapture, when some muddy stream of Europe flows in verse; but the author might as well incontinently drown himself in it, as lead the pastoral Schuylkill meandering through his poem. They can accompany the fop of an English play in his lounge through Bond-street,

* Paul H. Musser, ed., *James Nelson Barker 1784–1858* (Philadelphia, 1929).

482

while an American personage, of the same cast, would most probably be knocked down, if he attempted a promenade in High-street. They find innumerable Columbianisms in language, too, in that city where all the world beside acknowledge the English tongue is spoken in its utmost purity. In fine, this unaccountable prejudice extends to every thing here; the farther, therefore, you remove from America, the nearer you approach to their favour. Take my advice, then; burn your book, write a melo-drame, and lay your scene in the moon."

When my d—d good-natured friend had finished, I took his advice precisely as advice is usually taken; that is, I didn't take it at all, but carried my play to the manager and had it acted. To say that I found the assertions of my good-natured friend entirely false, would be disingenuous; but not to clear a kind public from any the least share of reproach would be ungrateful. The play was received with, to say no more, all the polite and urbane toleration that the only sanguine friend I had, i.e., myself, could expect; and has been repeated oftener than once, without experiencing any diminution of public favour. But it was not difficult to discover the *anti*-Longinuses that my good-natured friend mentioned. They were as conspicuous as illiberality, ill nature, and ill manners could make them. While the benign Dispenser of light and life is thanked by the creature he makes happy, there are who even would propitiate evil deities, from whom they may fear harm. While I gratefully bend to a kind public, what shall I offer on the altars of hostile demons? Contempt: 'tis all I have. May the sacrifice be propitious! (1807)